That's Entertainment

© Copyright 1975 by HAL LEONARD PUBLISHING CORPORATION, Winona, MN 55987
Made in U.S.A.   International Copyright Secured   All Rights Reserved
A Learning Unlimited® Product, 8112 W. Bluemound Rd., Milwaukee, WI 53213

Introduction

The Kimball Organ Company presents THAT'S ENTERTAINMENT . . . a special edition in the Kimball Entertainer songbook series. In this book, you'll find hit songs from the movies, highlights from the best of Broadway, a collection of well-known inspirational songs, plus many all-time favorite standards . . . all adding up to 100 great melodies.

Each arrangement has been simplified for easy play and adapted for use with the Magic Chord feature on the Entertainer unit. Chords are indicated by boxed chord symbols placed above the music. An alternate chord is sometimes shown in parentheses. Use the alternate chord in place of the boxed chord if you have it on your Magic Chord unit.

There also is a Registration Number suggested for each song. These numbers correspond to the numbers on the Registration Chart in your Kimball Owner's Manual. Set up either the suggested registration, or another one of your choice, select a Swinger rhythm . . . then have fun!

CONTENTS

FROM THE MOVIES

Easy To Love	9
Everything's Coming Up Roses	22
Exodus Song, The	12
Foggy Day, A	36
Georgy Girl	10
Gigi	18
I Concentrate On You	32
In The Still Of The Night	28
Love Is Here To Stay	40
Love Walked In	35
Nice Work If You Can Get It	42
Rosalie	26
Shall We Dance	46
Slap That Bass	38
Sonny Boy	14
Stay As Sweet As You Are	24
Thank Heaven For Little Girls	20
That's Entertainment	6
They All Laughed	44
3rd Man Theme, The	16
True Love	30

BEST OF BROADWAY

Allez-Vous-En, Go Away	138
Bewitched	106
Camelot	88
C'est Magnifique	134
Come Back To Me	116
Comedy Tonight	50
Do I Love You?	140
Don't Rain On My Parade	91
Falling In Love With Love	104
Follow Me	84
From This Moment On	142
Get Me To The Church On Time	72
How Are Things In Glocca Morra?	118
How To Handle A Woman	80
I Could Have Danced All Night	64
I Could Write A Book	108
I Didn't Know What Time It Was	112
I Got Plenty O' Nuttin'	128
I Love Paris	132
I Loves You Porgy	130
I See Your Face Before Me	62
I Talk To The Trees	78
I've Grown Accustomed To Her Face	66
If Ever I Would Leave You	86
If I Ruled The World	52
If This Isn't Love	122
It's All Right With Me	136
Look To The Rainbow	145
My Cup Runneth Over	60
My Funny Valentine	102
Old Devil Moon	120
On A Clear Day (You Can See Forever)	114
On The Street Where You Live	74
People	96
Rain In Spain, The	68
September Song	56
Small World	98
Speak Low	58
Sugar	100
Summertime	126
They Call The Wind Maria	82
Thrill Is Gone, The	54
With A Little Bit Of Luck	76
Woman Is A Sometime Thing, A	124
Wouldn't It Be Loverly	70
You Are Woman	94
You're Nearer	110

FOR INSPIRATION

Amazing Grace	149
Didn't He Shine	150
Jesus Made Me Higher	154
Me and Jesus	152
One More Song For Jesus	148
Shall We Gather At The River	155
Sun Of My Soul	153

ALL-TIME FAVORITES

Best Things In Life Are Free, The	183
Blueberry Hill	198
By Myself	172
Darling, Je Vous Aime Beaucoup	196
Did You Ever See A Dream Walking?	176
Everything I Love	206
Friendship	180
Harbor Lights	160
I Can't Get Started	162
I've Got You Under My Skin	190
It Ain't Necessarily So	200
It's De-lovely	184
Life Is Just A Bowl Of Cherries	203
Little Old Lady	194
Love Thy Neighbor	174
Mutual Admiration Society	164
My Heart Belongs To Daddy	186
Paris In The Spring	178
Ridin' High	204
Roses Of Picardy	166
Sunny Side Up	168
Try To Remember	158
Way Of Love, The	193
World Is Waiting For The Sunrise, The	170
You'd Be So Nice To Come Home To	188

From the Movies

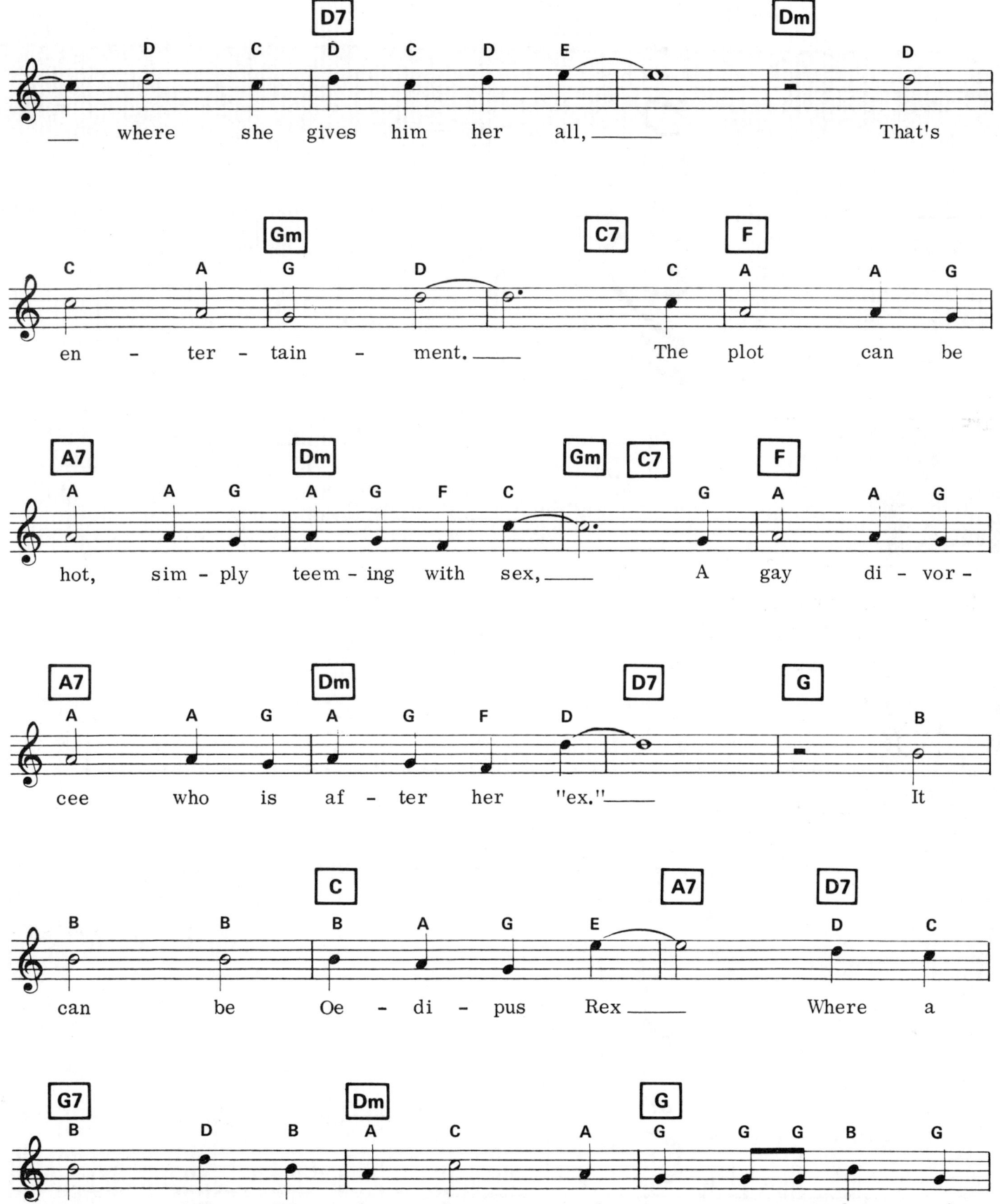

8

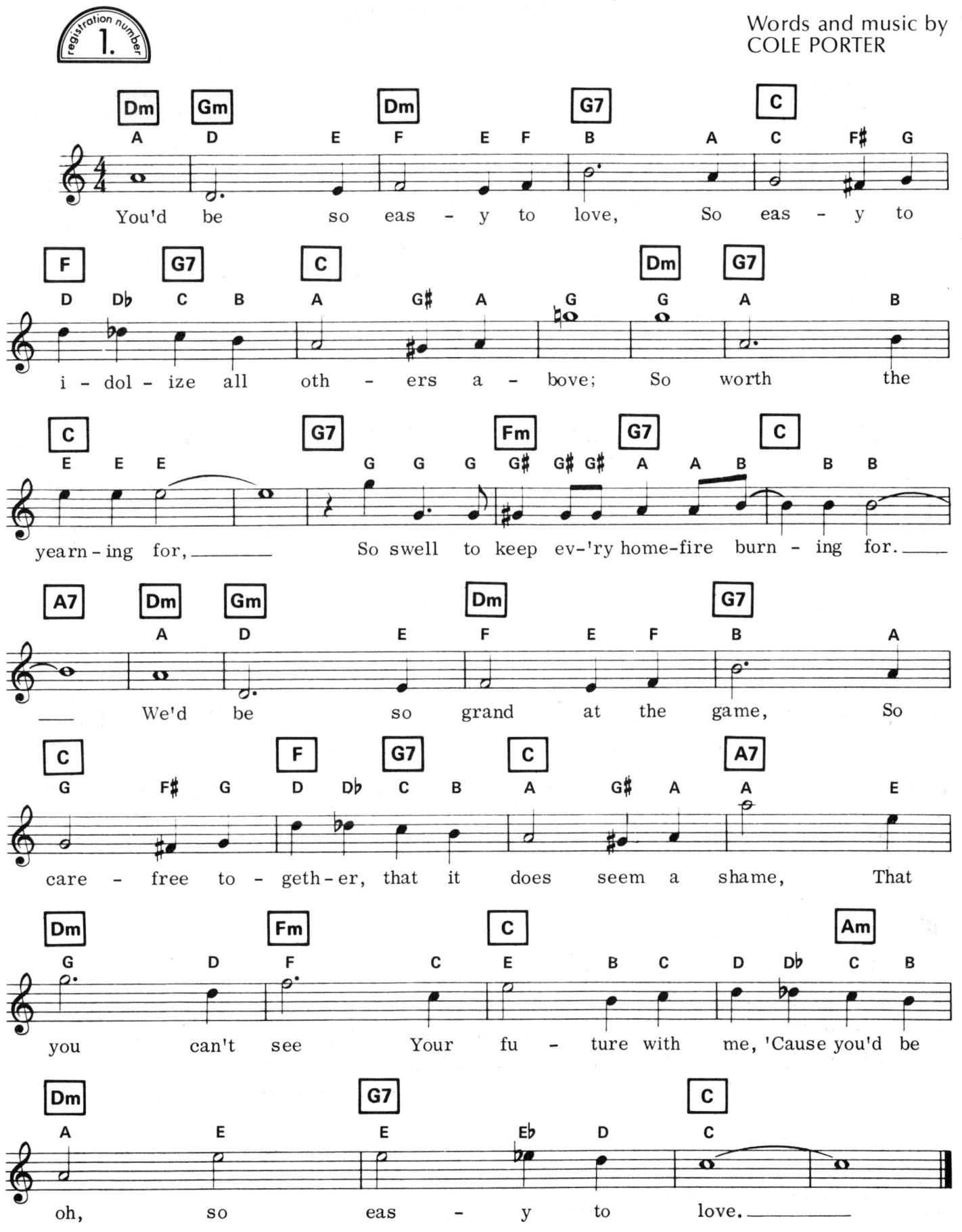

GEORGY GIRL

Words by JIM DALE
Music by TOM SPRINGFIELD

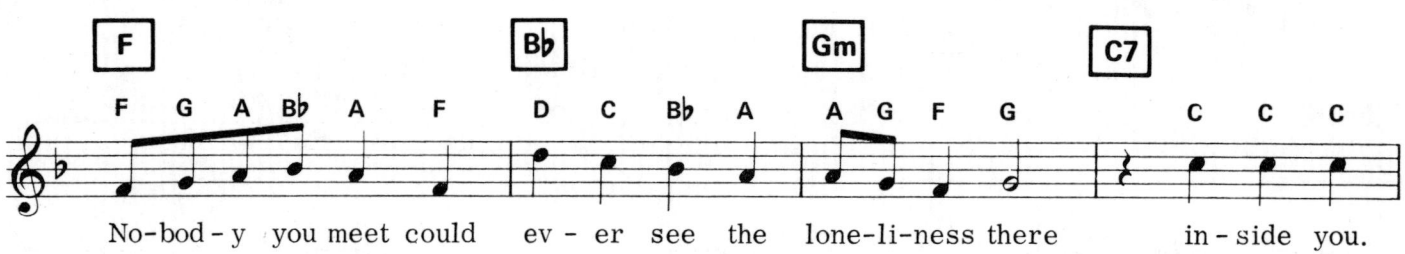

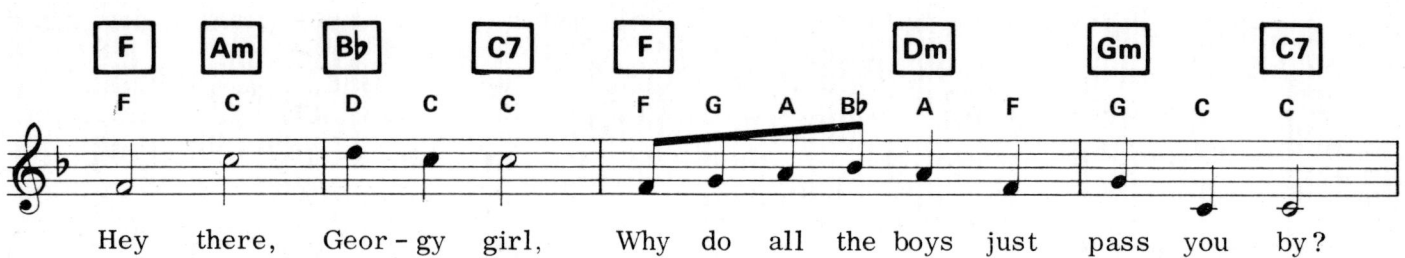

Copyright © 1966 & 1970 by Springfield Music, Ltd., London
Chappell & Co., Inc., publisher
Used by HAL LEONARD PUBLISHING CORPORATION, Winona, MN 55987 by Permission
Made in U.S.A.   International Copyright Secured   All Rights Reserved

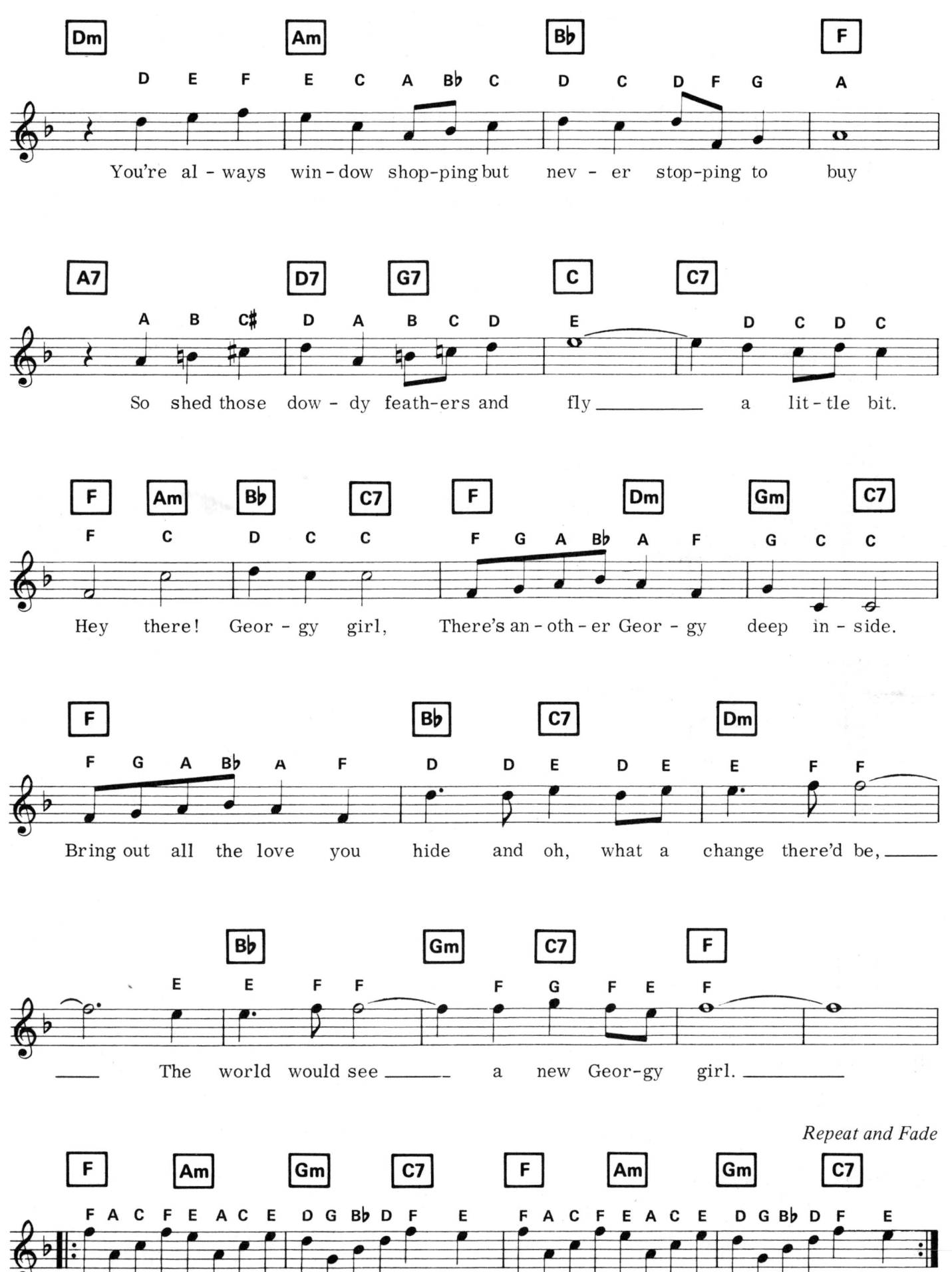

THE EXODUS SONG

ERNEST GOLD

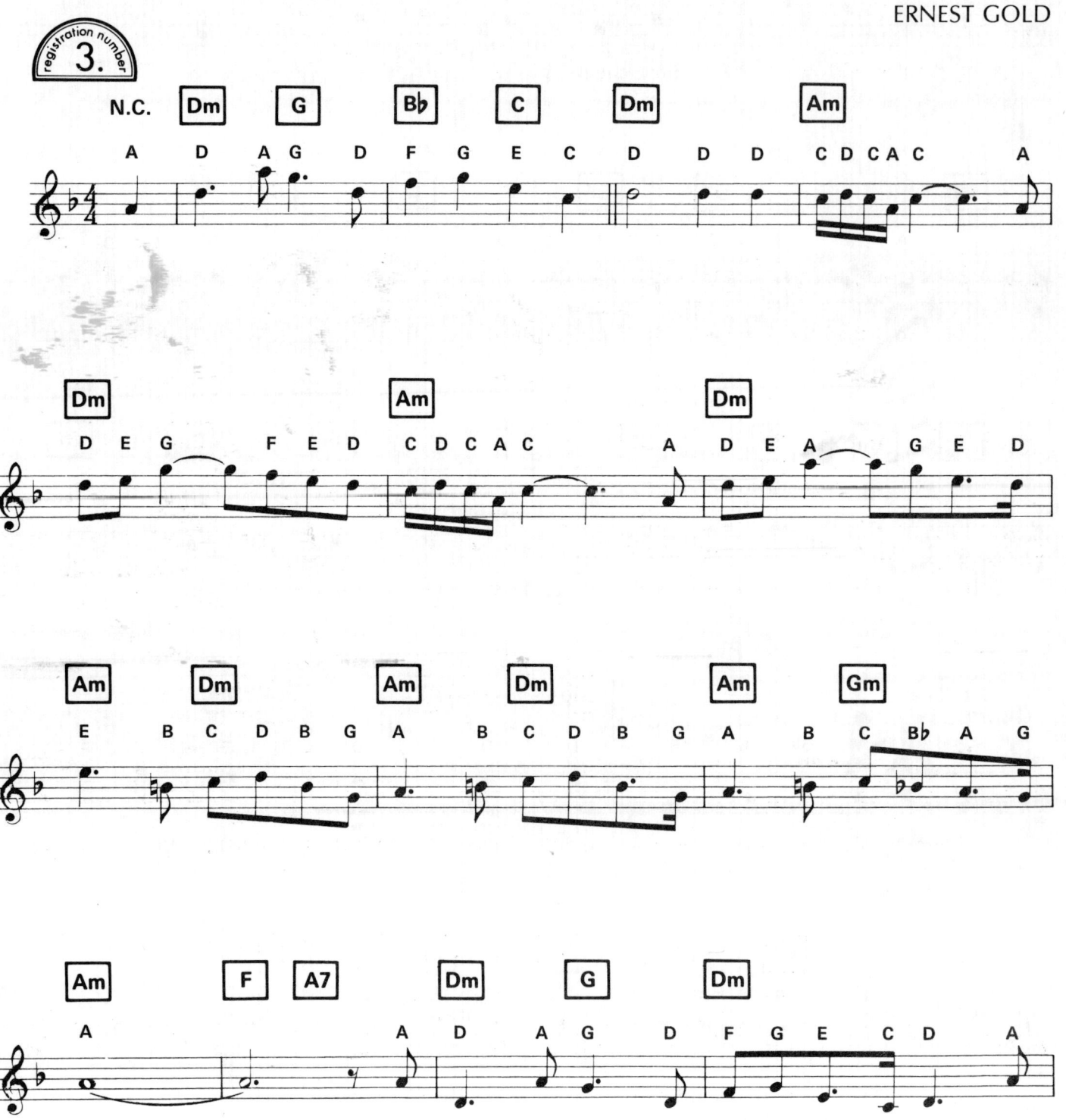

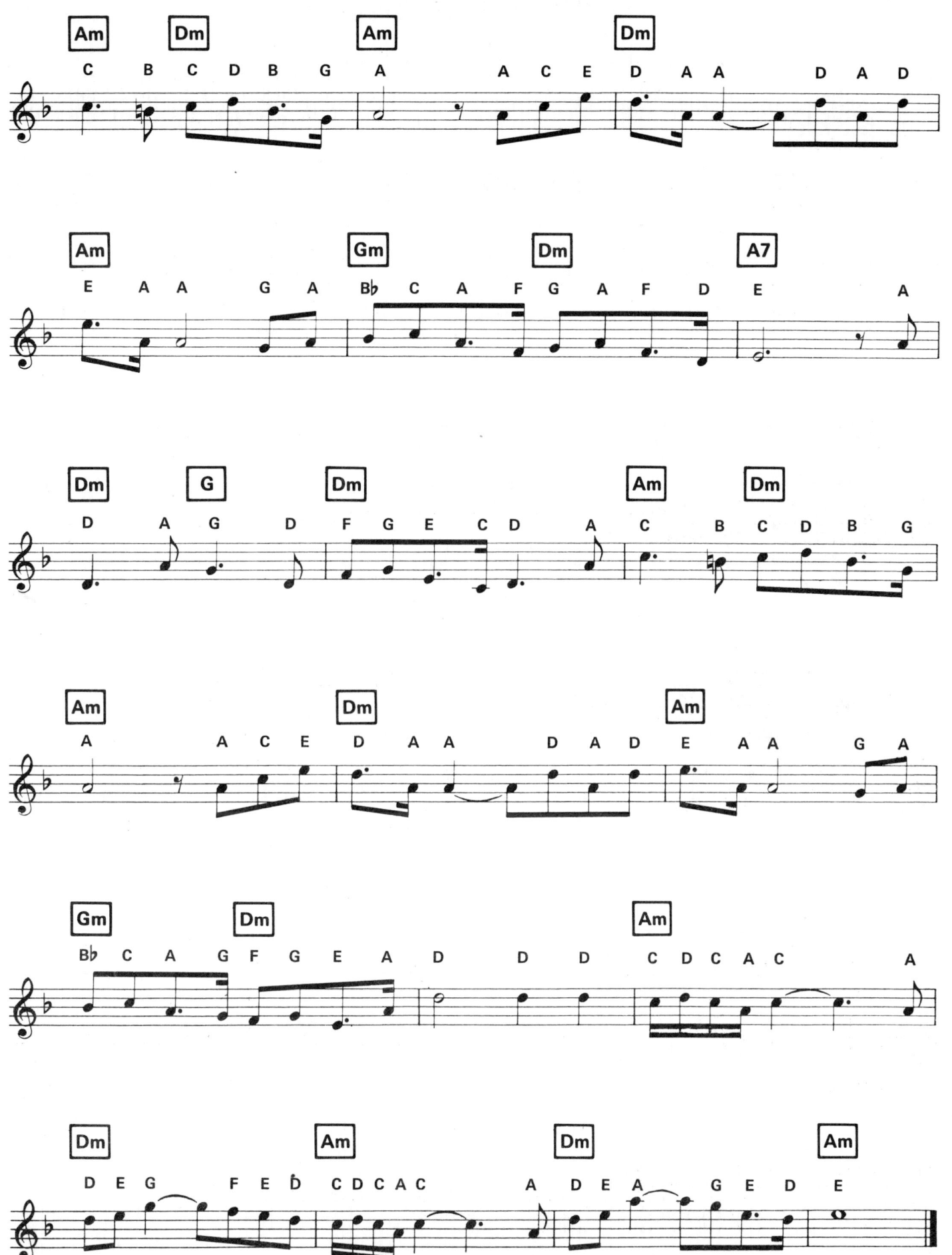

SONNY BOY

**Words and Music by
AL JOLSON, B.G. DeSYLVA,
LEW BROWN & RAY HENDERSON**

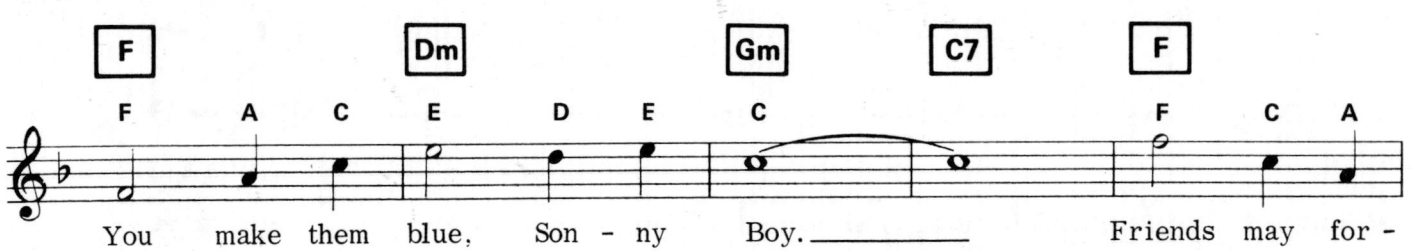

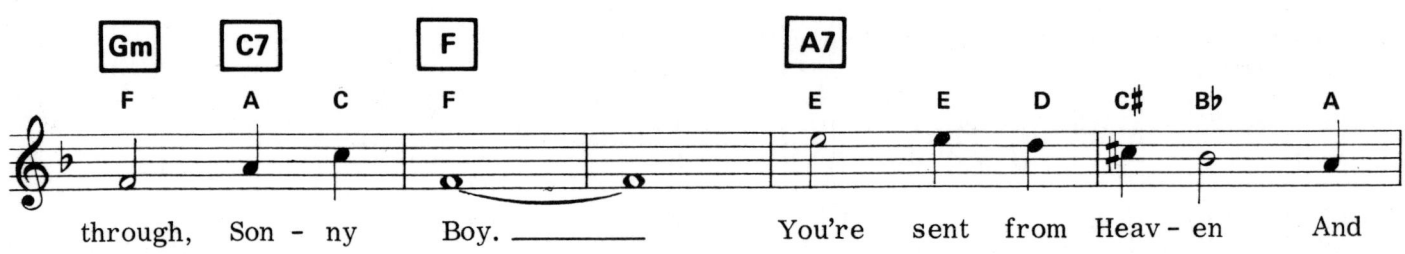

Copyright©1928 by DeSylva, Brown & Henderson, Inc.
Copyright Renewed, assigned to Chappell & Co., Inc.
Published in the United States by joint agreement with Anne-Rachel Music Corporation and Chappell & Co., Inc.
Used by HAL LEONARD PUBLISHING CORPORATION, Winona, MN 55987 by Permission
Made in U.S.A.   International Copyright Secured   All Rights Reserved

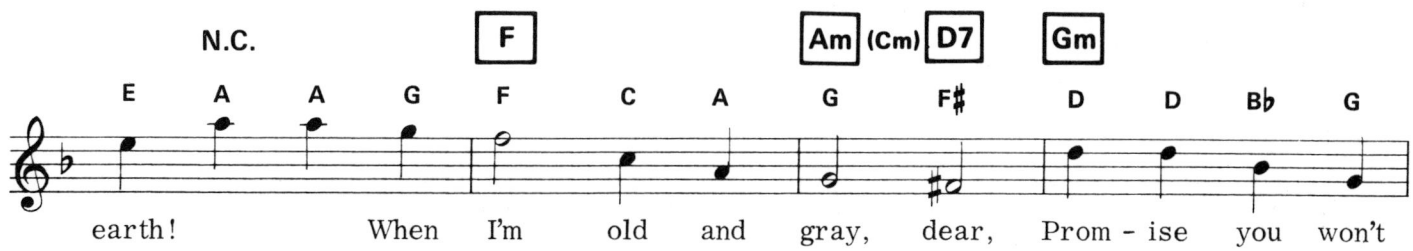
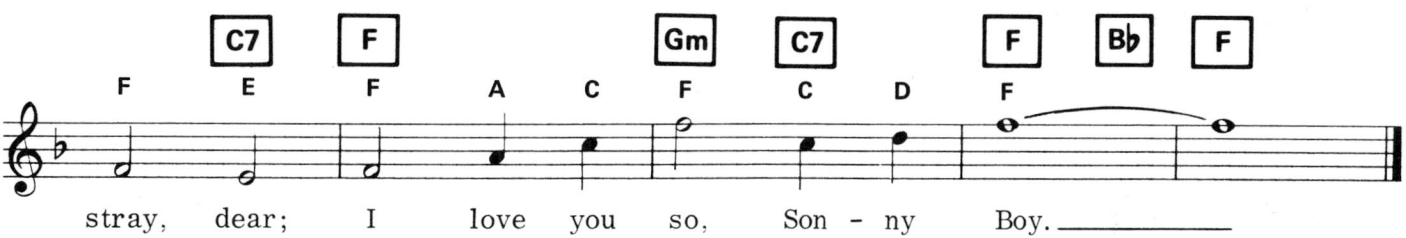

THE 3rd MAN THEME

ANTON KARAS

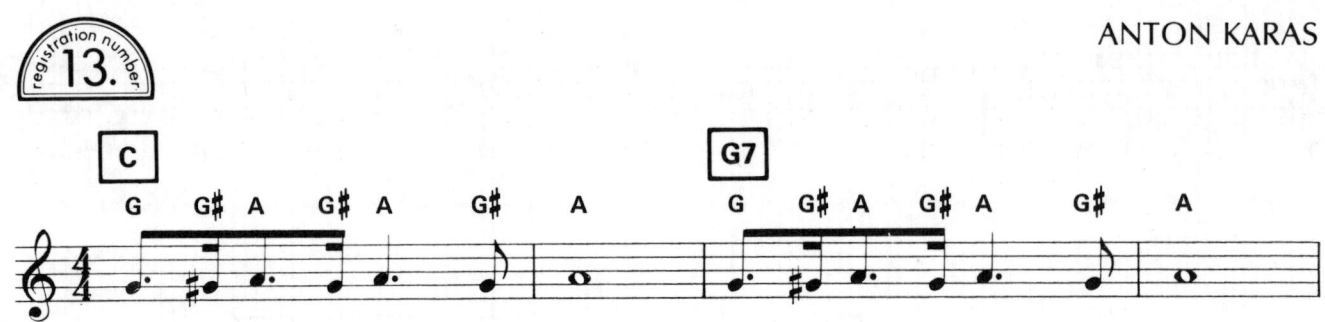

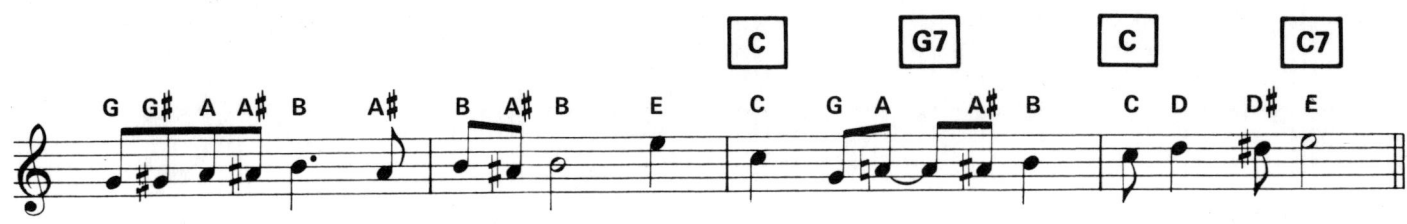

Copyright©1949 & 1970 by British Lion Films Limited, London
Chappell & Co., Inc., owner of publication and allied rights throughout the Western Hemisphere
Used by HAL LEONARD PUBLISHING CORPORATION, Winona, MN 55987 by Permission
Made in U.S.A.   International Copyright Secured   All Rights Reserved

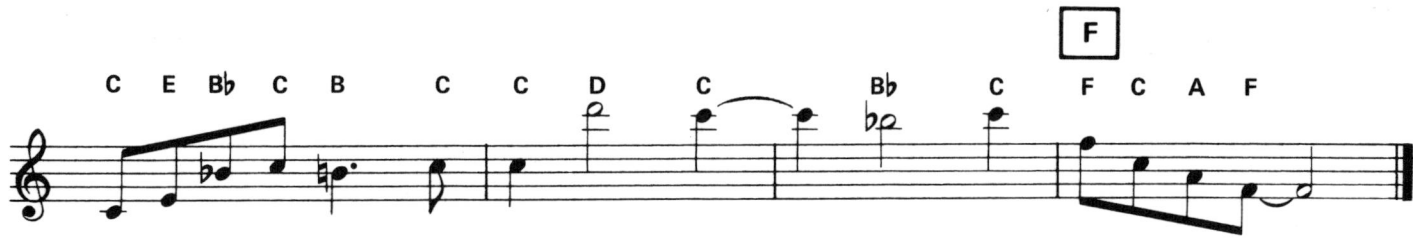

GIGI

Words by ALAN JAY LERNER
Music by FREDERICK LOEWE

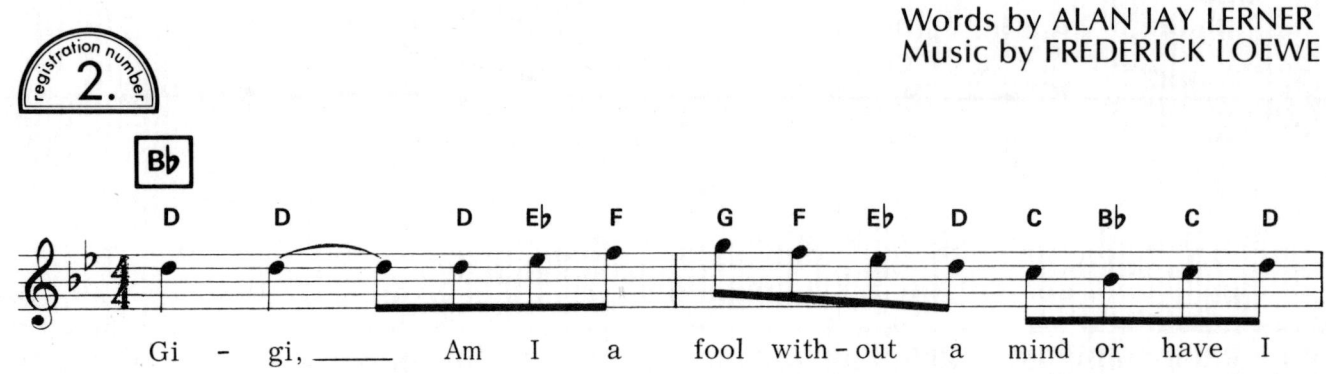

Gi - gi, ___ Am I a fool with-out a mind or have I

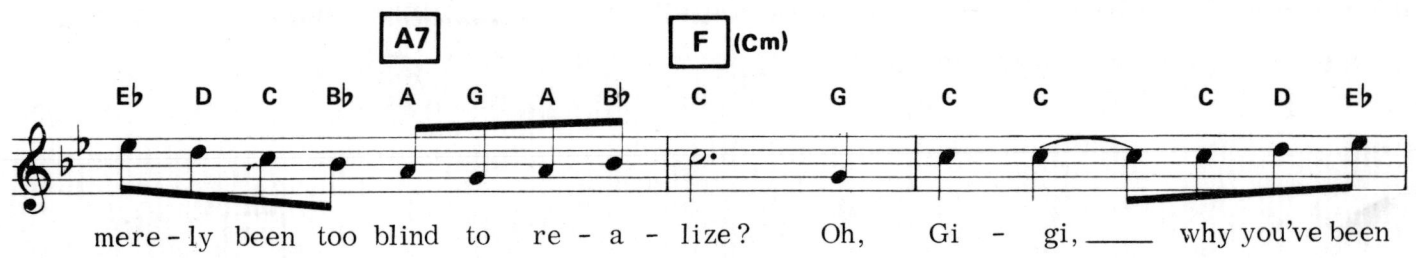

mere-ly been too blind to re-a-lize? Oh, Gi-gi, ___ why you've been

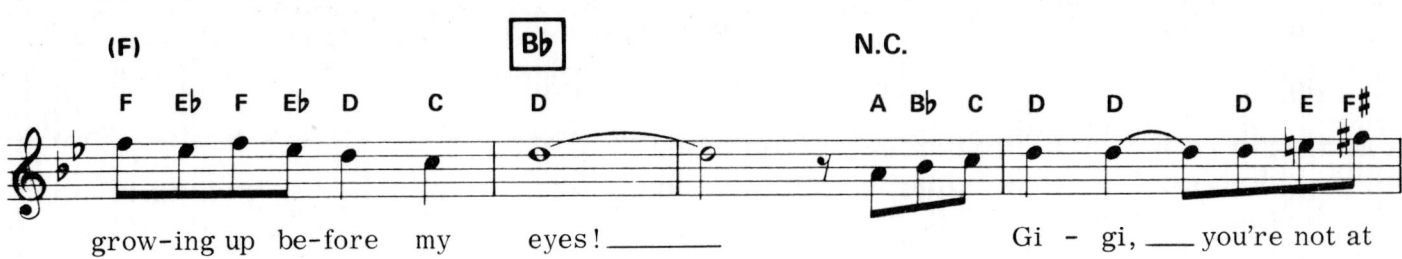

grow-ing up be-fore my eyes! ___ Gi-gi, ___ you're not at

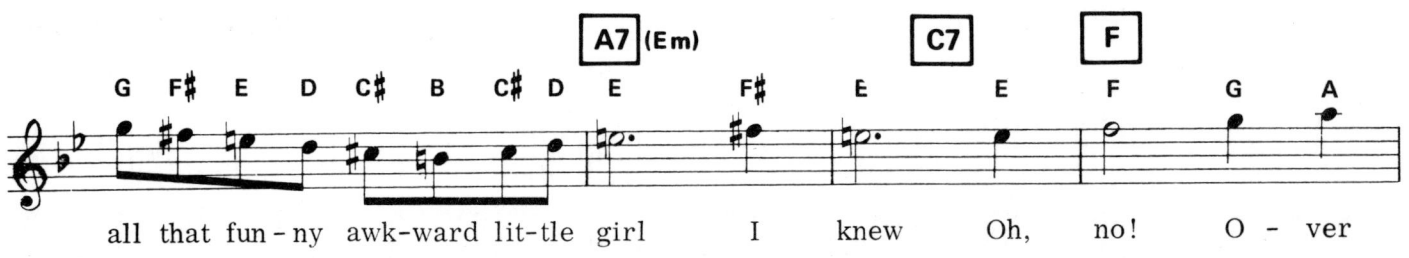

all that fun-ny awk-ward lit-tle girl I knew Oh, no! O-ver

Copyright ©1957 (unpub.), 1958 & 1970 by Chappell & Co., Inc.
Used by HAL LEONARD PUBLISHING CORPORATION, Winona, MN 55987 by Permission
Made in U.S.A. International Copyright Secured All Rights Reserved

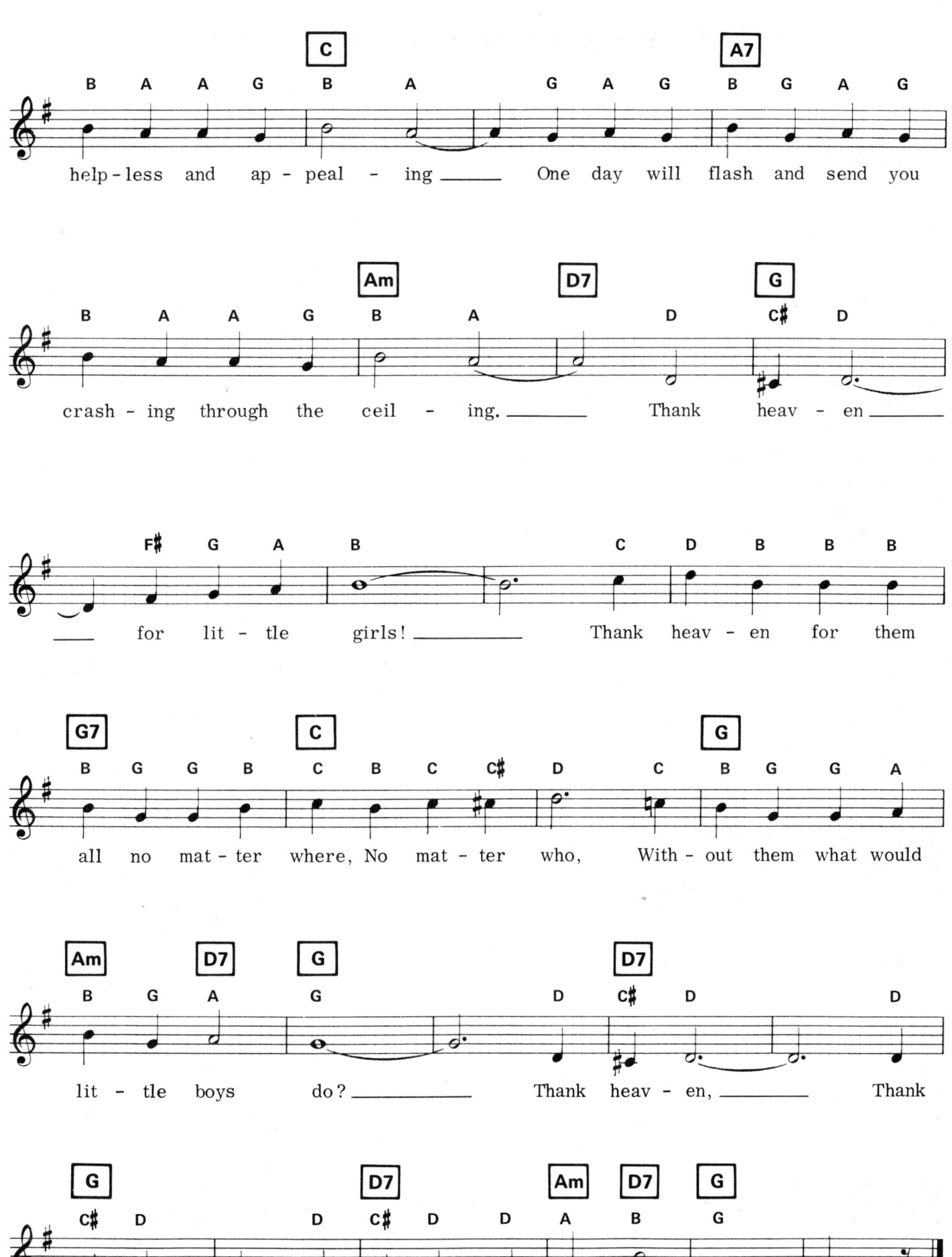

EVERYTHING'S COMING UP ROSES

Words by STEPHEN SONDHEIM
Music by JULE STYNE

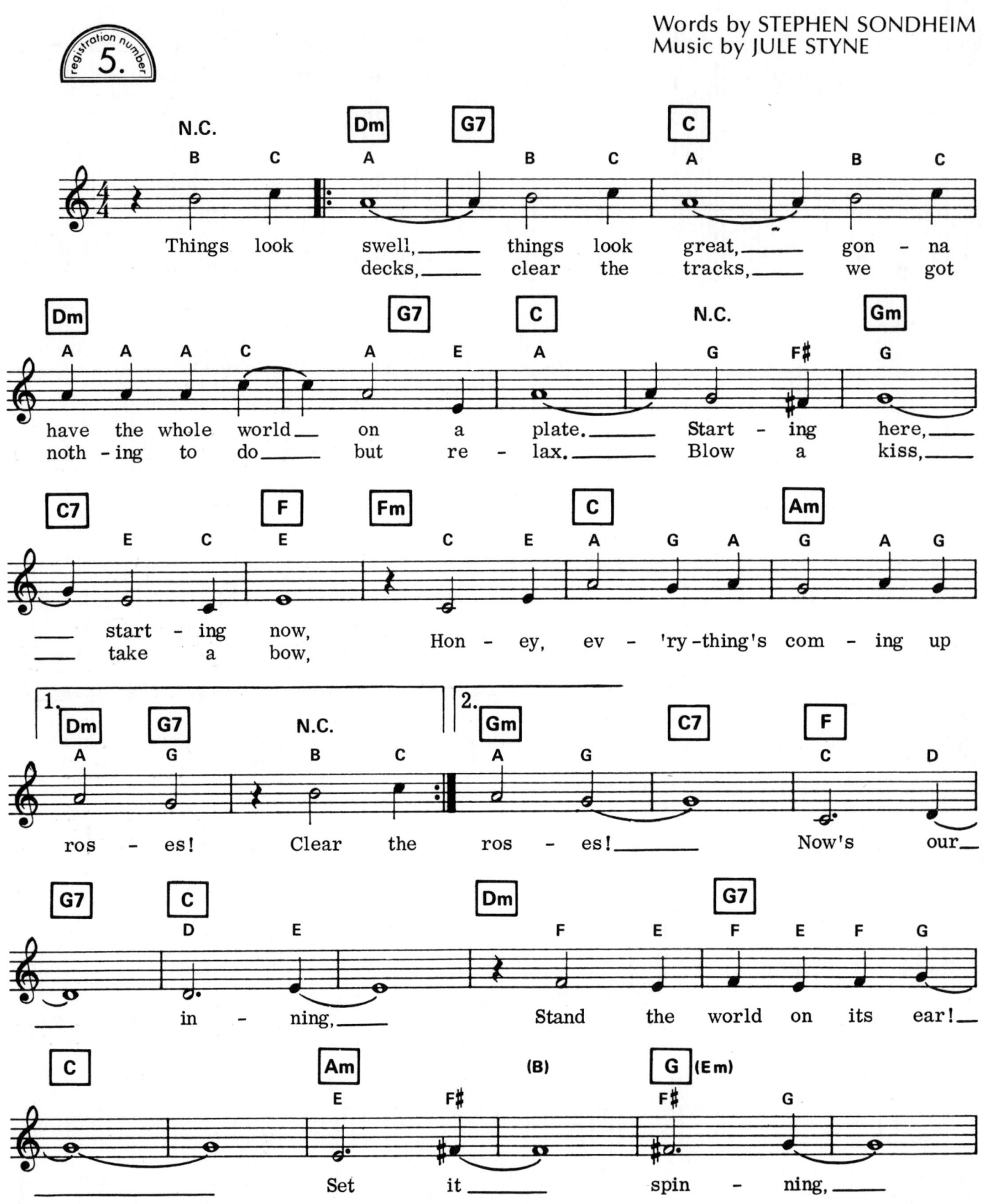

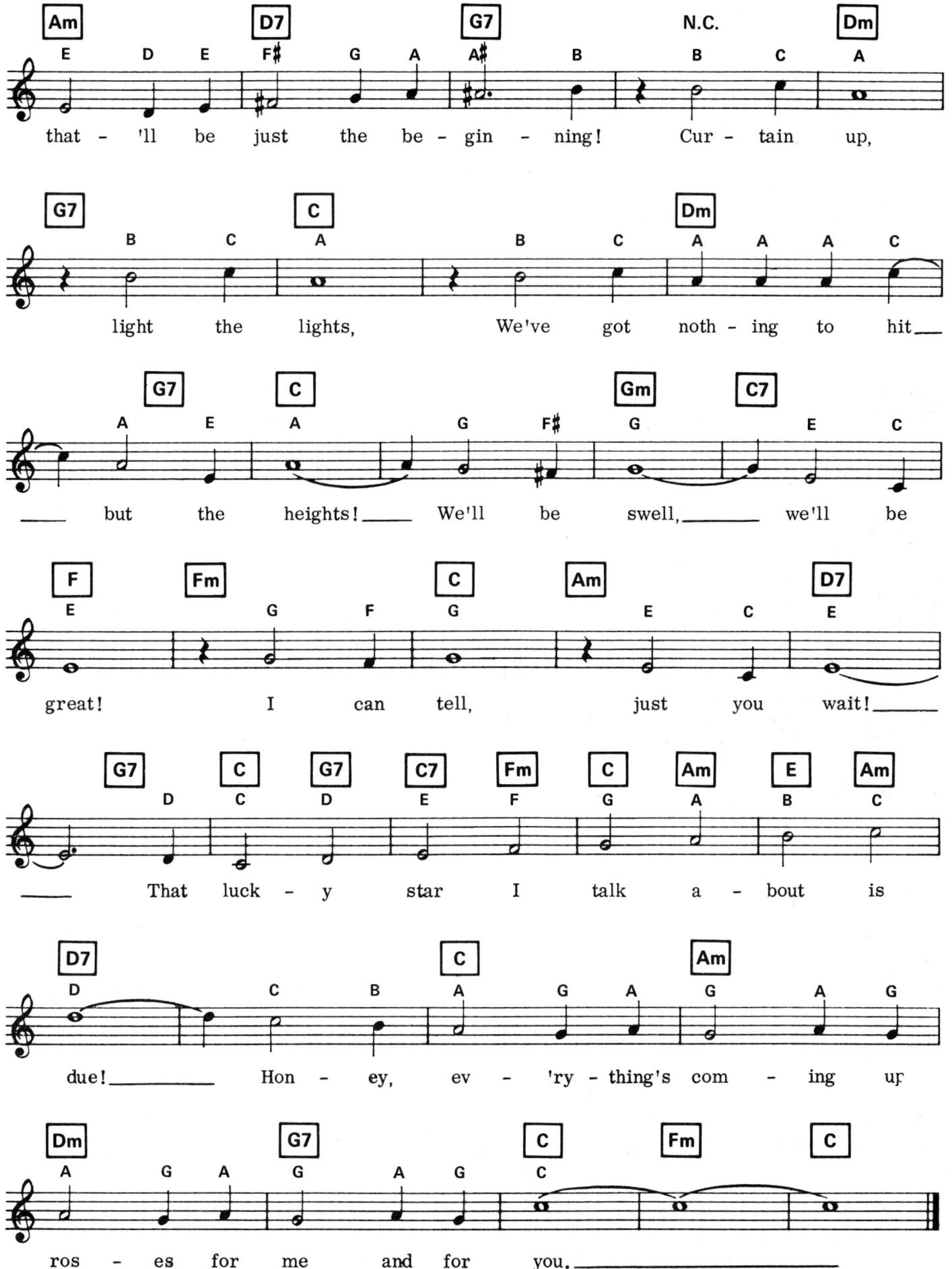

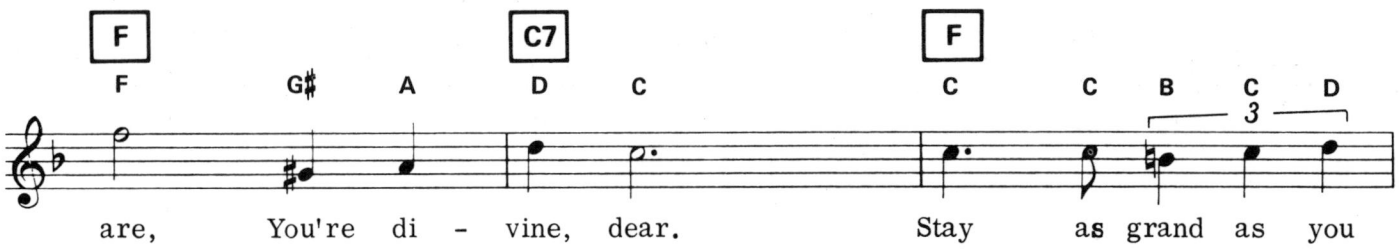

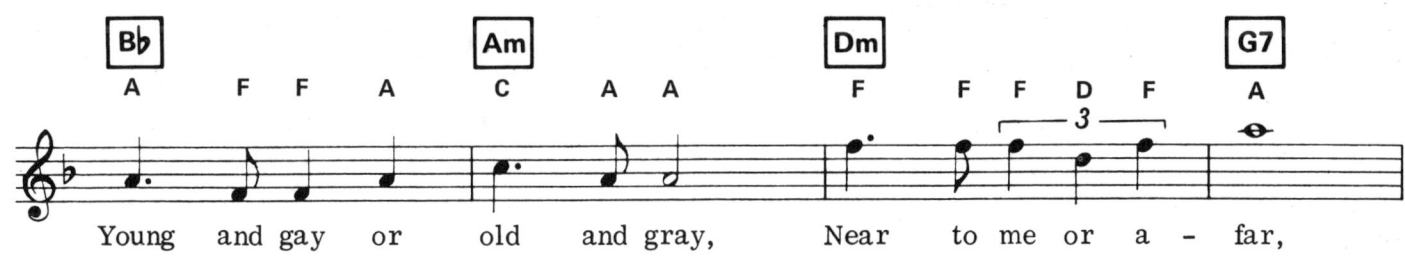
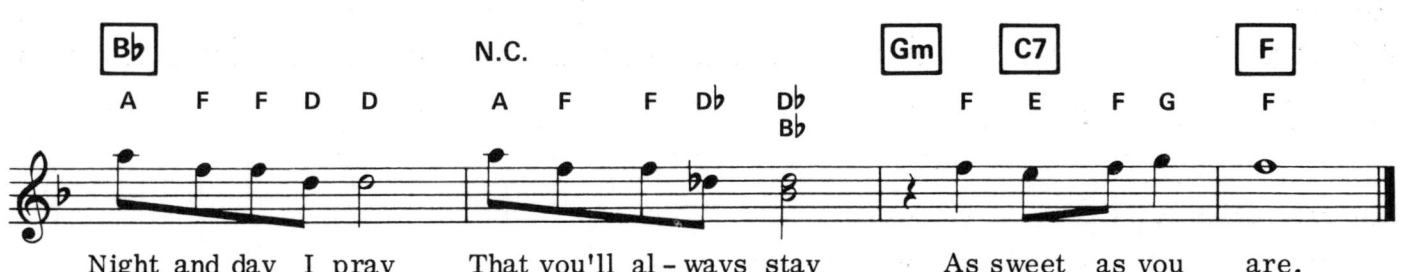

ROSALIE

Words and Music by
COLE PORTER

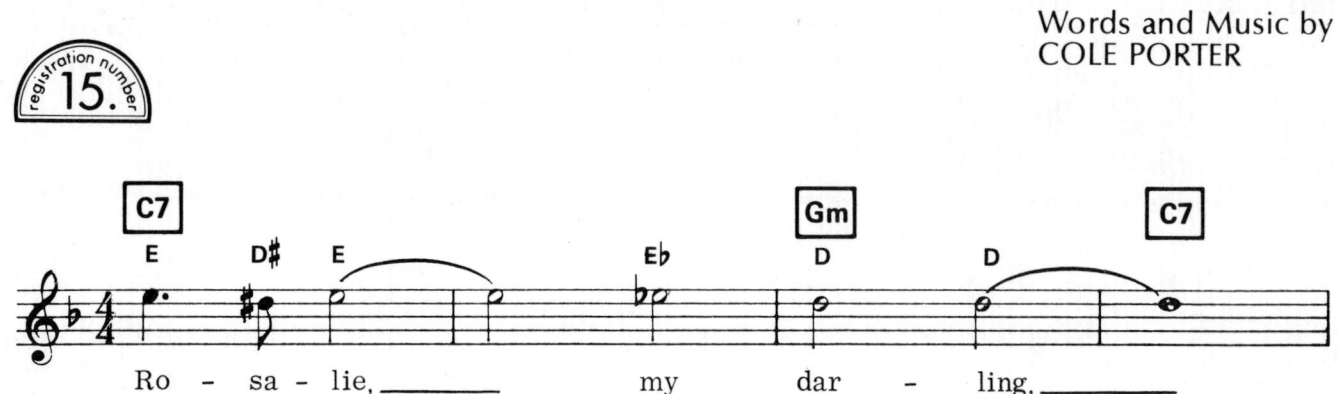

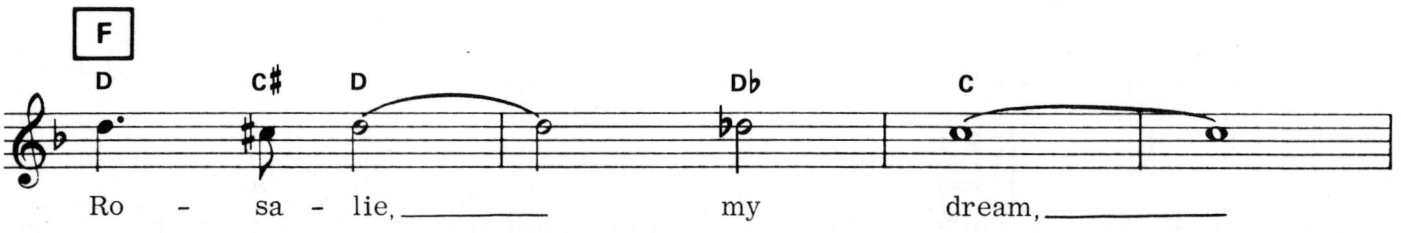

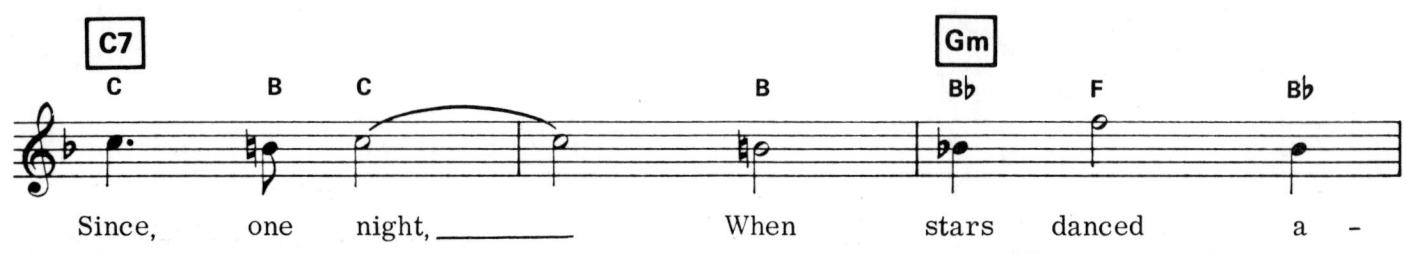

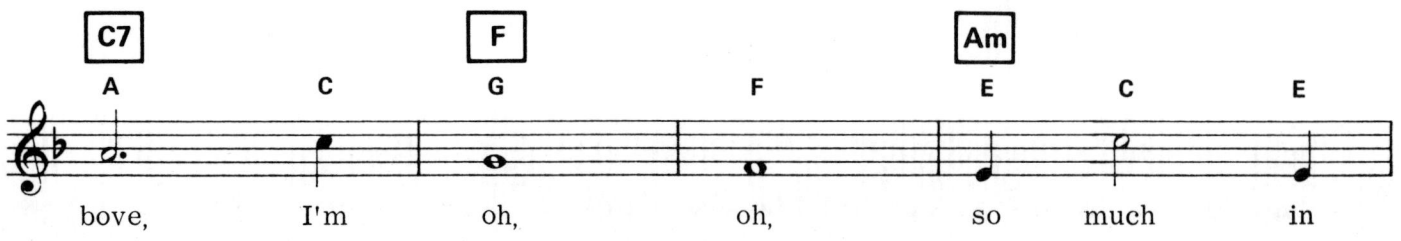

Copyright©1937 by Chappell & Co., Inc., New York, N.Y.
Copyright Renewed
Used by HAL LEONARD PUBLISHING CORPORATION, Winona, MN 55987 by Permission
Made in U.S.A.   International Copyright Secured   All Rights Reserved

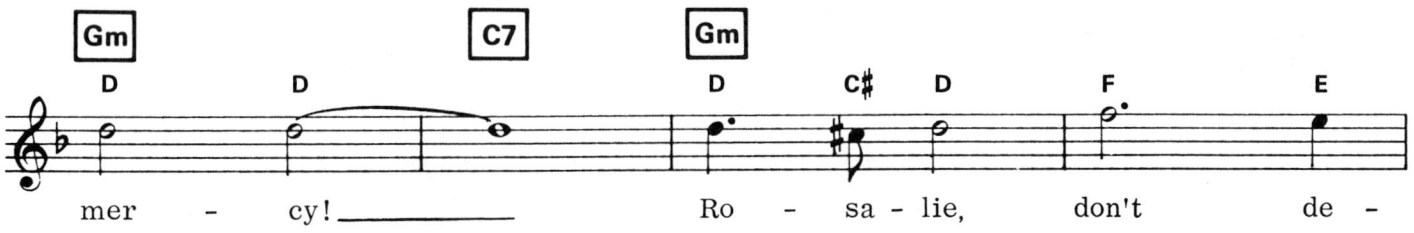

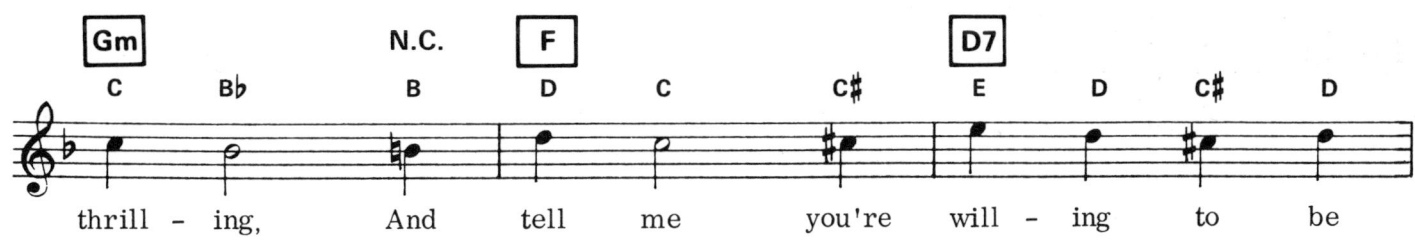
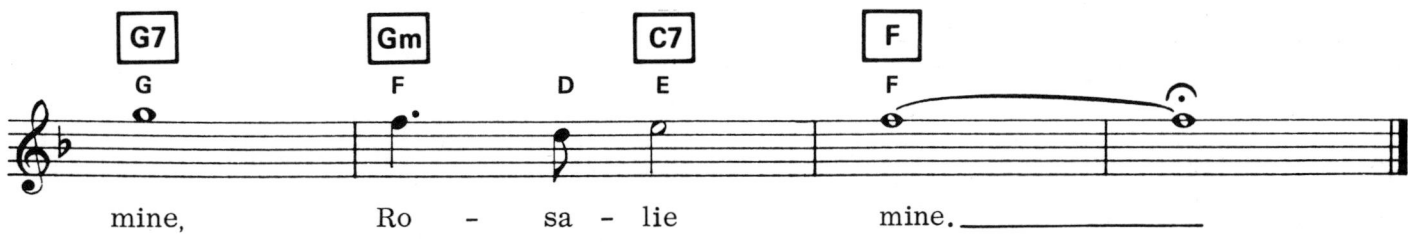

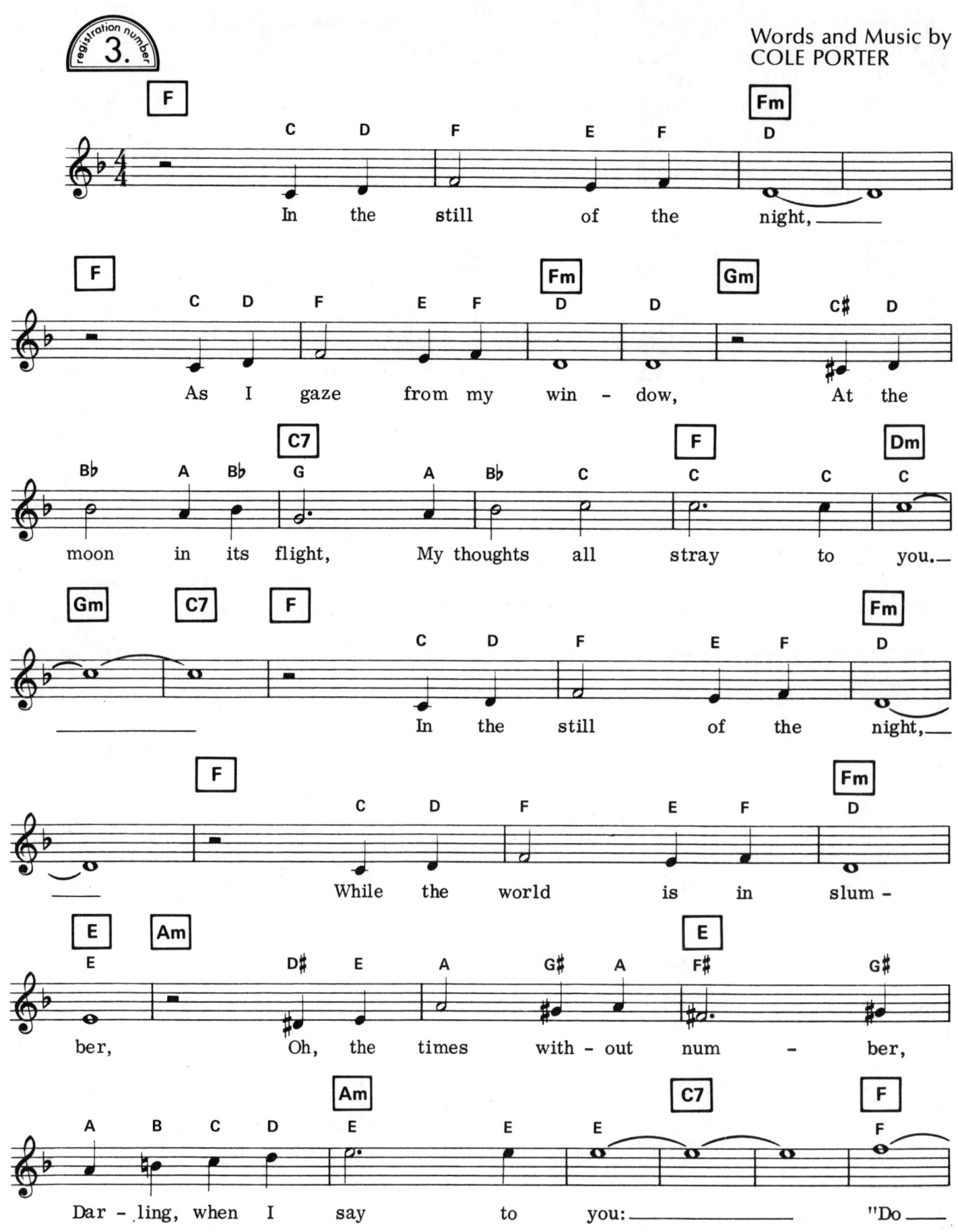

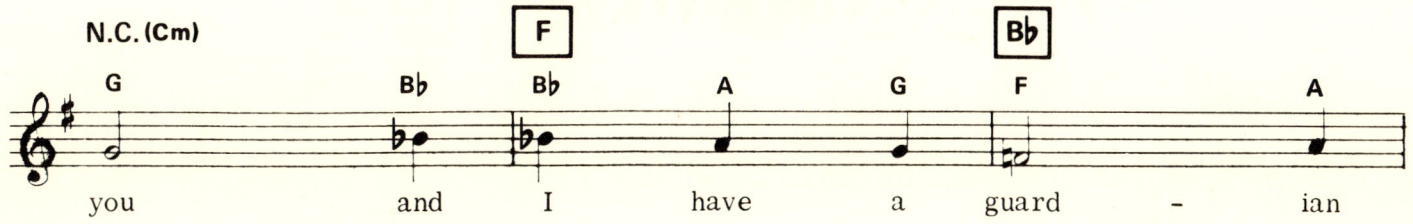
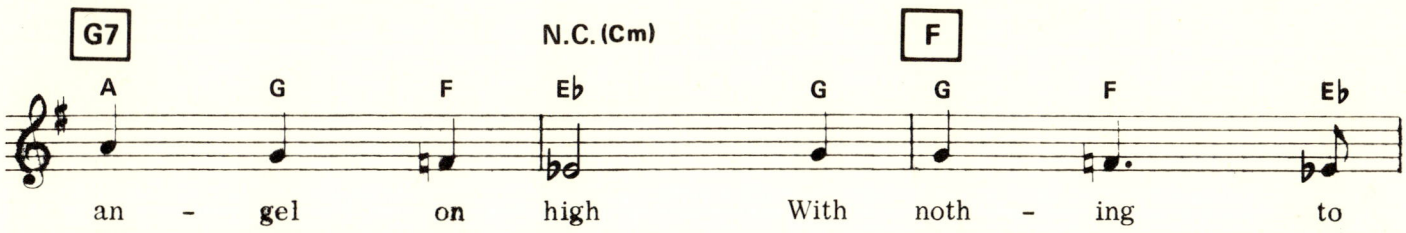
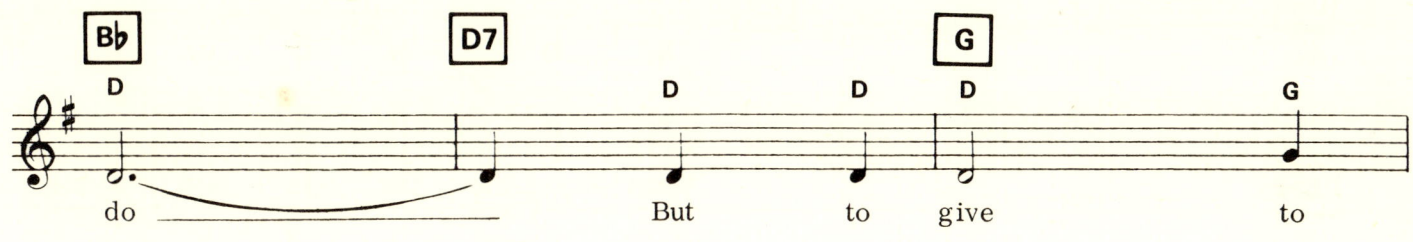
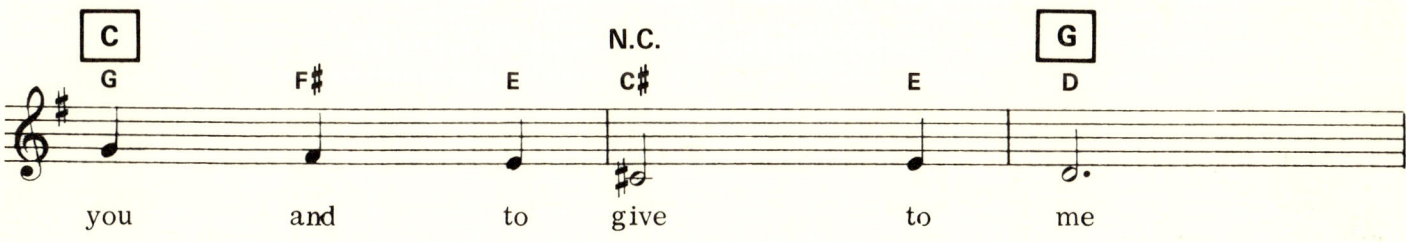
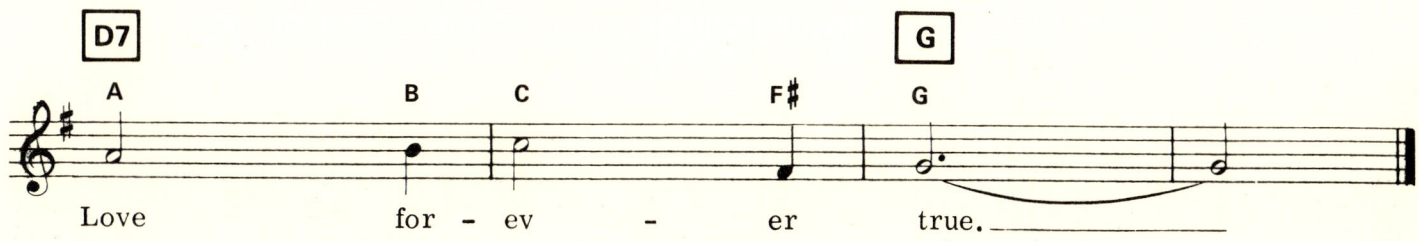

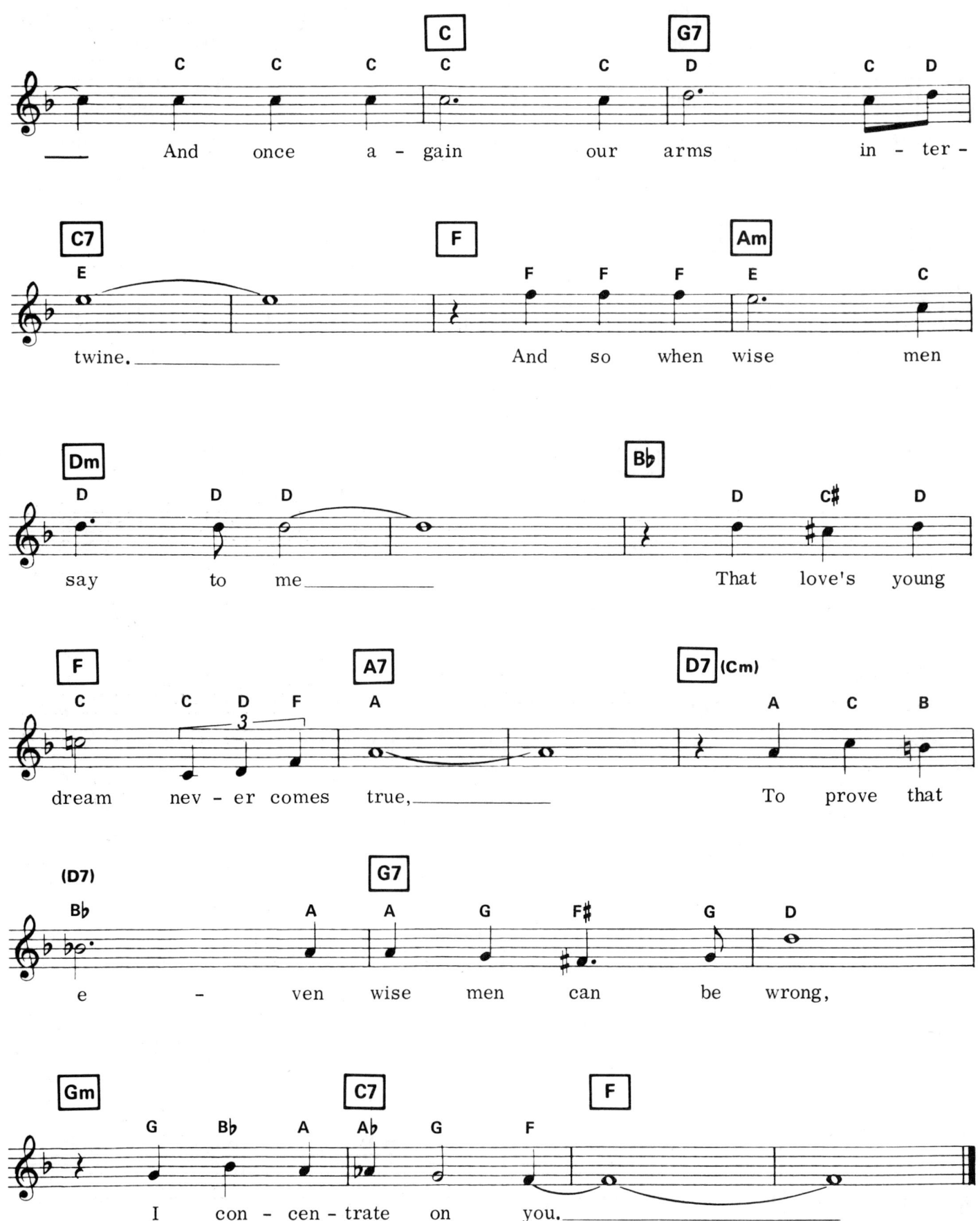

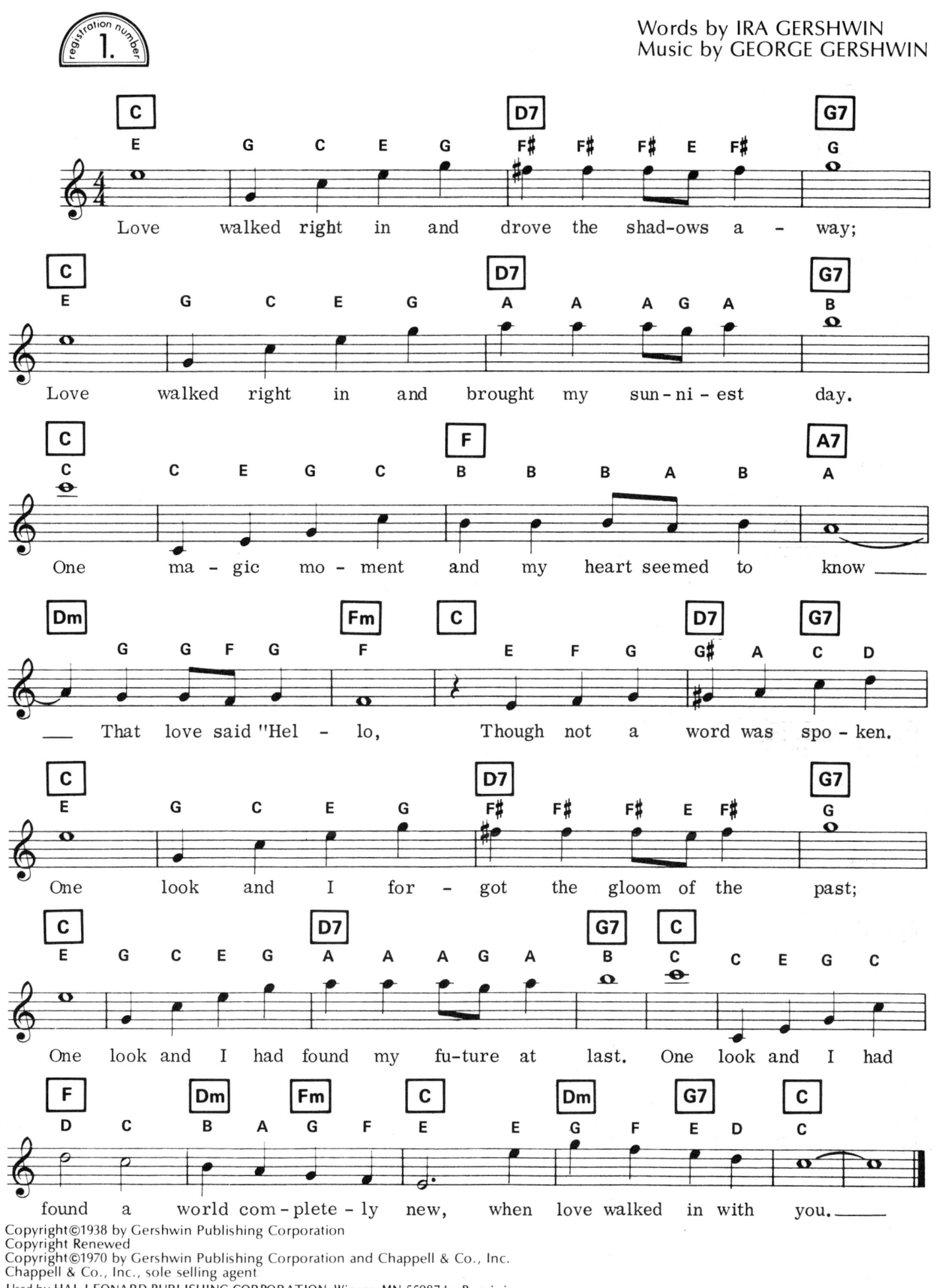

A FOGGY DAY

Words by IRA GERSHWIN
Music by GEORGE GERSHWIN

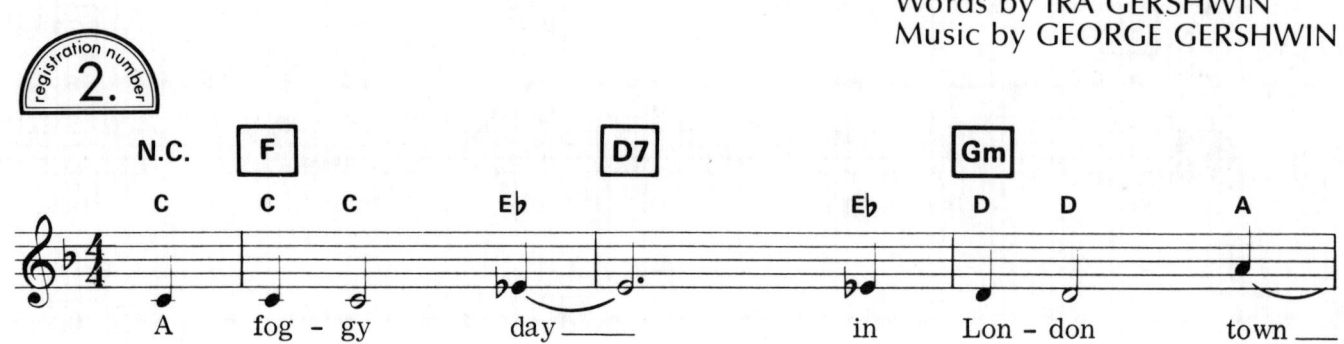

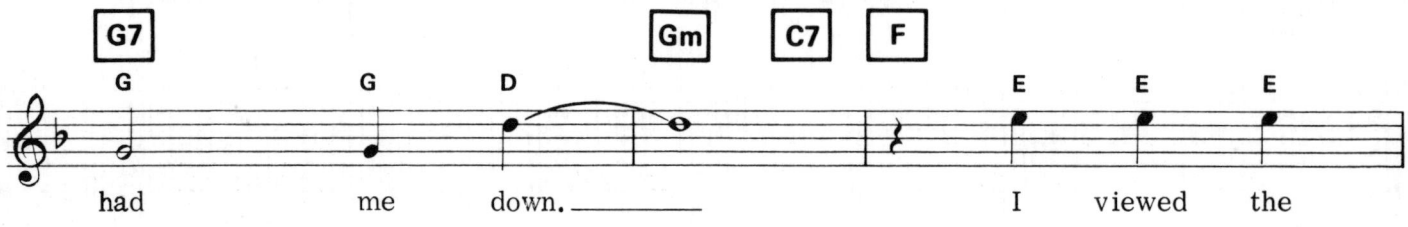

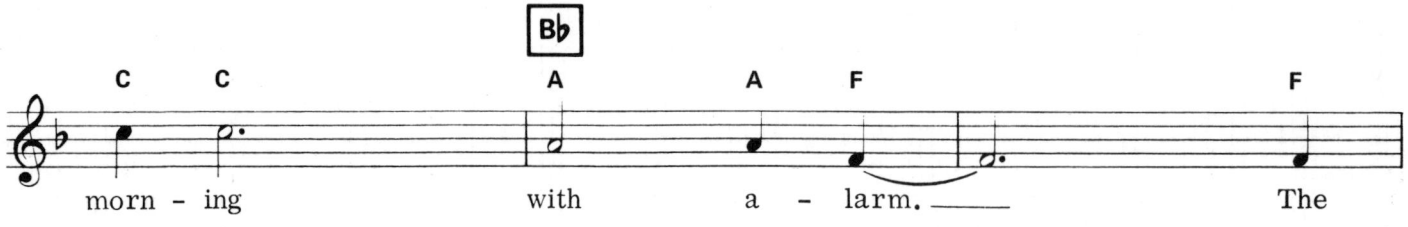

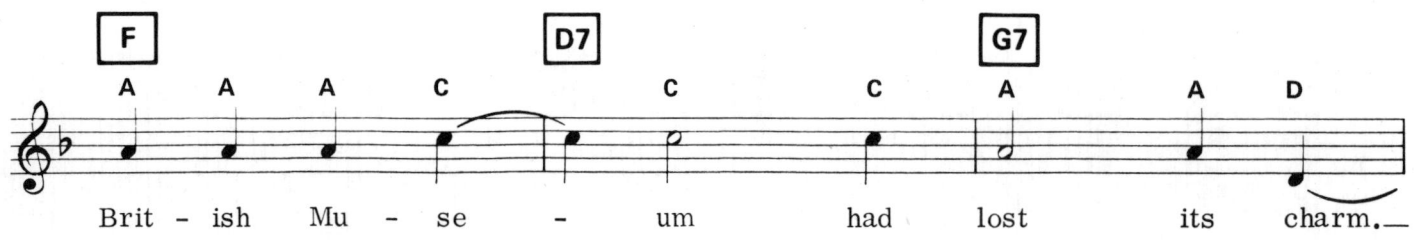

Copyright ©1937 by Gershwin Publishing Corporation
Copyright Renewed
Copyright ©1970 by Gershwin Publishing Corporation and Chappell & Co., Inc.
Chappell & Co., Inc., sole selling agent
Used by HAL LEONARD PUBLISHING CORPORATION, Winona, MN 55987 by Permission
Made in U.S.A.   International Copyright Secured   All Rights Reserved

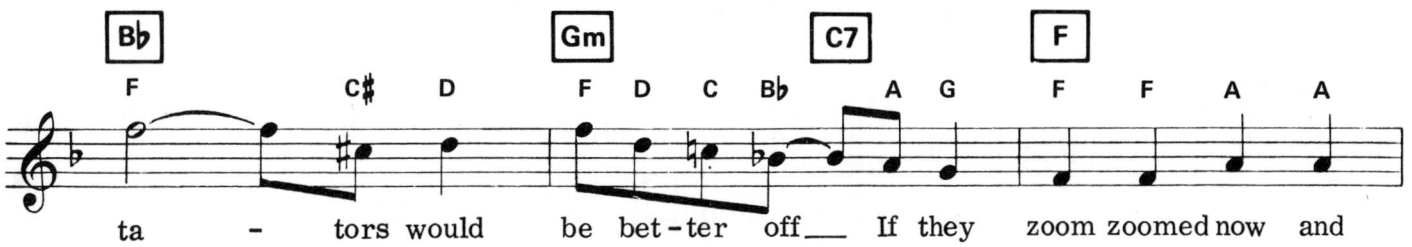
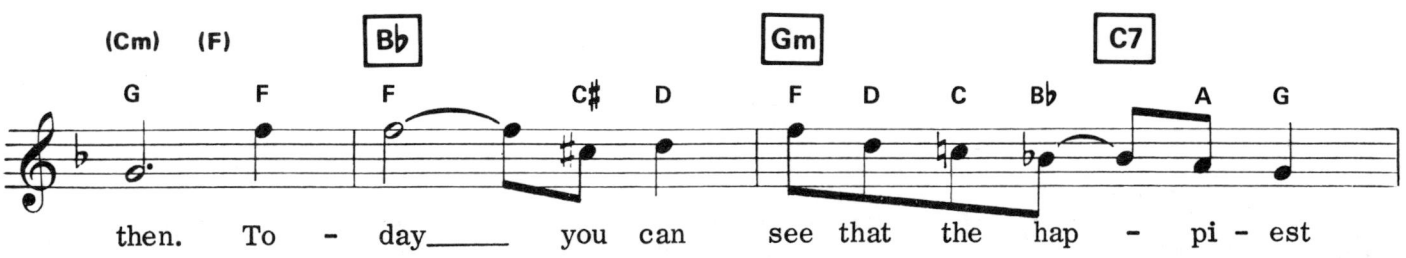

LOVE IS HERE TO STAY

Words by IRA GERSHWIN
Music by GEORGE GERSHWIN

It's ver-y clear Our love is here to stay;

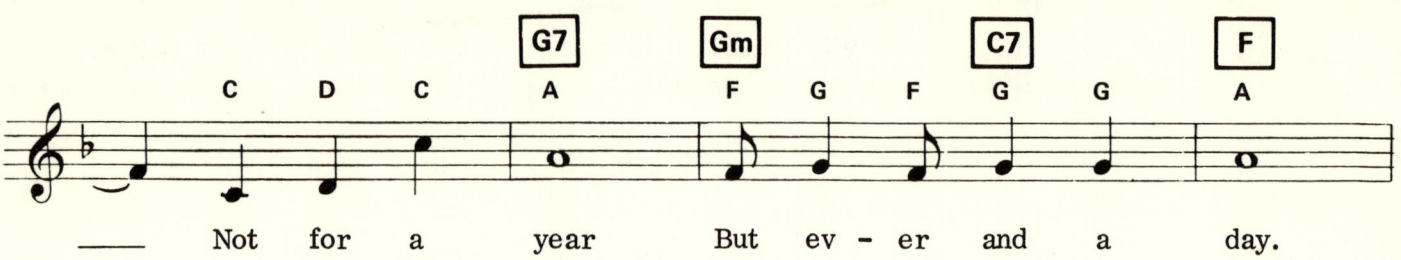
Not for a year But ev-er and a day.

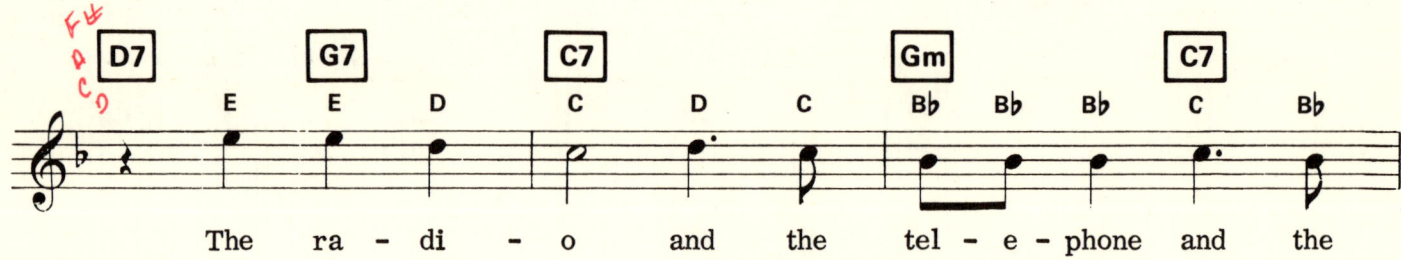
The ra-di-o and the tel-e-phone and the

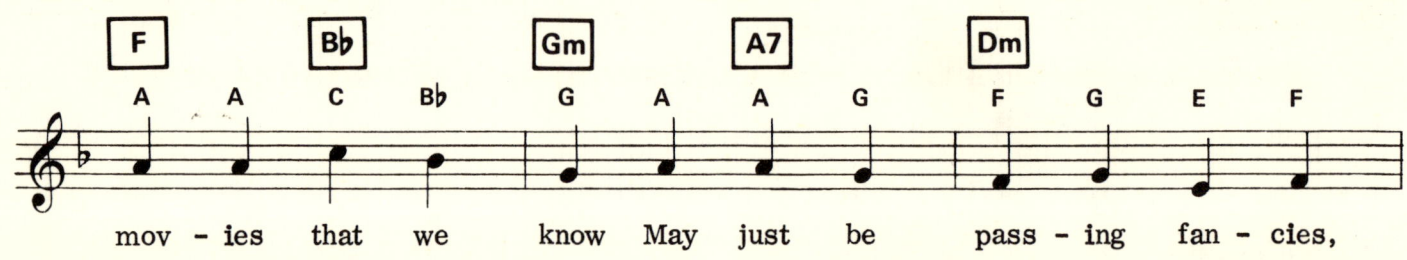
mov-ies that we know May just be pass-ing fan-cies,

Copyright © 1938 by Gershwin Publishing Corporation
Copyright Renewed
Chappell & Co., Inc., sole selling agent
Used by HAL LEONARD PUBLISHING CORPORATION, Winona, MN 55987 by Permission
Made in U.S.A.   International Copyright Secured   All Rights Reserved

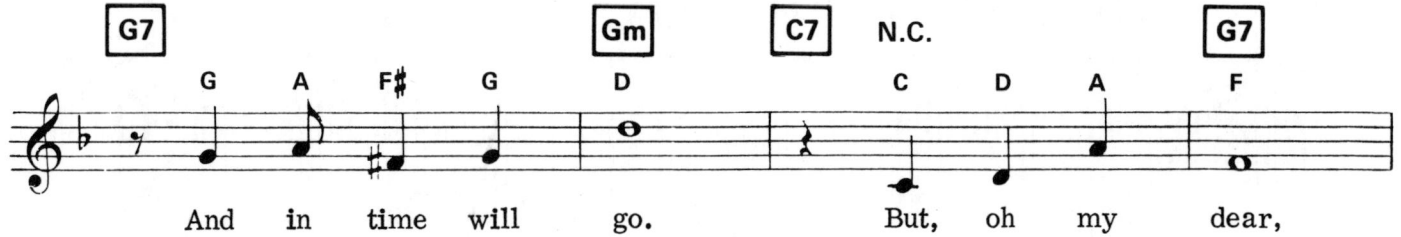
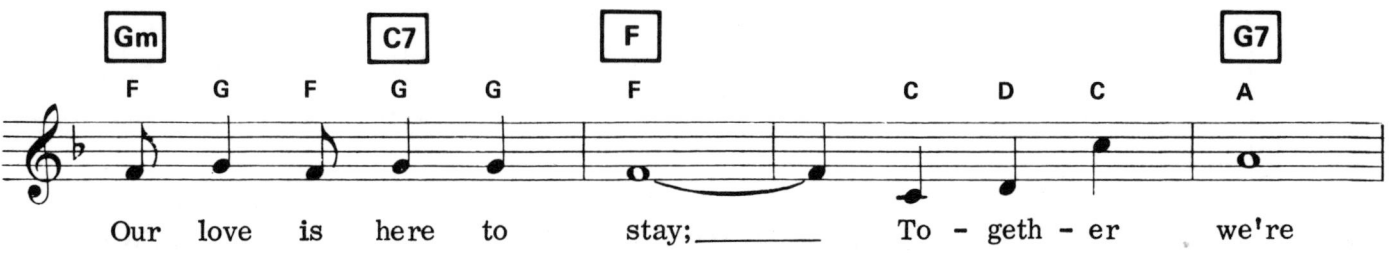
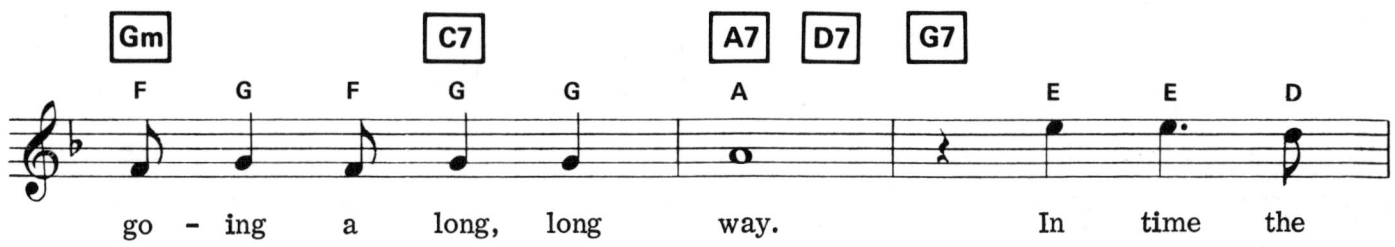

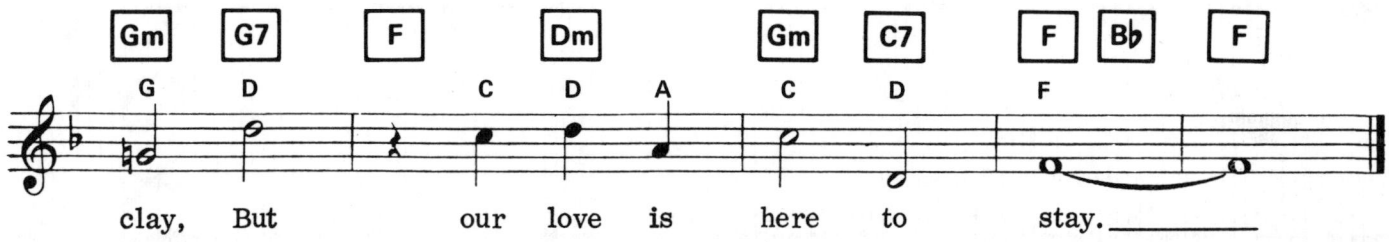

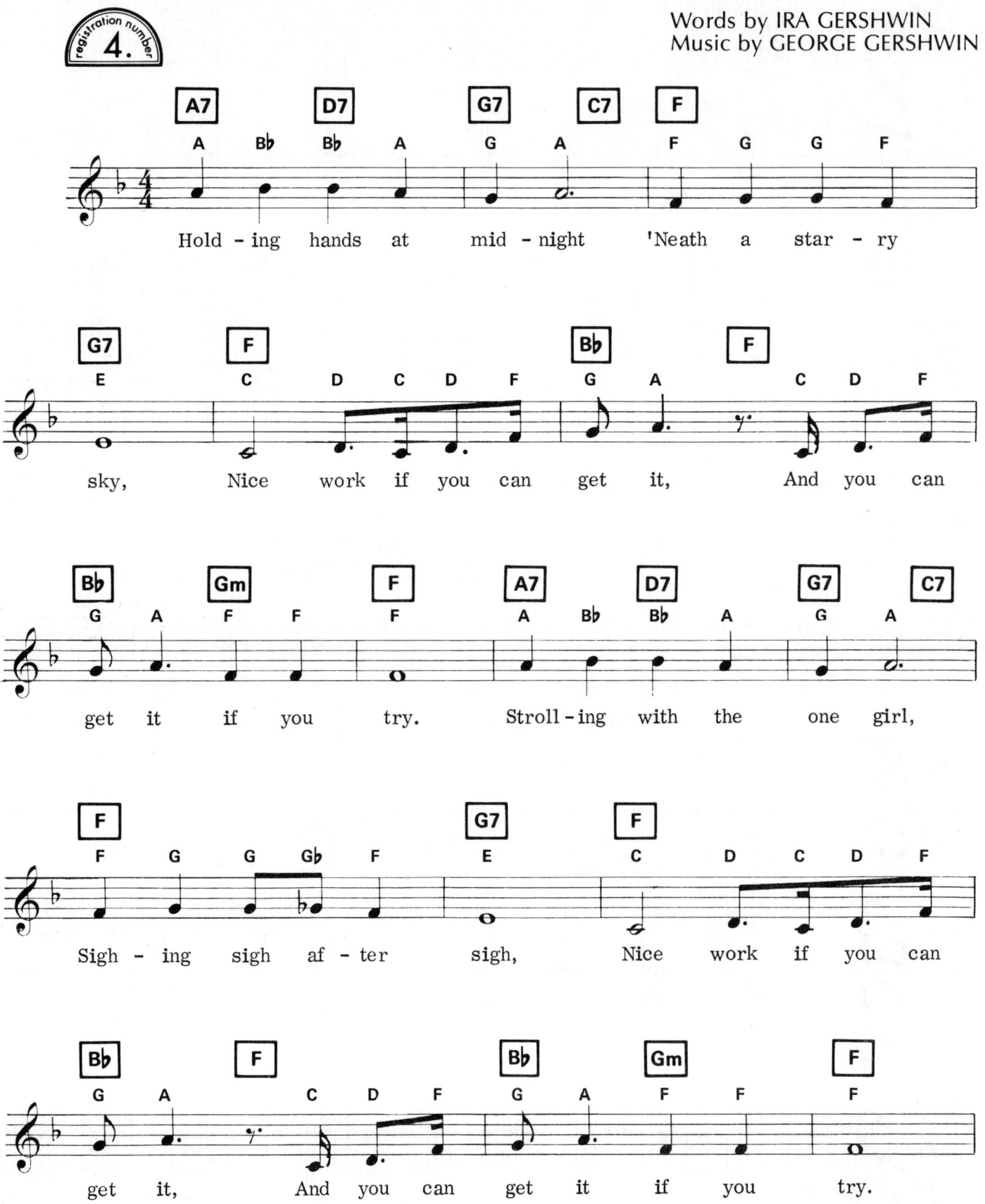

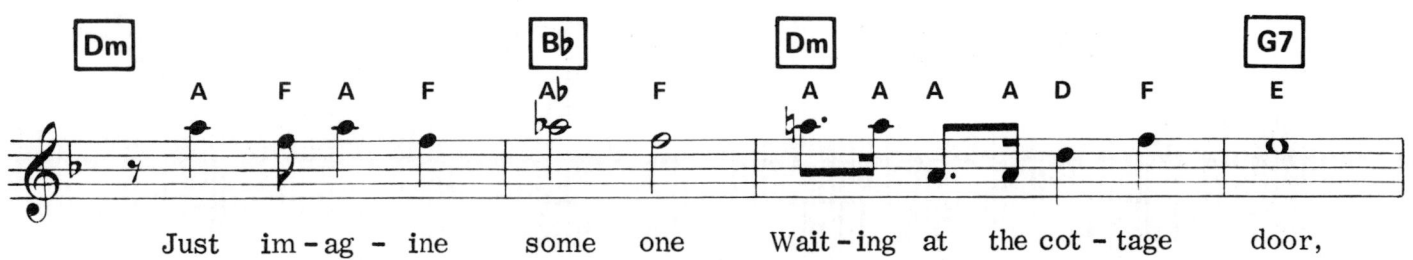
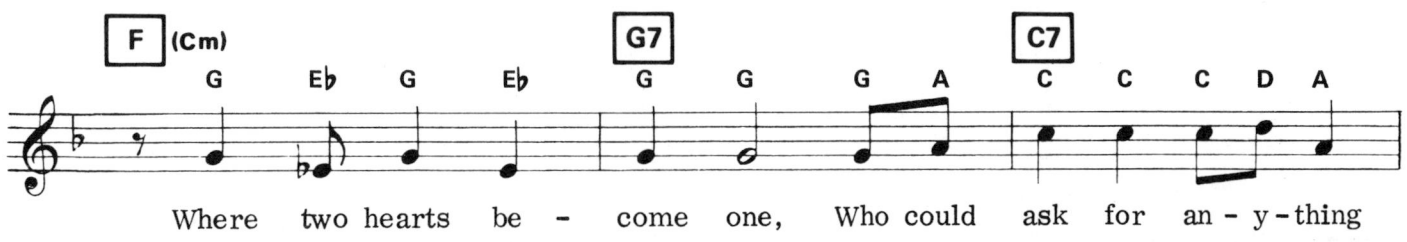

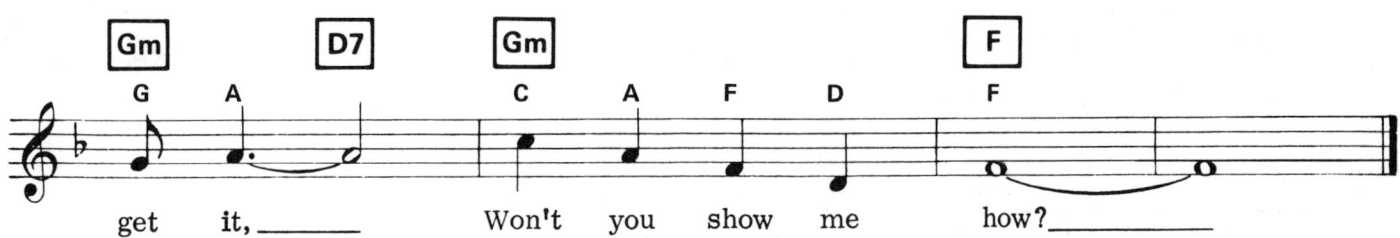

THEY ALL LAUGHED

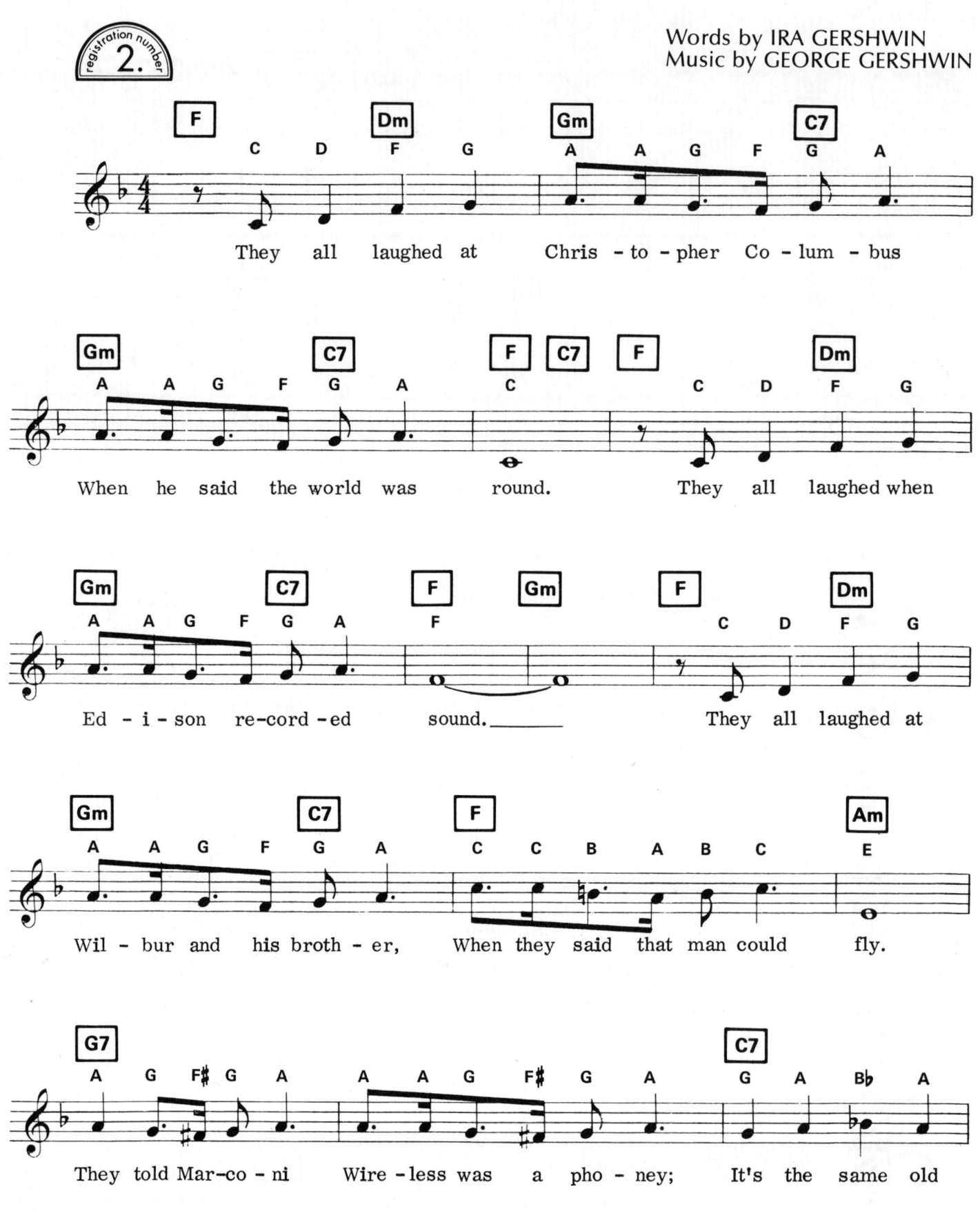

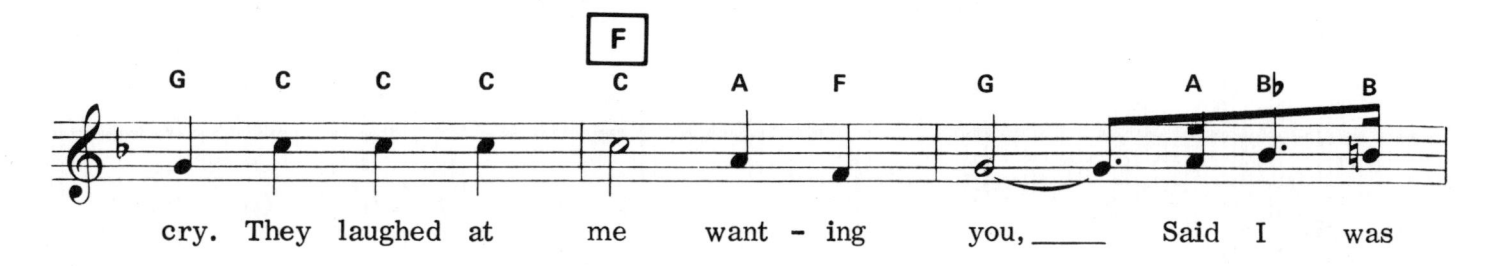

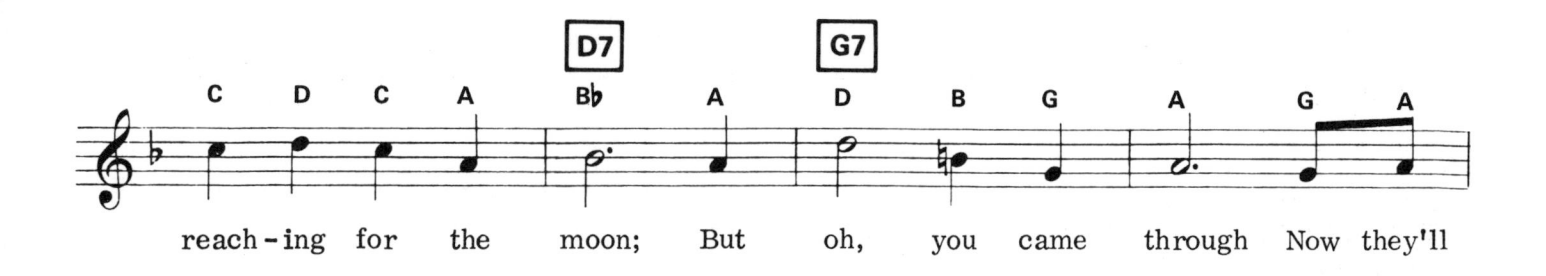

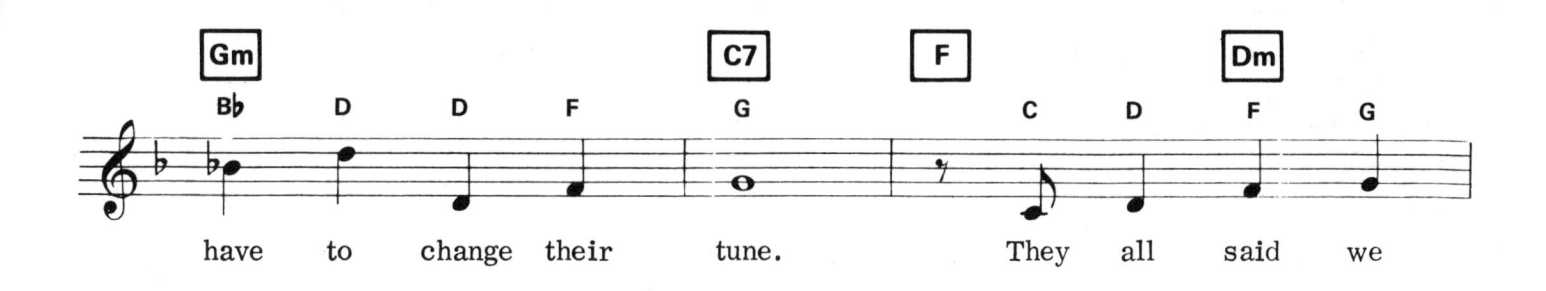

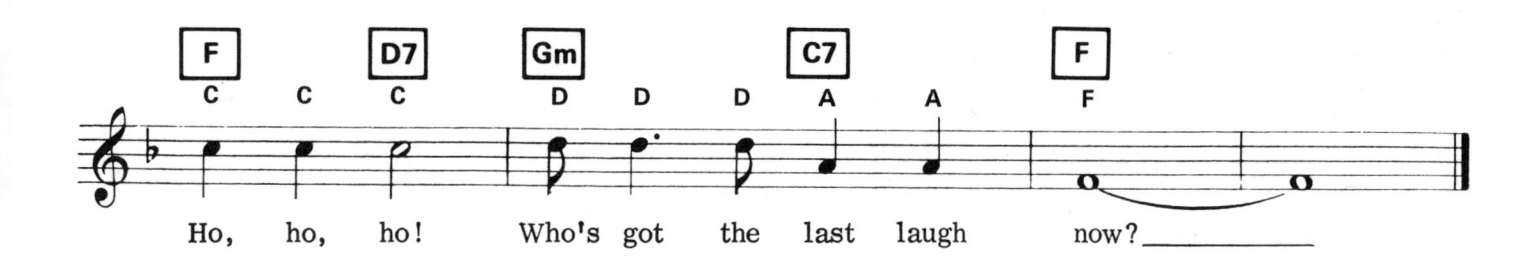

cry. They laughed at me want-ing you,____ Said I was reach-ing for the moon; But oh, you came through Now they'll have to change their tune. They all said we nev-er could be hap-py, They laughed at us and how! But Ho, ho, ho! Who's got the last laugh now?____

SHALL WE DANCE

Words by IRA GERSHWIN
Music by GEORGE GERSHWIN

registration number 3.

Shall we dance, Or keep on mop-ing? Shall we dance, and walk on air? Shall we give in to des-pair, Or shall we dance with nev-er a care?

Copyright © 1936 by Gershwin Publishing Corporation
Copyright Renewed
Chappell & Co., Inc., sole selling agent
Used by HAL LEONARD PUBLISHING CORPORATION, Winona, MN 55987 by Permission
Made in U.S.A.   International Copyright Secured   All Rights Reserved

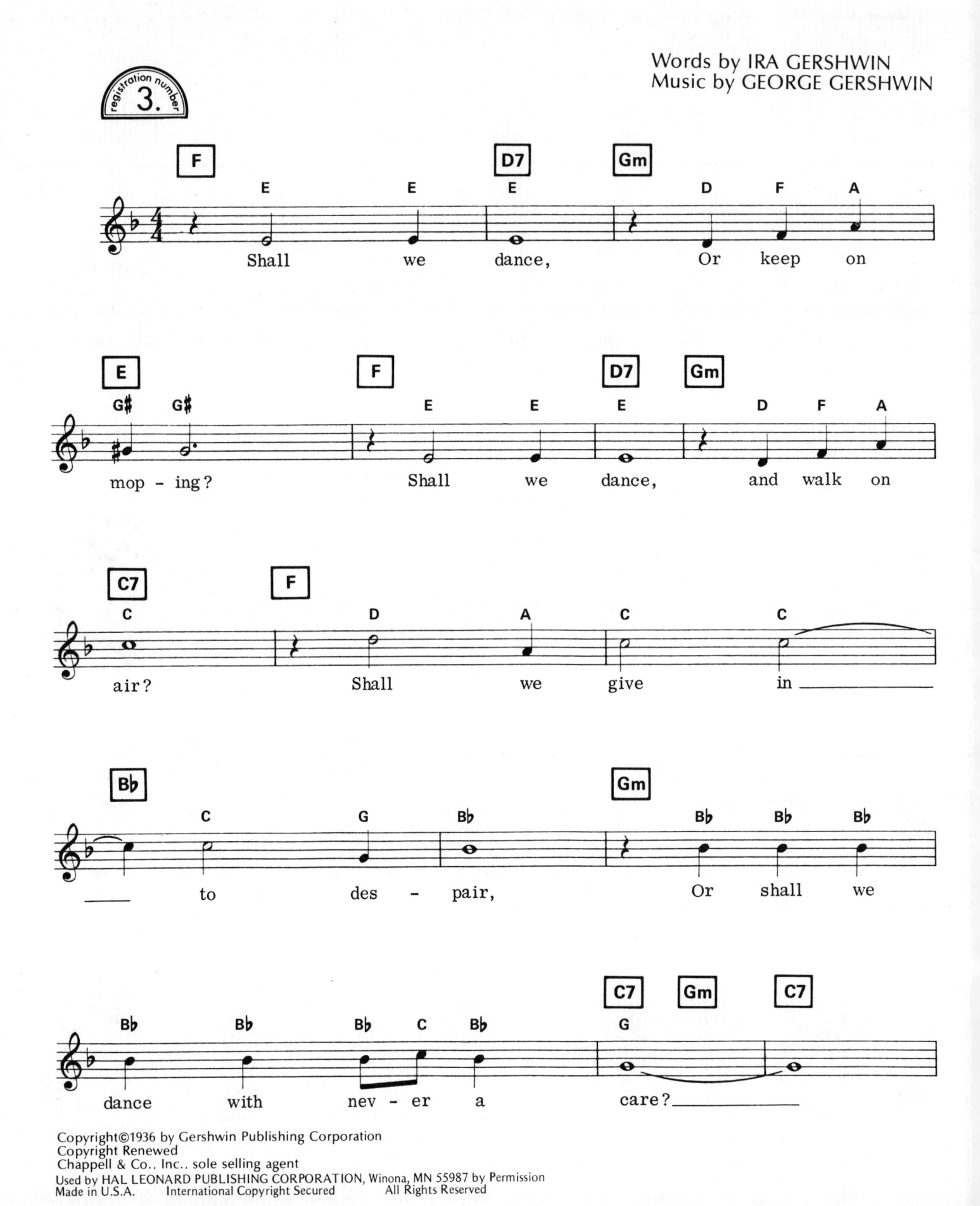

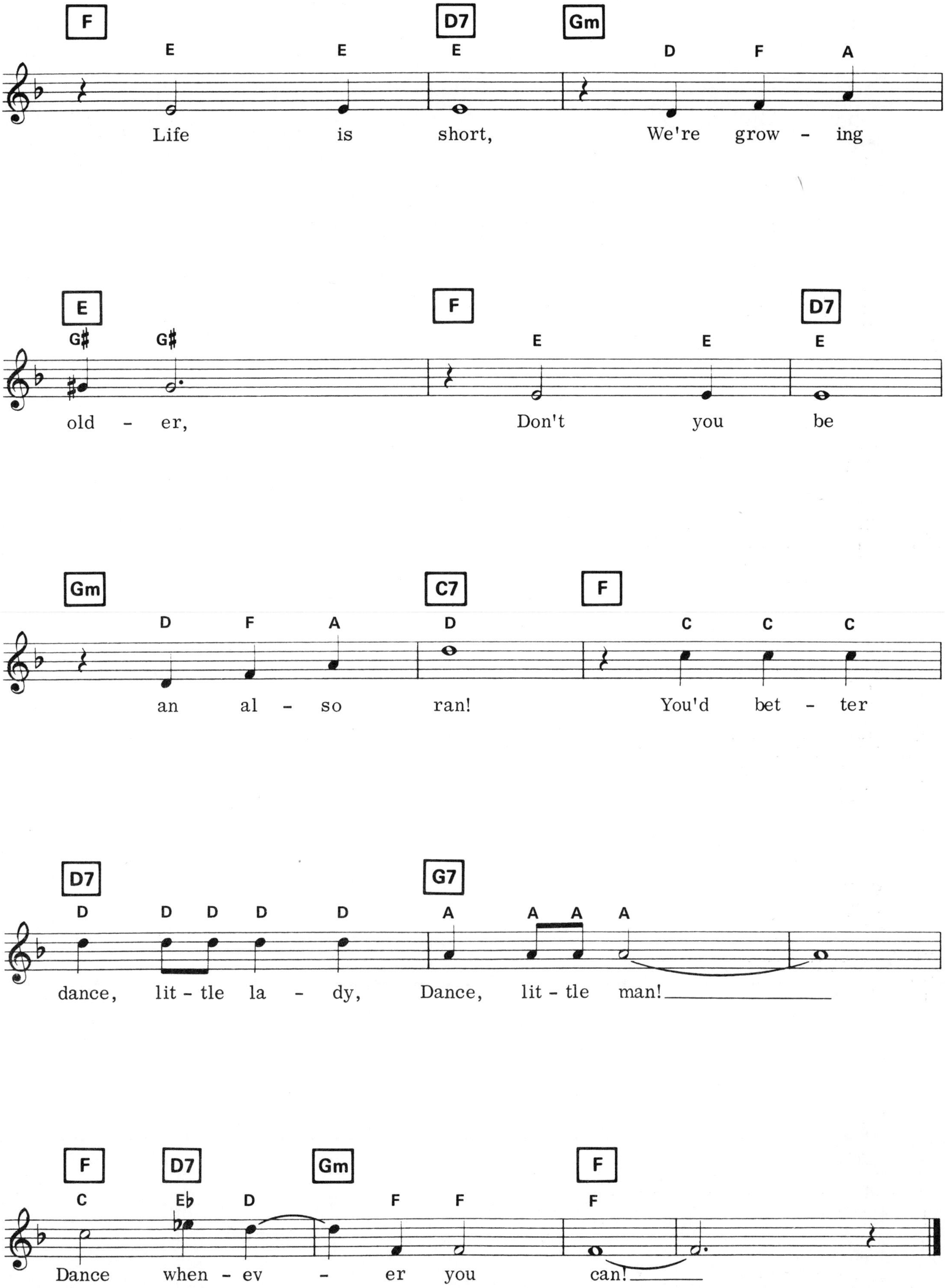
F
D7
Gm
E E E D F A
Life is short, We're grow - ing
E
F
D7
G♯ G♯ E E E
old - er, Don't you be
Gm
C7
F
D F A D C C C
an al - so ran! You'd bet - ter
D7
G7
D D D D D A A A A
dance, lit - tle la - dy, Dance, lit - tle man!
F
D7
Gm
F
C E♭ D F F F
Dance when - ev - er you can!

Best of Broadway

COMEDY TONIGHT

Words and Music by
STEPHEN SONDHEIM

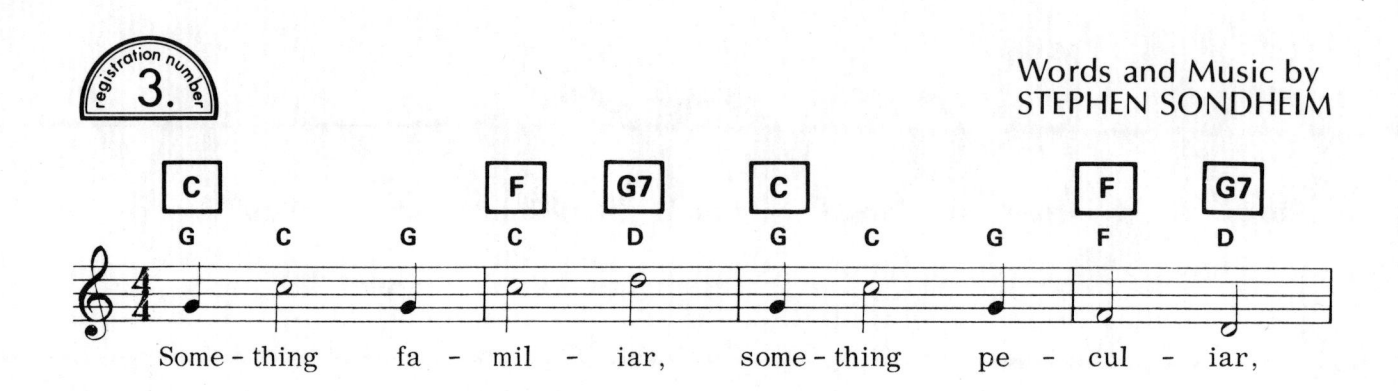

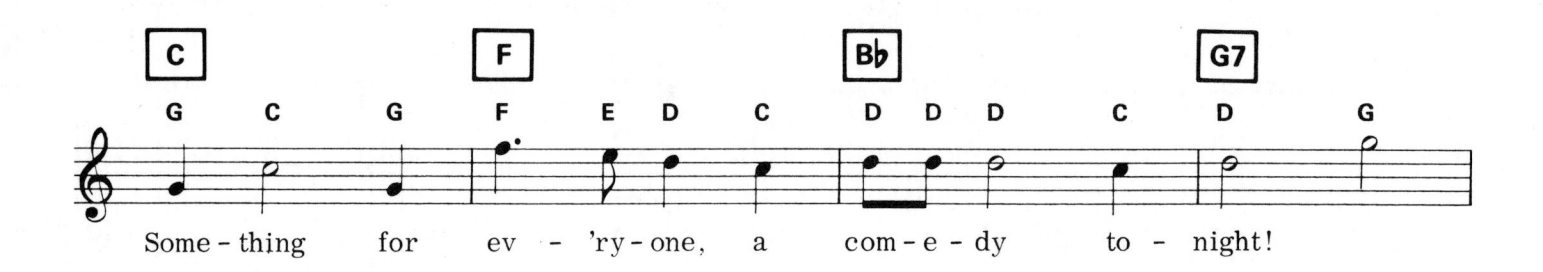

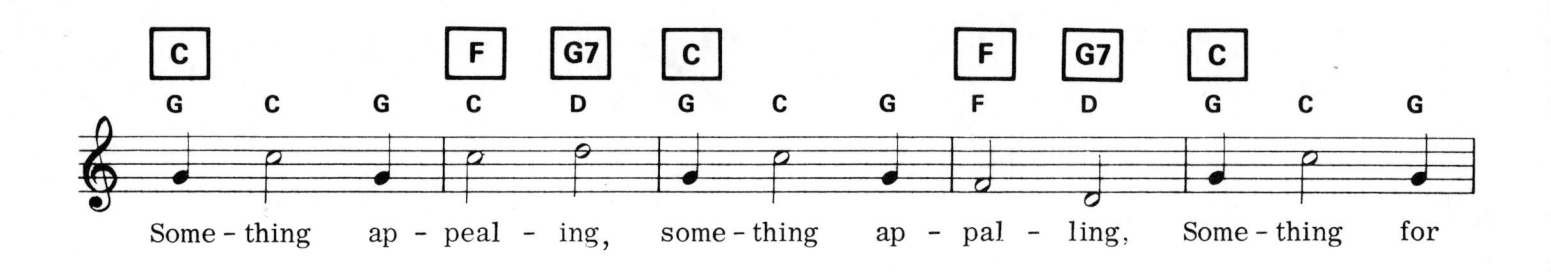

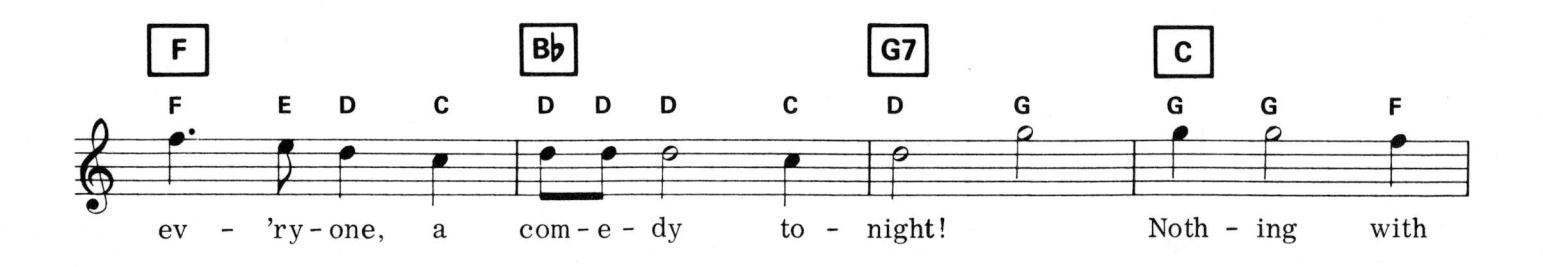

Some-thing fa-mil-iar, some-thing pe-cul-iar,
Some-thing for ev-'ry-one, a com-e-dy to-night!
Some-thing ap-peal-ing, some-thing ap-pal-ling, Some-thing for
ev-'ry-one, a com-e-dy to-night! Noth-ing with

Copyright © 1962 by Stephen Sondheim
Burthen Music Company, Inc., owner of publication and allied rights throughout the world
Chappell & Co., Inc., sole selling agent
Used by HAL LEONARD PUBLISHING CORPORATION, Winona, MN 55987 by Permission
Made in U.S.A.   International Copyright Secured   All Rights Reserved

kings, Nothing with crowns. Bring on the lovers, liars and clowns! Old situations, new complications, Nothing portentous or polite; Tragedy tomorrow, comedy tonight.

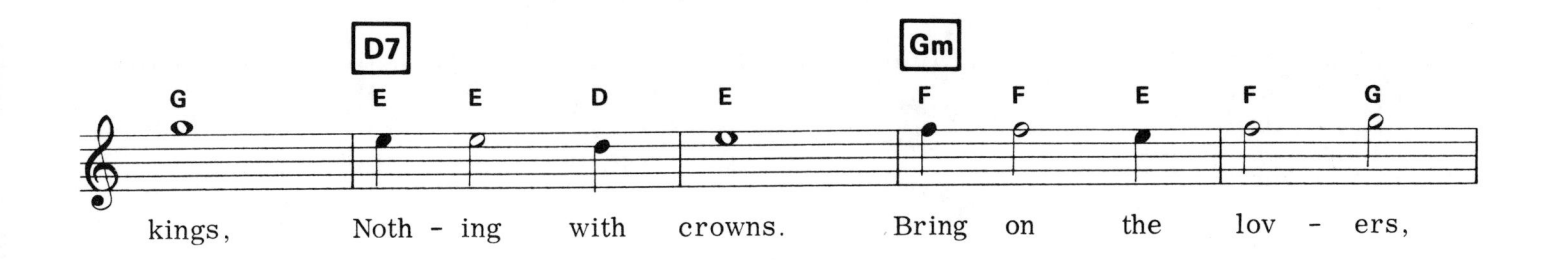

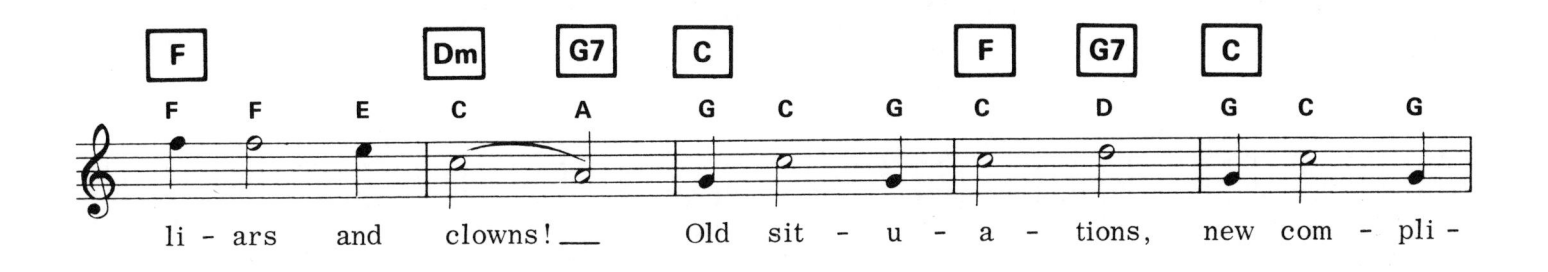

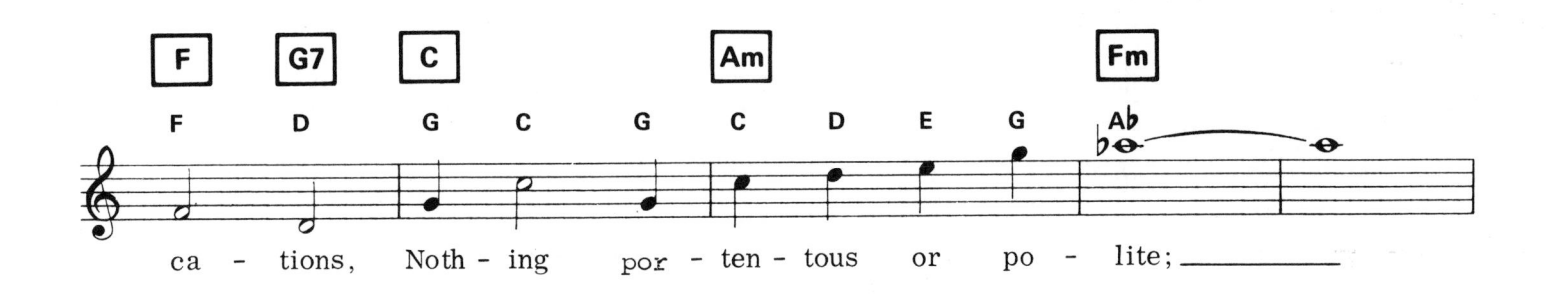

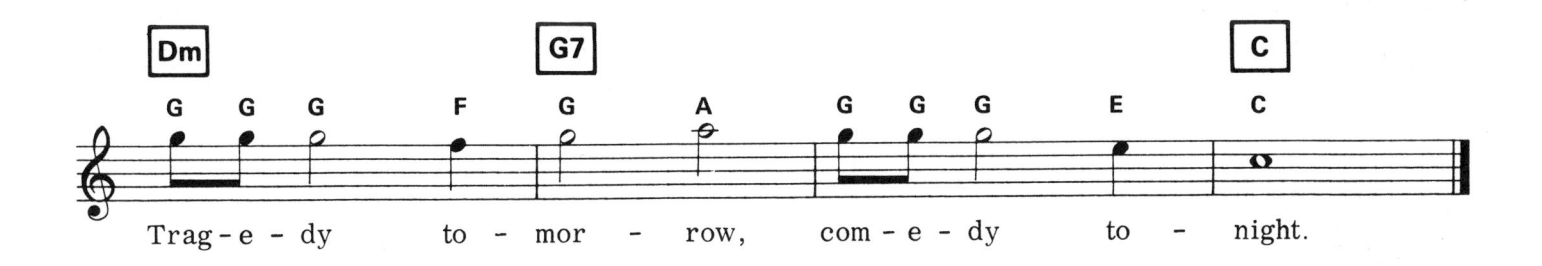

IF I RULED THE WORLD

Words by LESLIE BRICUSSE
Music by CYRIL ORNADEL

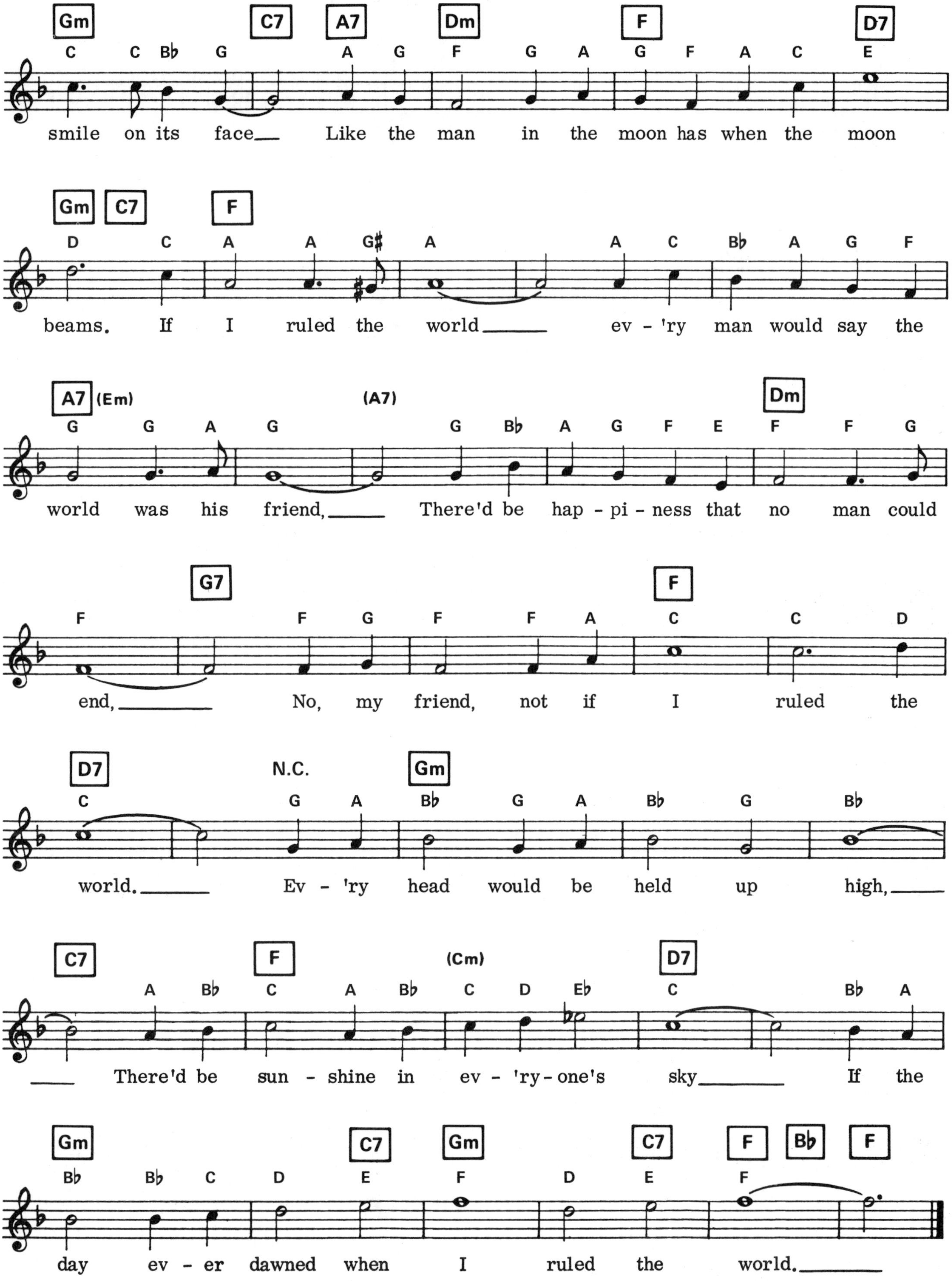
Gm C7 A7 Dm F D7
C C B♭ G A G F G A G F A C E
smile on its face__ Like the man in the moon has when the moon
Gm C7 F
D C A A G♯ A A C B♭ A G F
beams. If I ruled the world___ ev - 'ry man would say the
A7 (Em) (A7) Dm
G G A G G B♭ A G F E F F G
world was his friend,___ There'd be hap - pi - ness that no man could
G7 F
F F G F F A C C D
end,___ No, my friend, not if I ruled the
D7 N.C. Gm
C G A B♭ G A B♭ G B♭
world.___ Ev - 'ry head would be held up high,___
C7 F (Cm) D7
A B♭ C A B♭ C D E♭ C B♭ A
___ There'd be sun - shine in ev - 'ry - one's sky___ If the
Gm C7 Gm C7 F B♭ F
B♭ B♭ C D E F D E F
day ev - er dawned when I ruled the world.___

54

THE THRILL IS GONE

Words and Music by
LEW BROWN and RAY HENDERSON

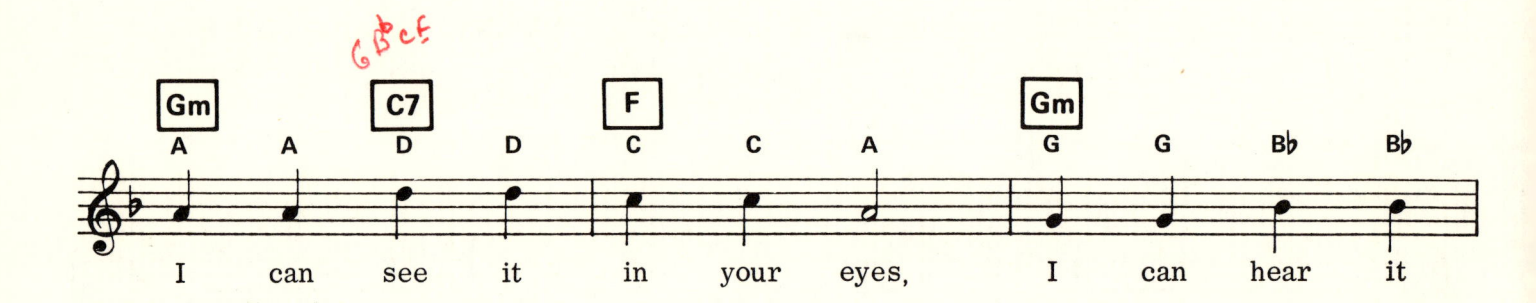

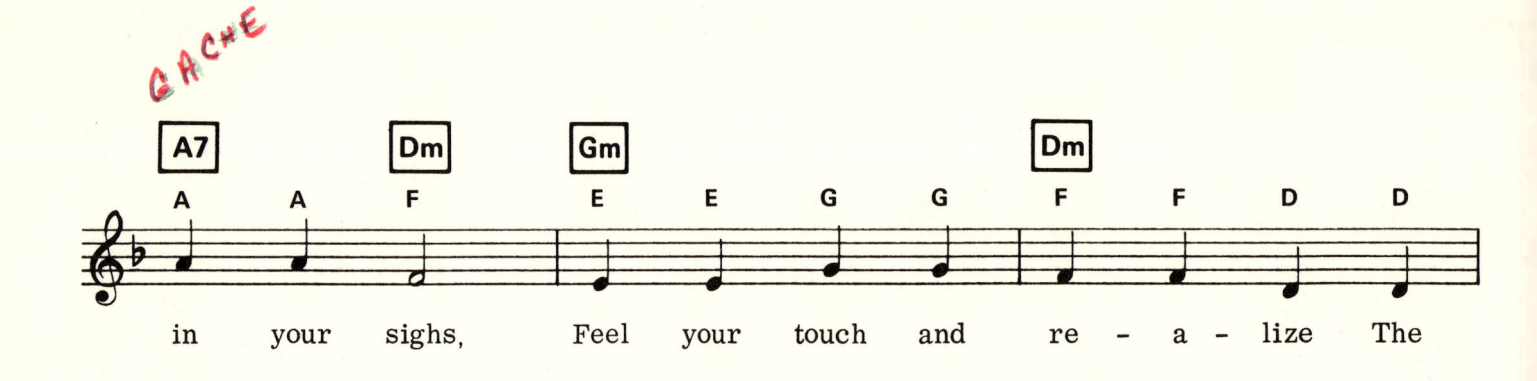

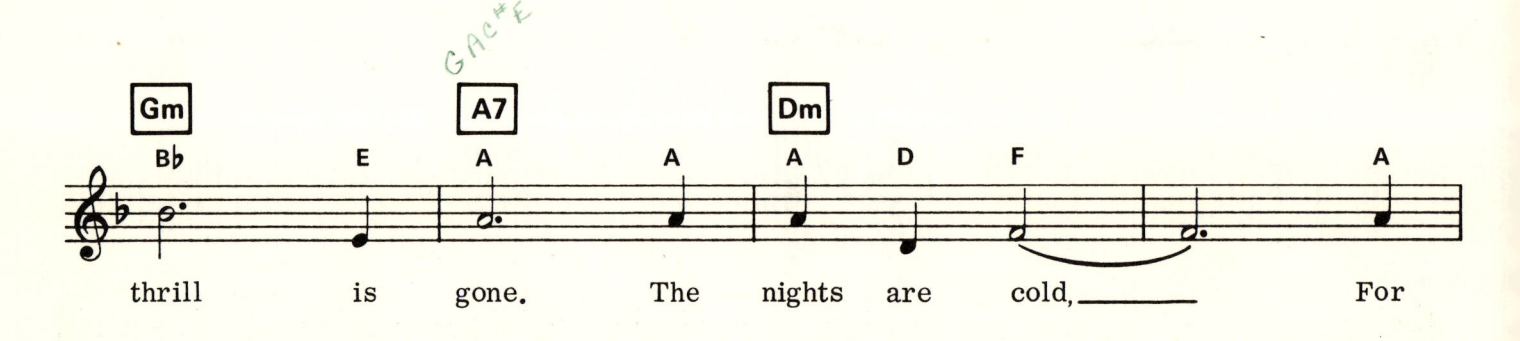

registration number 2.

N.C.	**Dm**		**G7**	
A	A D F		A A D F	

The thrill is gone! ___ The thrill is gone! ___

GBcE

Gm	**C7**	**F**	**Gm**	
A A	D D	C C A	G G B♭ B♭

I can see it in your eyes, I can hear it

GAC#E

A7	**Dm**	**Gm**	**Dm**	
A A	F	E E G G	F F D D

in your sighs, Feel your touch and re - a - lize The

GAC#E

Gm	**A7**	**Dm**		
B♭	E A	A A D F	A

thrill is gone. The nights are cold, ___ For

Copyright©1931 by DeSylva, Brown & Henderson, Inc.
Copyright Renewed, assigned to Chappell & Co., Inc.
Used by HAL LEONARD PUBLISHING CORPORATION, Winona, MN 55987 by Permission
Made in U.S.A.   International Copyright Secured   All Rights Reserved

G7 Gm C7 F
A D F A A D D C C A
love is old, Love was grand when love was new,
Gm A7 Dm Gm
G G B♭ B♭ A A F E E G G
Birds were sing - ing, Skies were blue. Now it don't ap -
C A C# E
Dm Gm A7 F
F F D D B♭ A B♭ A F E
peal to you, The thrill is gone. This is the
G# B E
Dm E Dm Gm
F E E D E D C B♭
end, So why pre - tend And let it
Dm N.C. A7 Dm
A F G E♭ A E G F D
lin - ger on? The thrill is gone.

SEPTEMBER SONG

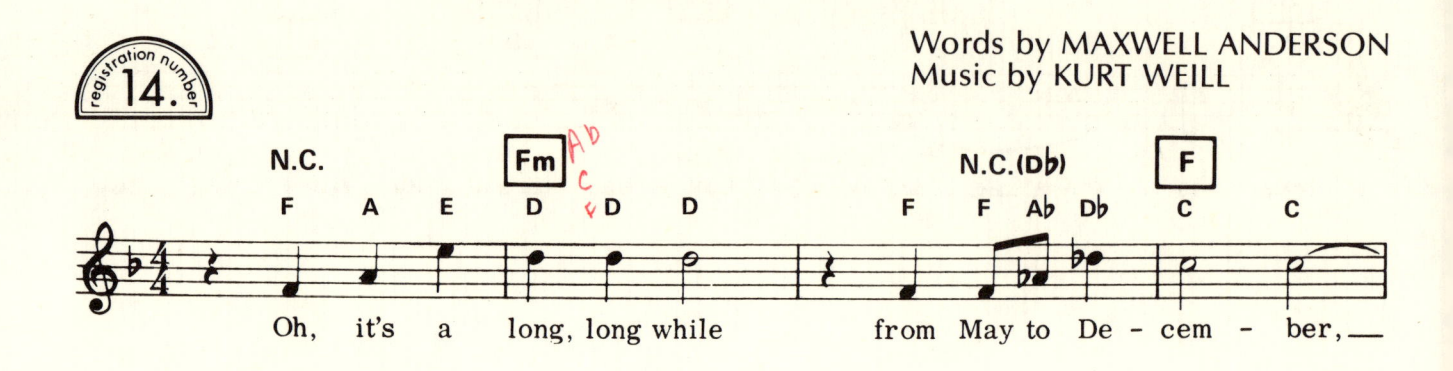

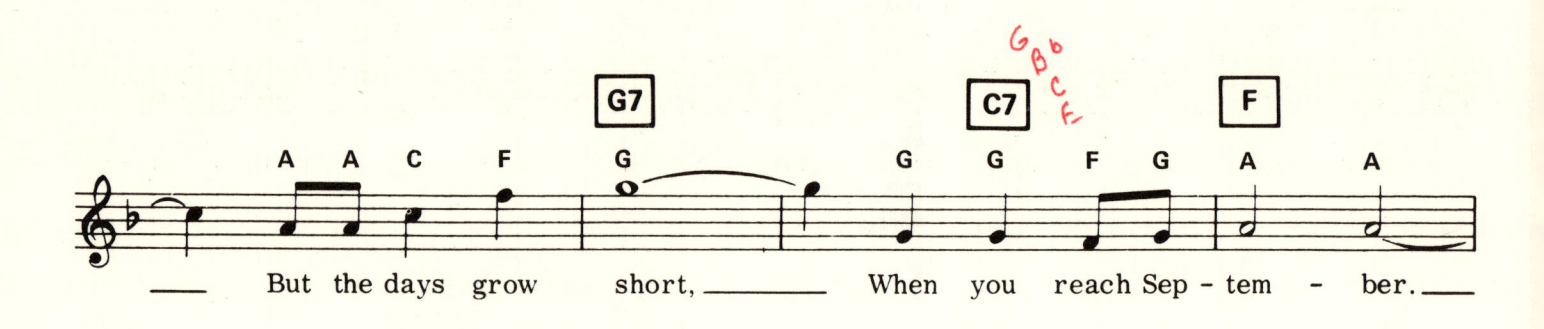

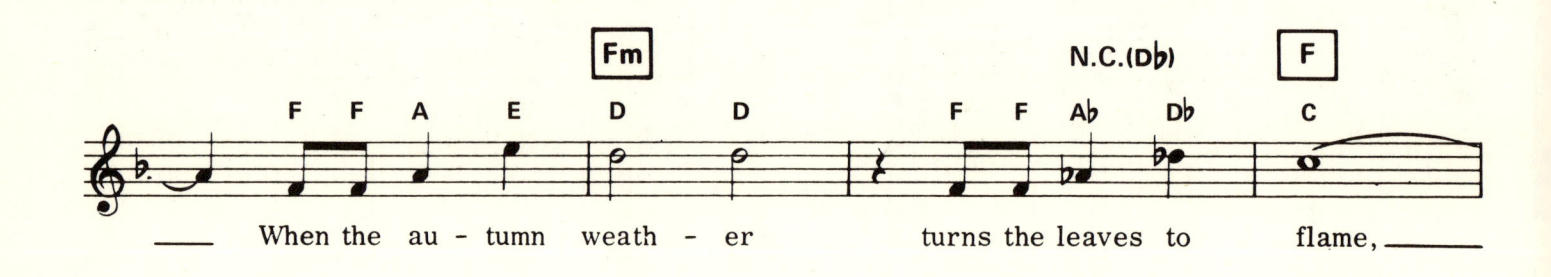

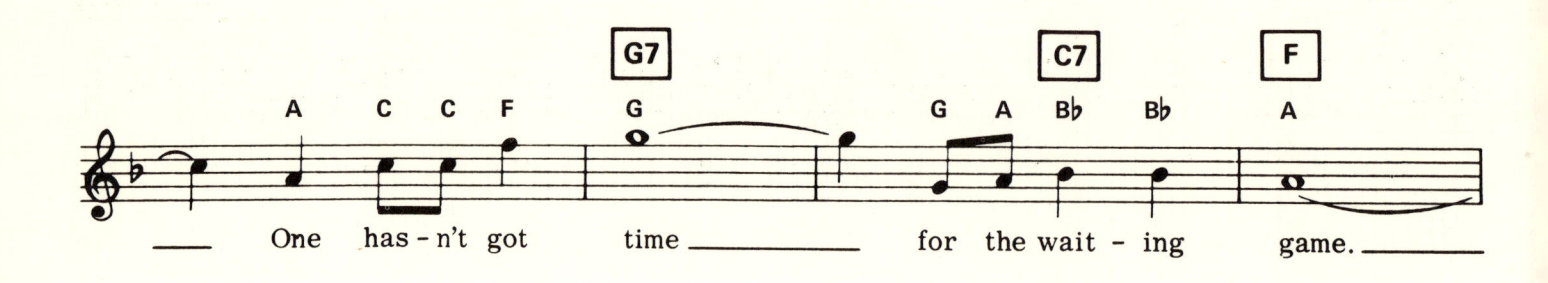

Words by MAXWELL ANDERSON
Music by KURT WEILL

registration number 14.

N.C.	Fm		N.C.(Db)	F
F A E	D D D		F F Ab Db	C C

Oh, it's a long, long while from May to De - cem - ber,

	G7			F
A A C F	G		G G F G A	A

But the days grow short, When you reach Sep - tem - ber.

	Fm		N.C.(Db)	F
F F A E	D D		F F Ab Db	C

When the au - tumn weath - er turns the leaves to flame,

	G7		C7	F
A C C F	G		G A Bb Bb	A

One has - n't got time for the wait - ing game.

Copyright©1938 by DeSylva, Brown & Henderson, Inc.
Copyright Renewed, assigned to Chappell & Co., Inc.
Copyright©1970 by Chappell & Co., Inc.
Used by Hal Leonard Publishing Corporation, Winona, MN 55987 by Permission
Made in U.S.A.   International Copyright Secured   All Rights Reserved

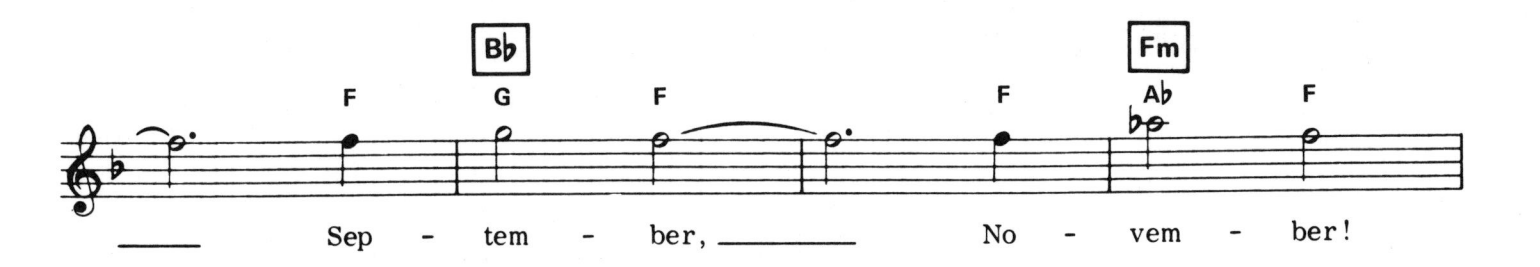

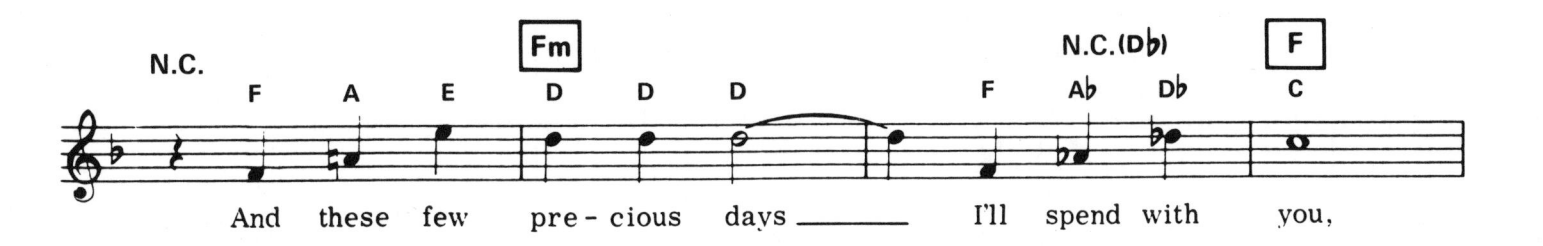

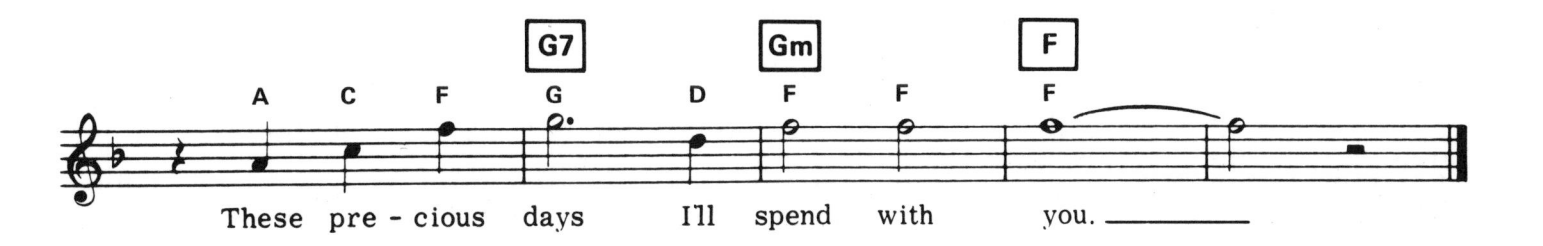

Oh, the days dwindle down to a precious few, September, November! And these few precious days I'll spend with you, These precious days I'll spend with you.

SPEAK LOW

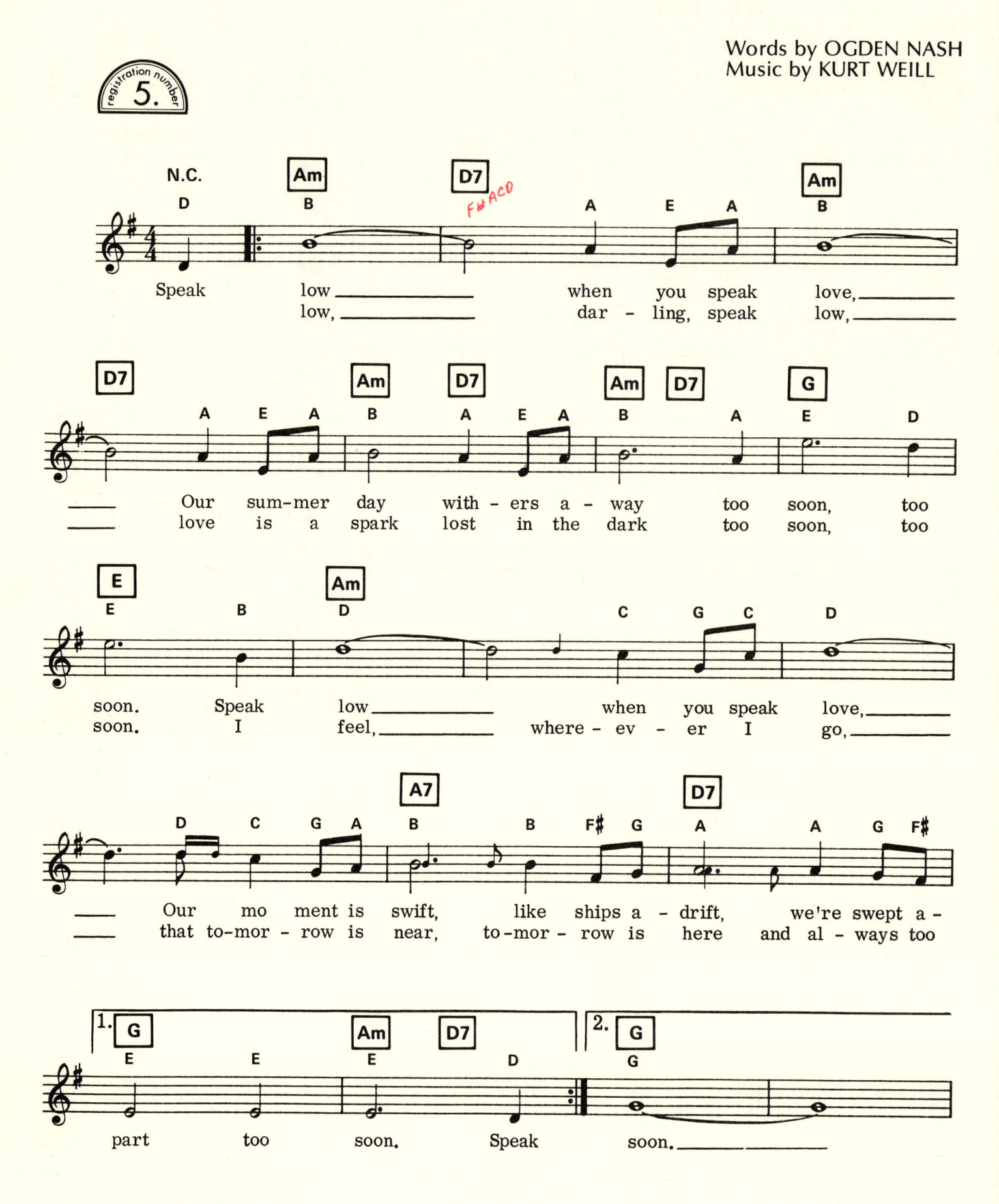

Words by OGDEN NASH
Music by KURT WEILL

Speak low _____ when you speak love, _____
low, _____ dar-ling, speak low, _____
Our sum-mer day with-ers a-way too soon, too
love is a spark lost in the dark too soon, too
soon. Speak low _____ when you speak love, _____
soon. I feel, _____ where-ev-er I go, _____
Our mo-ment is swift, like ships a-drift, we're swept a-
that to-mor-row is near, to-mor-row is here and al-ways too

1. part too soon. Speak
2. soon. _____

Copyright © 1943 by Chappell & Co., Inc.
Copyright Renewed
Copyright © 1970 by Chappell & Co., Inc.
Used by HAL LEONARD PUBLISHING CORPORATION, Winona, MN 55987 by Permission
Made in U.S.A.   International Copyright Secured   All Rights Reserved

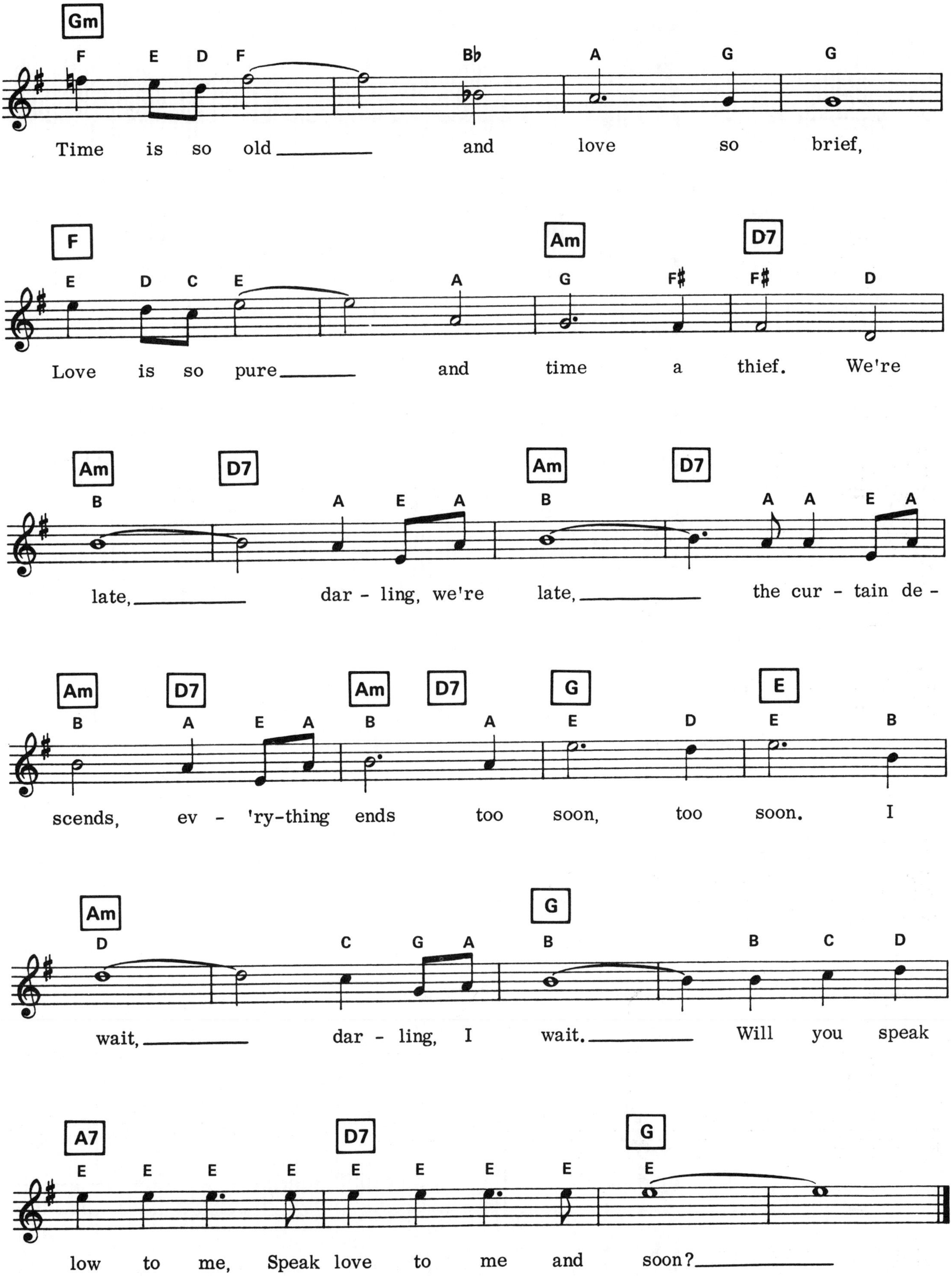
Gm
F E D F Bb A G G
Time is so old and love so brief,
F Am D7
E D C E A G F# F# D
Love is so pure and time a thief. We're
Am D7 Am D7
B A E A B A A E A
late, dar - ling, we're late, the cur - tain de -
Am D7 Am D7 G E
B A E A B A E D E B
scends, ev - 'ry-thing ends too soon, too soon. I
Am G
D C G A B B C D
wait, dar - ling, I wait. Will you speak
A7 D7 G
E E E E E E E E E
low to me, Speak love to me and soon?

MY CUP RUNNETH OVER

Words by TOM JONES
Music by HARVEY SCHMIDT

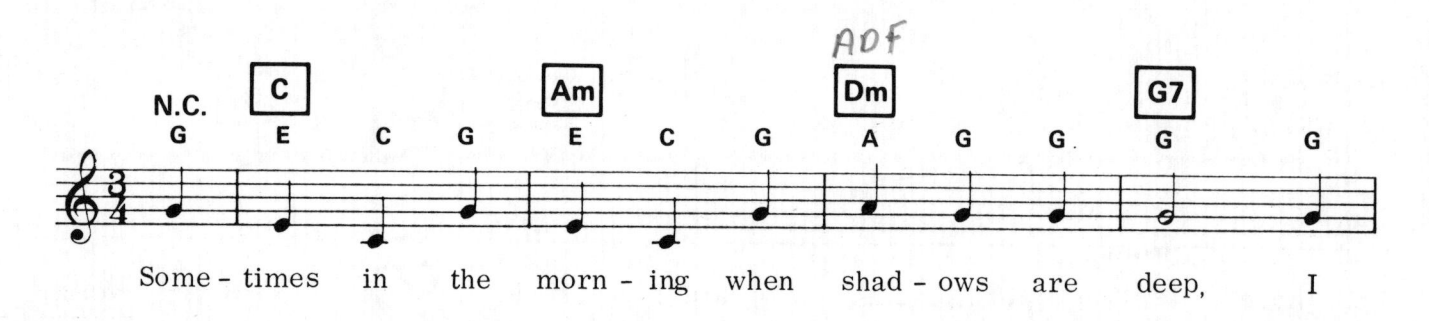

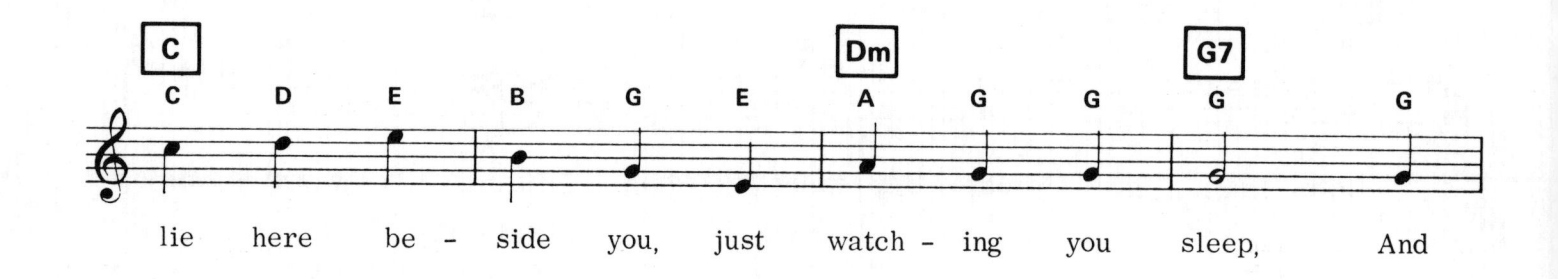

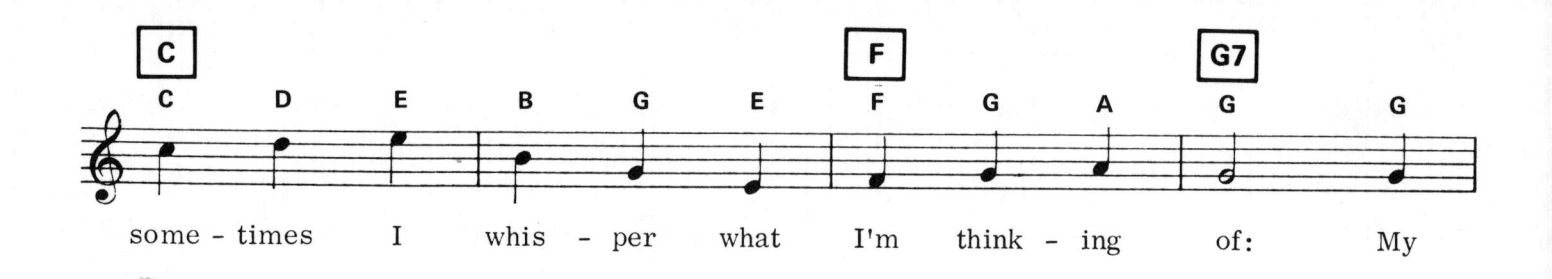

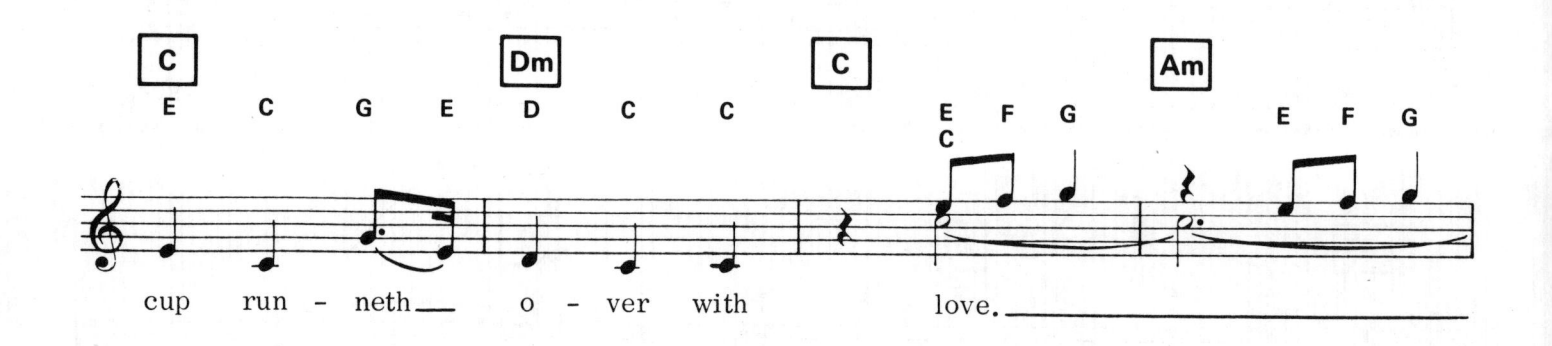

Some-times in the morn-ing when shad-ows are deep, I lie here be-side you, just watch-ing you sleep, And some-times I whis-per what I'm think-ing of: My cup run-neth__ o - ver with love.__

Copyright ©1966 & 1970 by Tom Jones and Harvey Schmidt
Portfolio Music, Inc., owner, Chappell & Co., Inc., administrator of publication and allied rights throughout the world
Used by HAL LEONARD PUBLISHING CORPORATION, Winona, MN 55987 by Permission
Made in U.S.A. International Copyright Secured All Rights Reserved

Sometimes in the ev-'ning when you do not see, I stud-y the small things you do con-stant-ly. I mem-or-ize mo-ments that I'm fond-est of: My cup run-neth o-ver with love.

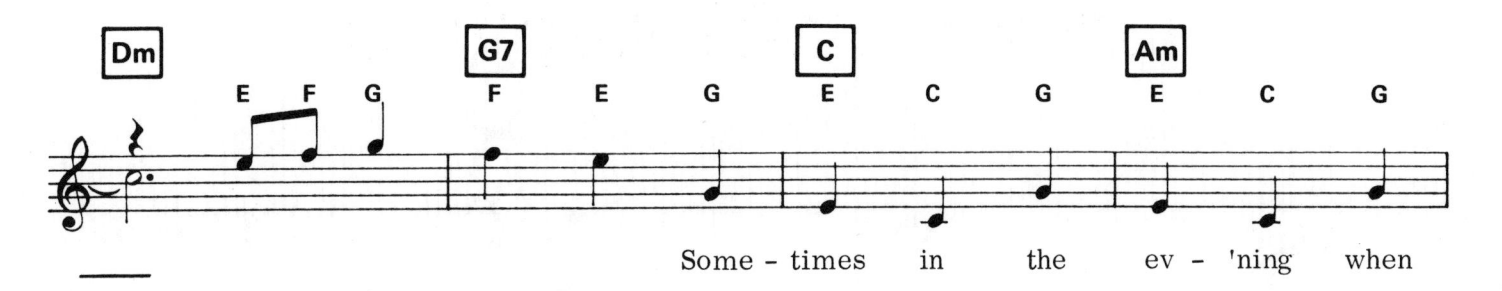

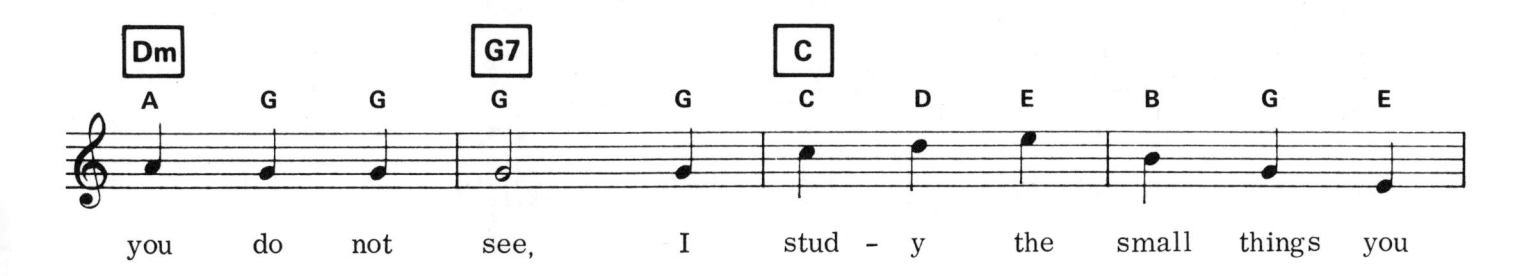

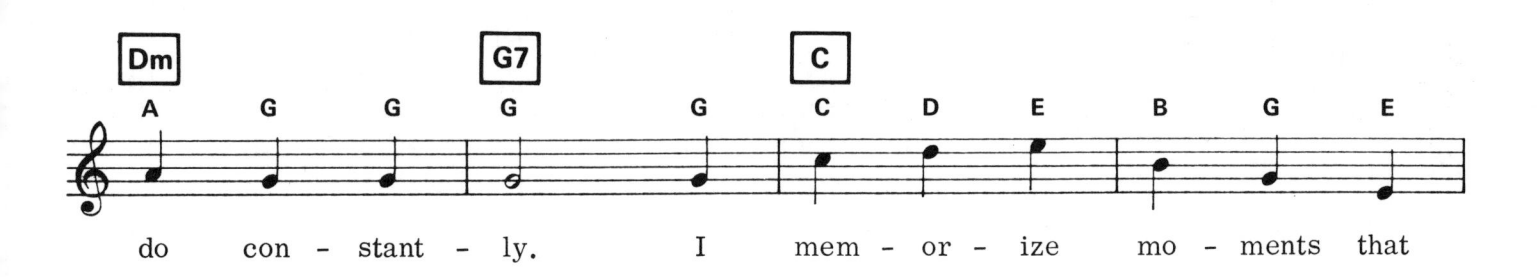

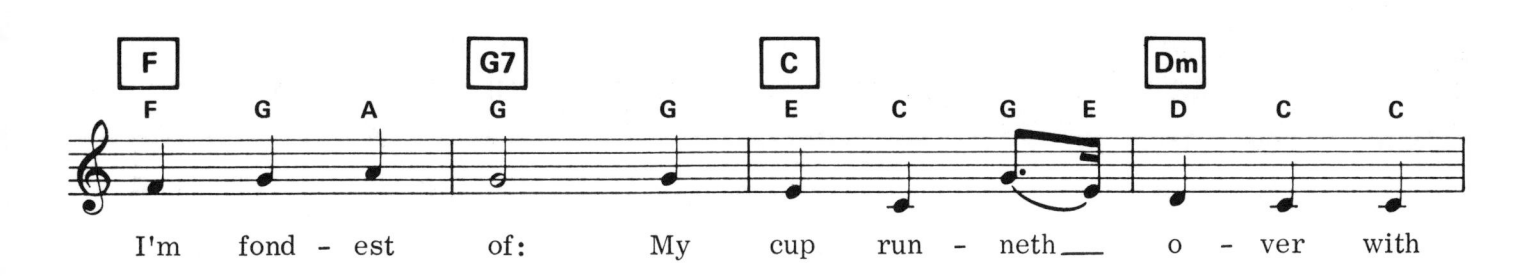

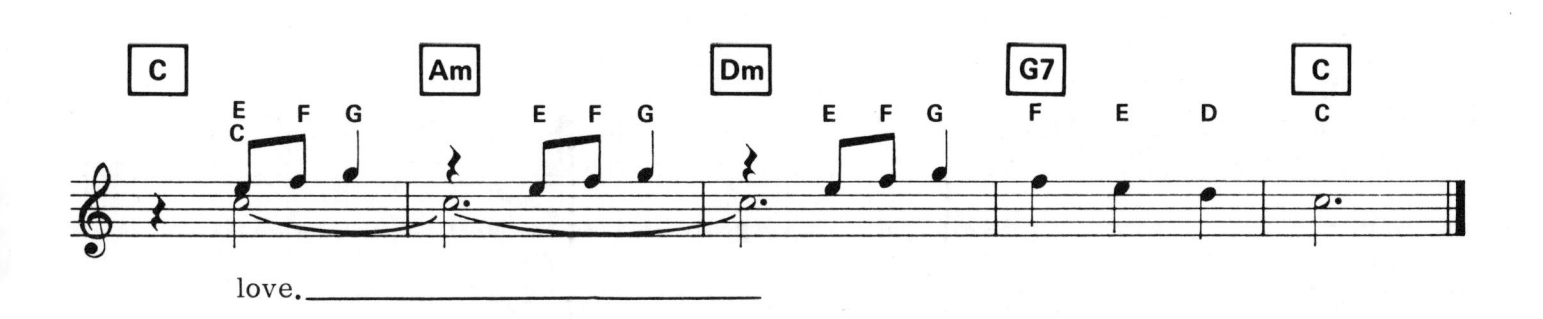

I SEE YOUR FACE BEFORE ME

Words by HOWARD DIETZ
Music by ARTHUR SCHWARTZ

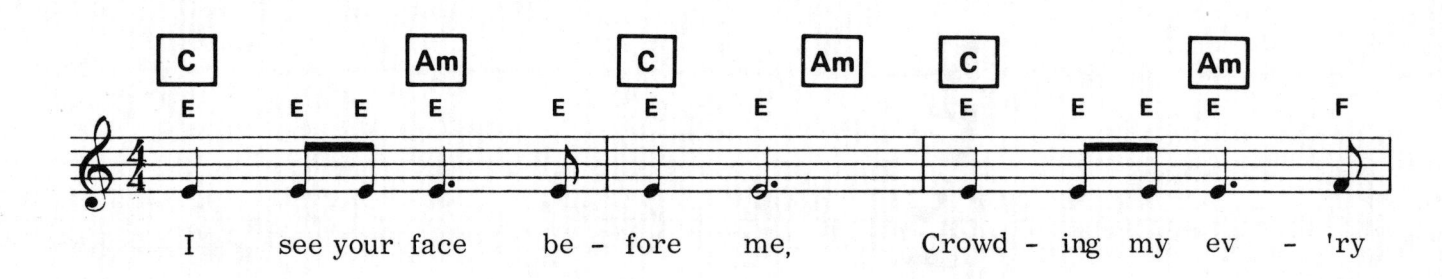

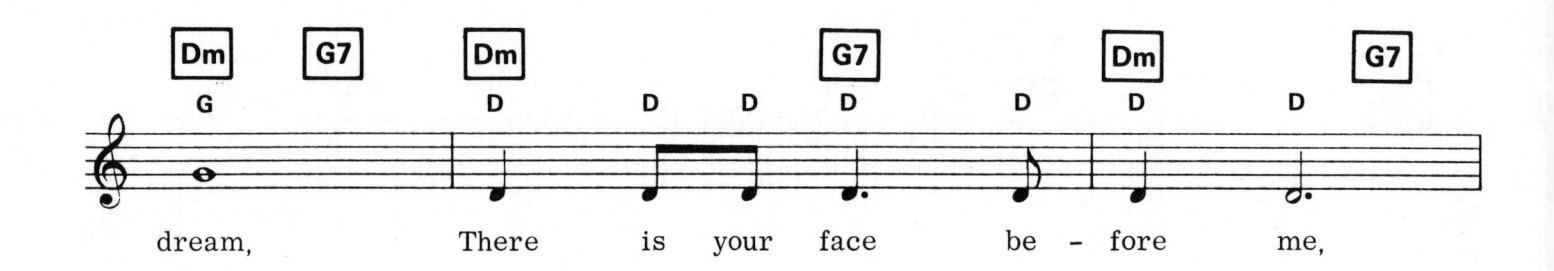

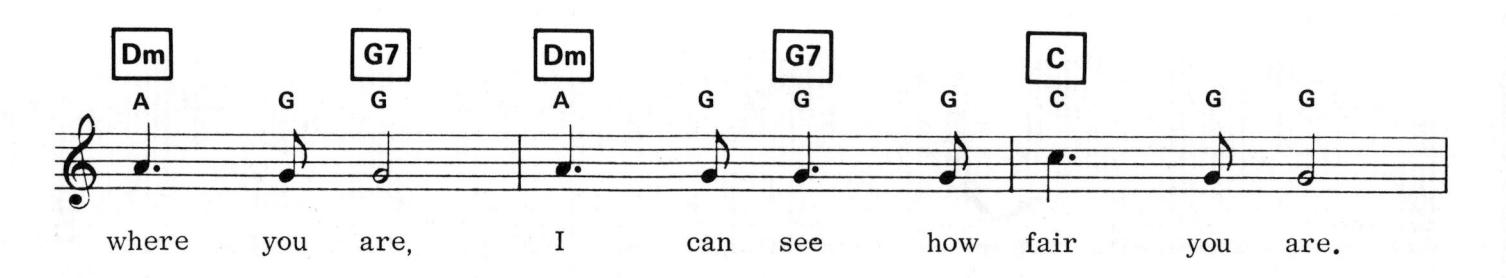

registration number 1.

I see your face be-fore me, Crowd-ing my ev-'ry dream, There is your face be-fore me, You are my on-ly theme. It does-n't mat-ter where you are, I can see how fair you are.

Copyright©1937 by DeSylva, Brown & Henderson, Inc.
Copyright Renewed, assigned to Chappell & Co., Inc.
Used by HAL LEONARD PUBLISHING CORPORATION, Winona, MN 55987 by Permission
Made in U.S.A. International Copyright Secured All Rights Reserved

I close my eyes and there you are, Al - ways.

If you could share the mag - ic, If you could see me too.

There would be noth - ing trag - ic In all my dreams of you.

Would that my love could haunt you so; know - ing I want you so,

I can't e - rase your beau - ti - ful face be - fore me.

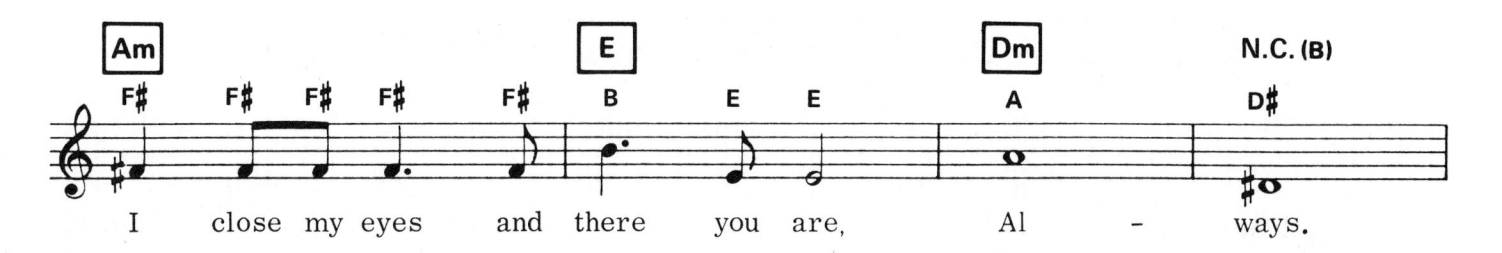

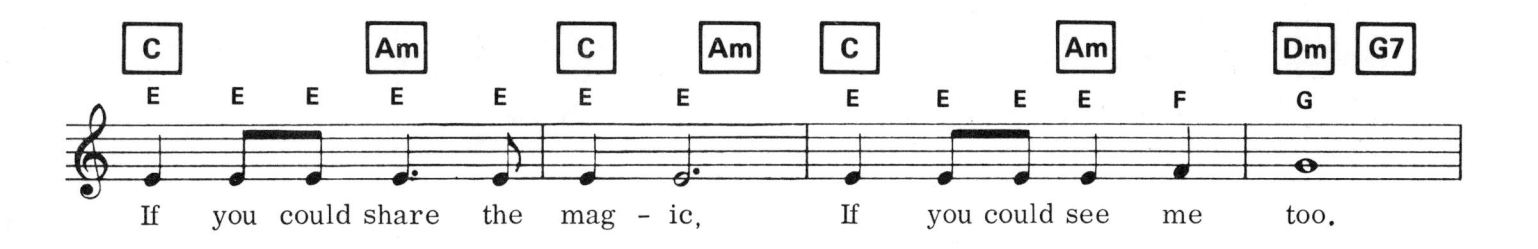

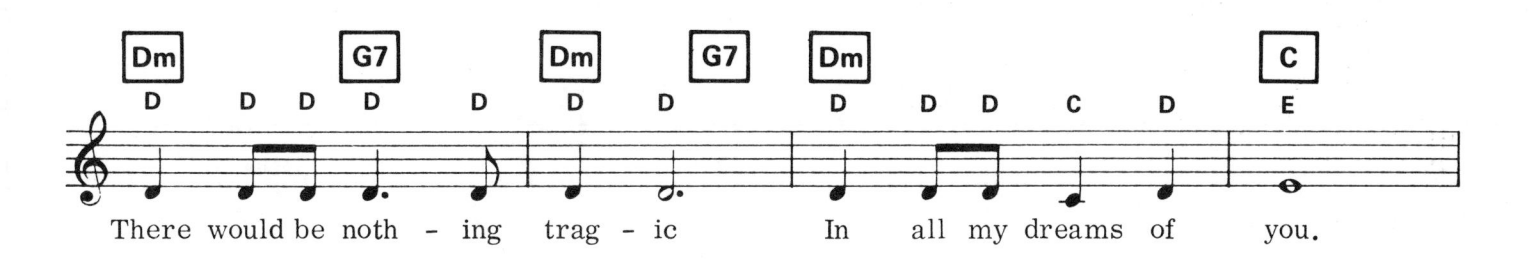

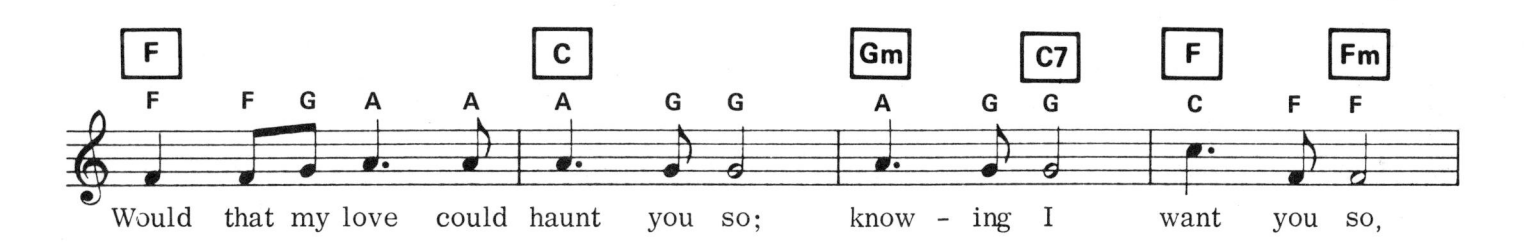

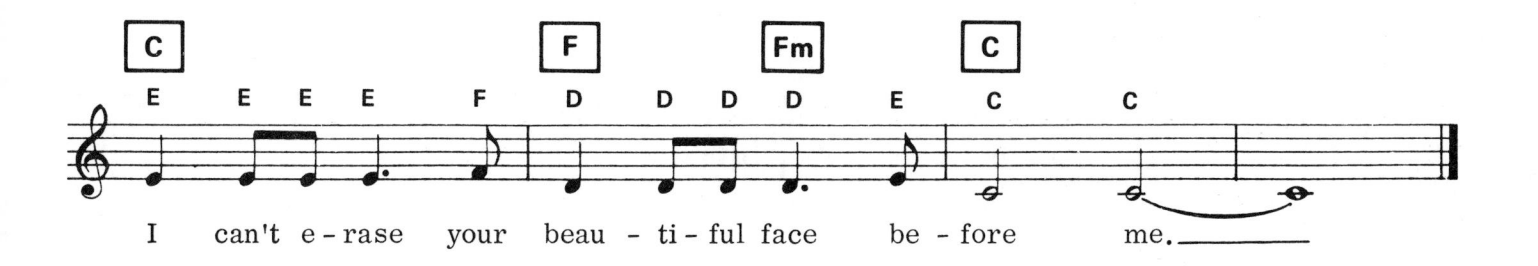

I COULD HAVE DANCED ALL NIGHT

Words by ALAN JAY LERNER
Music by FREDERICK LOEWE

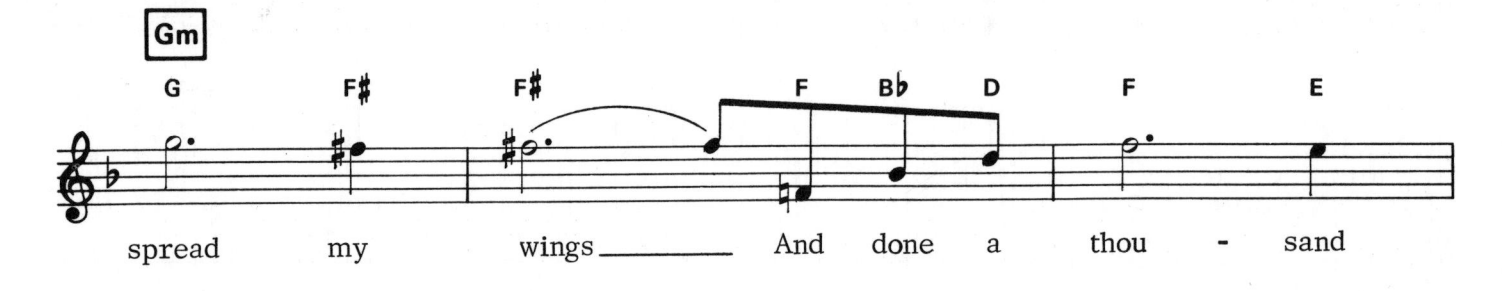

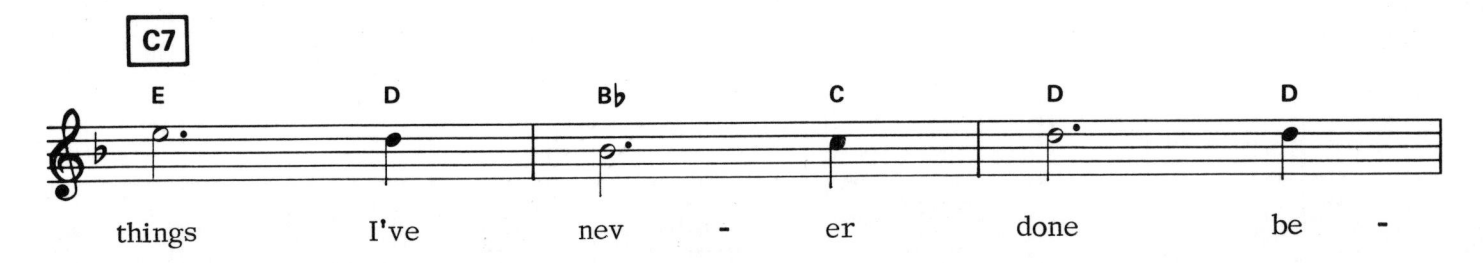

I could have danced all night! I could have danced all night! And still have begged for more. I could have spread my wings And done a thousand things I've nev-er done be-

Copyright ©1956 & 1968 by Alan Jay Lerner and Frederick Loewe
Chappell & Co., Inc., publisher and owner of allied rights throughout the world
Used by HAL LEONARD PUBLISHING CORPORATION, Winona, MN 55987 by Permission
Made in U.S.A.   International Copyright Secured   All Rights Reserved

fore._____ I'll nev-er know_____ what made it so ex-cit-ing,_____ why all at once my heart took flight._____ I on-ly know when he_____ be-gan to dance with me,_____ I could have danced, danced, danced_____ all night!_____

I'VE GROWN ACCUSTOMED TO HER FACE

Words by ALAN JAY LERNER
Music by FREDERICK LOEWE

I've grown ac-cus-tomed to her face. She al-most makes the day be-gin. I've grown ac-cus-tomed to the tune She whis-tles night and noon, Her smiles, her frowns, her ups, her downs are sec-ond na-ture to me now; Like breath-ing out and breath-ing in.

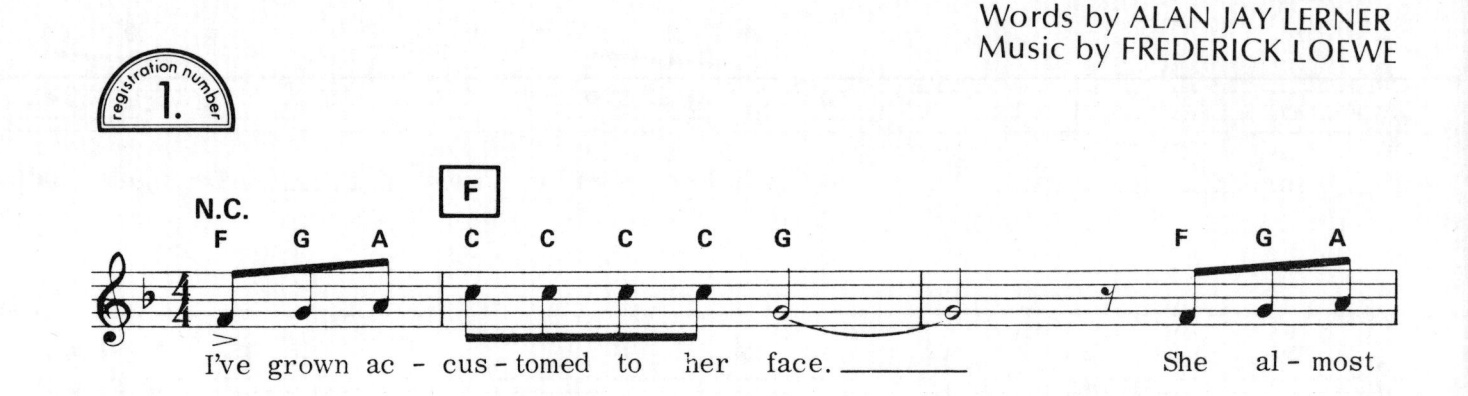

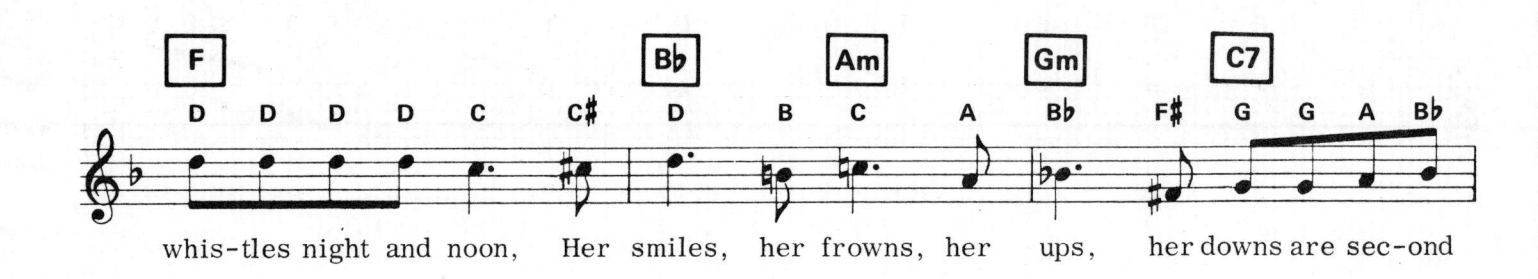

Copyright ©1956 & 1968 by Alan Jay Lerner and Frederick Loewe
Chappell & Co., Inc., publisher and owner of allied rights throughout the world
Used by HAL LEONARD PUBLISHING CORPORATION, Winona, MN 55987 by Permission
Made in U.S.A.   International Copyright Secured   All Rights Reserved

I was se-rene-ly in-de-pen-dent and con-tent be-fore we met, Sure-ly I could al-ways be that way a-gain and yet, I've grown ac-cus-tomed to her looks; Ac-cus-tomed to her voice; Ac-cus-tomed to her face.

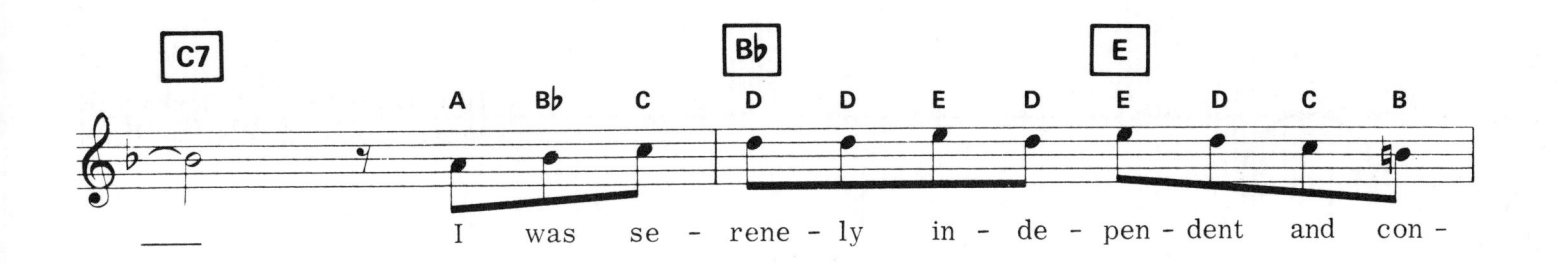

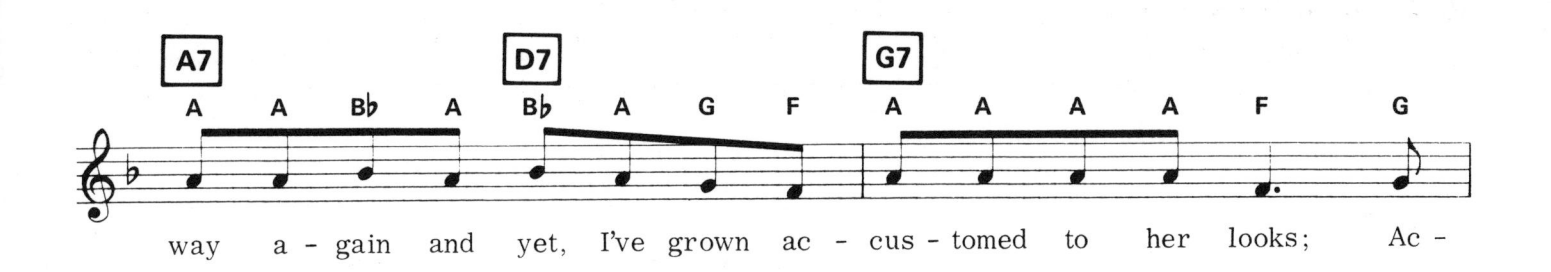

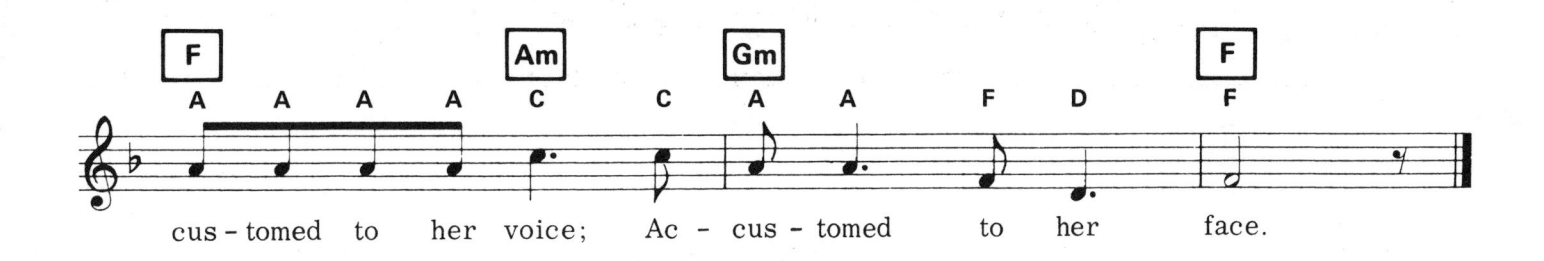

THE RAIN IN SPAIN

Words by ALAN JAY LERNER
Music by FREDERICK LOEWE

The rain in Spain stays main-ly in the plain. ___ I think she's got it! ___ The rain in Spain stays main-ly in the plain! ___ Now once a-gain, where does it rain? ___ On the plain, On the plain! And where's that sog-gy / blast-ed plain? In

Copyright © 1956 & 1968 by Alan Jay Lerner and Frederick Loewe
Chappell & Co., Inc., publisher and owner of allied rights throughout the world.
Used by HAL LEONARD PUBLISHING CORPORATION, Winona, MN 55987 by Permission
Made in U.S.A.   International Copyright Secured   All Rights Reserved

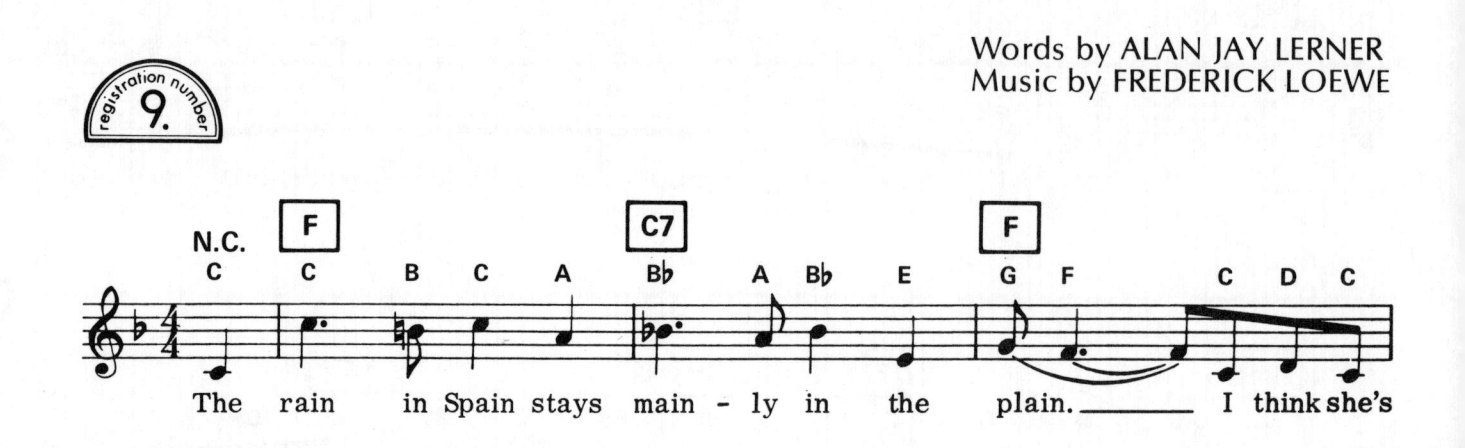

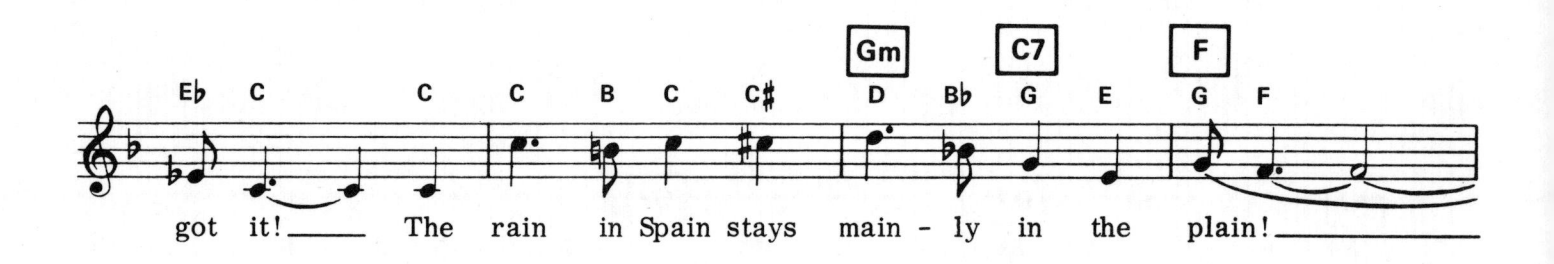

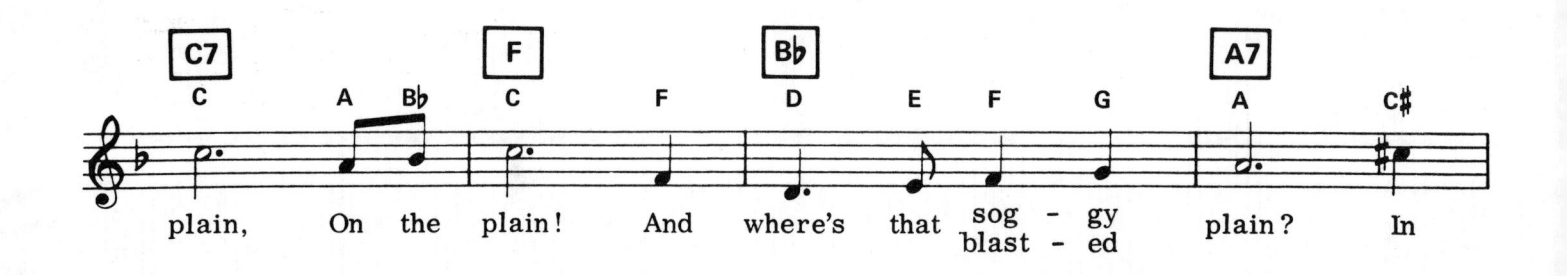

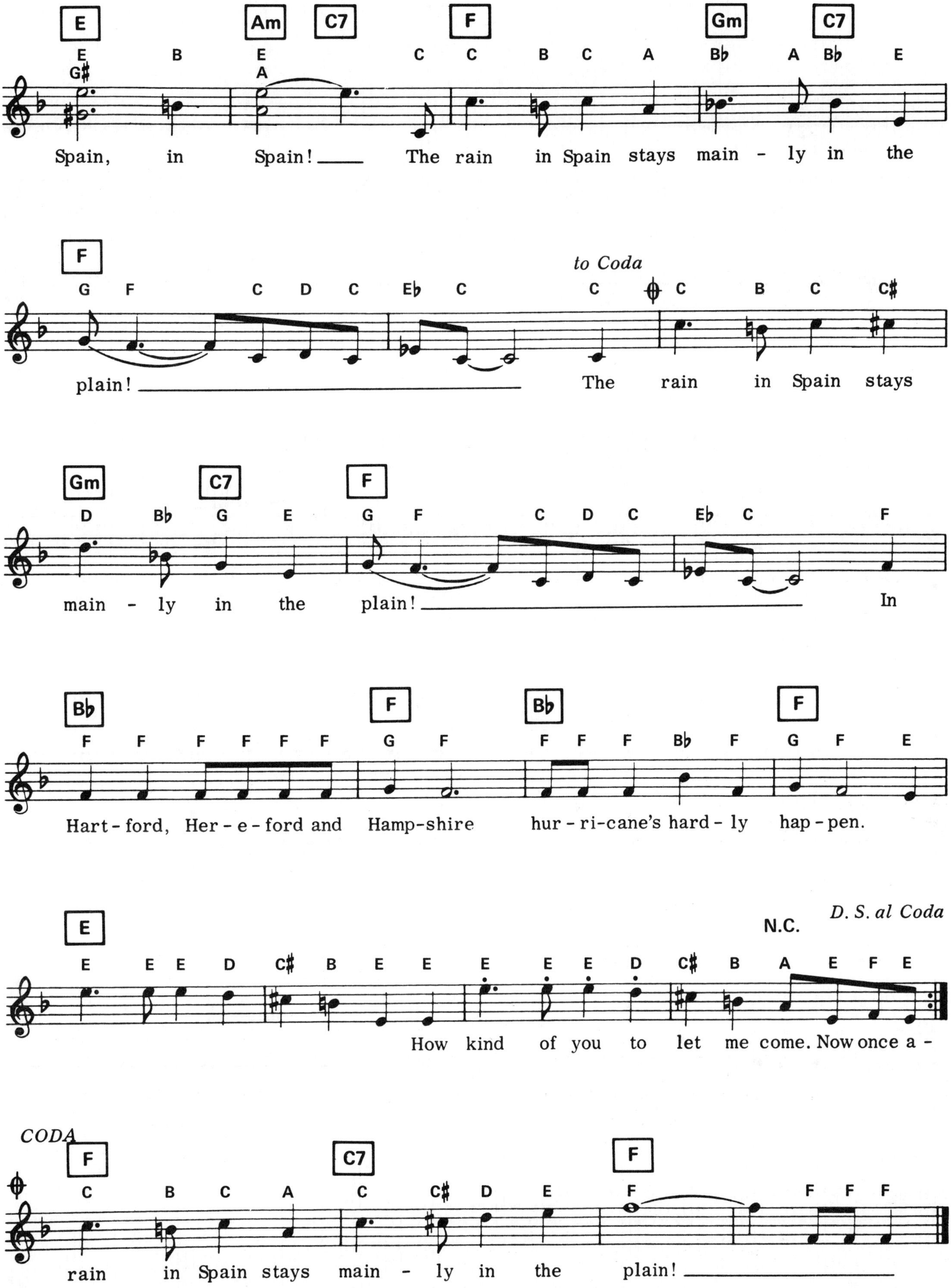
E Am C7 F Gm C7
Spain, in Spain! The rain in Spain stays main - ly in the
F
to Coda
plain! The rain in Spain stays
Gm C7 F
main - ly in the plain! In
B♭ F B♭ F
Hart - ford, Her - e - ford and Hamp-shire hur - ri-cane's hard - ly hap - pen.
E
N.C.
D. S. al Coda
How kind of you to let me come. Now once a -
CODA
F C7 F
rain in Spain stays main - ly in the plain!

WOULDN'T IT BE LOVERLY

Words by ALAN JAY LERNER
Music by FREDERICK LOEWE

registration number 1.

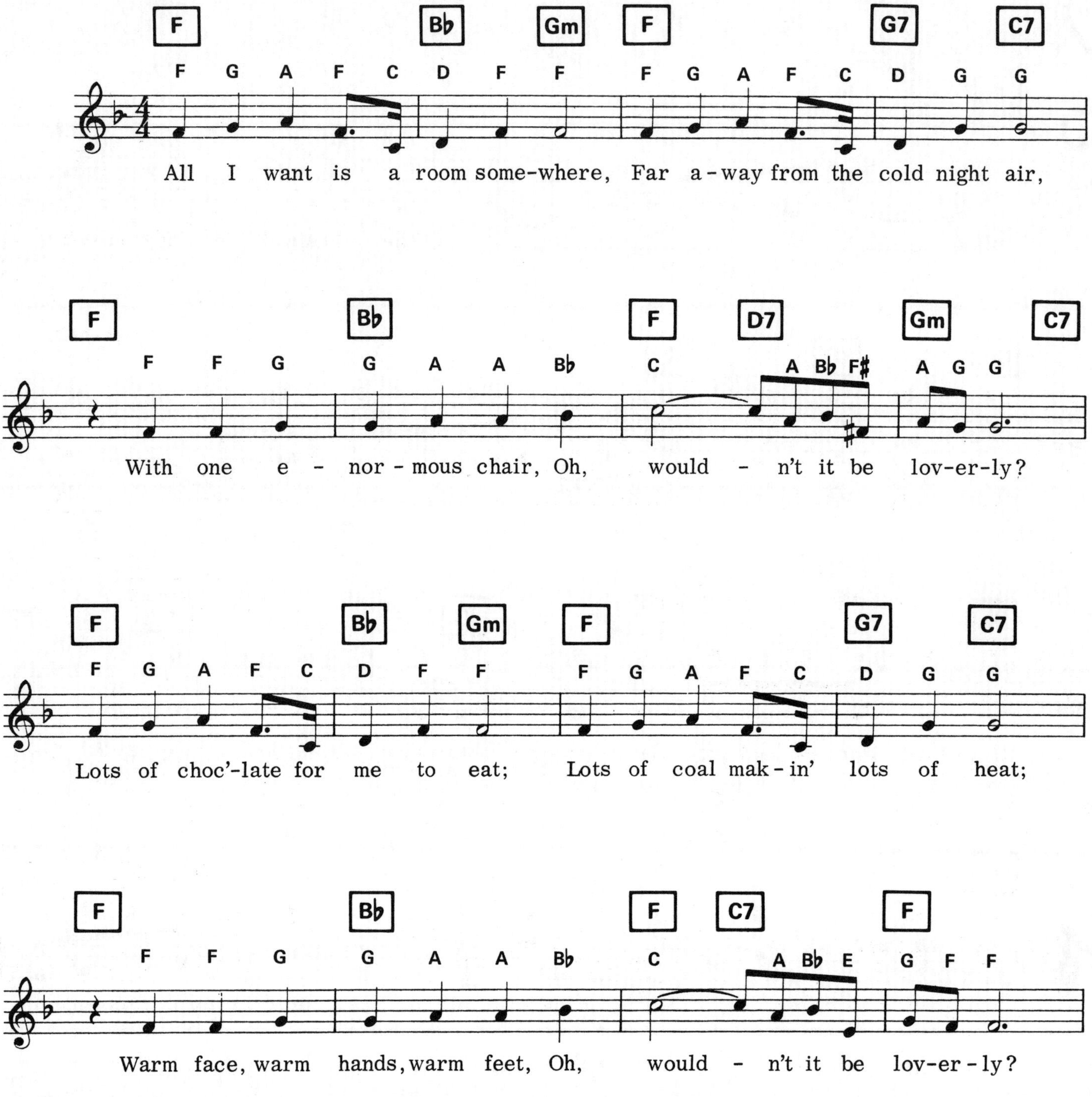

Oh, so lov-er-ly sit-tin' ab-so-bloom-in'-lute-ly still! I would nev-er budge 'til spring crept o-ver me win-der-sill. Some-one's head rest-in' on my knee; Warm and ten-der as he can be; Who takes good care of me, Oh, would-n't it be lov-er-ly? Lov-er-ly! Lov-er-ly!

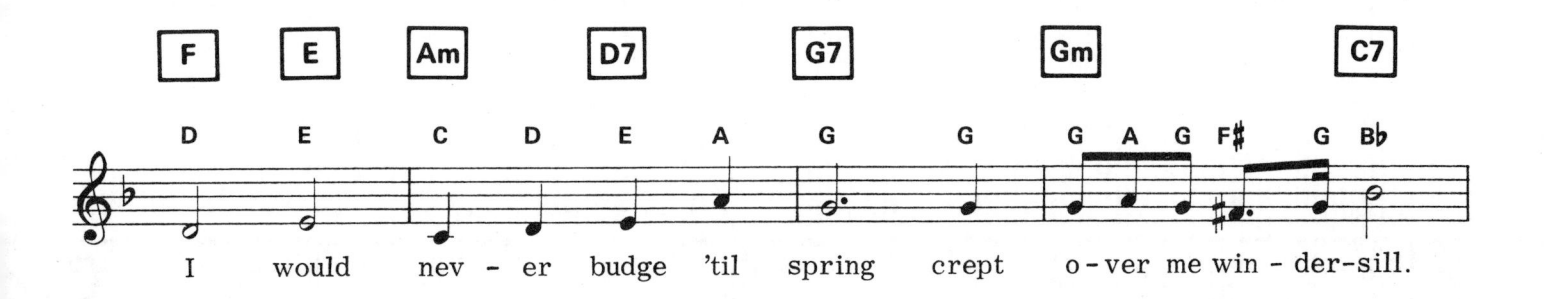

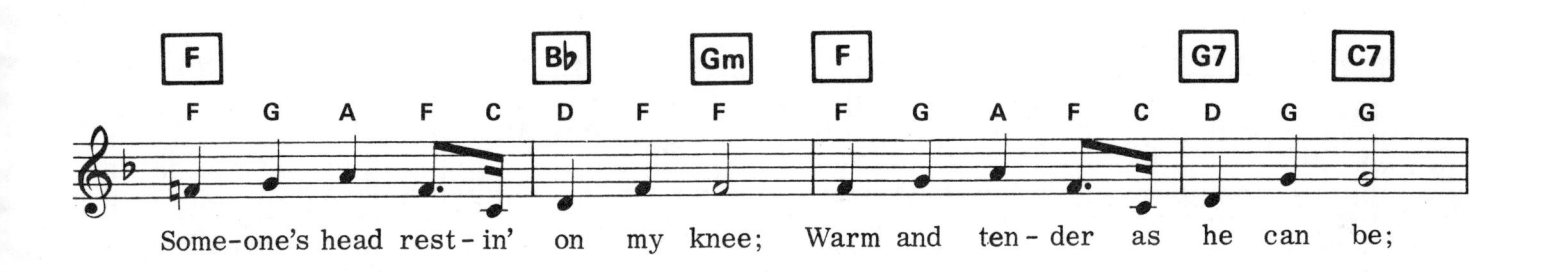

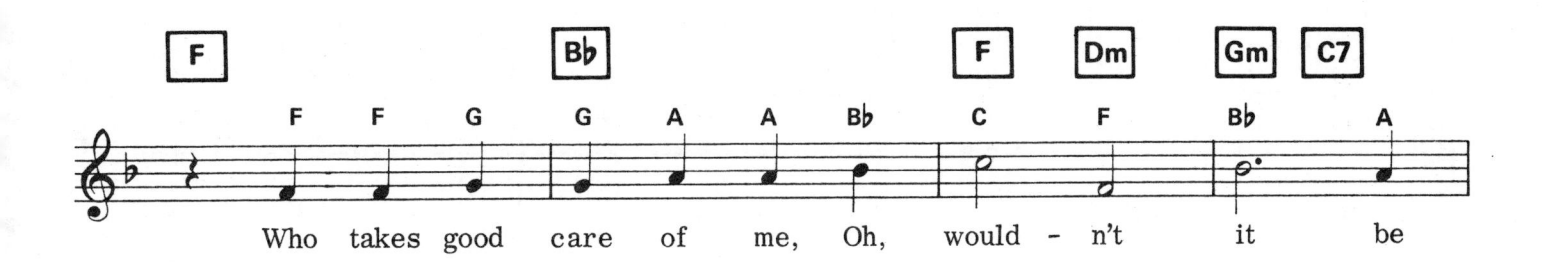

GET ME TO THE CHURCH ON TIME

Words by ALAN JAY LERNER
Music by FREDERICK LOEWE

I'm get-ting mar-ried in the morn-ing.
I got-ta be there in the morn-ing.

Ding! Dong! The bells are gon-na chime. Pull out the
Spruced up and look-ing in my prime. Girls come and

stop-per, Let's have a whop-per; But get me to the church on
kiss me; Show how you'll miss me, But get me to the church on

1. time!
2. time! If I am danc-ing,

Roll up the floor! If I am whis-tling,

Copyright ©1956 & 1968 by Alan Jay Lerner and Frederick Loewe
Chappell & Co., Inc., publisher and owner of allied rights throughout the world
Used by HAL LEONARD PUBLISHING CORPORATION, Winona, MN 55987 by Permission
Made in U.S.A.   International Copyright Secured   All Rights Reserved

whewt me out the door! ____ For I'm get-ting mar-ried in the morn-ing. ____ Ding! Dong! The bells are gon-na chime. ____ Kick up a rum-pus, But don't lose the com-pass; And get me to the church, Get me to the church. For Pete's sake, Get me to the church on time.

ON THE STREET WHERE YOU LIVE

Words by ALAN JAY LERNER
Music by FREDERICK LOEWE

I have of-ten walked down this street be-fore But the pave-ment al-ways stayed be-neath my feet be-fore. All at once am I sev-'ral sto-ries high, Know-ing I'm on the street where you live. Are there

li-lac trees in the heart of town? Can you hear a lark in an-y oth-er part of town? Does en-chant-ment pour out of ev-'ry door? no, it's just on the street where you live.

And, oh, the tow-er-ing feel-ing, Just to

Copyright © 1968 by Alan Jay Lerner and Frederick Loewe
Chappell & Co., Inc., publisher and owner of allied rights throughout the world
Used by HAL LEONARD PUBLISHING CORPORATION, Winona, MN 55987 by Permission
Made in U.S.A.   International Copyright Secured   All Rights Reserved

know___ some-how you are near!___ The o-ver-pow-er-ing feel-ing___ that an-y sec-ond you may sud-den-ly ap-pear!___ Peo-ple stop and stare,___ they don't both-er me,___ For there's no-where else on earth that I would rath-er be.___ Let the time go by.___ I won't care if I___ can be here on the street where you live.___

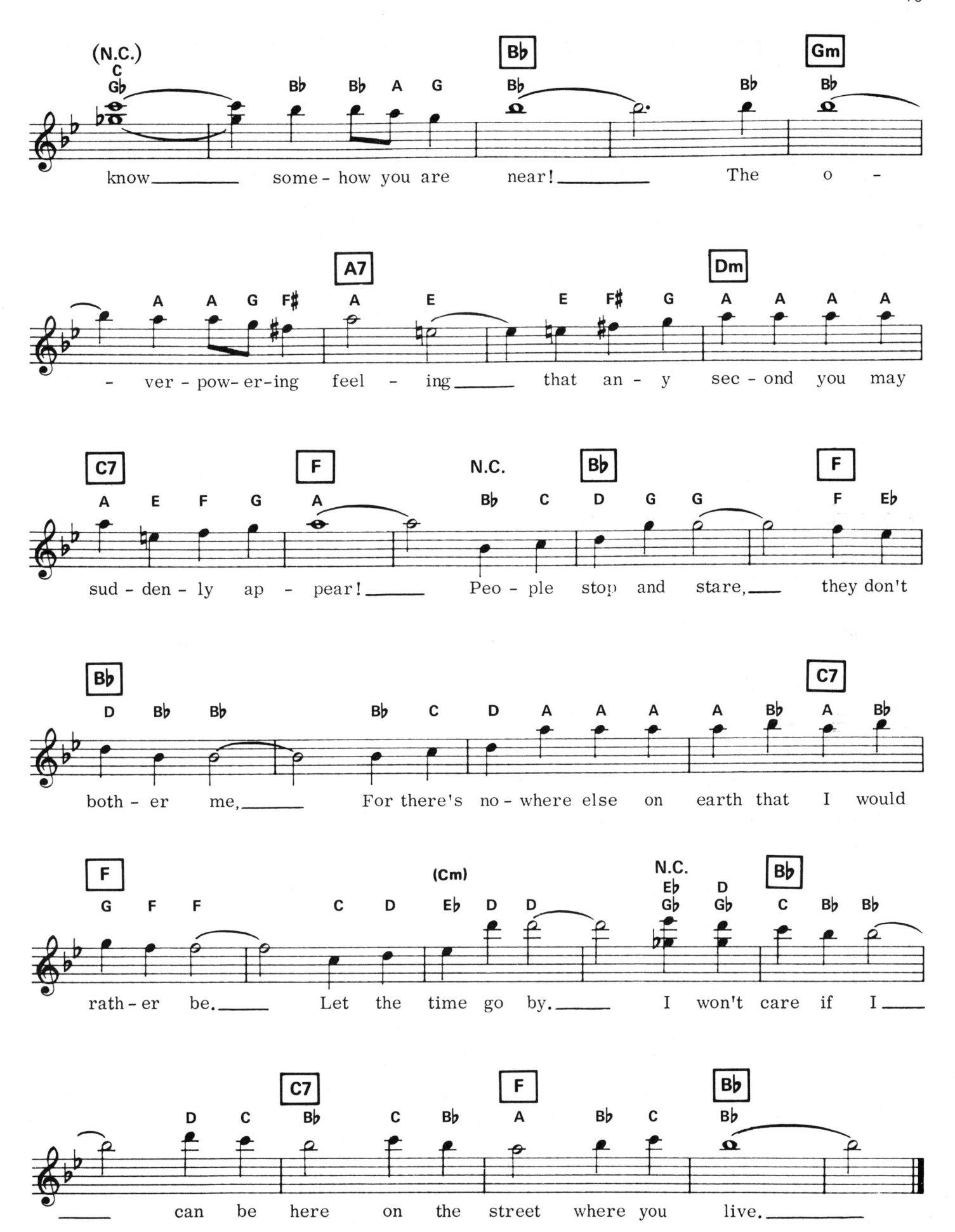

WITH A LITTLE BIT OF LUCK

registration number 3.

Words by ALAN JAY LERNER
Music by FREDERICK LOEWE

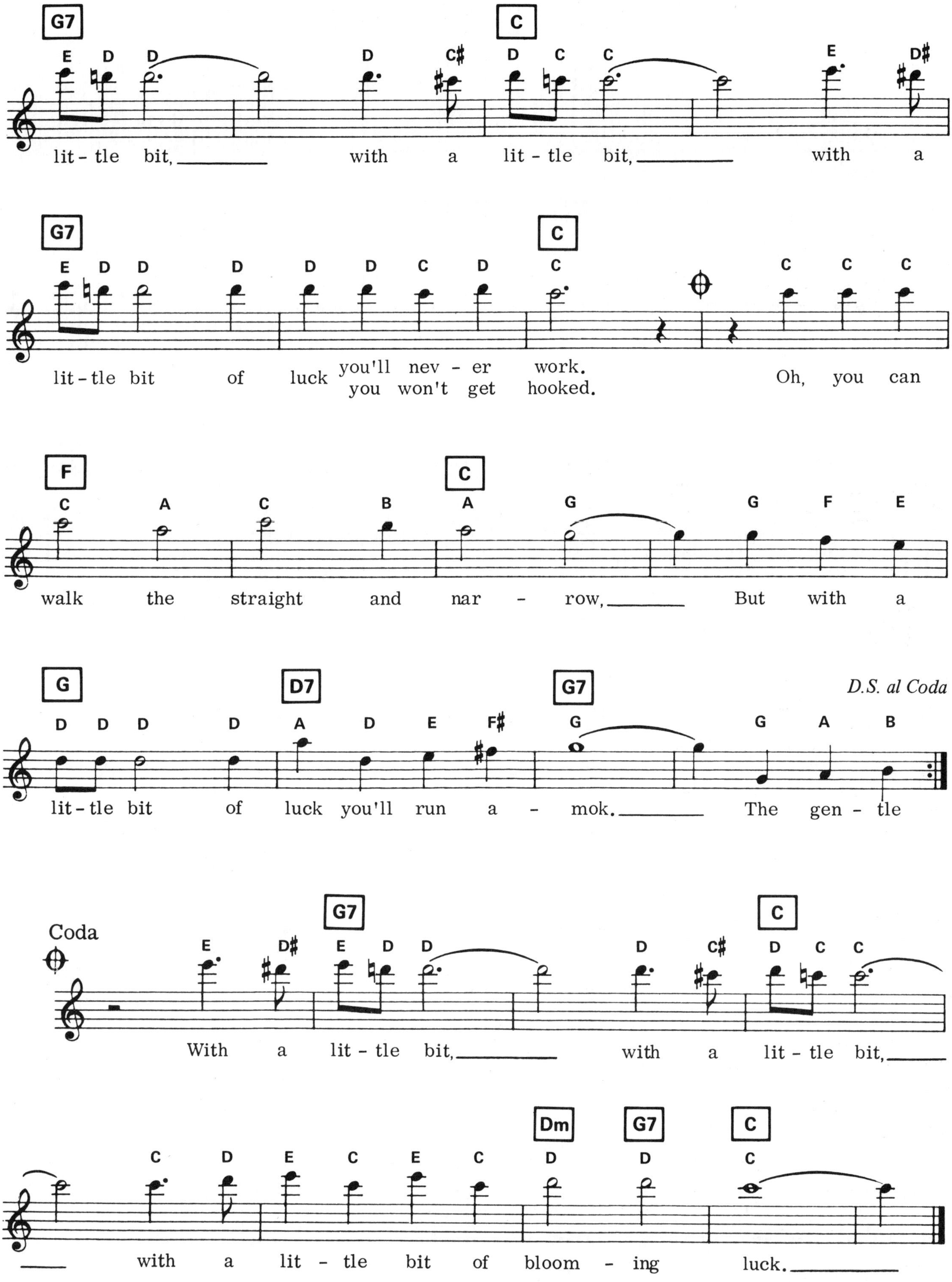
G7 C
E D D D C♯ D C C E D♯
lit - tle bit, with a lit - tle bit, with a
G7 C
E D D D D D C D C C C C
lit - tle bit of luck you'll nev - er work. Oh, you can
you won't get hooked.
F C
C A C B A G G F E
walk the straight and nar - row, But with a
G D7 G7 D.S. al Coda
D D D D A D E F♯ G G A B
lit - tle bit of luck you'll run a - mok. The gen - tle
Coda
G7 C
E D♯ E D D D C♯ D C C
With a lit - tle bit, with a lit - tle bit,
Dm G7 C
C D E C E C D D C
with a lit - tle bit of bloom - ing luck.

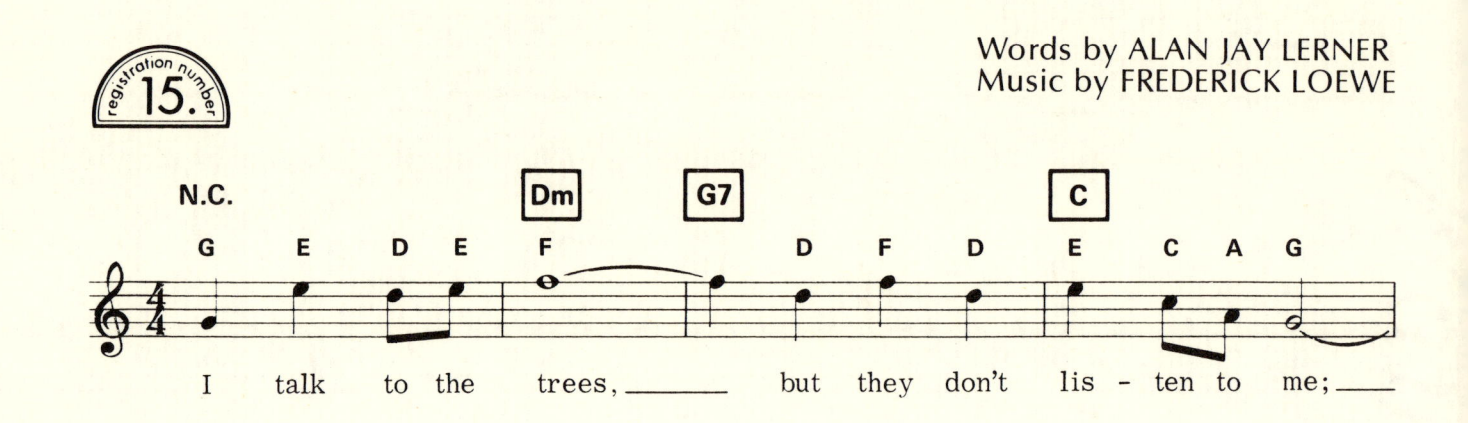

I TALK TO THE TREES

Words by ALAN JAY LERNER
Music by FREDERICK LOEWE

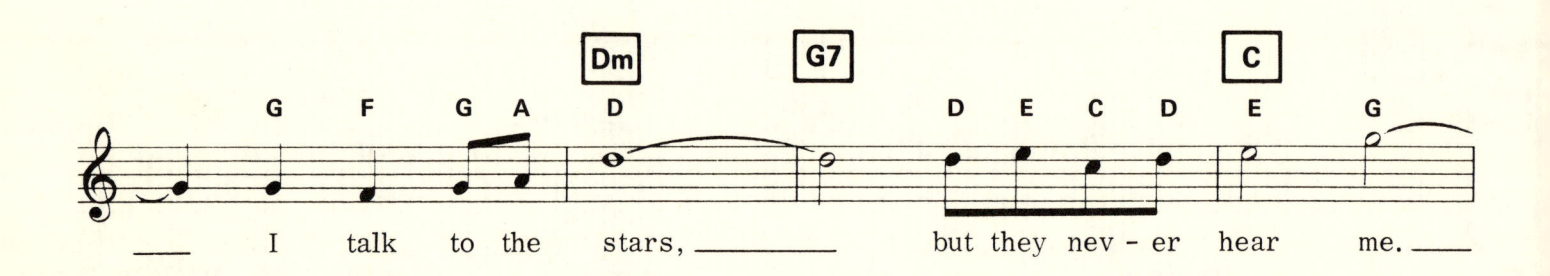

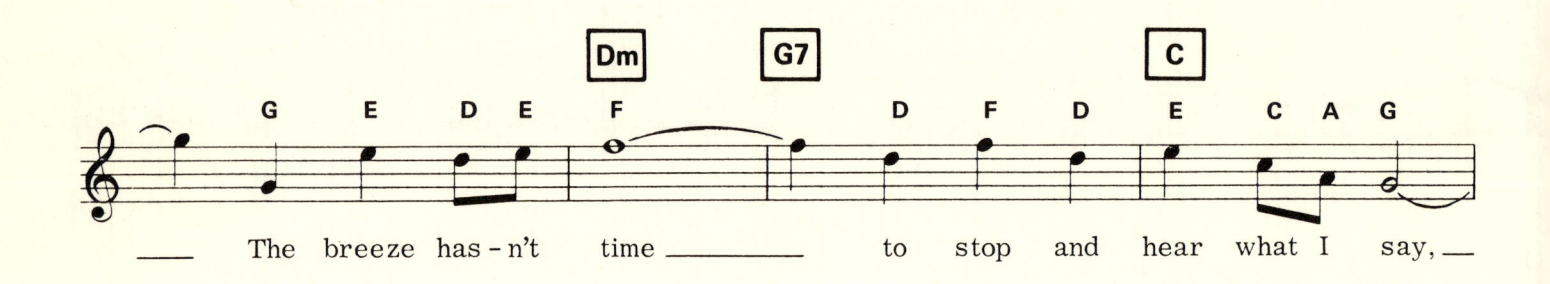

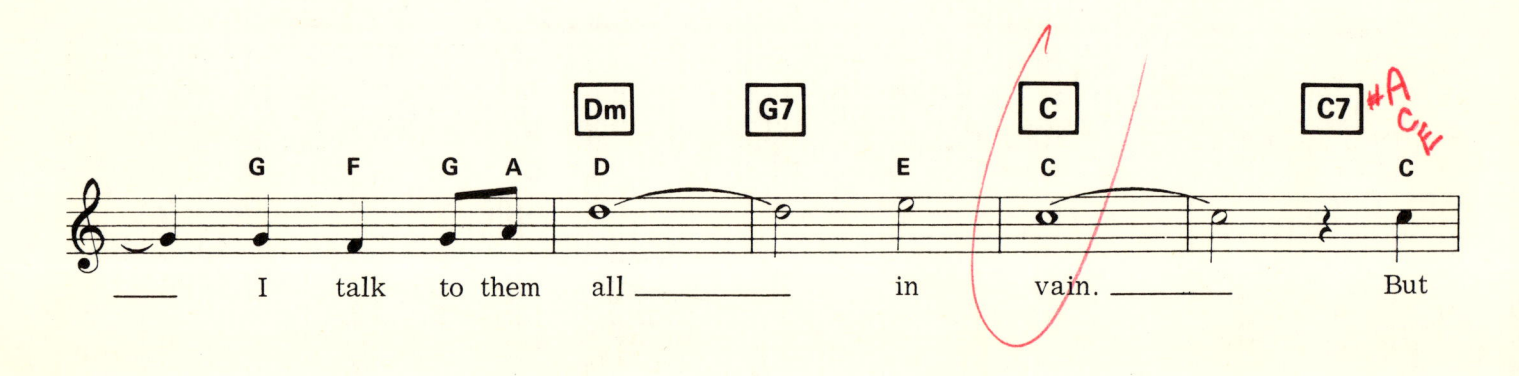

registration number 15.

N.C. | **Dm** | **G7** | **C**
I talk to the trees, but they don't lis-ten to me;

Dm | **G7** | **C**
I talk to the stars, but they nev-er hear me.

Dm | **G7** | **C**
The breeze has-n't time to stop and hear what I say,

Dm | **G7** | **C** | **C7**
I talk to them all in vain. But

Copyright ©1951 by Alan Jay Lerner and Frederick Loewe
Chappell & Co., Inc., publisher and owner of allied rights throughout the world
Used by HAL LEONARD PUBLISHING CORPORATION, Winona, MN 55987 by Permission
Made in U.S.A.   International Copyright Secured   All Rights Reserved

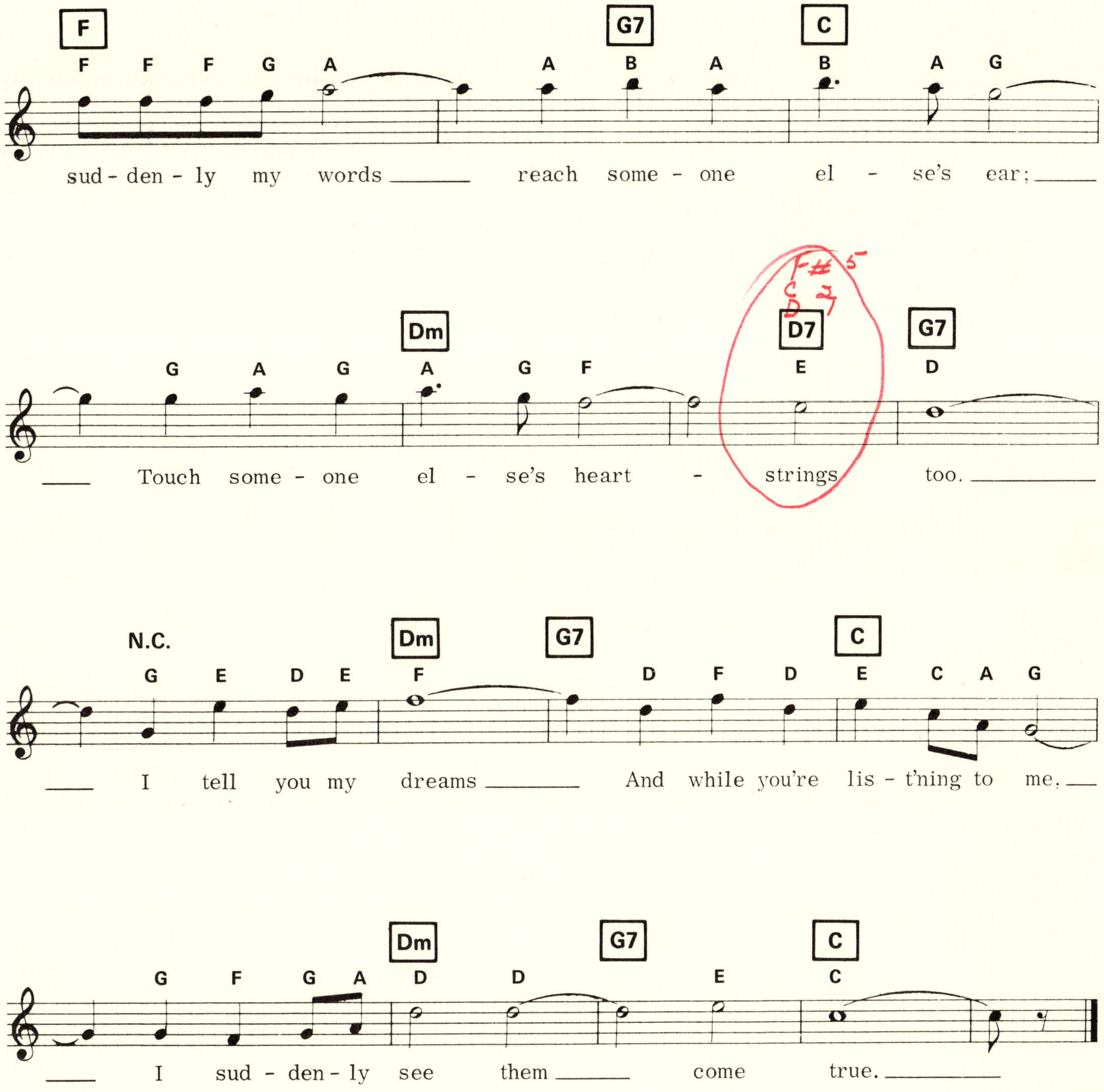
F G7 C
F F F G A A B A B A G
sud - den - ly my words reach some - one el - se's ear;
Dm D7 G7
G A G A G F E D
Touch some - one el - se's heart - strings too.
N.C. Dm G7 C
G E D E F D F D E C A G
I tell you my dreams And while you're lis - t'ning to me,
Dm G7 C
G F G A D D E C
I sud - den - ly see them come true.

HOW TO HANDLE A WOMAN

Words by ALAN JAY LERNER
Music by FREDERICK LOEWE

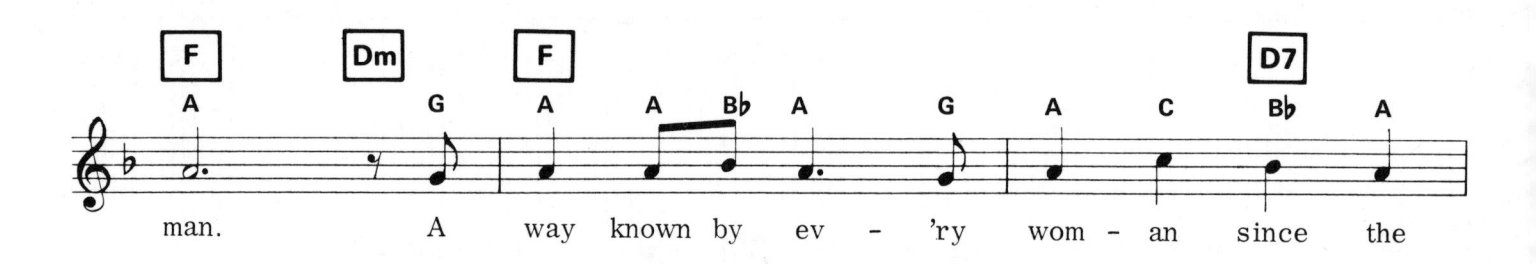

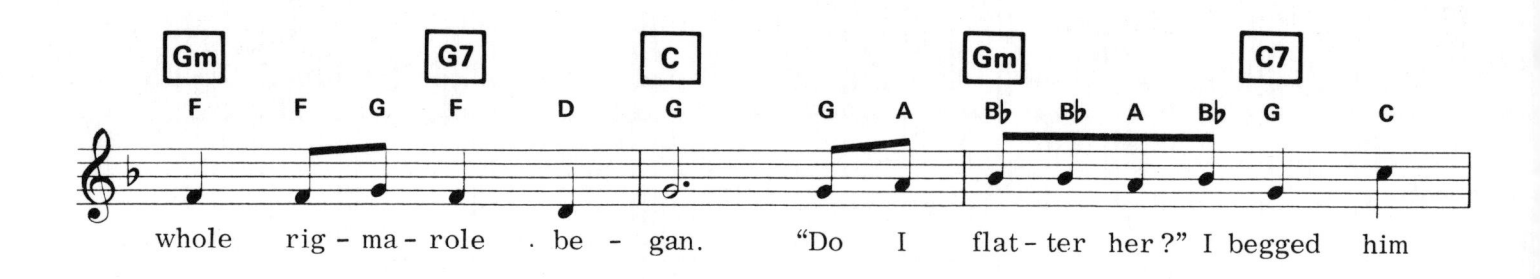

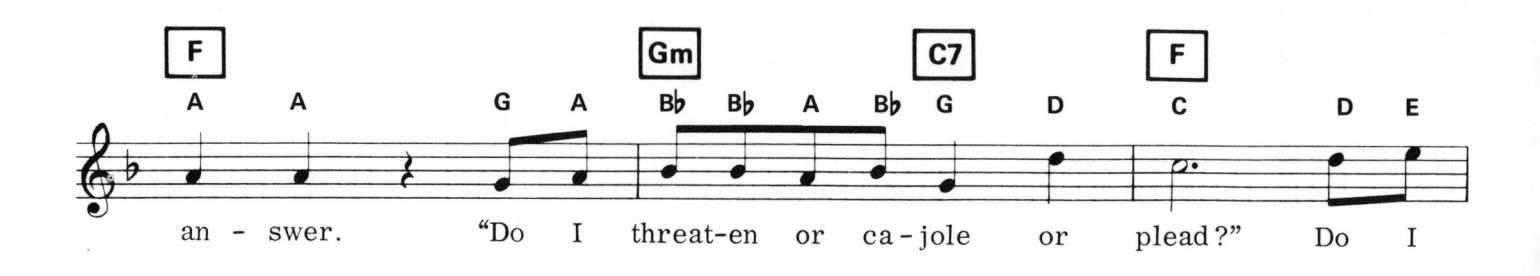

registration number 1.

How to han-dle a wom-an. There's a way, said a wise old man. A way known by ev-'ry wom-an since the whole rig-ma-role be-gan. "Do I flat-ter her?" I begged him an-swer. "Do I threat-en or ca-jole or plead?" Do I

Copyright © 1960 by Alan Jay Lerner and Frederick Loewe
Chappell & Co., Inc., publisher and owner of allied rights throughout the world
Used by HAL LEONARD PUBLISHING CORPORATION, Winona, MN 55987 by Permission
Made in U.S.A.   International Copyright Secured   All Rights Reserved

brood or play the gay ro-man-cer?" Said he, smil-ing, "No, in-deed." How to han-dle a wom-an, Mark me well, I will tell you, sir, "The way to han-dle a wom-an is to love her,___ Sim-ply love her,___ ___ Mere-ly love her, love her, love her!"___

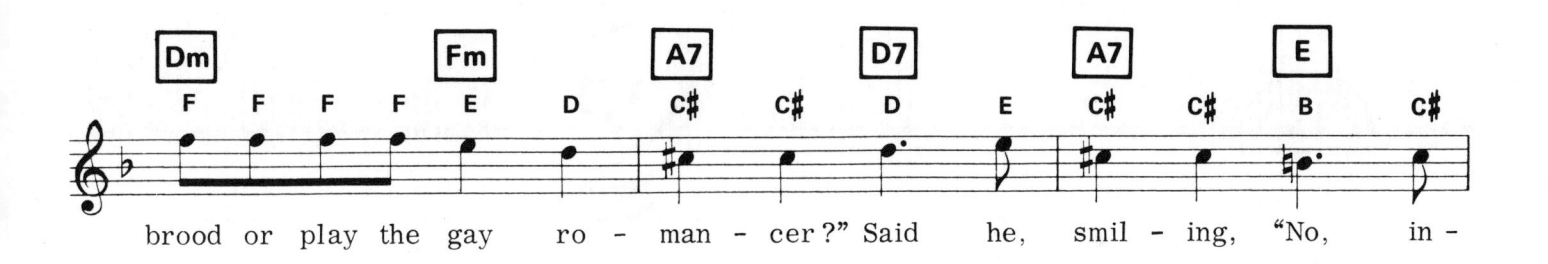

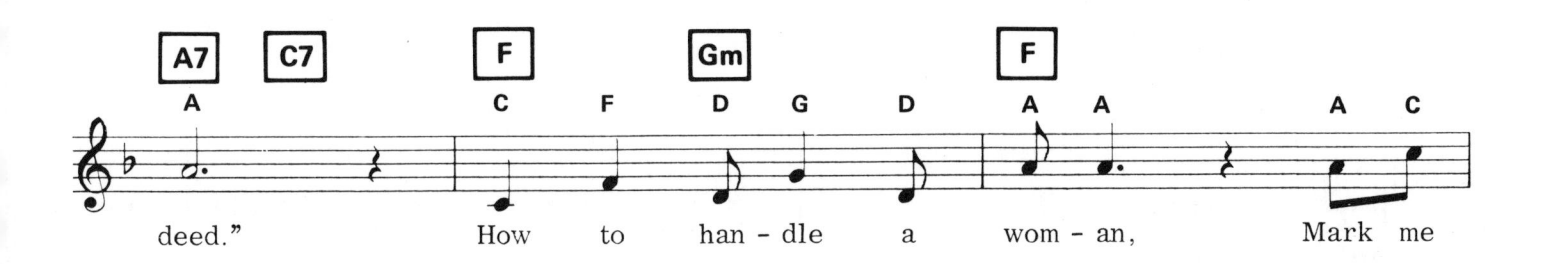

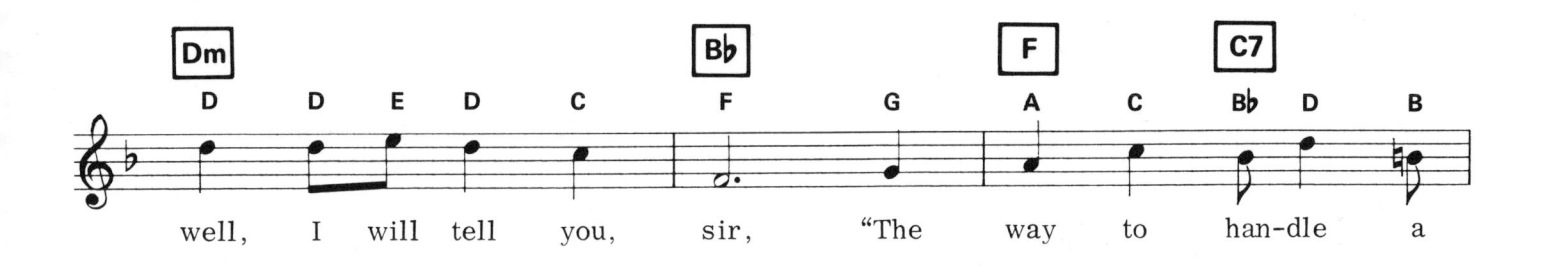

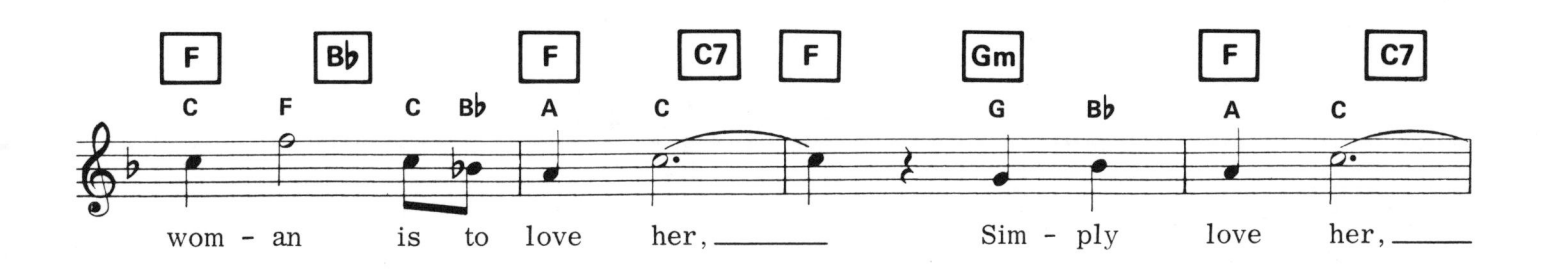

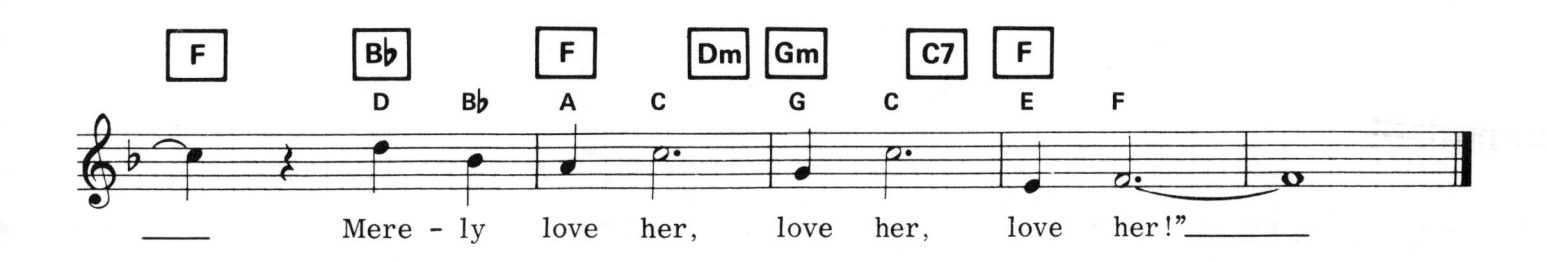

THEY CALL THE WIND MARIA

Words by ALAN JAY LERNER
Music by FREDERICK LOEWE

registration number 13.

Start oct low

A - way out here they got a name for wind, and rain and fi - re. The rain is Tess, the fire is Joe, And they call the wind Ma - ri - a. ____ Ma - ri - a blows the stars a - round, And sends the clouds a - fly - in'. Ma - ri - a makes the

Copyright ©1951 by Alan Jay Lerner and Frederick Loewe
Chappell & Co., Inc., publisher and owner of allied rights throughout the world
Used by HAL LEONARD PUBLISHING CORPORATION, Winona, MN 55987 by Permission
Made in U.S.A.   International Copyright Secured   All Rights Reserved

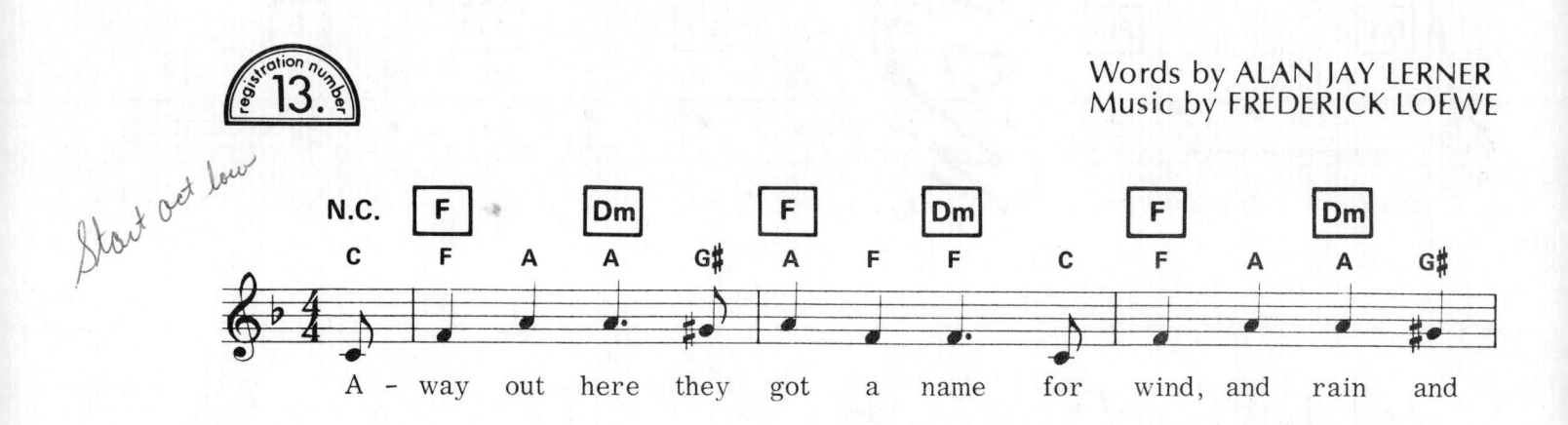

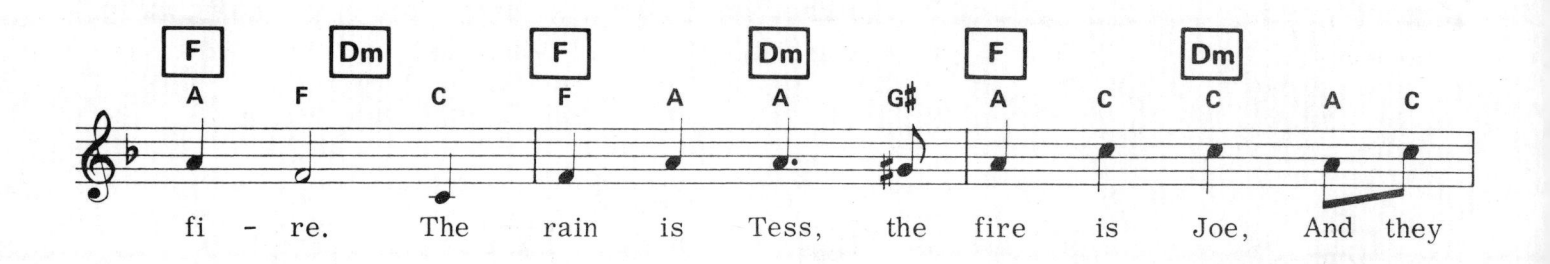

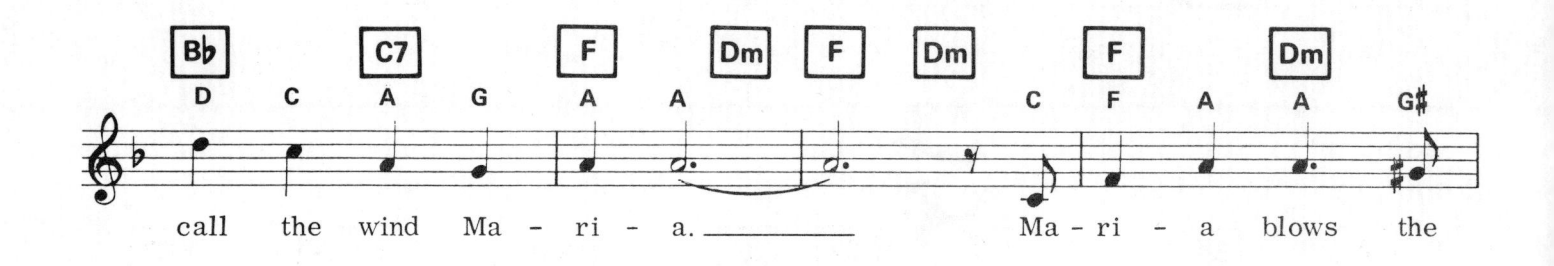

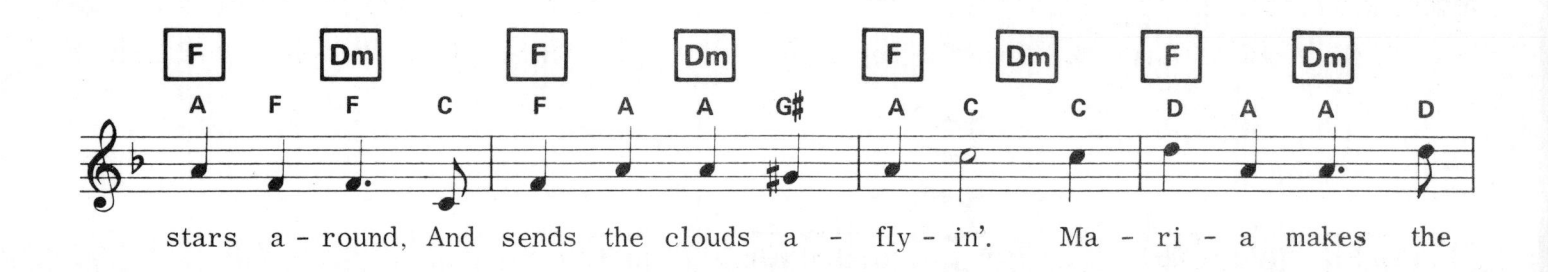

moun - tain sound   Like folks were up there dy - in'._____ Ma -

ri - a!_____   Ma - ri - a!_____   They call the

wind Ma - ri - a!_____   Ma - ri - a!_____   Ma -

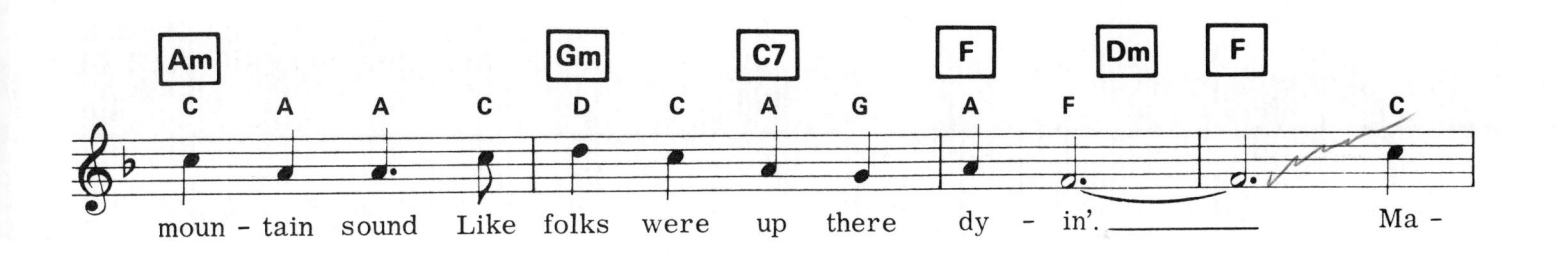

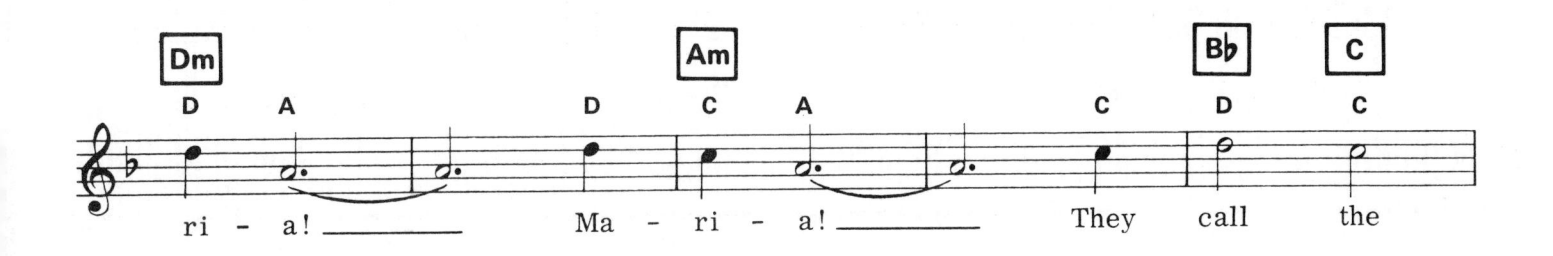

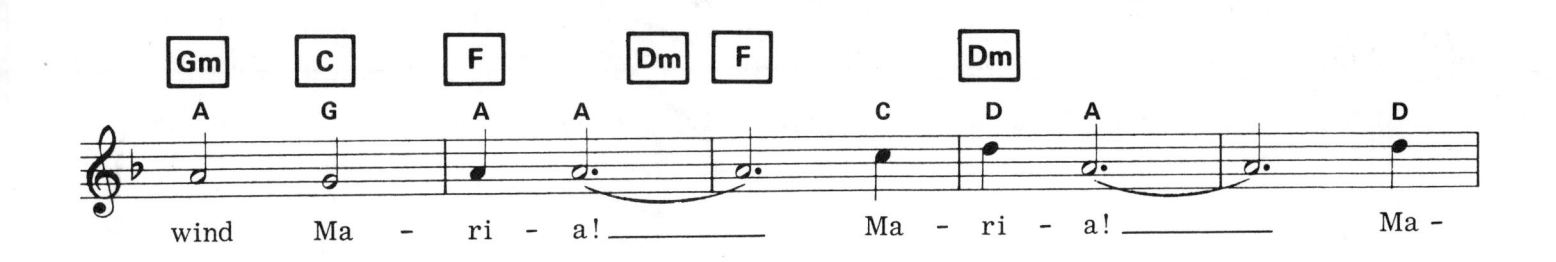

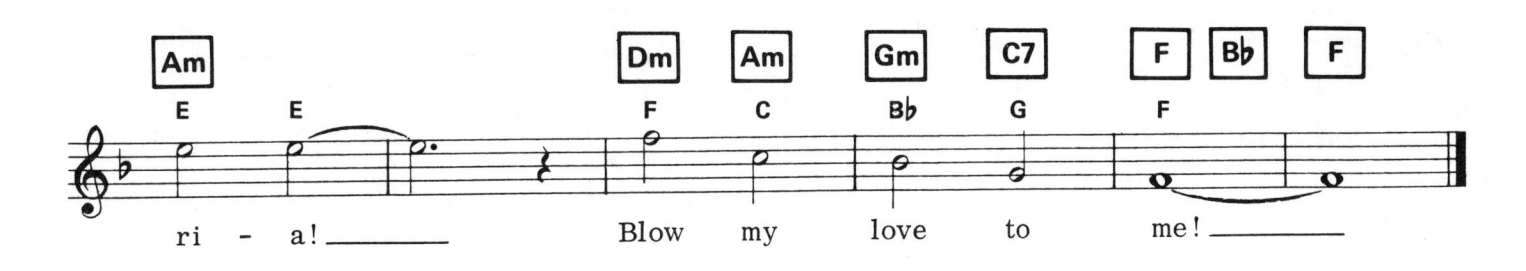

ri - a!_____   Blow my love to me!_____

FOLLOW ME

Words by ALAN JAY LERNER
Music by FREDERICK LOEWE

registration number 1.

Through the clouds gray with years; O-ver hills wet with tears; To a world young and free We shall fly. Fol-low me. A-pril green ev-'ry-where; A-pril's song al-ways there. Come and hear. Come and see. Fol-low me. To the tree where our hopes hang

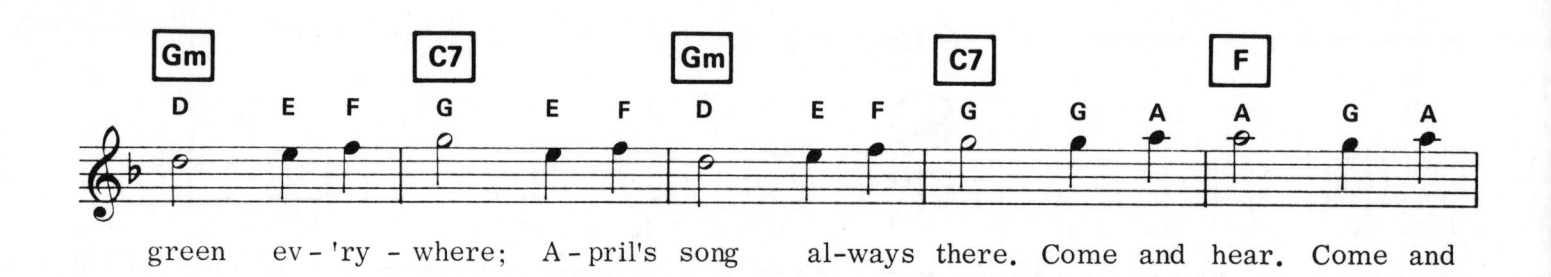

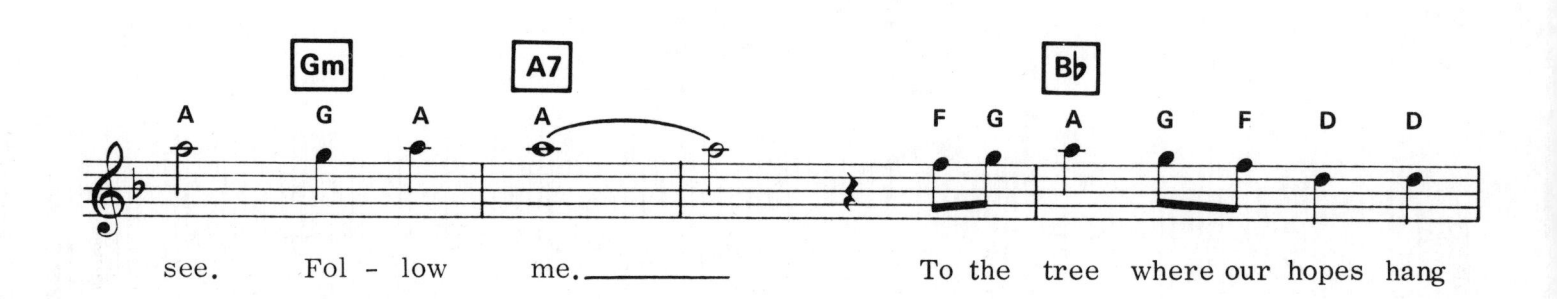

Copyright © 1960 & 1967 by Alan Jay Lerner and Frederick Loewe
Chappell & Co., Inc., owner of publication and allied rights throughout the world
Used by HAL LEONARD PUBLISHING CORPORATION, Winona, MN 55987 by Permission
Made in U.S.A.   International Copyright Secured   All Rights Reserved

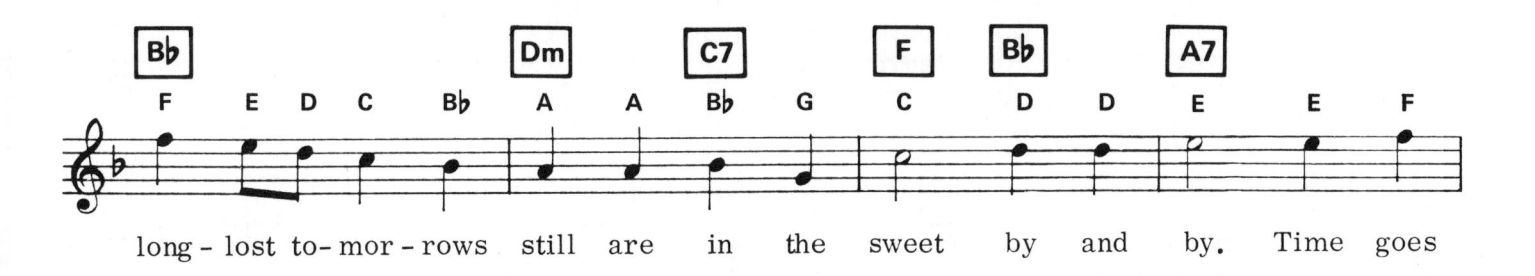

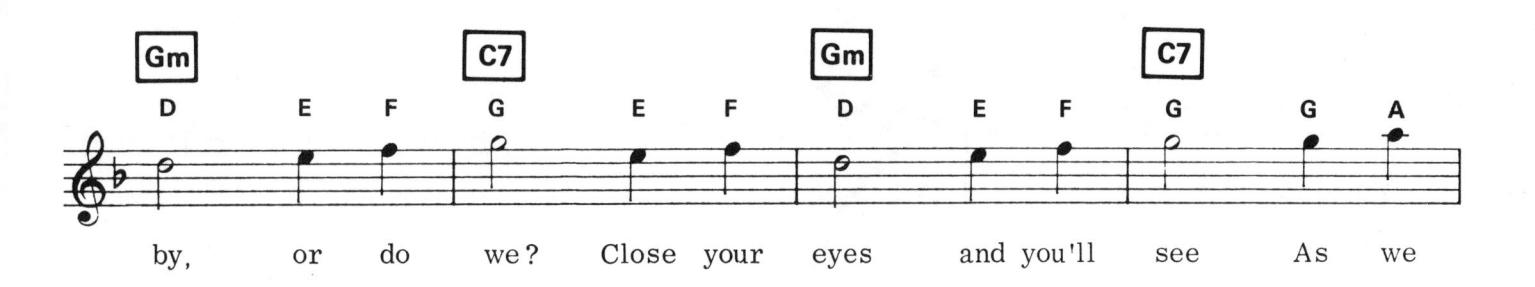

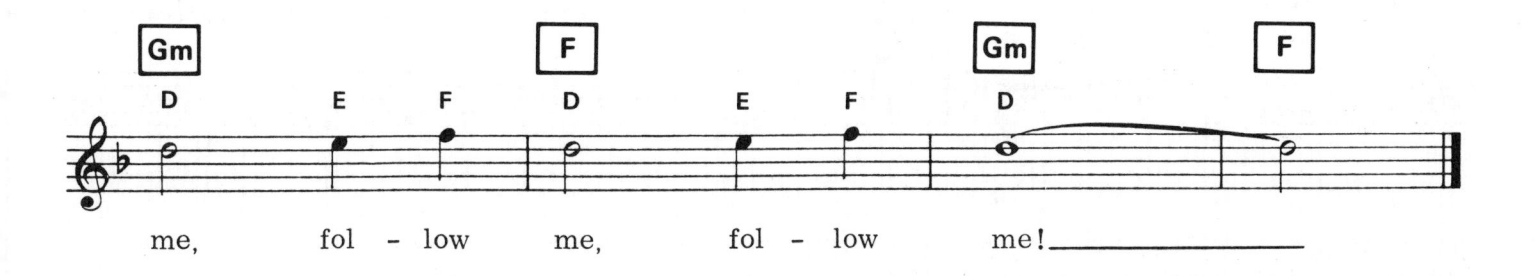

high; To the dream that should nev - er die; Where our long-lost to-mor-rows still are in the sweet by and by. Time goes by, or do we? Close your eyes and you'll see As we were we can be. Weep no more. Fol - low me. Fol - low me, fol - low me, fol - low me!

IF EVER I WOULD LEAVE YOU

Words by ALAN JAY LERNER
Music by FREDERICK LOEWE

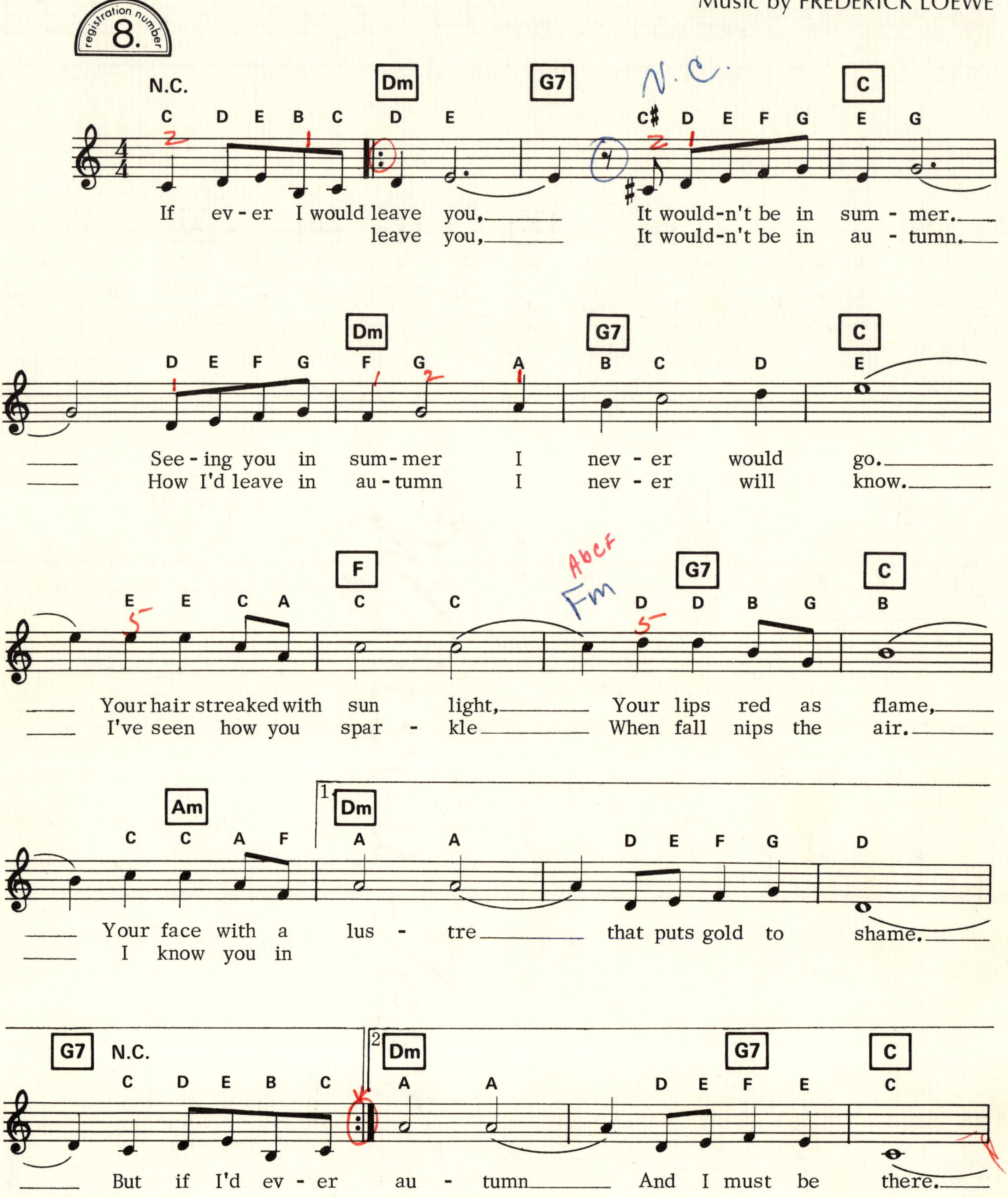

G# BE
N.C. E
B C D E E E E E E E E F# G#
And could I leave you run-ning mer-ri-ly through the snow?
N.C. E N.C. E
D# E F# G# G# G# G# G# G# A B G# A B
Or on a win-try eve-ning when you catch the fi-re's glow?
G7 N.C. Dm G7 C
C D E B C D E C# D E F G E G
If ev-er I would leave you, How could it be in spring-time.
Dm G7 C
D E F G F G A B C D E
Know-ing you in spring I'm be-witched by you so?
F Fm C
E E C A C C C D E C A♭ C
Oh, no! Not in spring-time! Sum-mer, win-ter or fall!
D7 Dm G7 C
C D E B C D E B C
No nev-er could I leave you at all!

CAMELOT

Words by ALAN JAY LERNER
Music by FREDERICK LOEWE

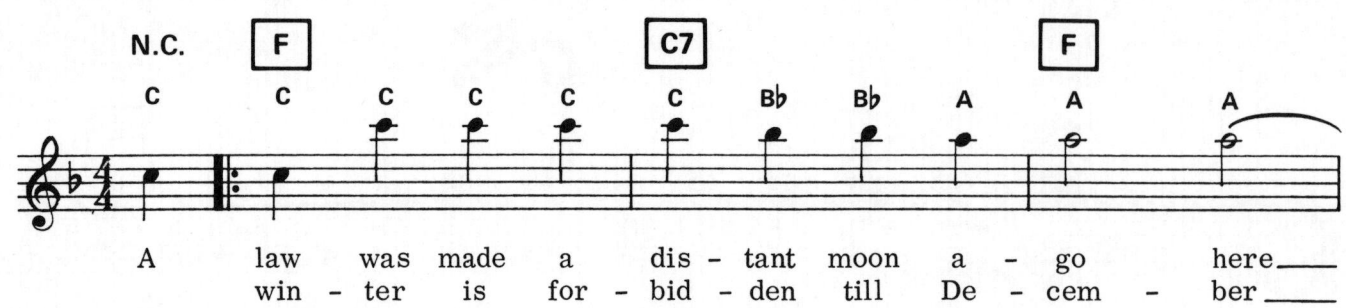

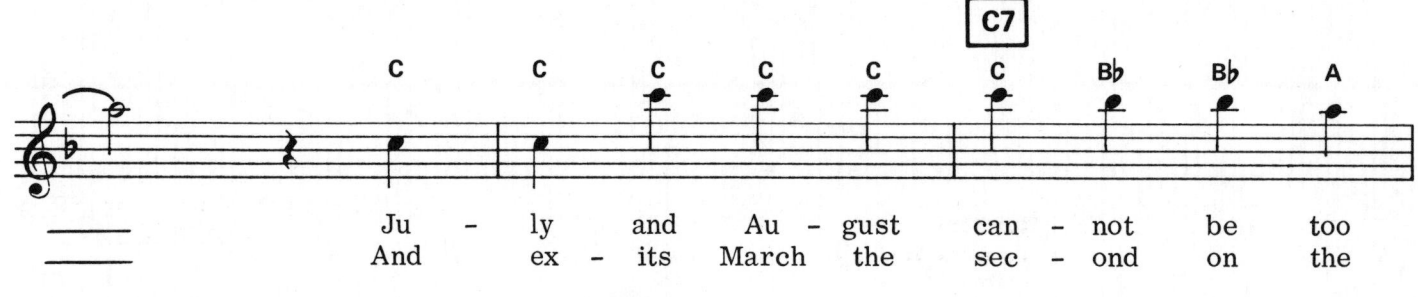

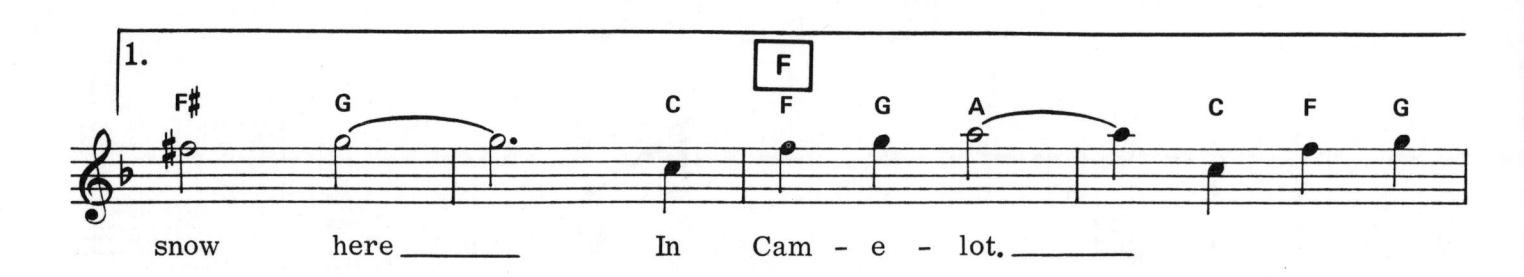

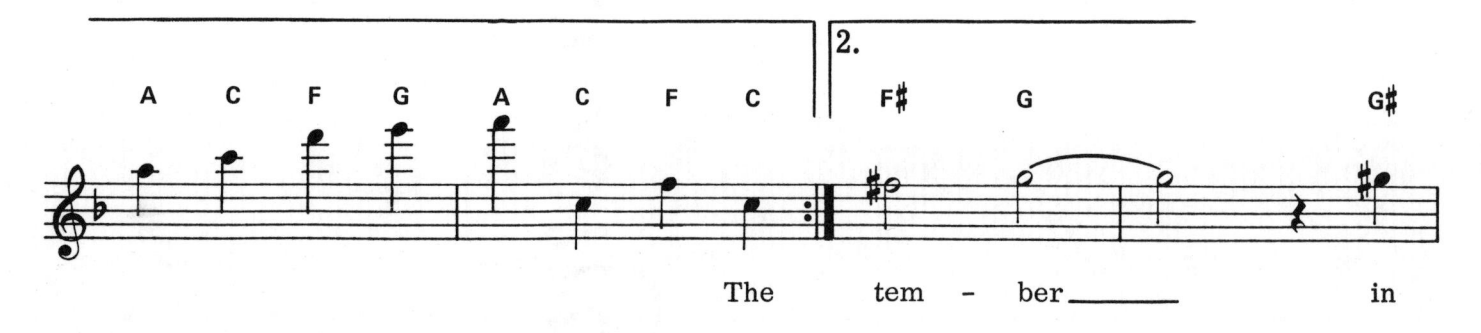

registration number 4.

A law was made a distant moon ago here___ Ju-ly and Au-gust can-not be too hot;___ And there's a le-gal lim-it to the snow here___ In Cam-e-lot.___

winter is for-bid-den till De-cem-ber___ And ex-its March the sec-ond on the dot.___ By or-der sum-mer lin-gers through Sep- tem-ber___ in

Copyright © 1960 & 1967 by Alan Jay Lerner and Frederick Loewe
Chappell & Co., Inc., owner of publication and allied rights throughout the world
Used by HAL LEONARD PUBLISHING CORPORATION, Winona, MN 55987 by Permission
Made in U.S.A.   International Copyright Secured   All Rights Reserved

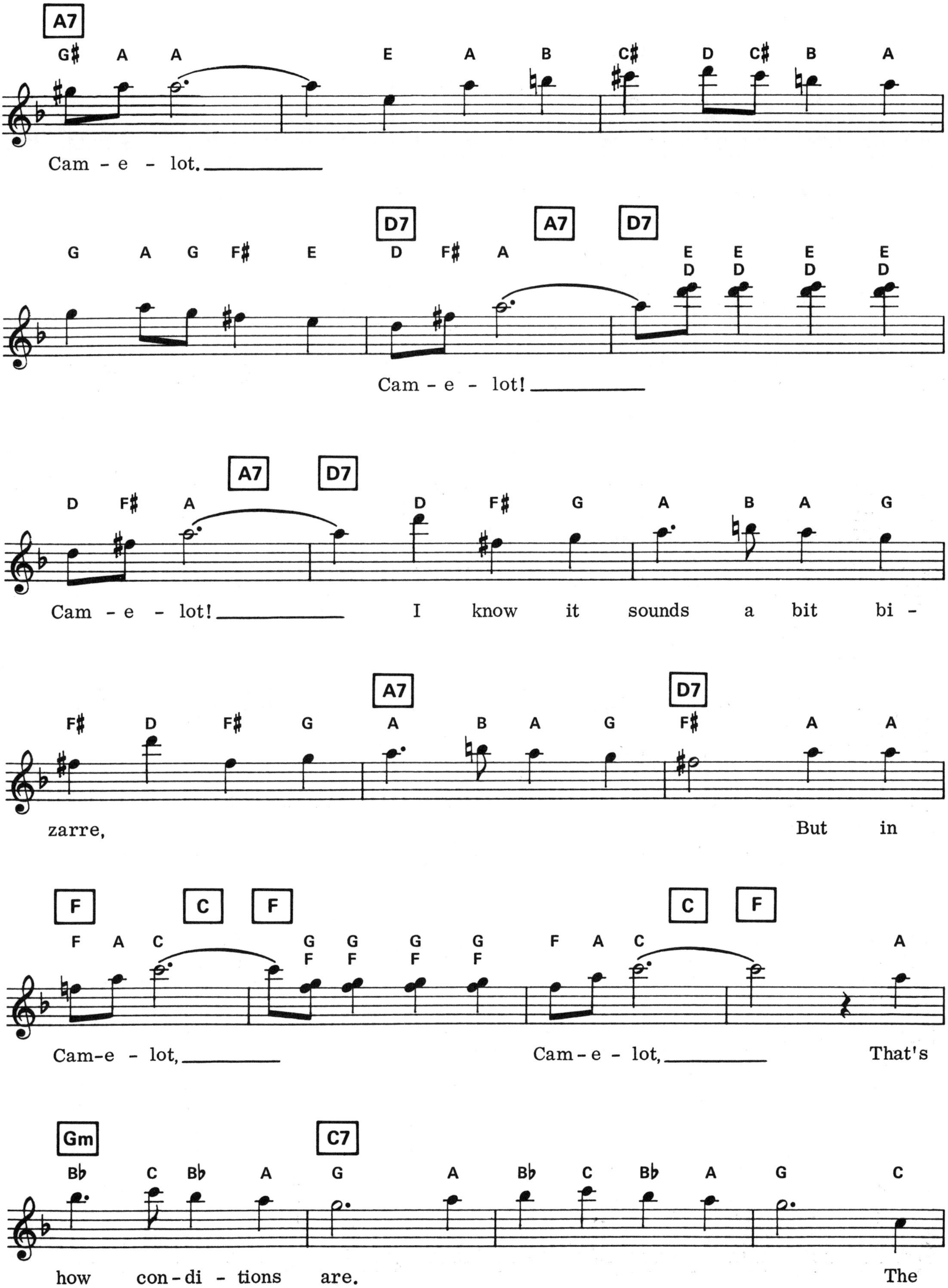
A7
G♯ A A E A B C♯ D C♯ B A
Cam - e - lot.
D7 A7 D7
G A G F♯ E D F♯ A E D E D E D E D
Cam - e - lot!
A7 D7
D F♯ A D F♯ G A B A G
Cam - e - lot! I know it sounds a bit bi -
A7 D7
F♯ D F♯ G A B A G F♯ A A
zarre, But in
F C F C F
F A C G F G F G F G F F A C A
Cam-e - lot, Cam - e - lot, That's
Gm C7
B♭ C B♭ A G A B♭ C B♭ A G C
how con - di - tions are. The

rain may nev-er fall till af-ter sun-down. By

eight the morn-ing fog must dis-ap-pear. In

short, there's sim-ply not a more con-gen-ial spot For

hap-p'ly-ev-er-aft-er-ing than here in

Cam - e - lot!

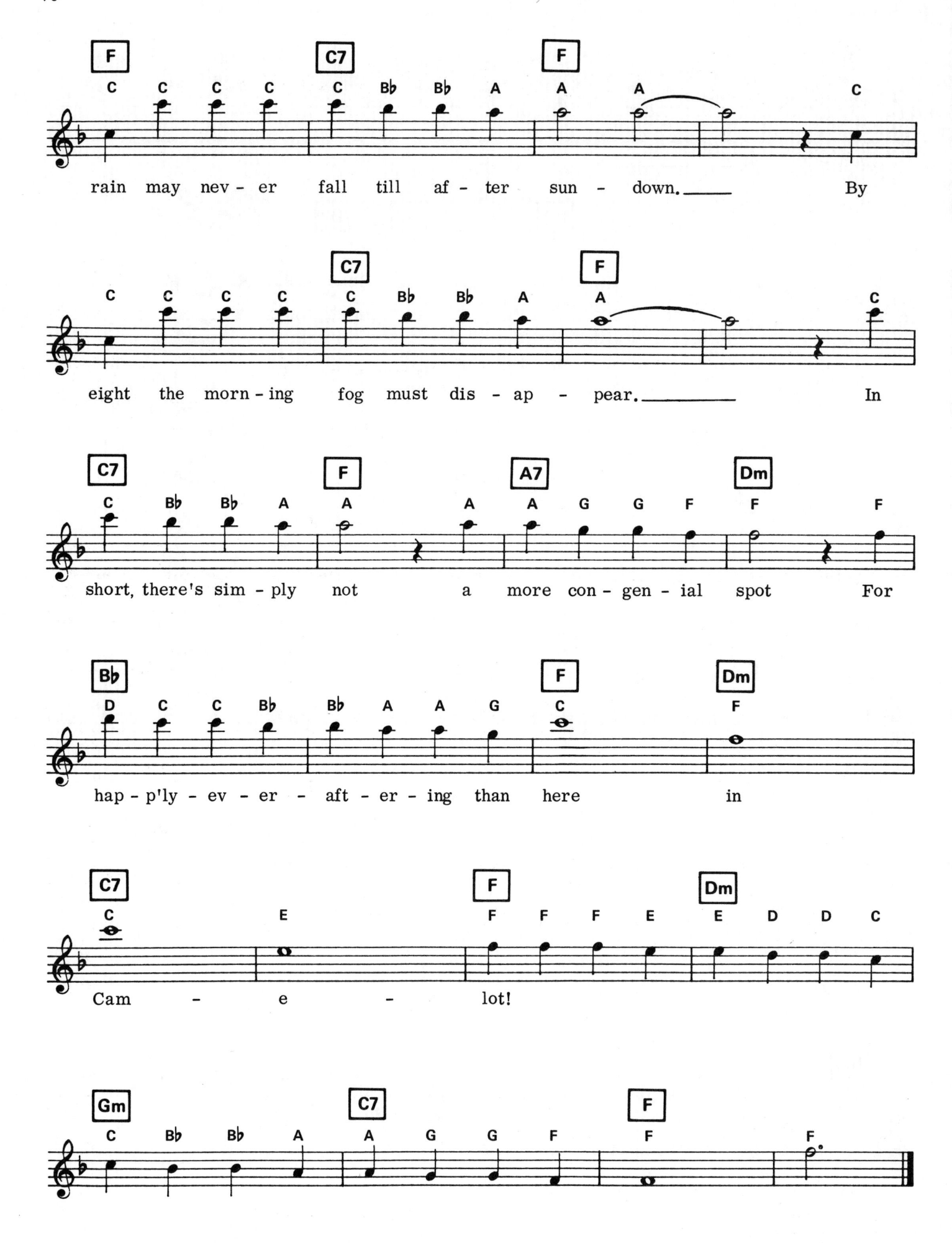

DON'T RAIN ON MY PARADE

Words by BOB MERRILL
Music by JULE STYNE

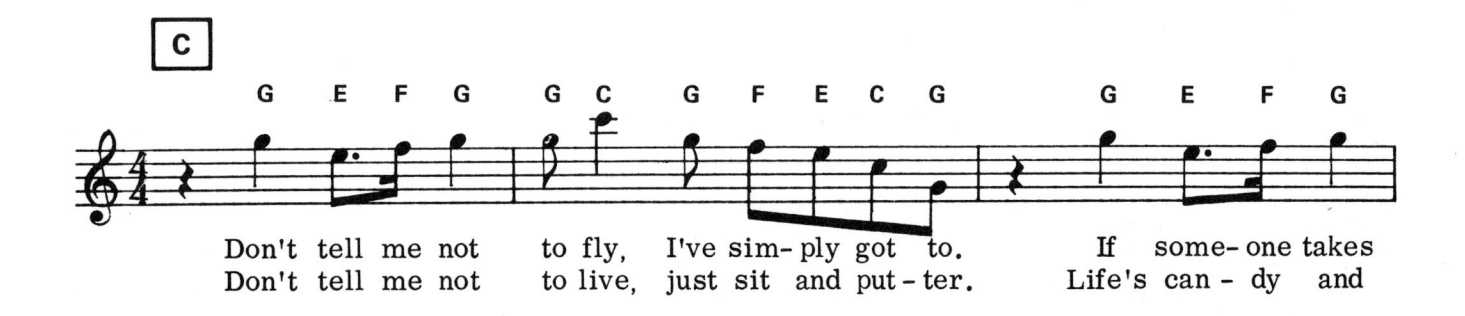

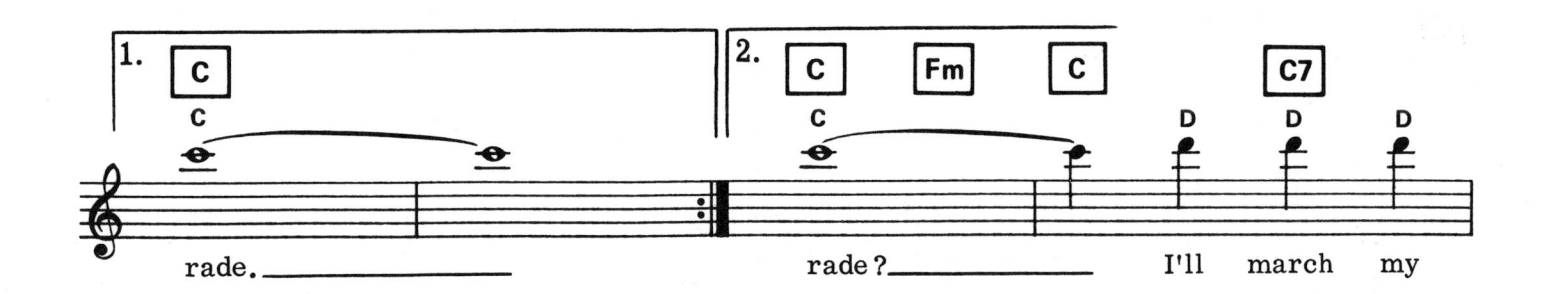

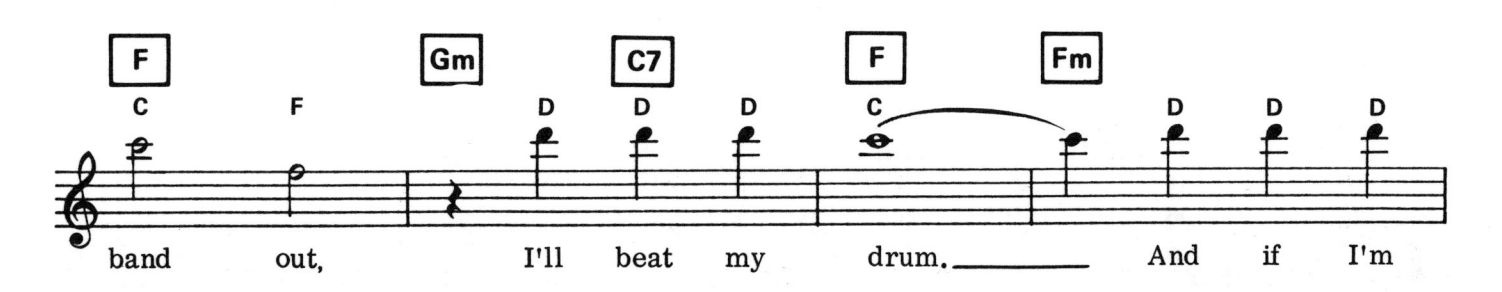

registration number 5.

Don't tell me not to fly, I've sim-ply got to. If some-one takes
Don't tell me not to live, just sit and put-ter. Life's can-dy and

a spill, it's me and not you. Don't bring a-round a cloud to rain on my pa-
the sun's a ball of but-ter. Who told you you're al-lowed to rain on my pa-

1. rade.

2. rade? I'll march my

band out, I'll beat my drum. And if I'm

Copyright © 1963 & 1968 by Bob Merrill and Jule Styne
Chappell-Styne, Inc., and Wonderful Music Corp., owners of publication and allied rights throughout the world
Chappell & Co., Inc., sole and exclusive agent

Used by HAL LEONARD PUBLISHING CORPORATION, Winona, MN 55987 by Permission
Made in U.S.A.   International Copyright Secured   All Rights Reserved

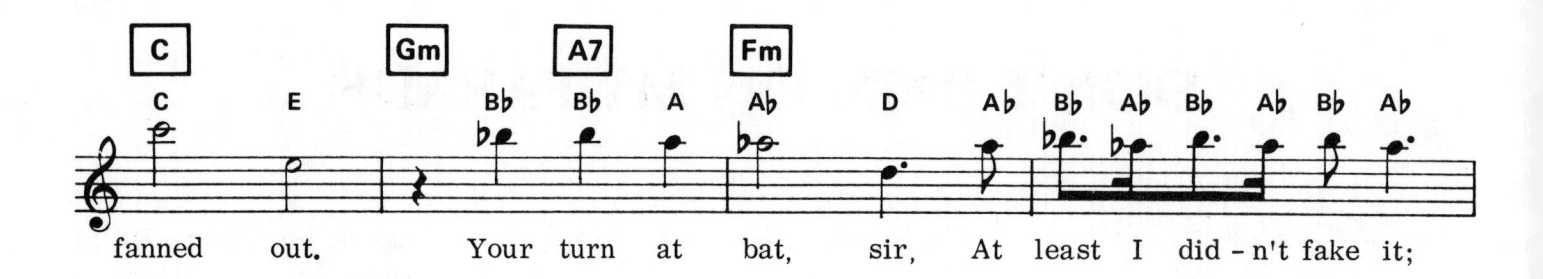

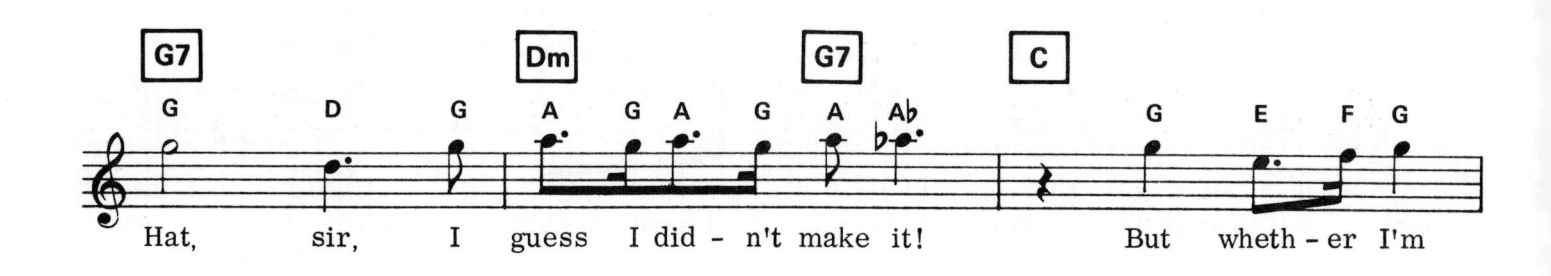

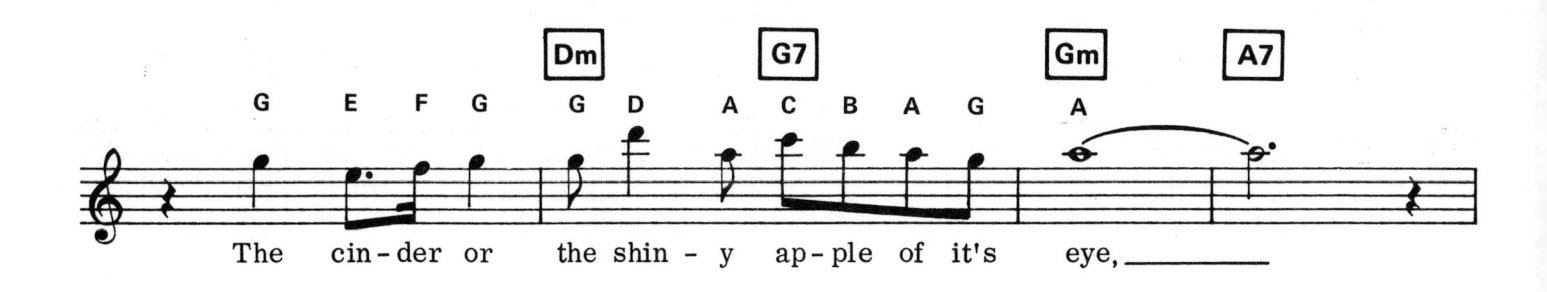

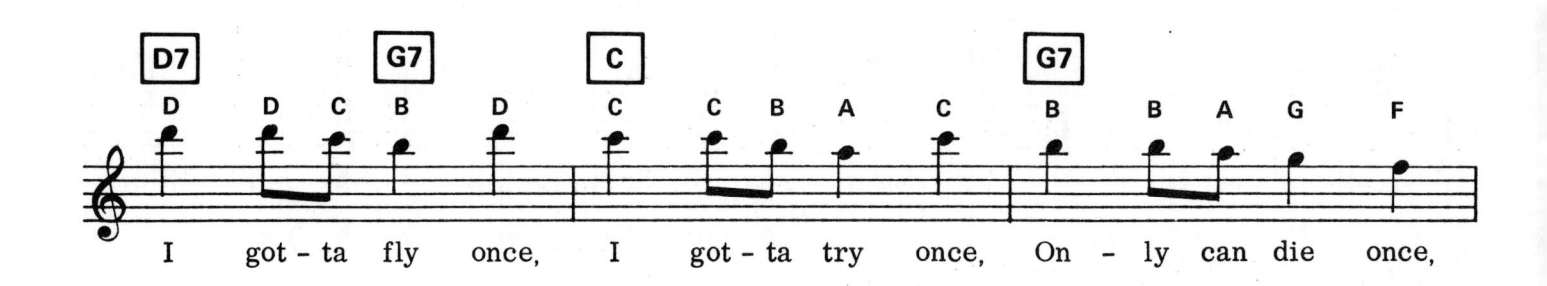

fanned out. Your turn at bat, sir, At least I did-n't fake it; Hat, sir, I guess I did-n't make it! But wheth-er I'm the rose of sheer per-fec-tion Or freck-le on the nose of life's com-plex-ion, The cin-der or the shin-y ap-ple of it's eye, I got-ta fly once, I got-ta try once, On-ly can die once,

C D7 G7 C Am
Right, sir? Ooh, love is juic - y, Juic - y and you see
N.C. (B) E G7 C
I got - ta have my bite, sir. Get read - y for
N.C. (D♭)
me, love, 'cause I'm a "com - er". I sim-ply got - ta march, my heart's a drum - mer.
C Am Dm
No - bod - y, no, no - bod - y Is gon - na
C G7 C
rain on my pa - rade.

YOU ARE WOMAN

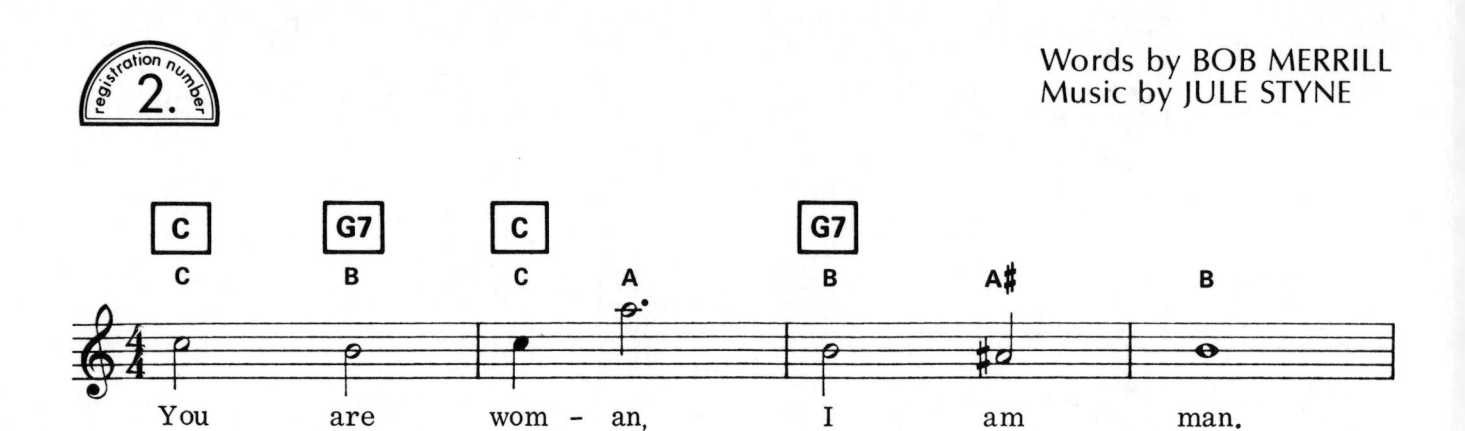

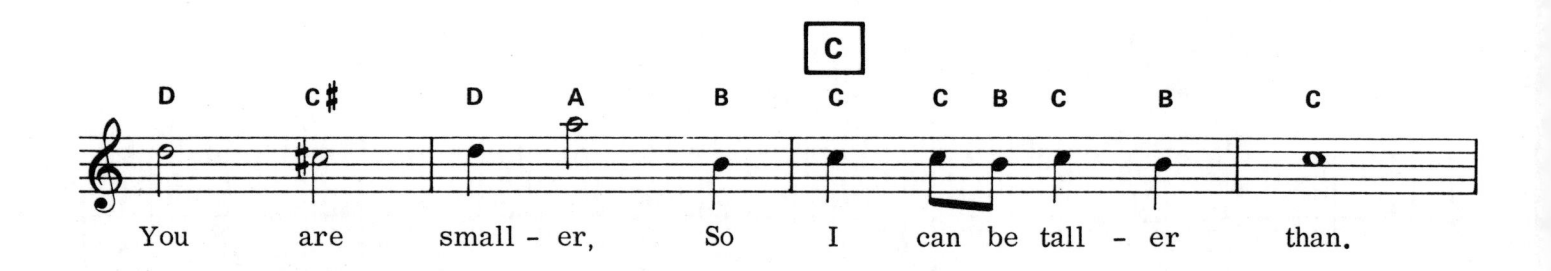

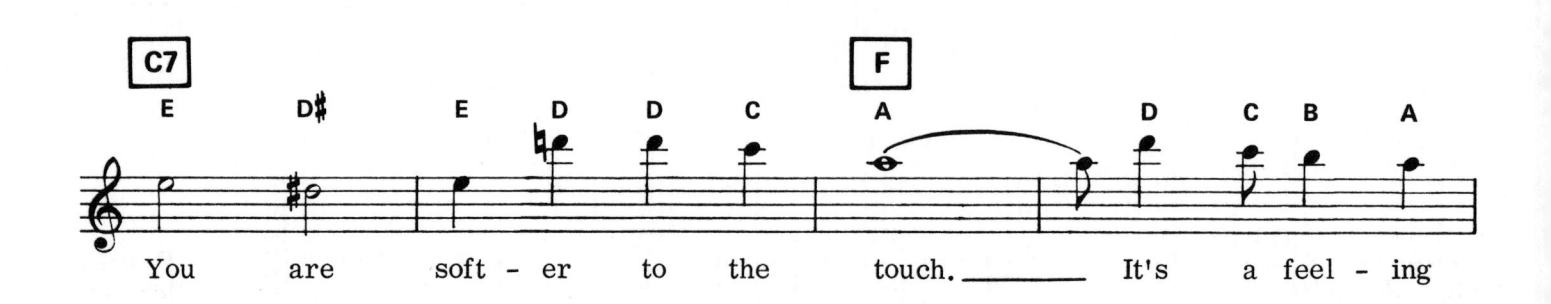

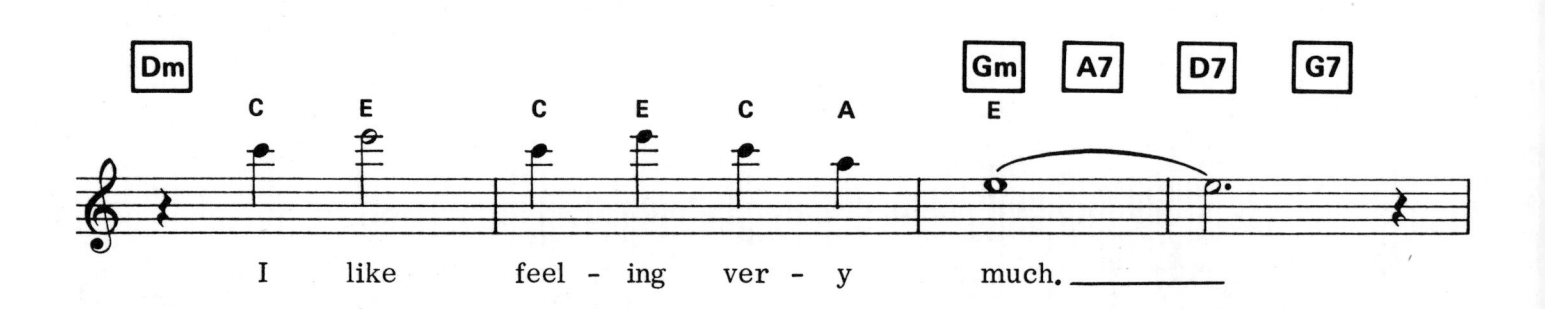

Words by BOB MERRILL
Music by JULE STYNE

You are wom-an, I am man.

You are small-er, So I can be tall-er than.

You are soft-er to the touch. It's a feel-ing

I like feel-ing ver-y much.

Copyright © 1963 & 1968 by Bob Merrill and Jule Styne
Chappell-Styne, Inc. and Wonderful Music Corp., owners of publication and allied rights throughout the world
Chappell & Co., Inc., sole and exclusive agent

Used by HAL LEONARD PUBLISHING CORPORATION, Winona, MN 55987 by Permission
Made in U.S.A.   International Copyright Secured   All Rights Reserved

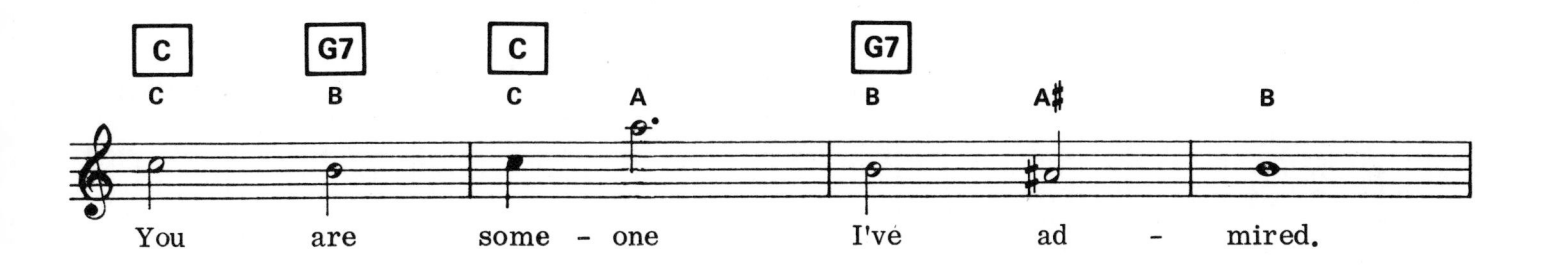

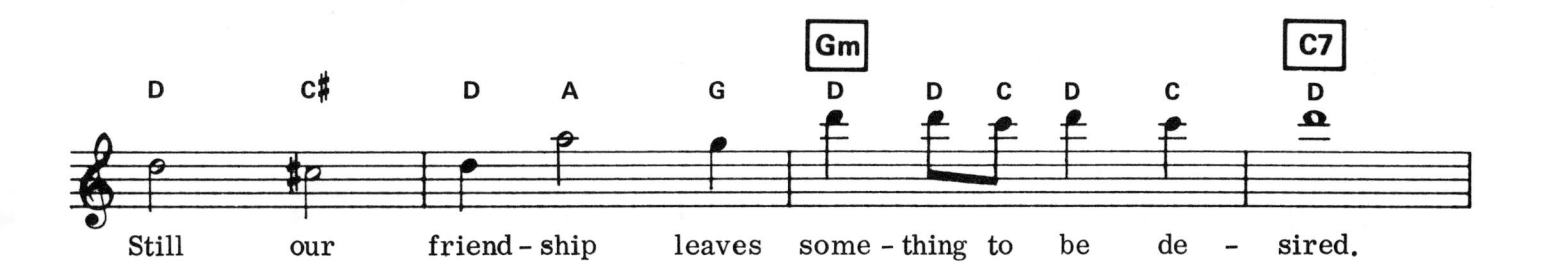

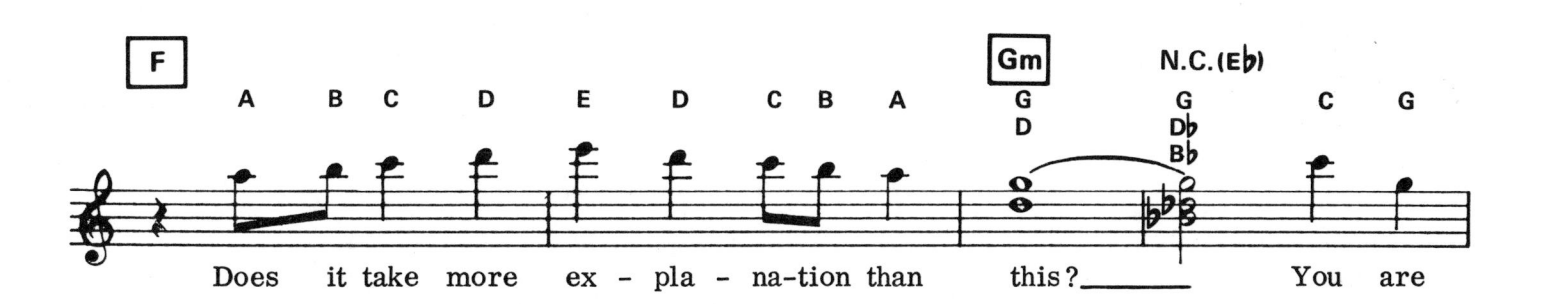

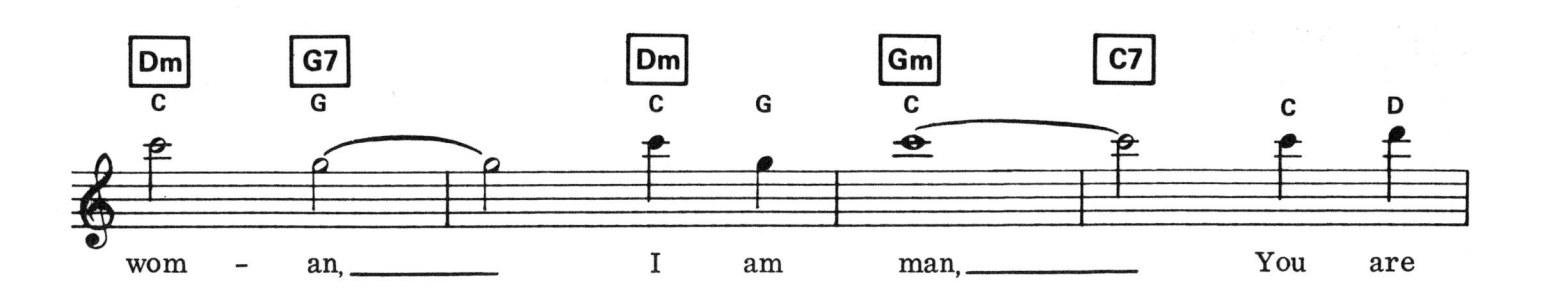

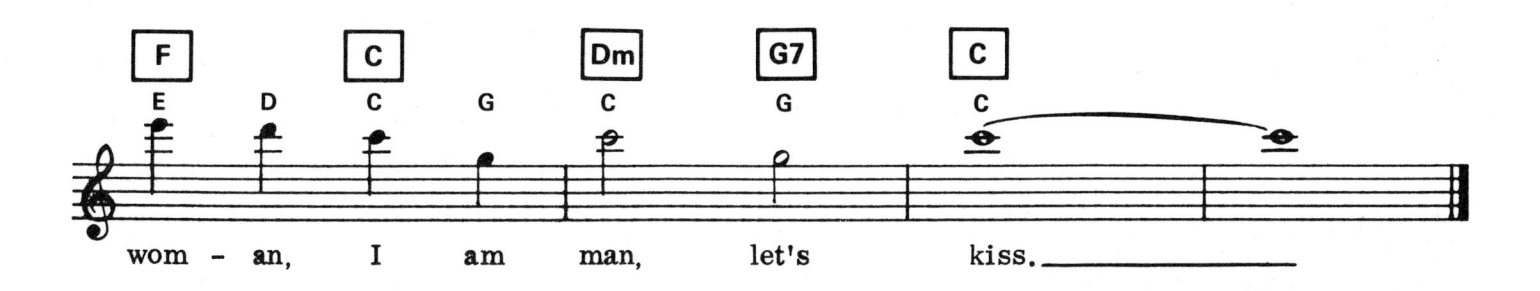

You are some-one I've ad-mired. Still our friend-ship leaves some-thing to be de-sired. Does it take more ex-pla-na-tion than this? You are wom-an, I am man, You are wom-an, I am man, let's kiss.

PEOPLE

Words by BOB MERRILL
Music by JULE STYNE

registration number 8

Peo - ple, peo-ple who need peo - ple Are the luck - i - est peo - ple in the world. We're chil - dren need-ing oth - er chil - dren And yet, let - ting our grown up pride Hide all the need in - side, Act - ing more like chil - dren, than chil - dren. Lov - ers

Copyright © 1963 & 1968 by Bob Merrill and Jule Styne
Chappell-Styne, Inc. and Wonderful Music Corp., owners of publication and allied rights throughout the world
Chappell & Co., Inc., sole and exclusive agent
Used by HAL LEONARD PUBLISHING CORPORATION, Winona, MN 55987 by Permission
Made in U.S.A.   International Copyright Secured   All Rights Reserved

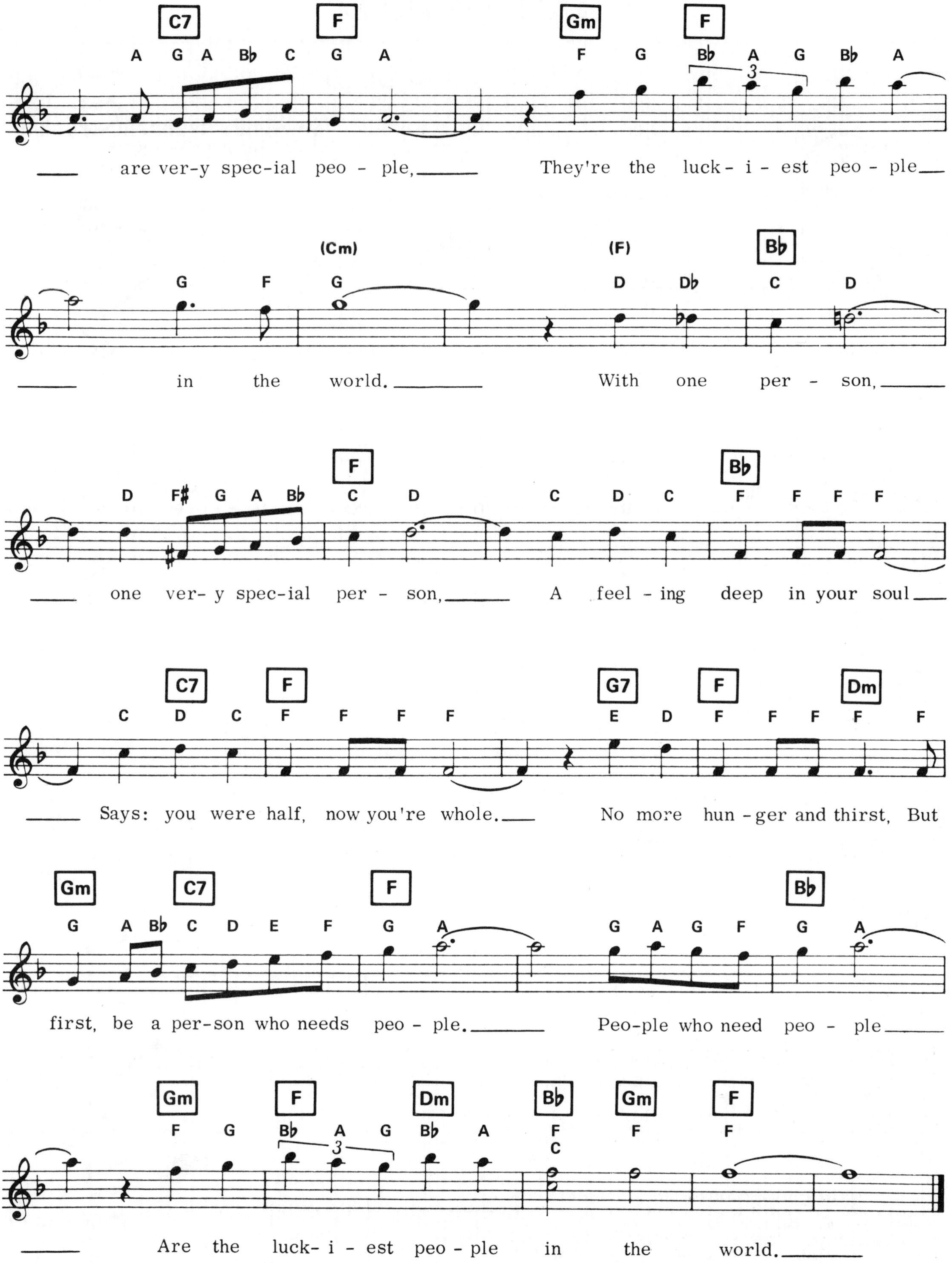
C7 F Gm F
A G A B♭ C G A F G B♭ A G B♭ A
are ver-y spec-ial peo - ple, They're the luck- i - est peo - ple
(Cm) (F) B♭
G F G D D♭ C D
in the world. With one per - son,
F B♭
D F♯ G A B♭ C D C D C F F F F
one ver- y spec-ial per - son, A feel - ing deep in your soul
C7 F G7 F Dm
C D C F F F F E D F F F F F
Says: you were half, now you're whole. No more hun - ger and thirst, But
Gm C7 F B♭
G A B♭ C D E F G A G A G F G A
first, be a per-son who needs peo - ple. Peo-ple who need peo - ple
Gm F Dm B♭ Gm F
F G B♭ A G B♭ A F C F F
Are the luck- i - est peo - ple in the world.

SMALL WORLD

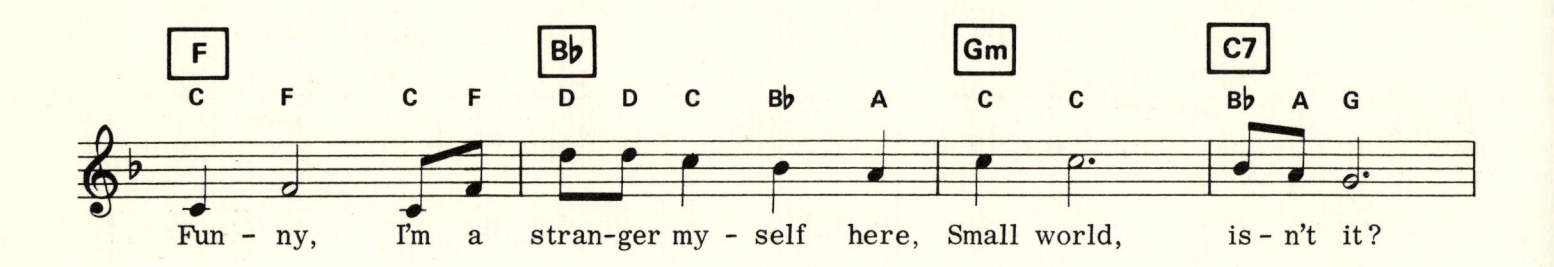

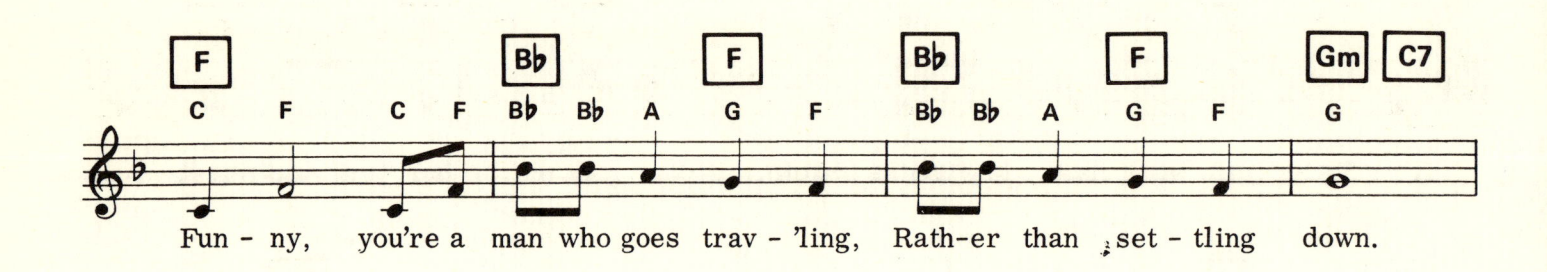

Words by STEPHEN SONDHEIM
Music by JULE STYNE

Fun - ny, you're a stran-ger who's come here, Come from an - oth - er town.

Fun - ny, I'm a stran-ger my - self here, Small world, is - n't it?

Fun - ny, you're a man who goes trav - 'ling, Rath-er than set - tling down.

Fun - ny, 'cause I'd love to go trav - 'ling, Small world, is - n't it?

Copyright ©1959 by Norbeth Productions, Inc., and Stephen Sondheim
Williamson Music, Inc. and Stratford Music Corporation, owners of publication and allied rights throughout the world
Chappell & Co., Inc., sole selling agent
Used by HAL LEONARD PUBLISHING CORPORATION, Winona, MN 55987 by Permission
Made in U.S.A.   International Copyright Secured   All Rights Reserved

We have so much in com - mon, It's a phe-nom - e - non.

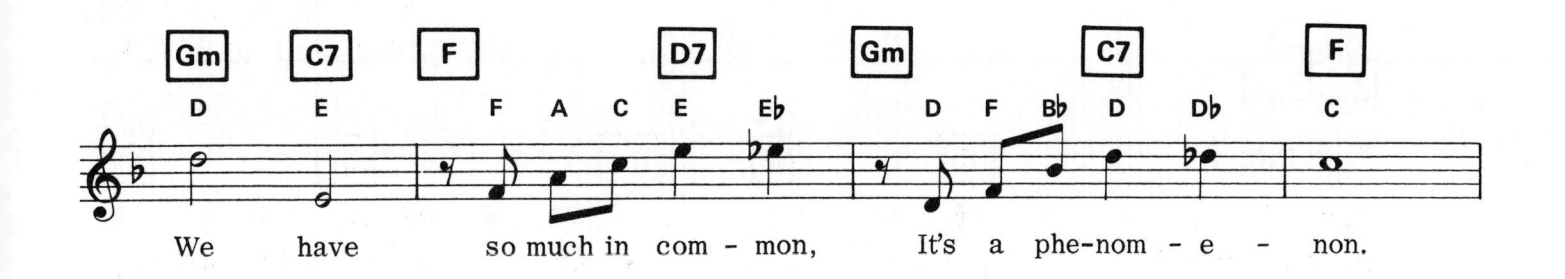

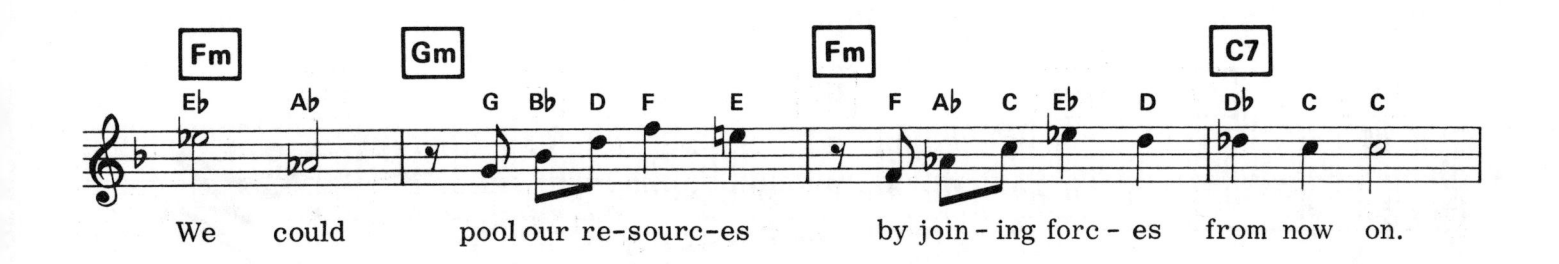

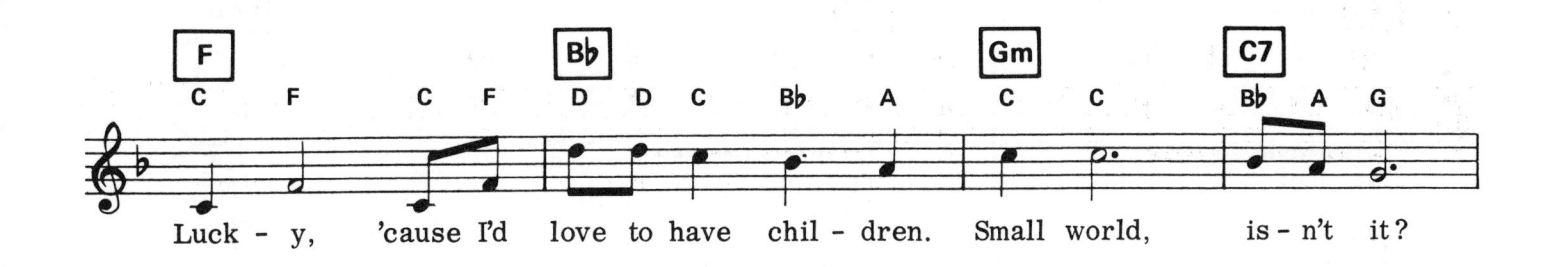

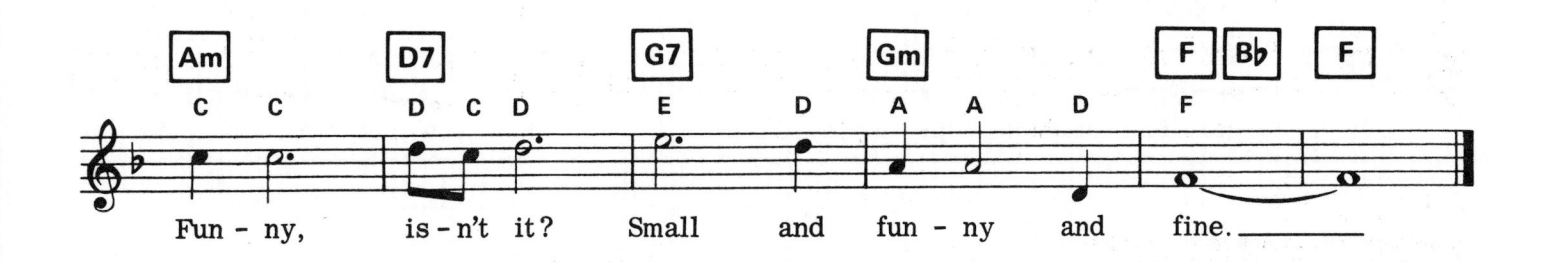

We could pool our re-sourc-es by join - ing forc - es from now on.

Luck - y, you're a man who likes chil - dren. That's an im - por - tant sign.

Luck - y, 'cause I'd love to have chil - dren. Small world, is - n't it?

Fun - ny, is - n't it? Small and fun - ny and fine.

SUGAR

Words by BOB MERRILL
Music by JULE STYNE

Do-ing it for Su-gar, I'm on-ly do-ing it for Su-gar. Al-though I do ad-mit when her heart is twink-ling that I get a sprink-ling of Su-gar. To-night I'm gon-na show her a time, a time that she's got to a-dore; Su-gar's one of those peo-ple that you just want to do

Copyright ©1972 by Bob Merrill and Jule Styne
Chappell & Co., Inc. and Merrill Music Corporation owners of publication and allied rights throughout the world
Used by HAL LEONARD PUBLISHING CORPORATION, Winona, MN 55987 by Permission
Made in U.S.A.   International Copyright Secured   All Rights Reserved

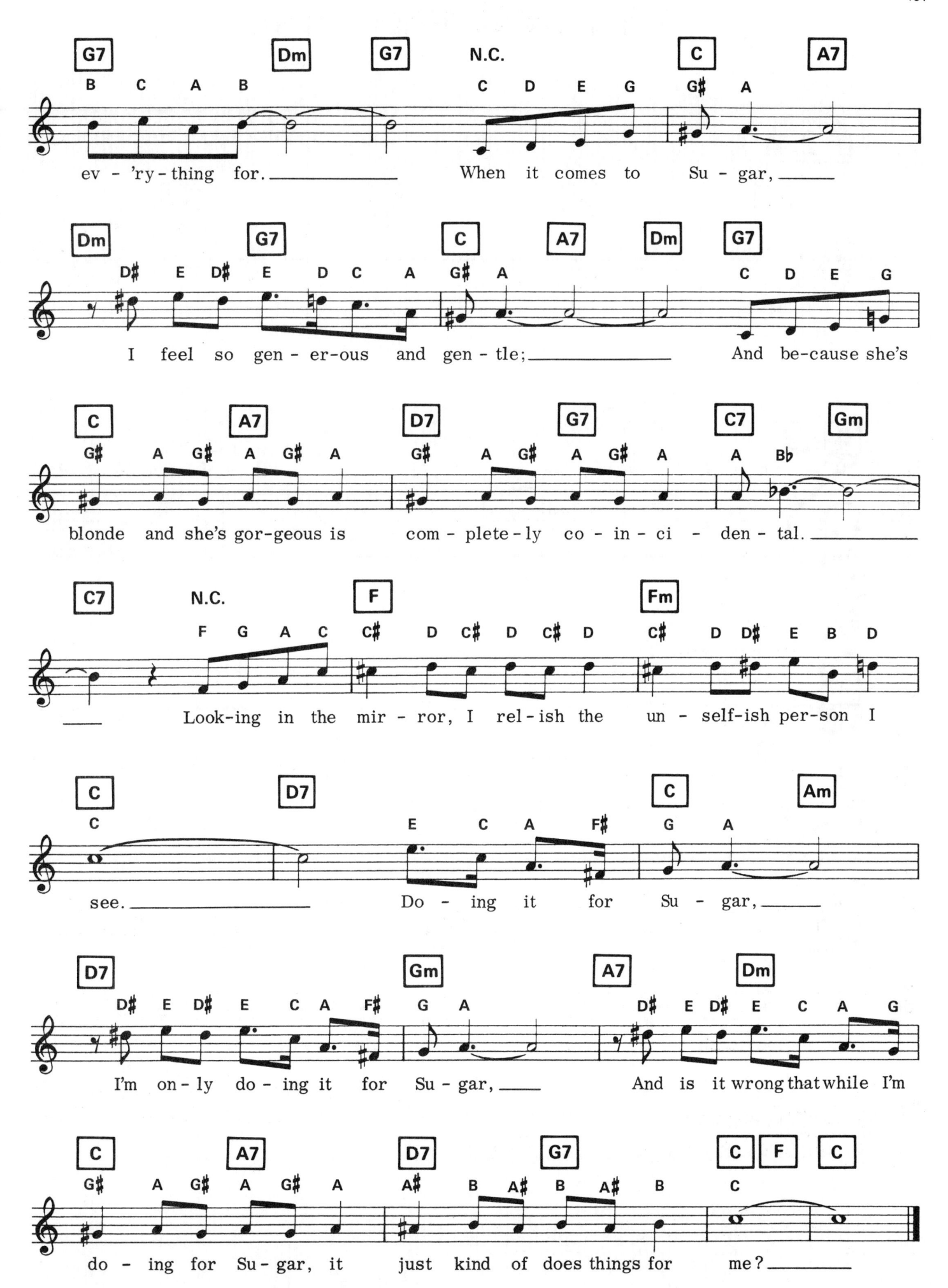

ev - 'ry-thing for.____ When it comes to Su - gar,____
I feel so gen - er-ous and gen - tle;____ And be-cause she's
blonde and she's gor-geous is com - plete-ly co - in - ci - den - tal.____
____ Look-ing in the mir - ror, I rel-ish the un - self-ish per-son I
see.____ Do - ing it for Su - gar,____
I'm on - ly do - ing it for Su - gar,____ And is it wrong that while I'm
do - ing for Su - gar, it just kind of does things for me?____

MY FUNNY VALENTINE

Words by LORENZ HART
Music by RICHARD RODGERS

registration number 2.

| Dm | A7 | Dm | A7 |
| D E F | E F E | D E F | E F E |

My fun-ny val-en-tine, Sweet com-ic val-en-tine,

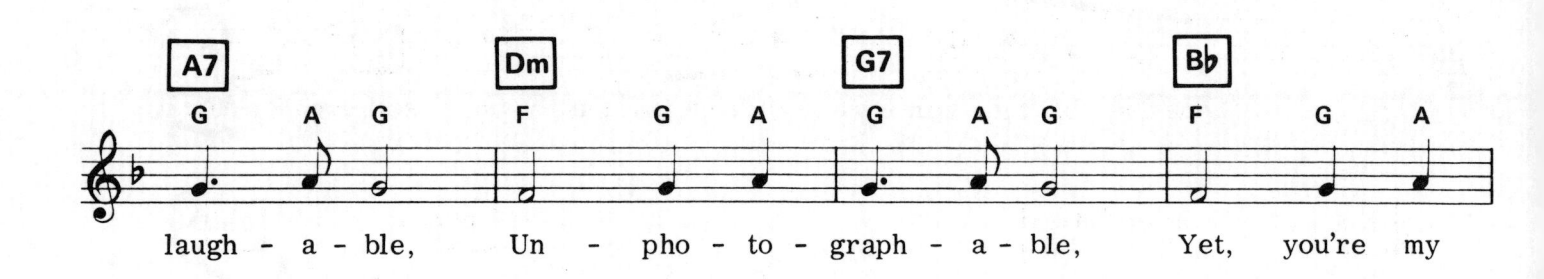

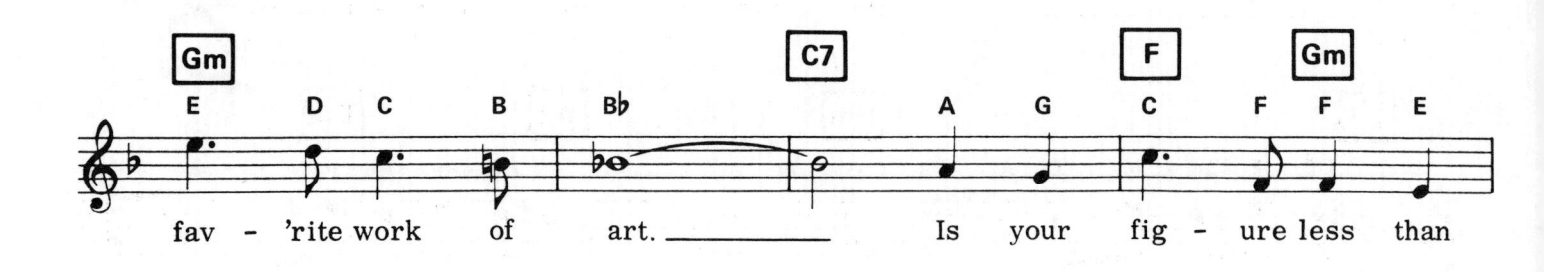

| Bb | Gm | A7 | Dm |
| D E F | C Bb A | G | F G A |

You make me smile with my heart.____ Your looks are

| A7 | Dm | G7 | Bb |
| G A G | F G A | G A G | F G A |

laugh-a-ble, Un-pho-to-graph-a-ble, Yet, you're my

| Gm | | C7 | F | Gm |
| E D C B | Bb | A G | C F | F E |

fav-'rite work of art.____ Is your fig-ure less than

Copyright © 1937 by Chappell & Co., Inc.
Copyright Renewed
Used by HAL LEONARD PUBLISHING CORPORATION, Winona, MN 55987 by Permission
Made in U.S.A. International Copyright Secured All Rights Reserved

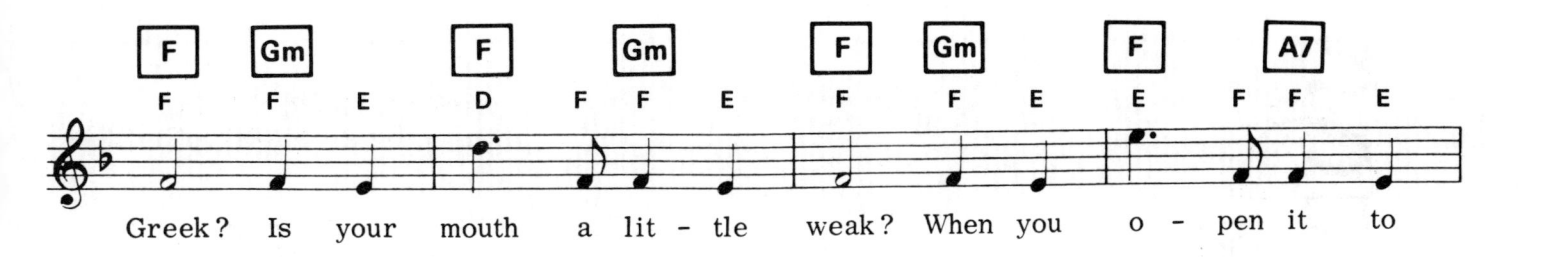

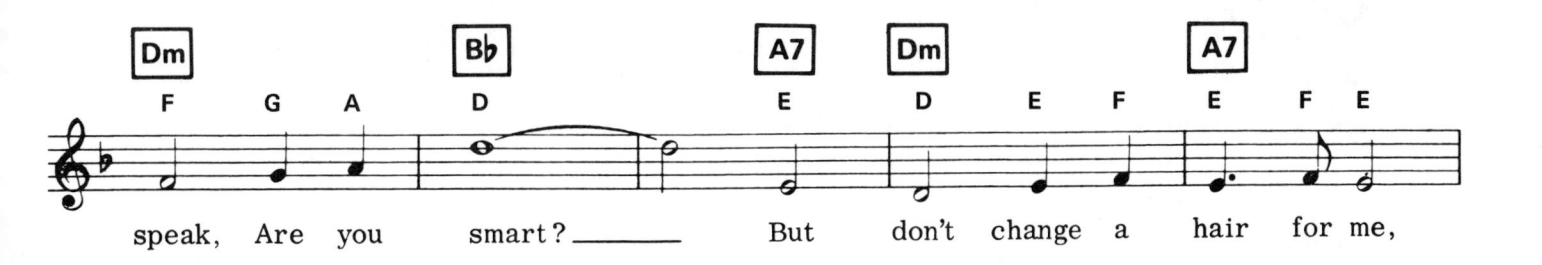

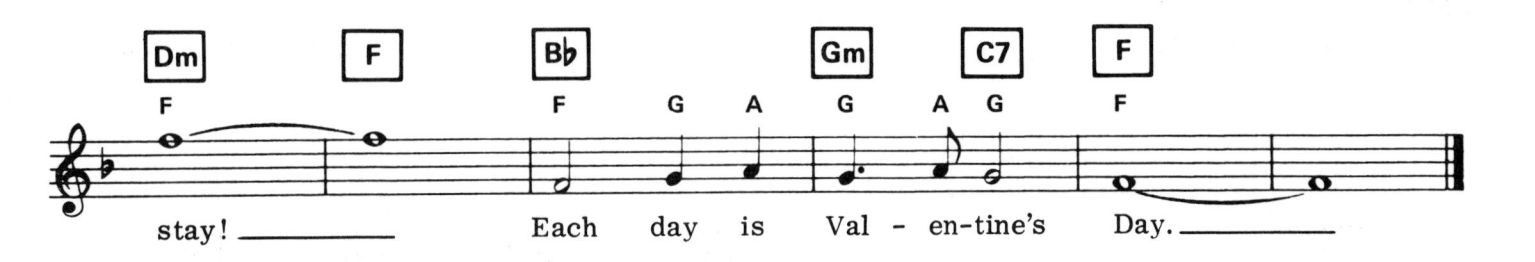

Greek? Is your mouth a lit-tle weak? When you o-pen it to speak, Are you smart? But don't change a hair for me, Not if you care for me. Stay lit-tle Val-en-tine, stay! Each day is Val-en-tine's Day.

FALLING IN LOVE WITH LOVE

Words by LORENZ HART
Music by RICHARD RODGERS

Fall-ing in love with love is fall-ing for make be-lieve. Fall-ing in love with love Is play-ing the fool. Car-ing too much is such a ju-ve-nile fan-cy.

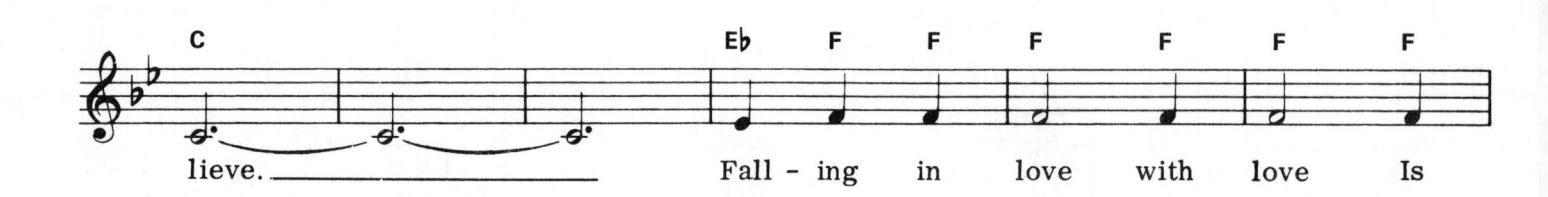

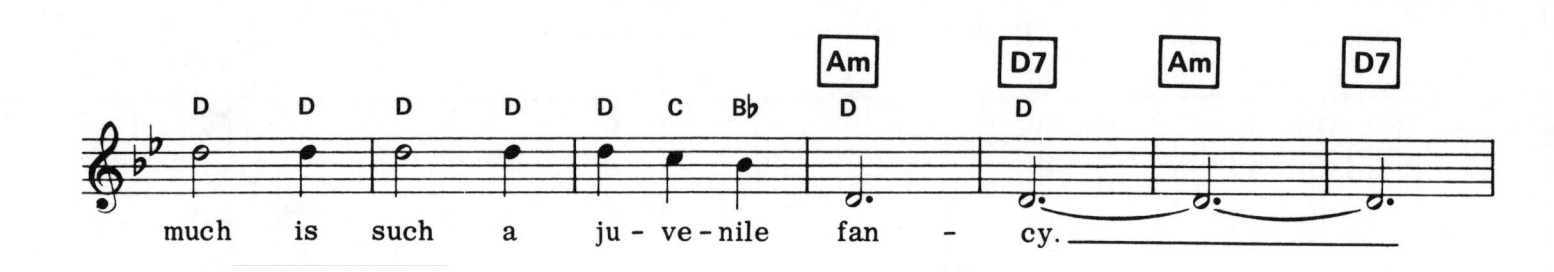

Copyright©1938 by Chappell & Co., Inc.
Copyright Renewed
Copyright©1970 by Chappell & Co., Inc.
Used by HAL LEONARD PUBLISHING CORPORATION, Winona, MN 55987 by Permission
Made in U.S.A.   International Copyright Secured   All Rights Reserved

Learn-ing to trust is just like chil-dren in school. I fell in love with love one night when the moon was full. I was un-wise with eyes un-a-ble to see. I fell in love with love, with love ev-er-last-ing. But love fell out with me.

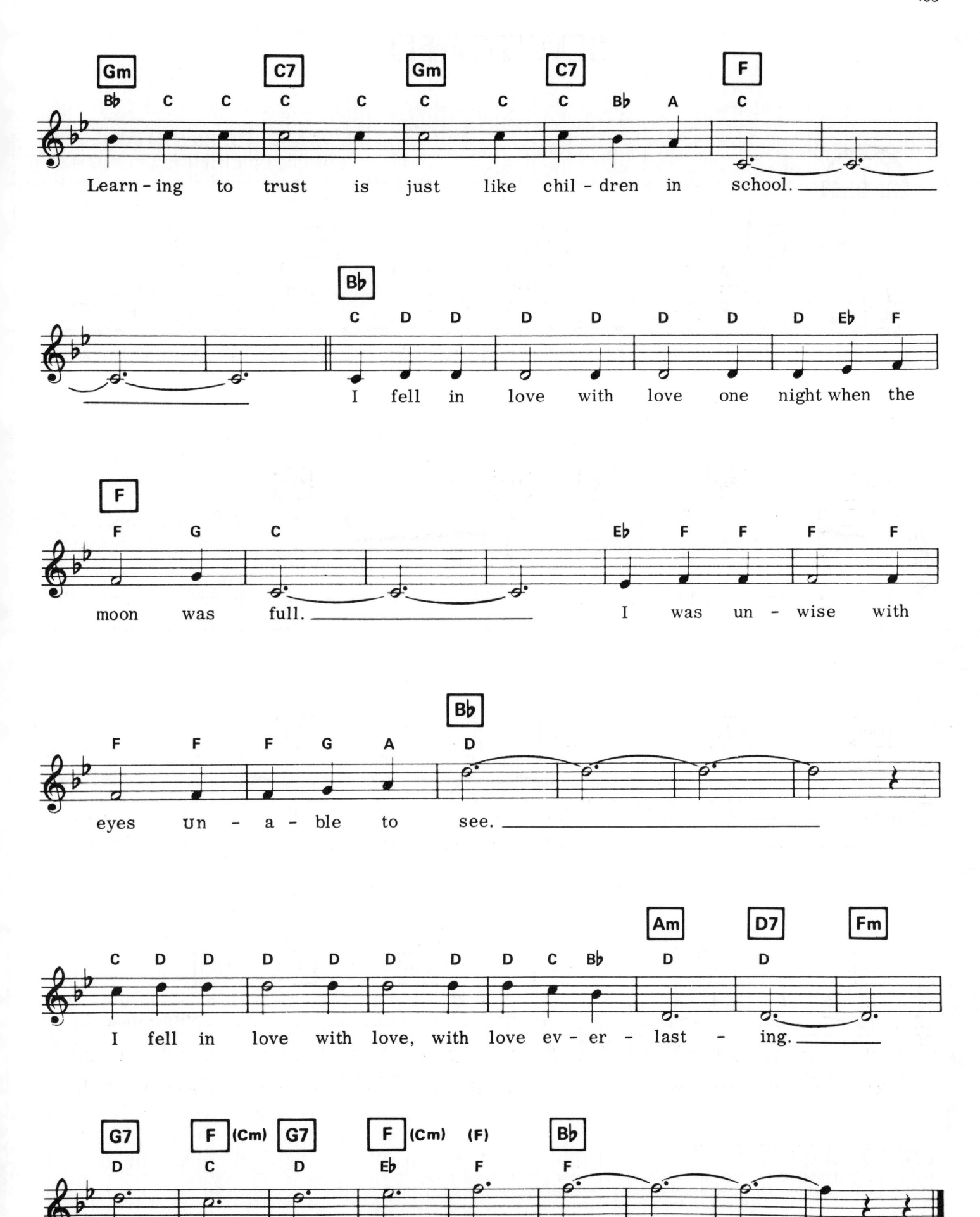

BEWITCHED

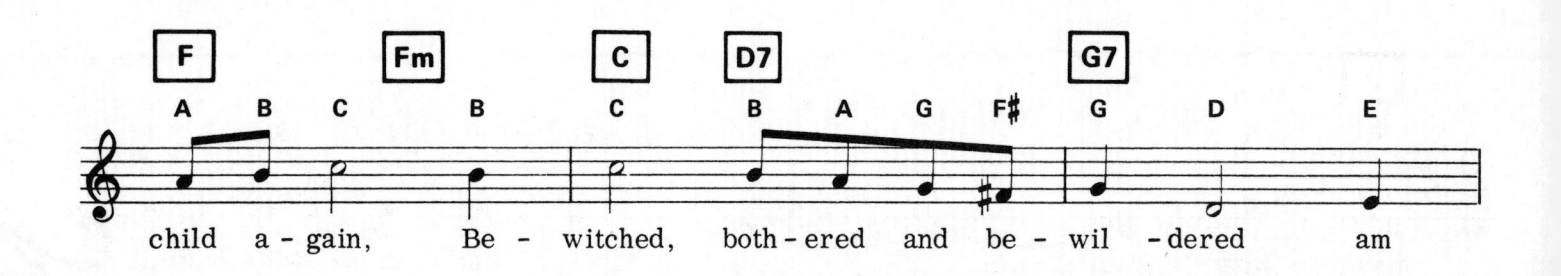

Words by LORENZ HART
Music by RICHARD RODGERS

I'm wild a-gain, Be-guiled a-gain, A sim-per-ing, whim-per-ing child a-gain, Be-witched, both-ered and be-wil-dered am I. _____ I could-n't sleep, And would-n't sleep, When love came and told me I should-n't sleep, Be-witched, both-ered and be-

Copyright © 1941 by Chappell & Co., Inc.
Copyright Renewed

Used by HAL LEONARD PUBLISHING CORPORATION, Winona, MN 55987 by Permission
Made in U.S.A. International Copyright Secured All Rights Reserved

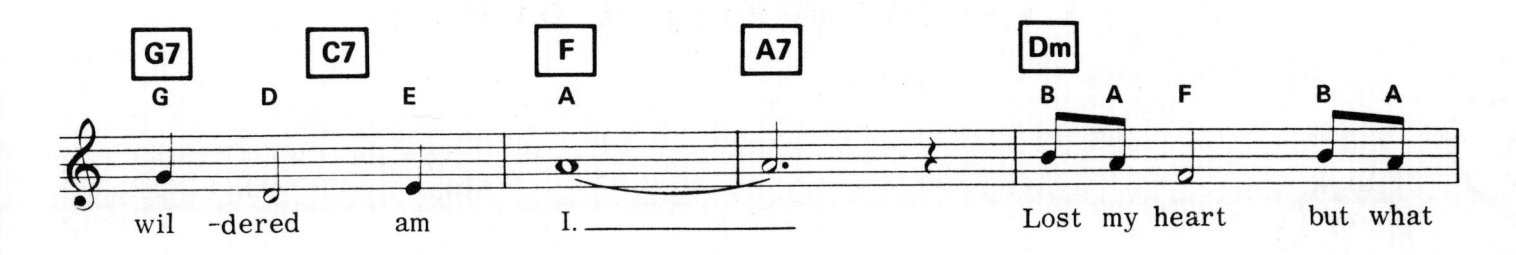

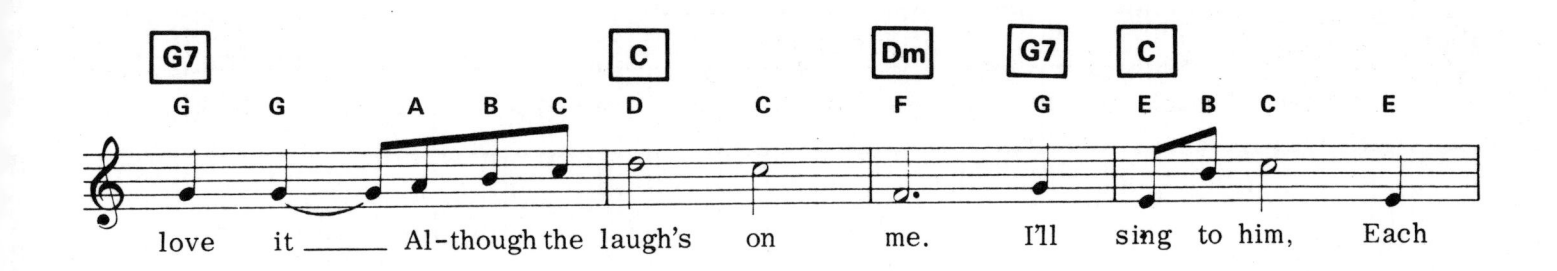

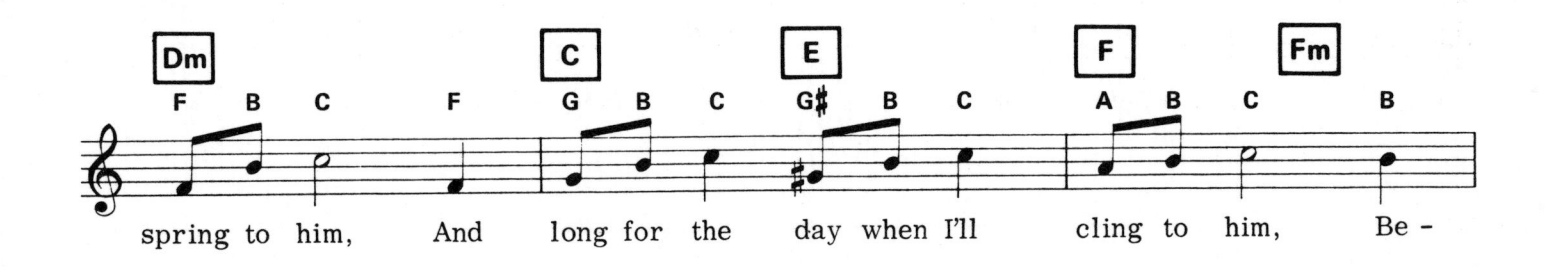

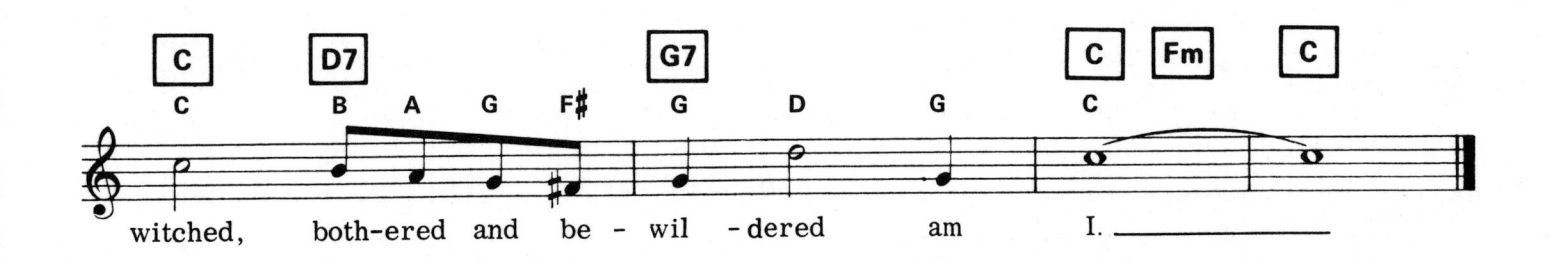

wil-dered am I. _____ Lost my heart but what of it? He is cold, I a-gree. He can laugh, but I love it _____ Al-though the laugh's on me. I'll sing to him, Each spring to him, And long for the day when I'll cling to him, Be-witched, both-ered and be-wil-dered am I. _____

I COULD WRITE A BOOK

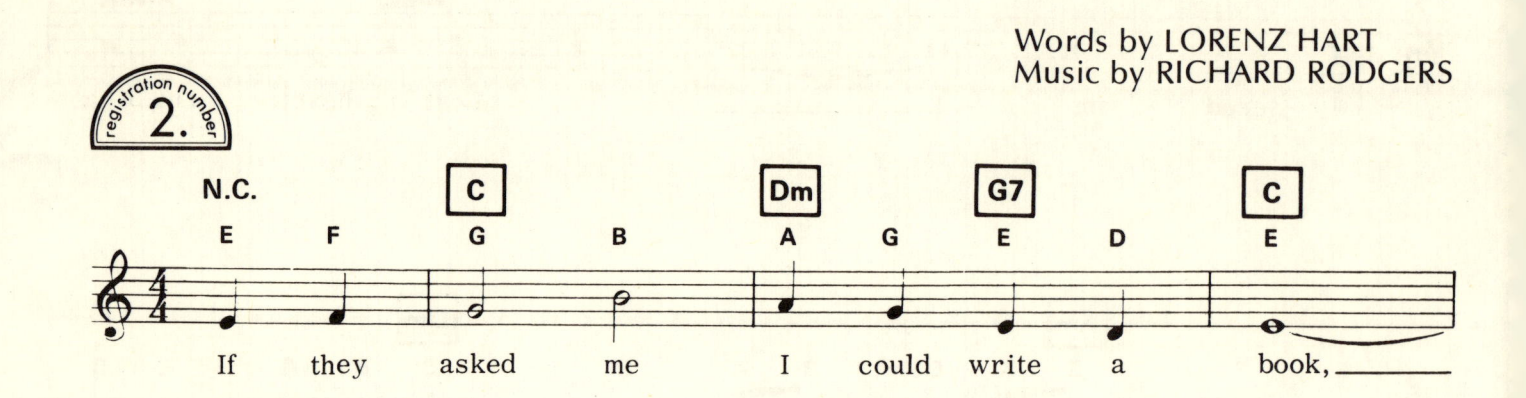

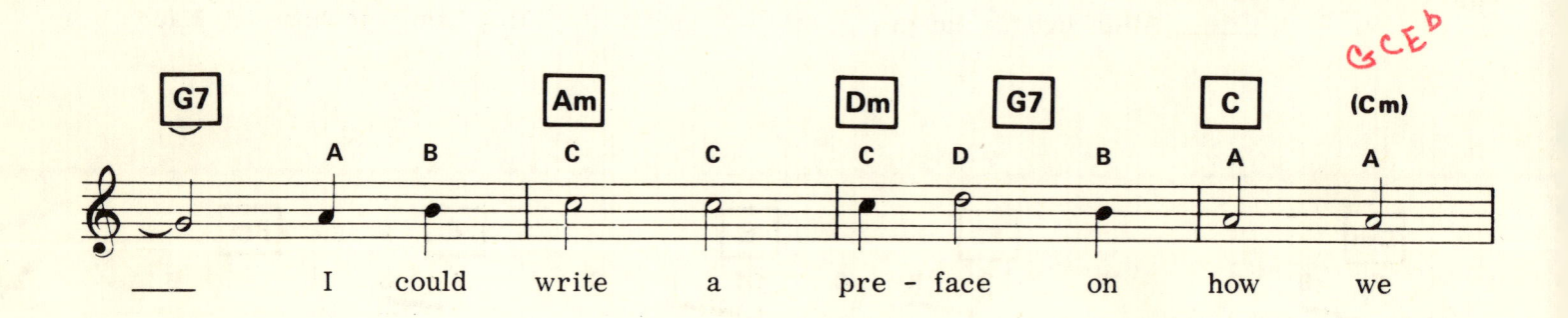

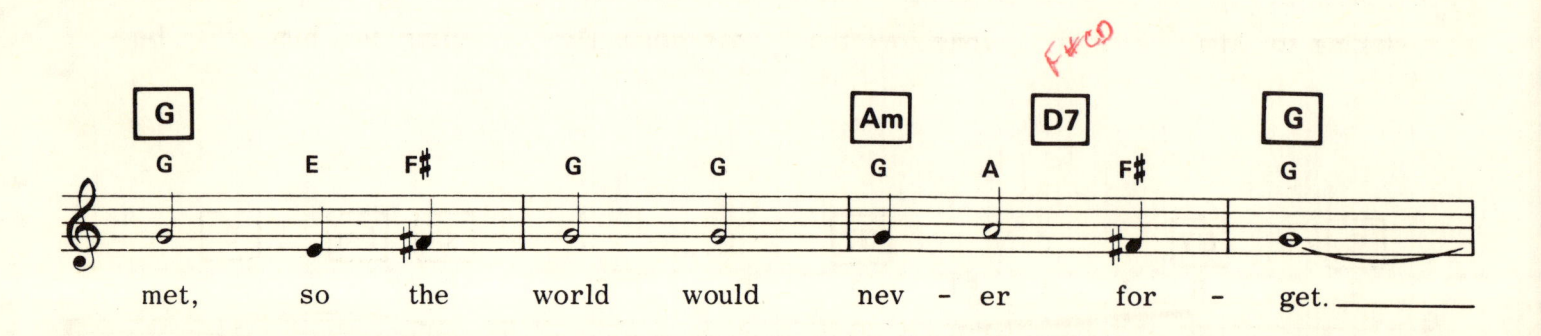

Words by LORENZ HART
Music by RICHARD RODGERS

registration number 2.

N.C. E F | **C** G B | **Dm** A G | **G7** E D | **C** E
If they asked me | I could write a | book,___

G E D | E G E D | **Am** E C | **Dm** E G
___ a-bout the way | you walk and | whis-per and | look,___

G7 A B | **Am** C C | **Dm** C D | **G7** B A | **C** A (Cm) A
GCE♭
___ I could write a | pre-face | on how we

G G E F♯ | G G | **Am** G A | **D7** F♯ | **G** G
F♯CD
met, so the | world would | nev-er for- | get.___

Copyright©1940 by Chappell & Co., Inc.
Copyright Renewed
Used by HAL LEONARD PUBLISHING CORPORATION, Winona, MN 55987 by Permission
Made in U.S.A.   International Copyright Secured   All Rights Reserved

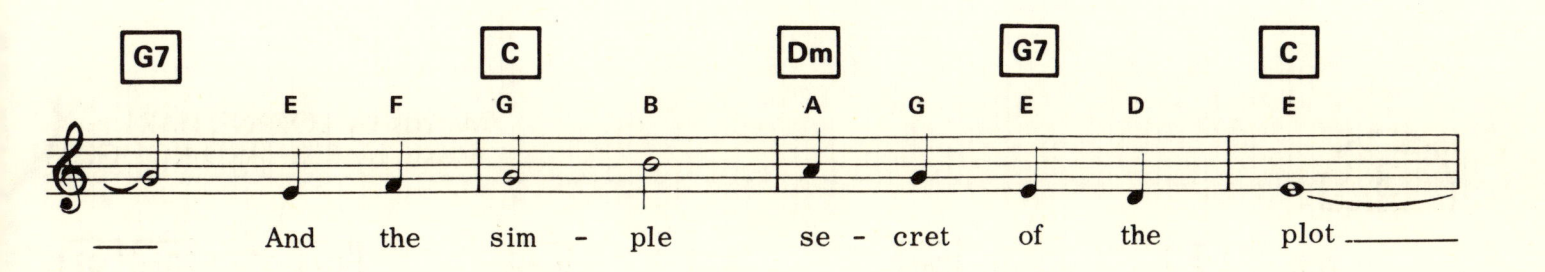

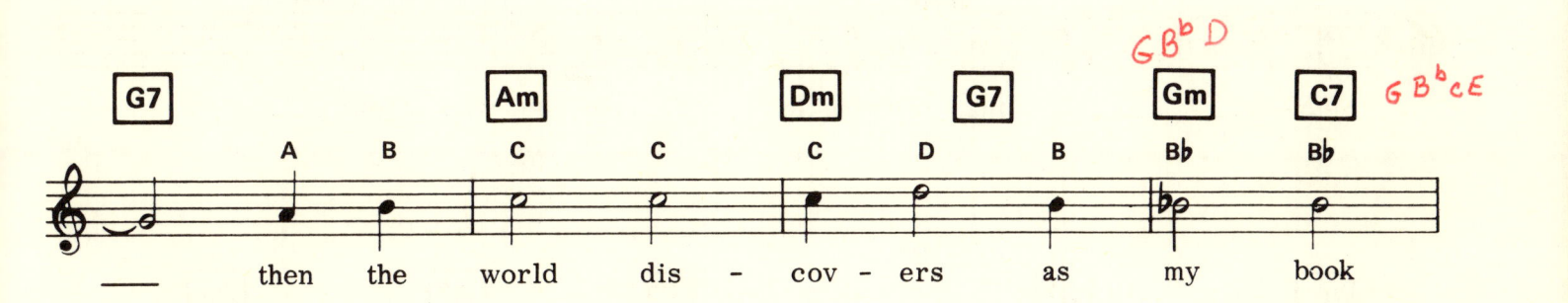

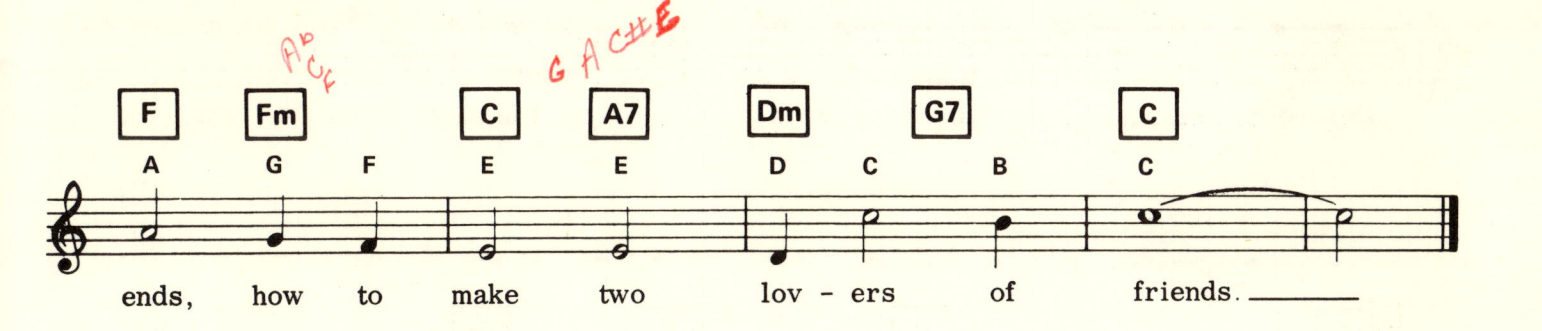

YOU'RE NEARER

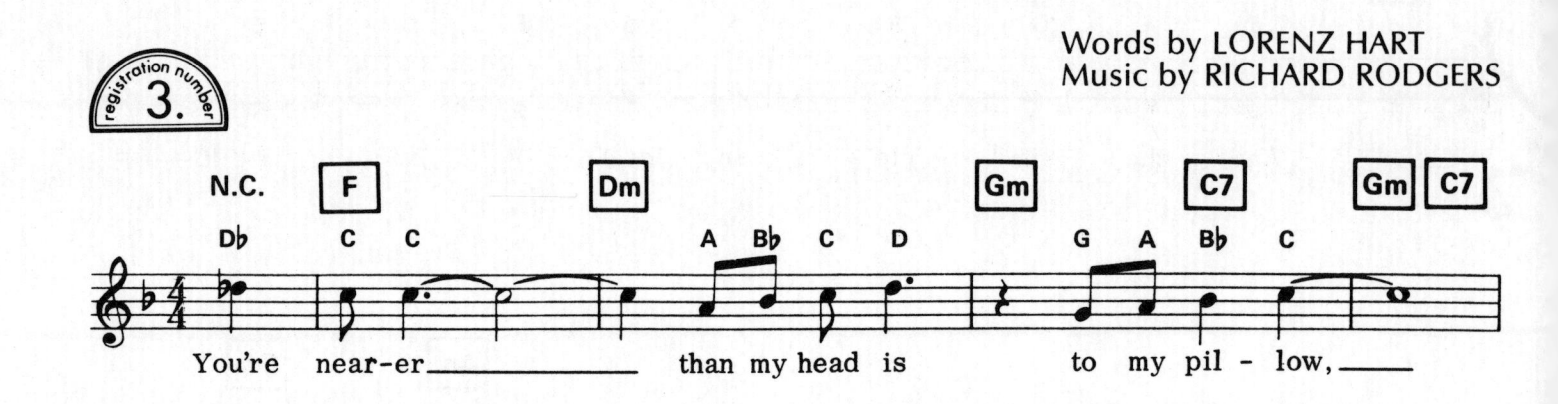

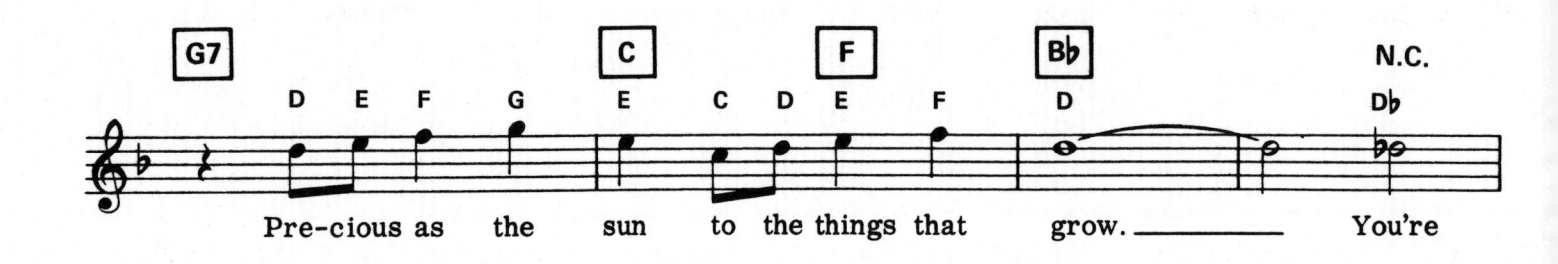

Words by LORENZ HART
Music by RICHARD RODGERS

You're near-er_____ than my head is to my pil - low,_____
Near-er_____ than the wind is to the wil - low;_____
Dear-er_____ than the rain is to the earth be - low.
Pre-cious as the sun to the things that grow._____ You're

Copyright © 1940 by Chappell & Co., Inc.
Copyright Renewed
Used by HAL LEONARD PUBLISHING CORPORATION, Winona, MN 55987 by Permission
Made in U.S.A.   International Copyright Secured   All Rights Reserved

near-er _____ than the i-vy to the wall is, _____

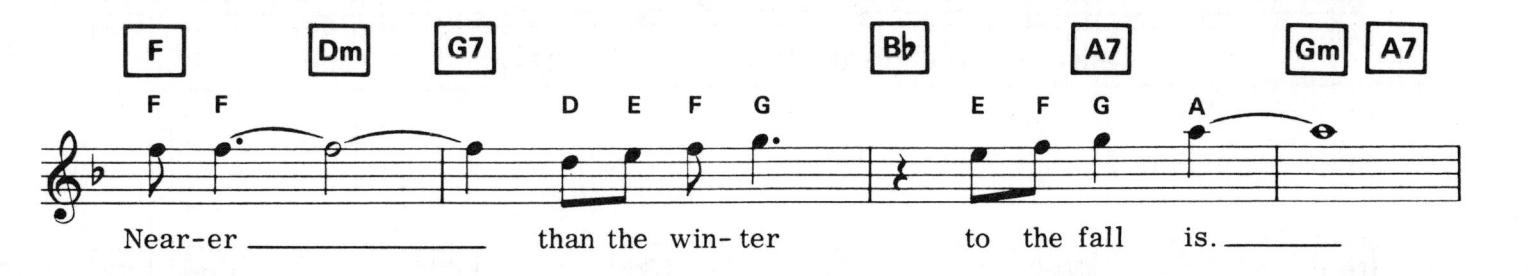

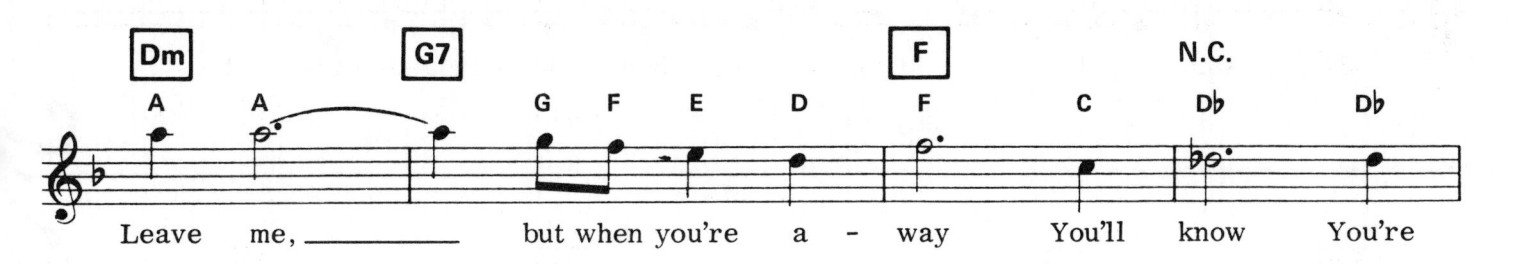

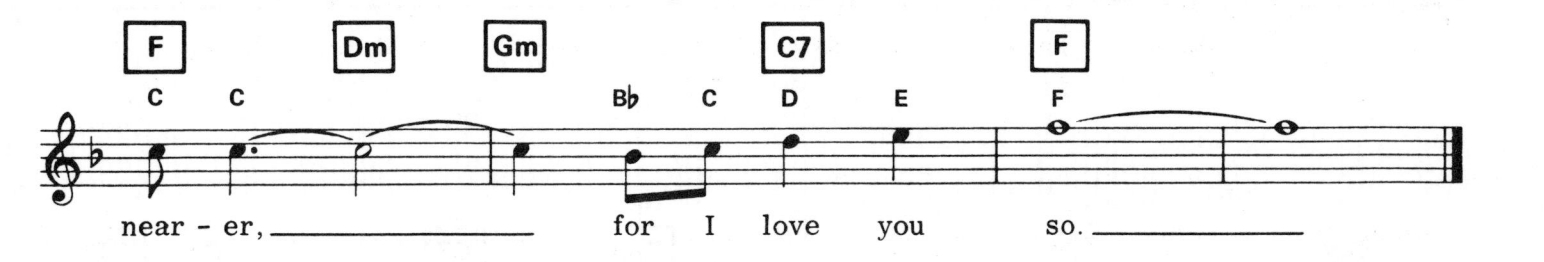

Near-er _____ than the win-ter to the fall is. _____

Leave me, _____ but when you're a-way You'll know You're

near-er, _____ for I love you so. _____

I DIDN'T KNOW WHAT TIME IT WAS

Words by LORENZ HART
Music by RICHARD RODGERS

I did-n't know what time it was, Then I met you.

Oh, what a love-ly time it was, How sub-lime it was too.

I did-n't know what day it was. You held my hand,

Warm like the month of May it was And I'll say it was grand.

Copyright © 1939 by Chappell & Co., Inc.
Copyright Renewed
Used by HAL LEONARD PUBLISHING CORPORATION, Winona, MN 55987 by Permission
Made in U.S.A.   International Copyright Secured   All Rights Reserved

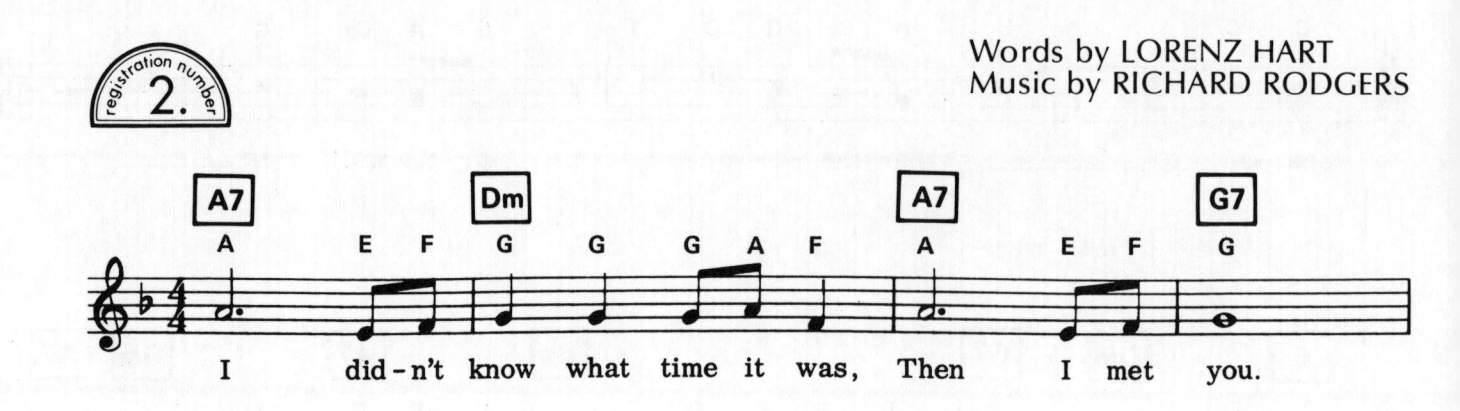

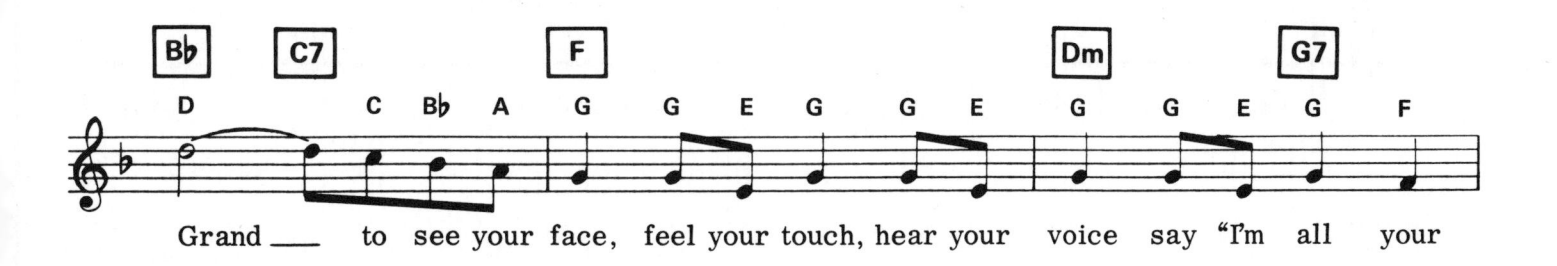

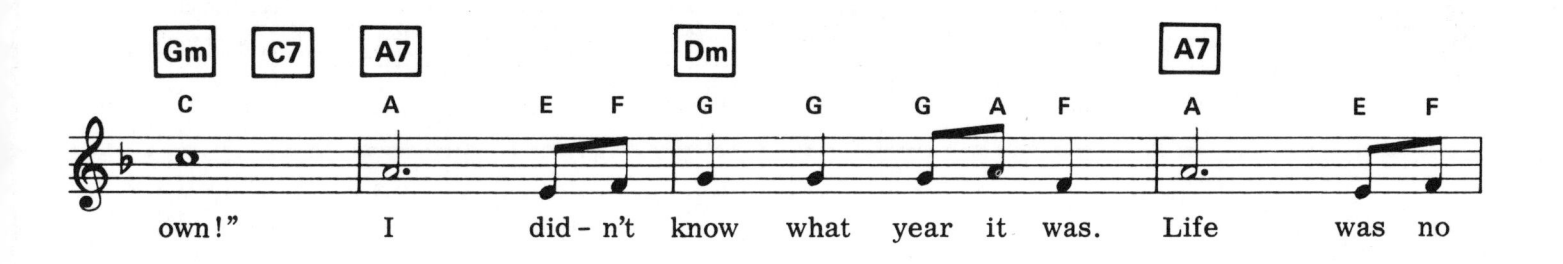

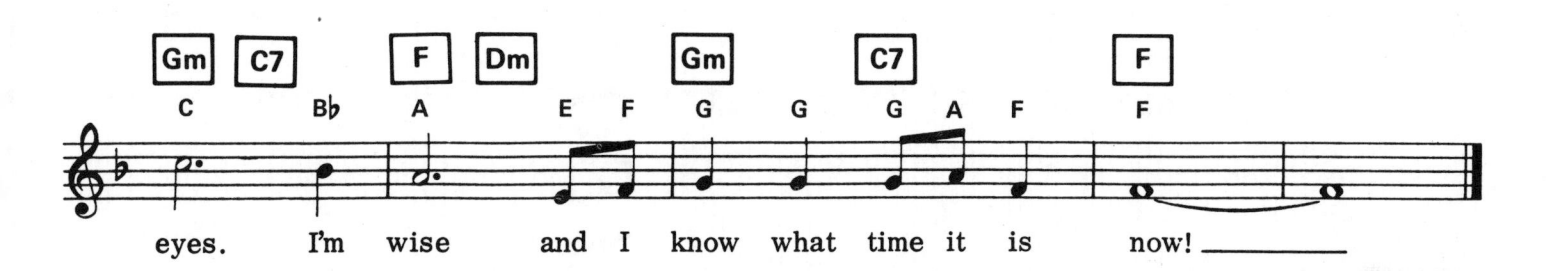

Grand __ to be a-live, to be young, to be mad, to be yours a - lone!

Grand __ to see your face, feel your touch, hear your voice say "I'm all your own!" I did-n't know what year it was. Life was no prize. I want-ed love and here it was shin-ing out of your eyes. I'm wise and I know what time it is now! _____

ON A CLEAR DAY (You Can See Forever)

Words by ALAN JAY LERNER
Music by BURTON LANE

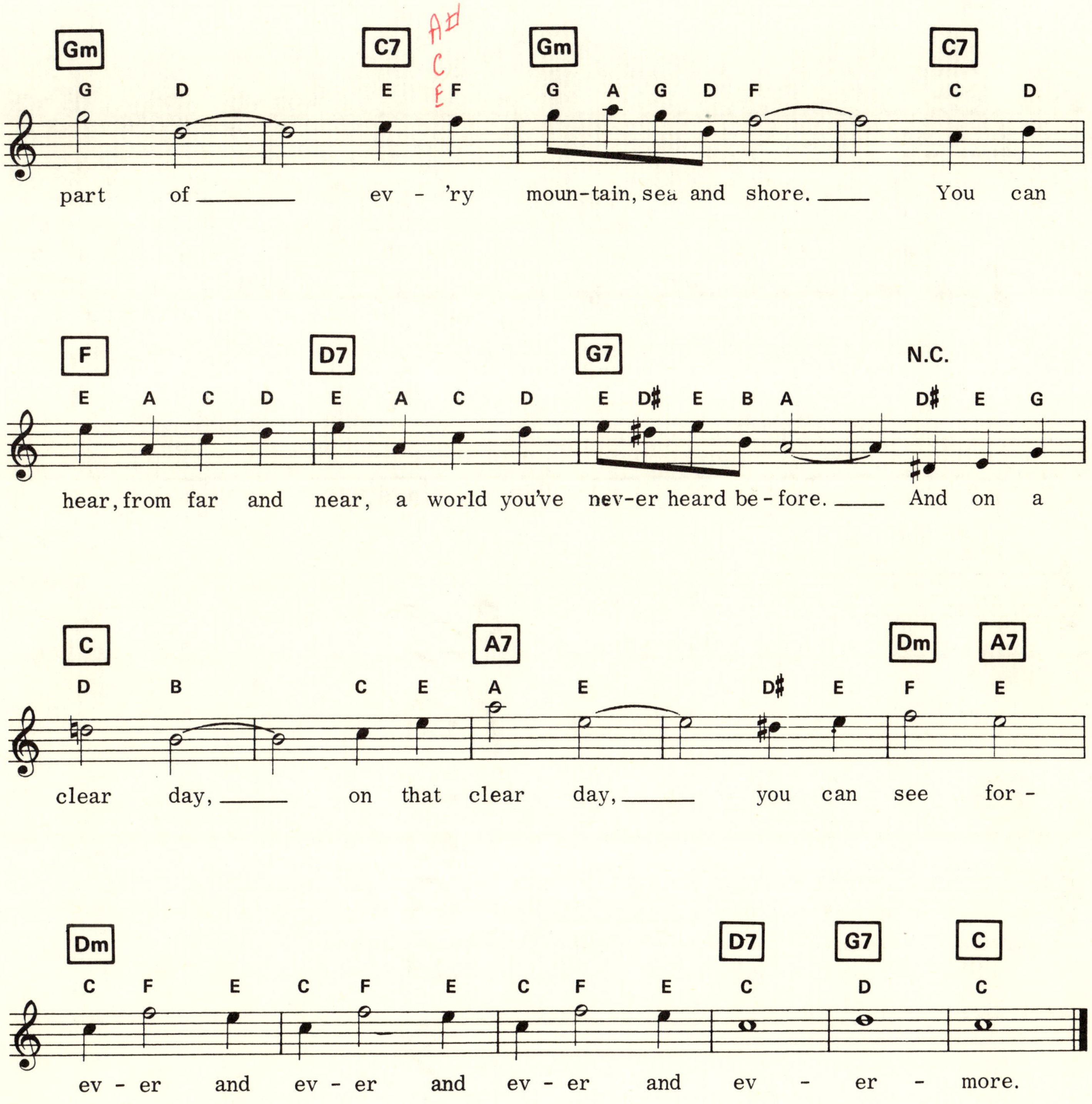
Gm C7 Gm C7
G D E F G A G D F C D
A♮ C E
part of ___ ev - 'ry moun-tain, sea and shore. ___ You can
F D7 G7 N.C.
E A C D E A C D E D♯ E B A D♯ E G
hear, from far and near, a world you've nev-er heard be-fore. ___ And on a
C A7 Dm A7
D B C E A E D♯ E F E
clear day, ___ on that clear day, ___ you can see for -
Dm D7 G7 C
C F E C F E C F E C D C
ev - er and ev - er and ev - er and ev - er - more.

COME BACK TO ME

Words by ALAN JAY LERNER
Music by BURTON LANE

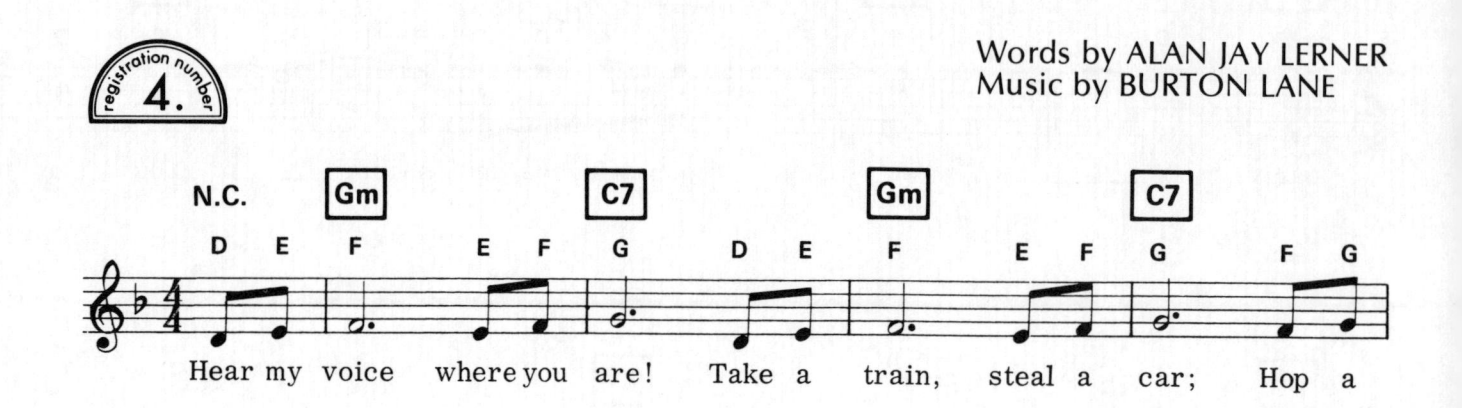

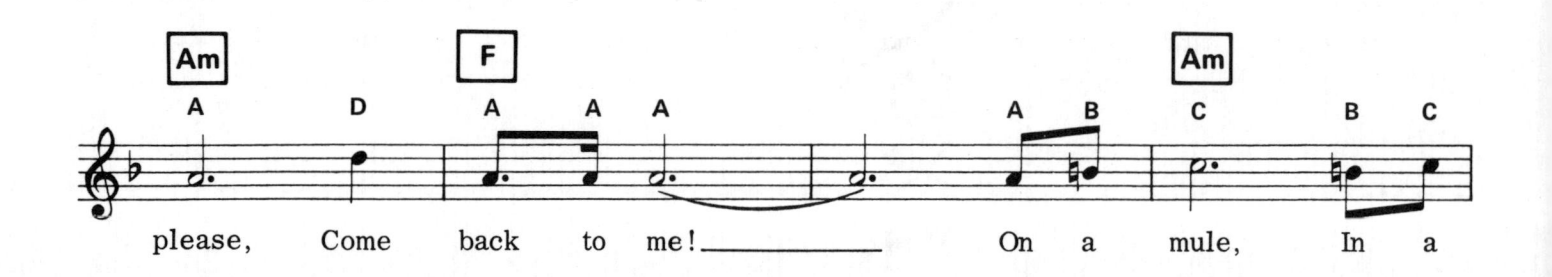

Hear my voice where you are! Take a train, steal a car; Hop a freight, Grab a star; Come back to me! Catch a plane, catch a breeze; On your hands, on your knees; Swim or fly, on-ly please, Come back to me! On a mule, In a

Copyright © 1965 by Alan Jay Lerner and Burton Lane
Chappell & Co., Inc., publisher and owner of allied rights throughout the world
Used by HAL LEONARD PUBLISHING CORPORATION, Winona, MN 55987 by Permission
Made in U.S.A.   International Copyright Secured   All Rights Reserved

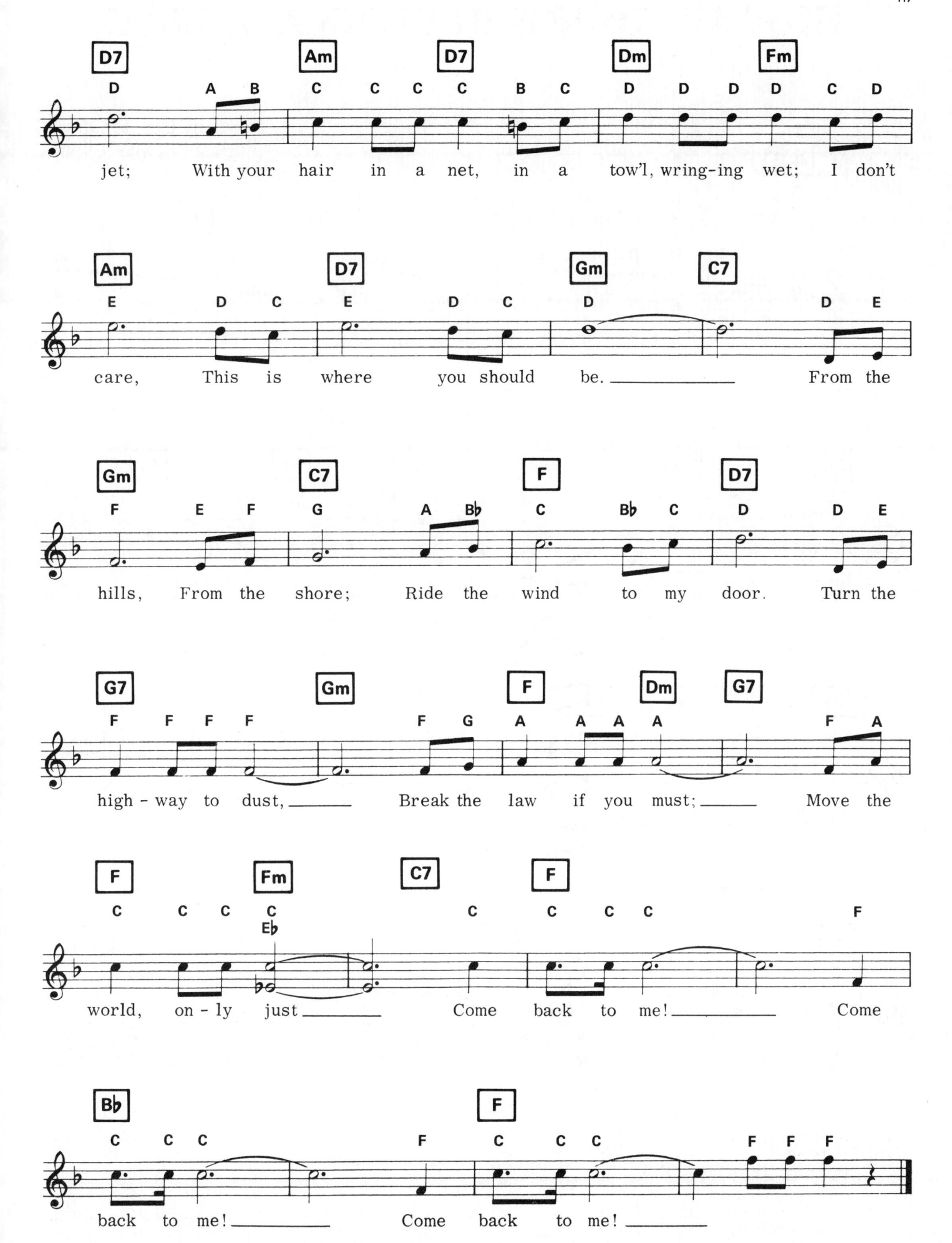

jet; With your hair in a net, in a tow'l, wring-ing wet; I don't care, This is where you should be. From the hills, From the shore; Ride the wind to my door. Turn the high-way to dust, Break the law if you must; Move the world, on-ly just Come back to me! Come back to me! Come back to me!

HOW ARE THINGS IN GLOCCA MORRA?

Words by E. Y. HARBURG
Music by BURTON LANE

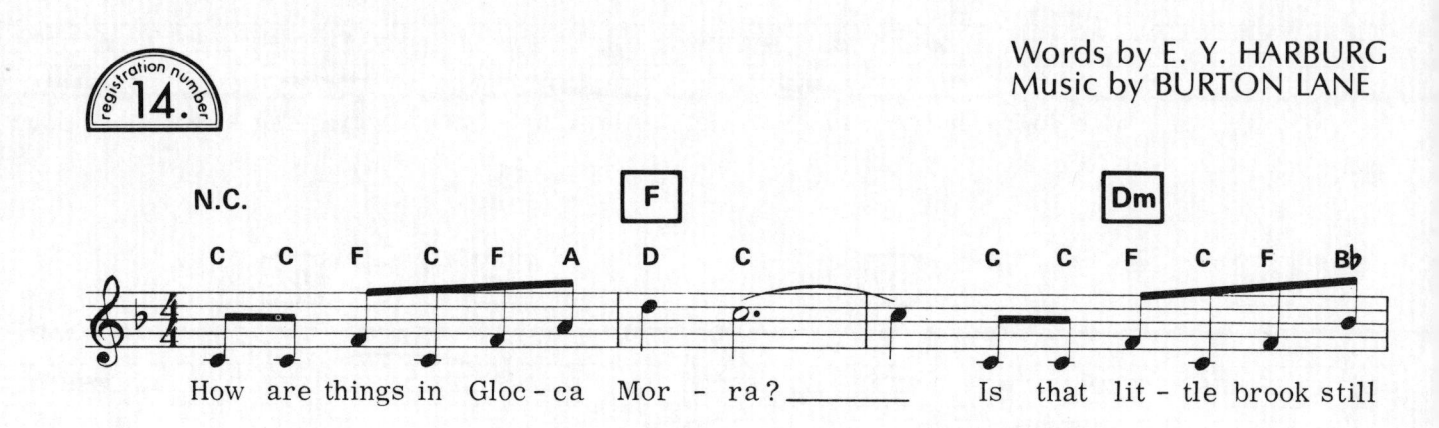

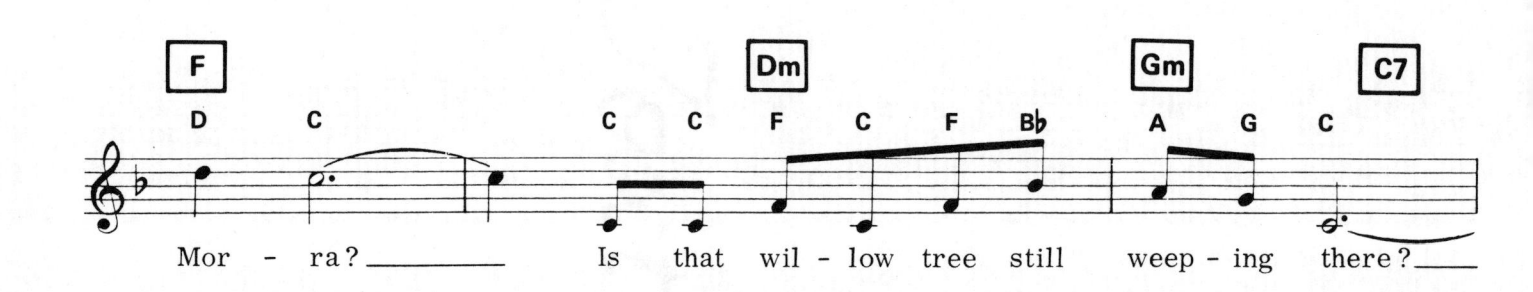

How are things in Gloc-ca Mor-ra? Is that lit-tle brook still leap-ing there? Does it still run down to Don-ny Cove, through Kil-ly begs, Kil-ker-ry and Kil-dare? How are things in Gloc-ca Mor-ra? Is that wil-low tree still weep-ing there?

Copyright © 1946 by Chappell & Co., Inc.
Copyright Renewed
Used by HAL LEONARD PUBLISHING CORPORATION, Winona, MN 55987 by Permission
Made in U.S.A.   International Copyright Secured   All Rights Reserved

Does that lassie with the twinklin' eye Come smilin' by And does she walk away, Sad and dreamy there not to see me there? So I ask each weeping willow and each brook along the way And each lass that comes a-sighin' Toora-lay, How are things in Glocca Morra this fine day?

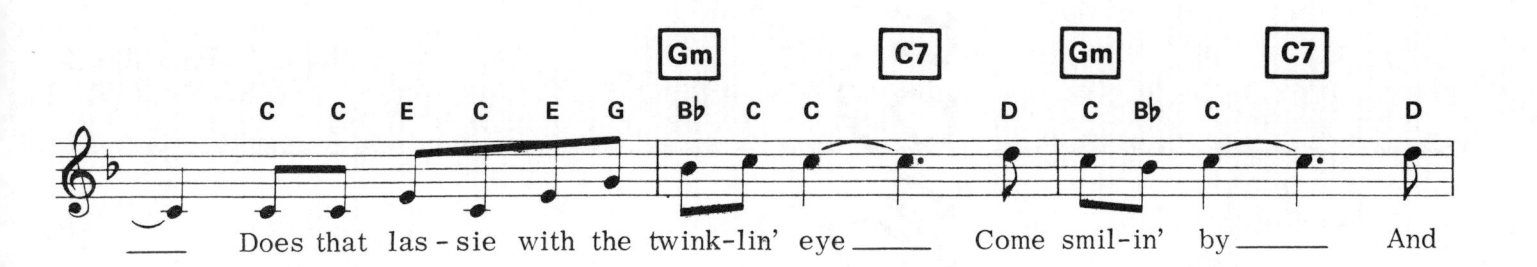

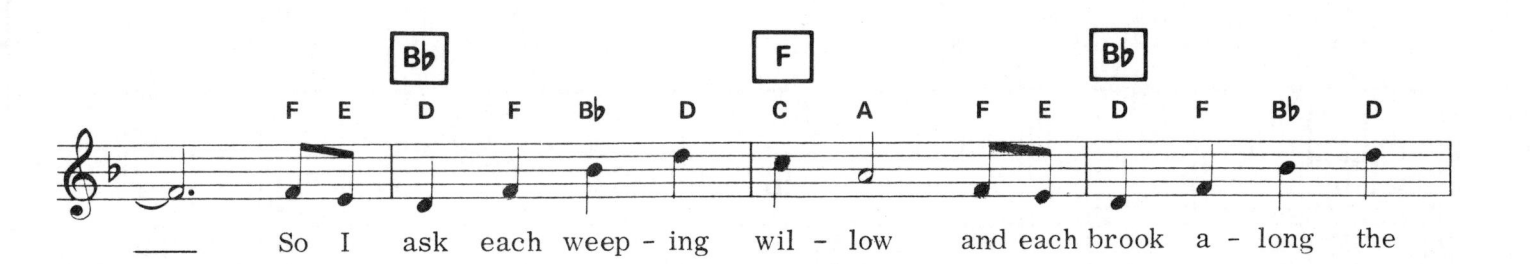

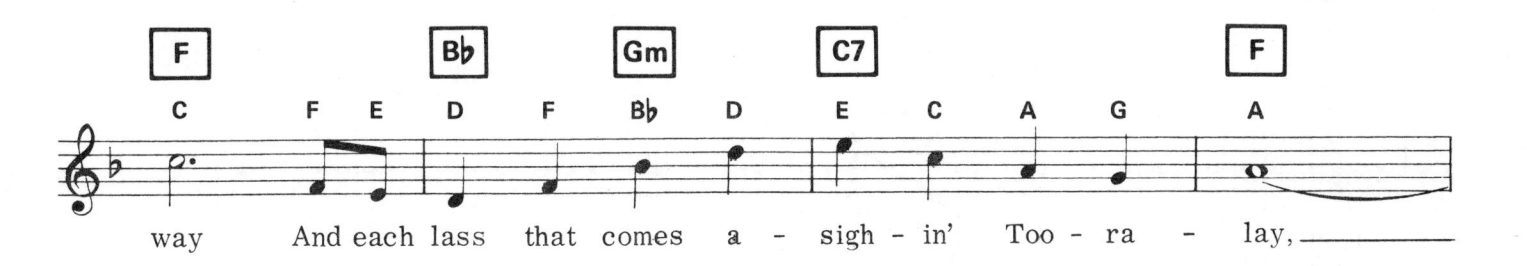

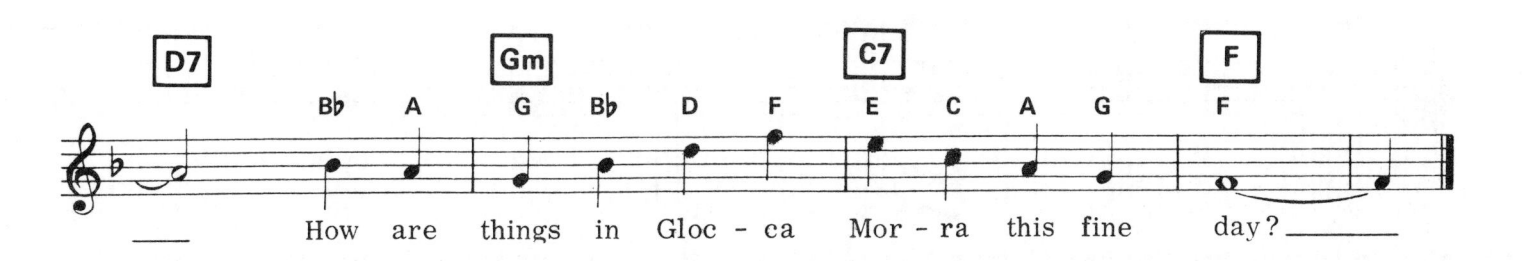

OLD DEVIL MOON

Words by E. Y. HARBURG
Music by BURTON LANE

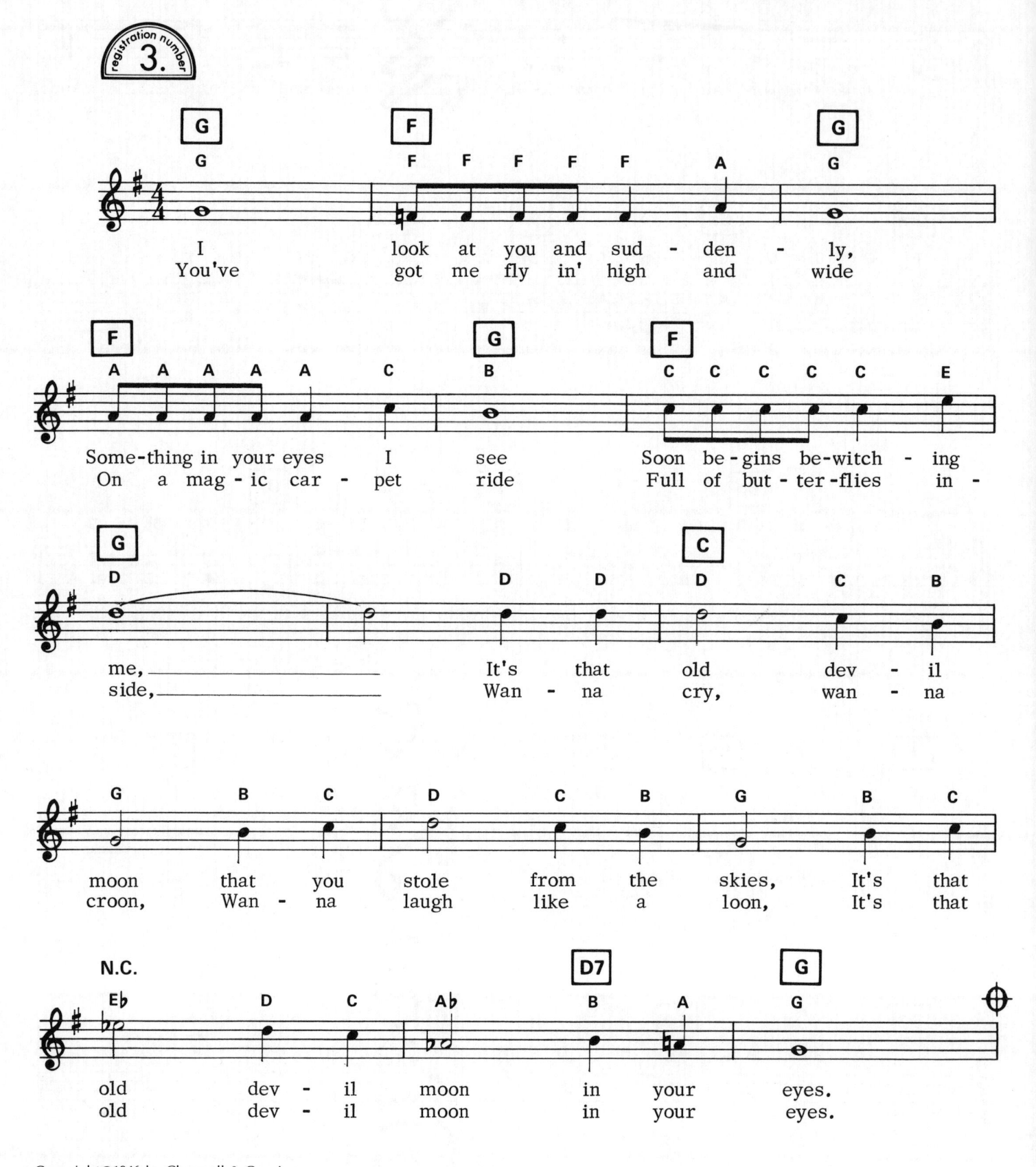

registration number 3.

I look at you and sud - den - ly,
You've got me fly in' high and wide

Some-thing in your eyes I see Soon be - gins be - witch - ing
On a mag - ic car - pet ride Full of but - ter - flies in -

me, It's that old dev - il
side, Wan - na cry, wan - na

moon that you stole from the skies, It's that
croon, Wan - na laugh like a loon, It's that

old dev - il moon in your eyes.
old dev - il moon in your eyes.

Copyright ©1946 by Chappell & Co., Inc.,
Copyright Renewed
Copyright ©1968 by Chappell & Co., Inc.,
Used by HAL LEONARD PUBLISHING CORPORATION, Winona, MN 55987 by Permission
Made in U.S.A.   International Copyright Secured   All Rights Reserved

121

You and your glance make this ro-mance too hot to han-dle.____ Stars in the night blaz-ing their light can't hold a can-dle____ to your raz-zle daz-zle

D.C. al Coda

⊕ *CODA* Just when I think I'm____ free as a dove____ Old dev-il moon deep in your eyes blinds me with love.____

IF THIS ISN'T LOVE

Words by E. Y. HARBURG
Music by BURTON LANE

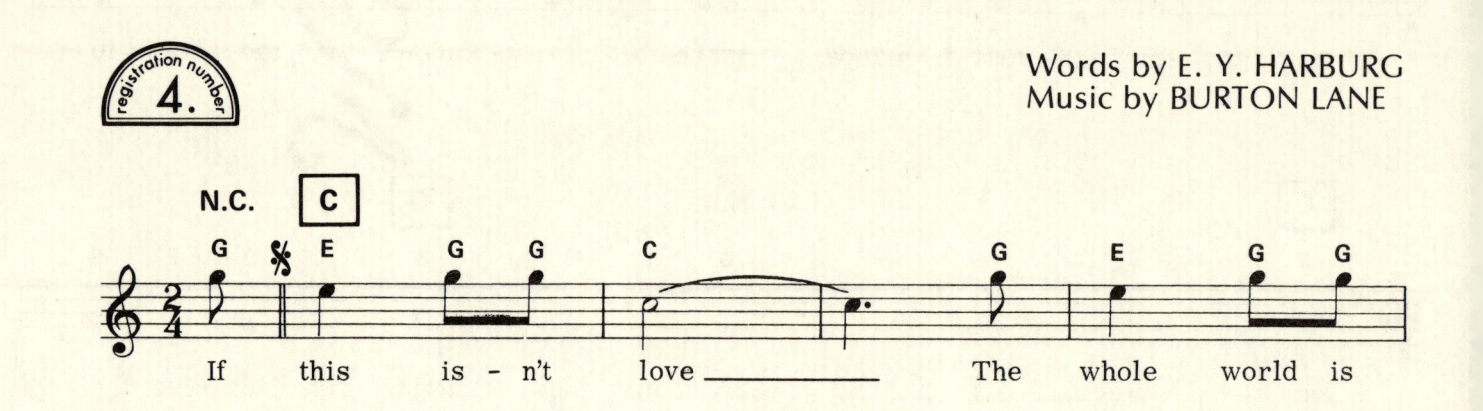

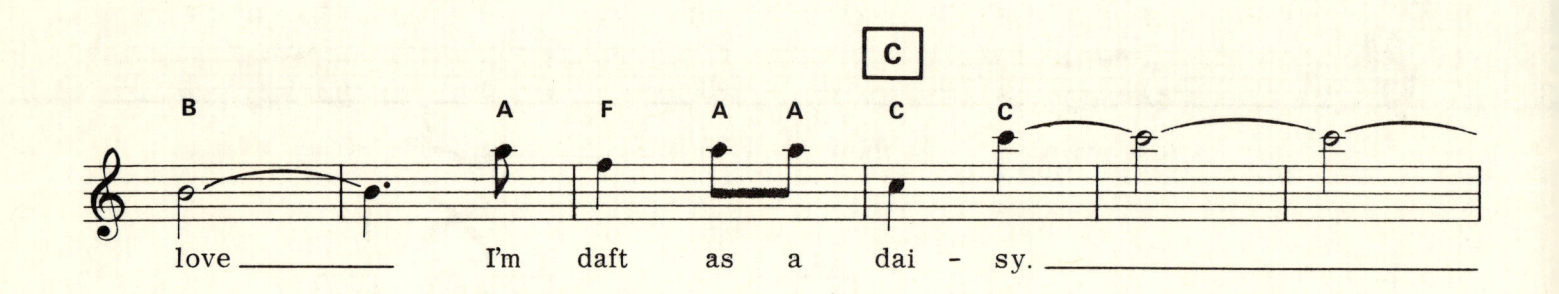

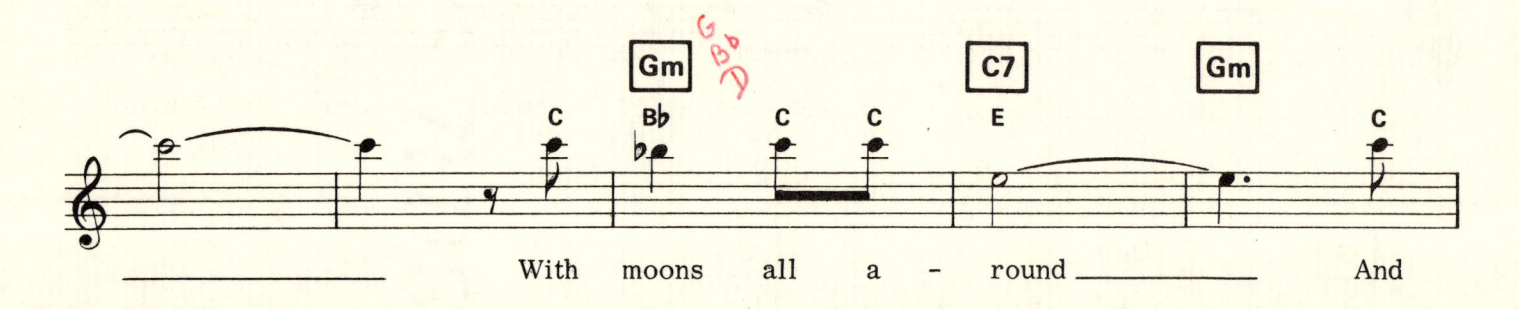

registration number 4.

If this is-n't love _____ The whole world is cra-zy. _____ If this is-n't love _____ I'm daft as a dai-sy. _____ With moons all a-round _____ And

Copyright © 1946 by Chappell & Co., Inc.
Copyright Renewed
Used by HAL LEONARD PUBLISHING CORPORATION, Winona, MN 55987 by Permission
Made in U.S.A.   International Copyright Secured   All Rights Reserved

cows jump-ing o - ver, _____ There's some-thing a - miss, and I'll eat my hat if this is-n't love. _____ I'm feel-ing like an ap - ple on top of Wil - liam Tell, With this I can-not grap - ple, be - cause, be - cause you're so a - dor - a - belle. If

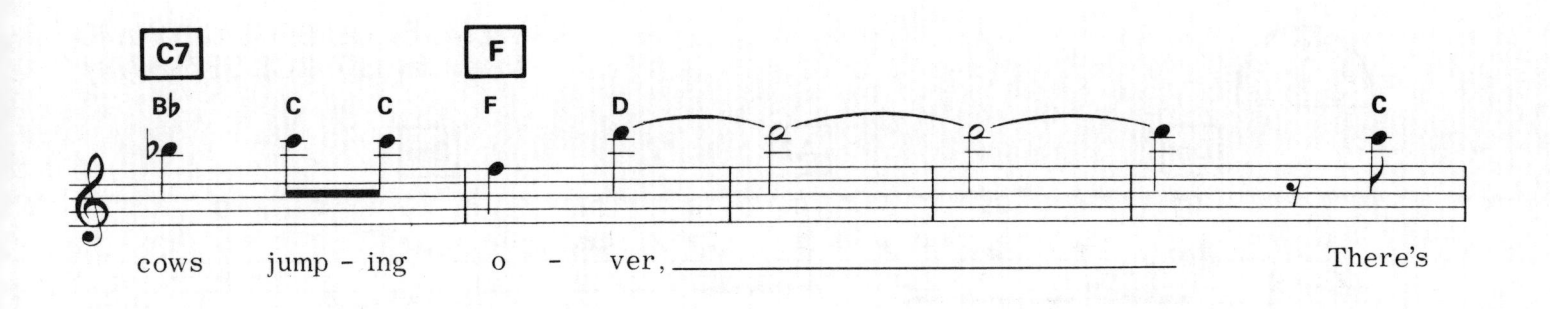

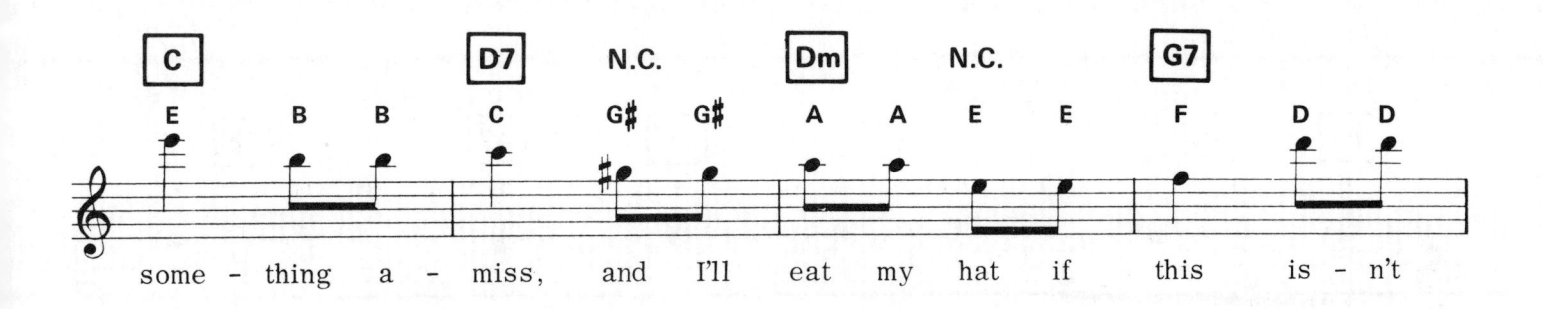

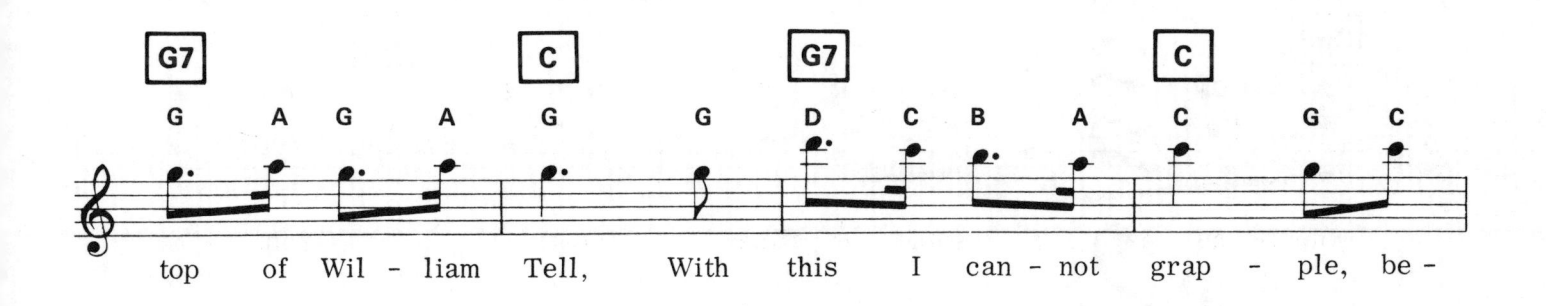

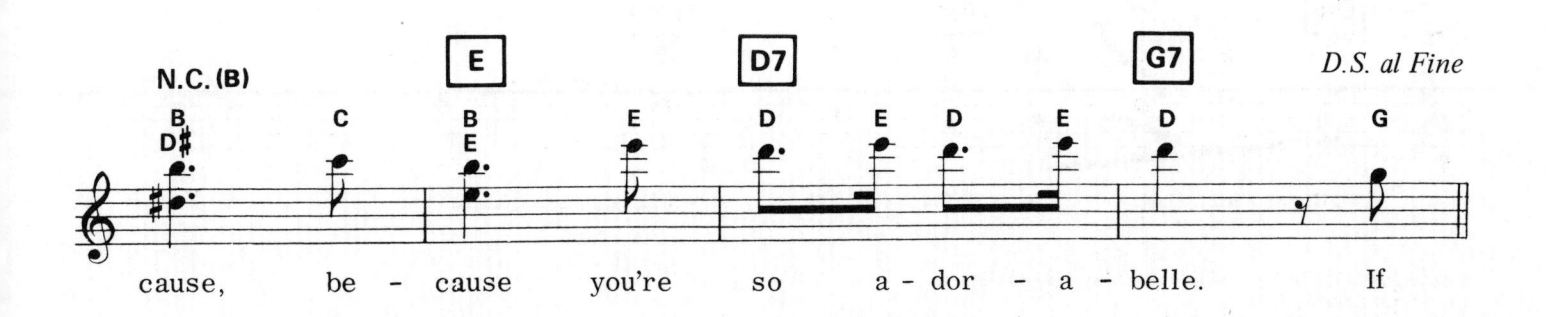

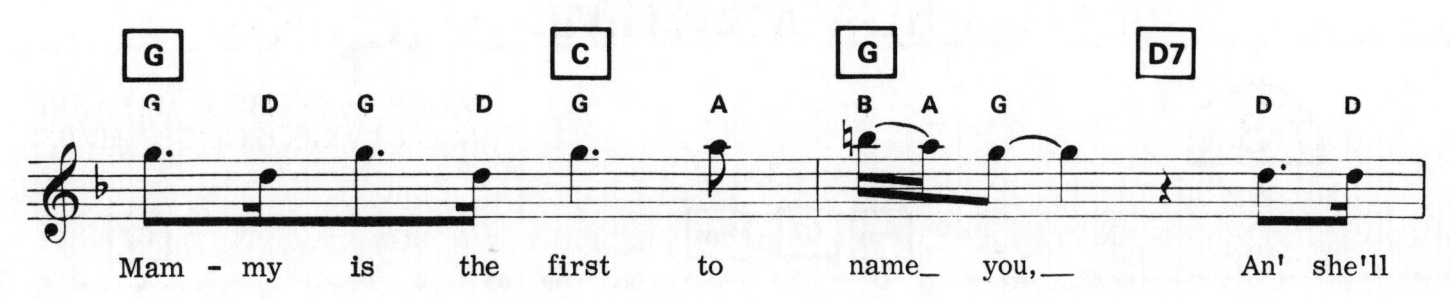

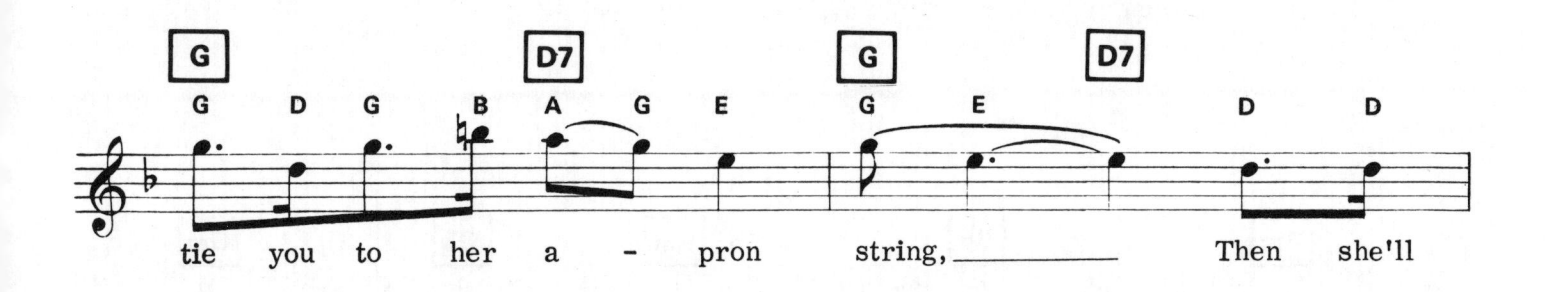

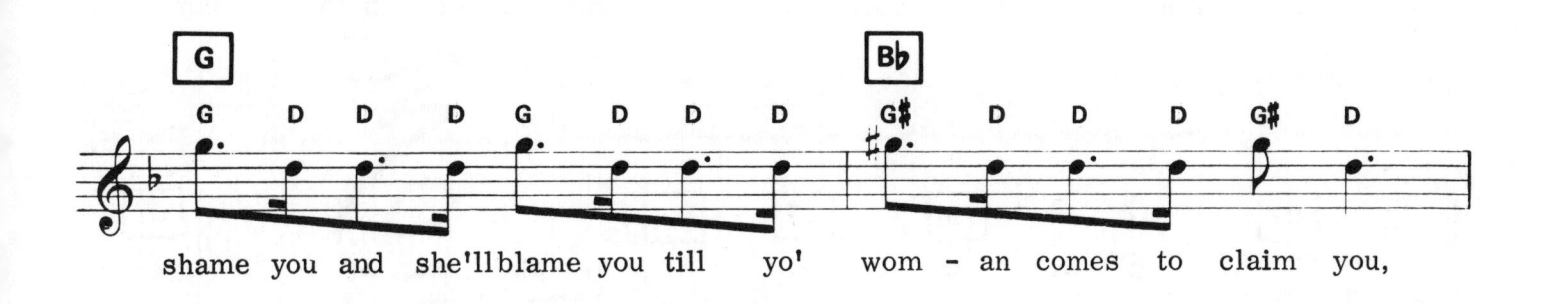

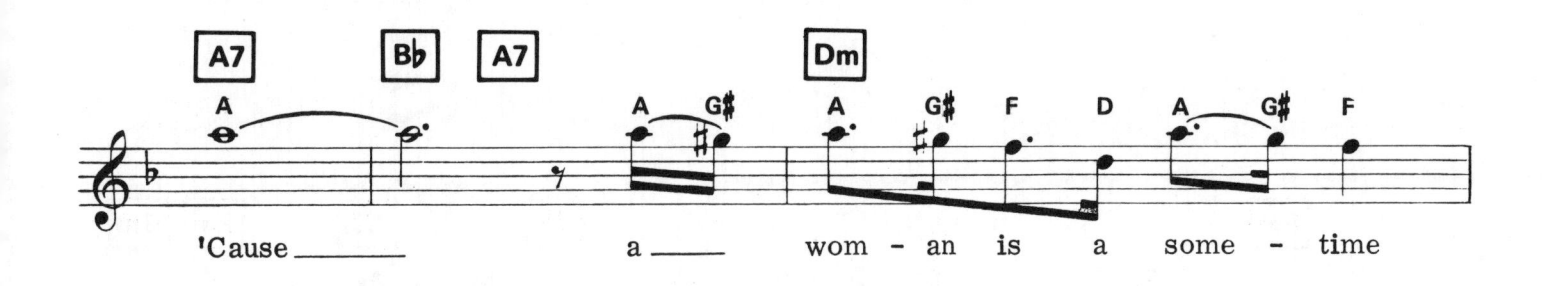

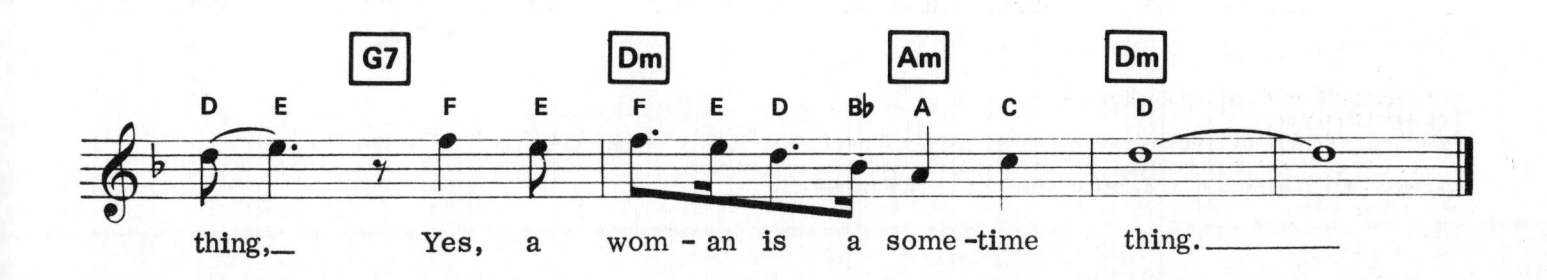

Mammy is the first to name you, An' she'll tie you to her apron string, Then she'll shame you and she'll blame you till yo' woman comes to claim you, 'Cause a woman is a some-time thing, Yes, a woman is a some-time thing.

SUMMERTIME

registration number 8.

Words by DU BOSE HEYWARD
Music by GEORGE GERSHWIN

Fm C7 Fm C7 Fm C7
C C A♭ C C C B♭ A♭ B♭ C A♭
3
One of these morn - in's you goin' to rise up
Fm C7 Fm B♭
F C C A♭ B♭ B♭ B♭
sing - in', Then you'll spread your wings
Fm G7 Gm C7 N.C.
A♭ F A♭ F A♭ G C C A♭
an' you'll take to the sky. But till that
Fm C7 Fm C7 Fm C7 Fm
C C B♭ A♭ B♭ C A♭ F C C
morn - in' there's a noth - in' can harm you With
B♭ C7 Fm Gm Fm Gm Fm
E♭ C E♭ F A♭ C B♭ A♭ F
Dad - dy an' Mam - my stand - in' by.

I GOT PLENTY O' NUTTIN'

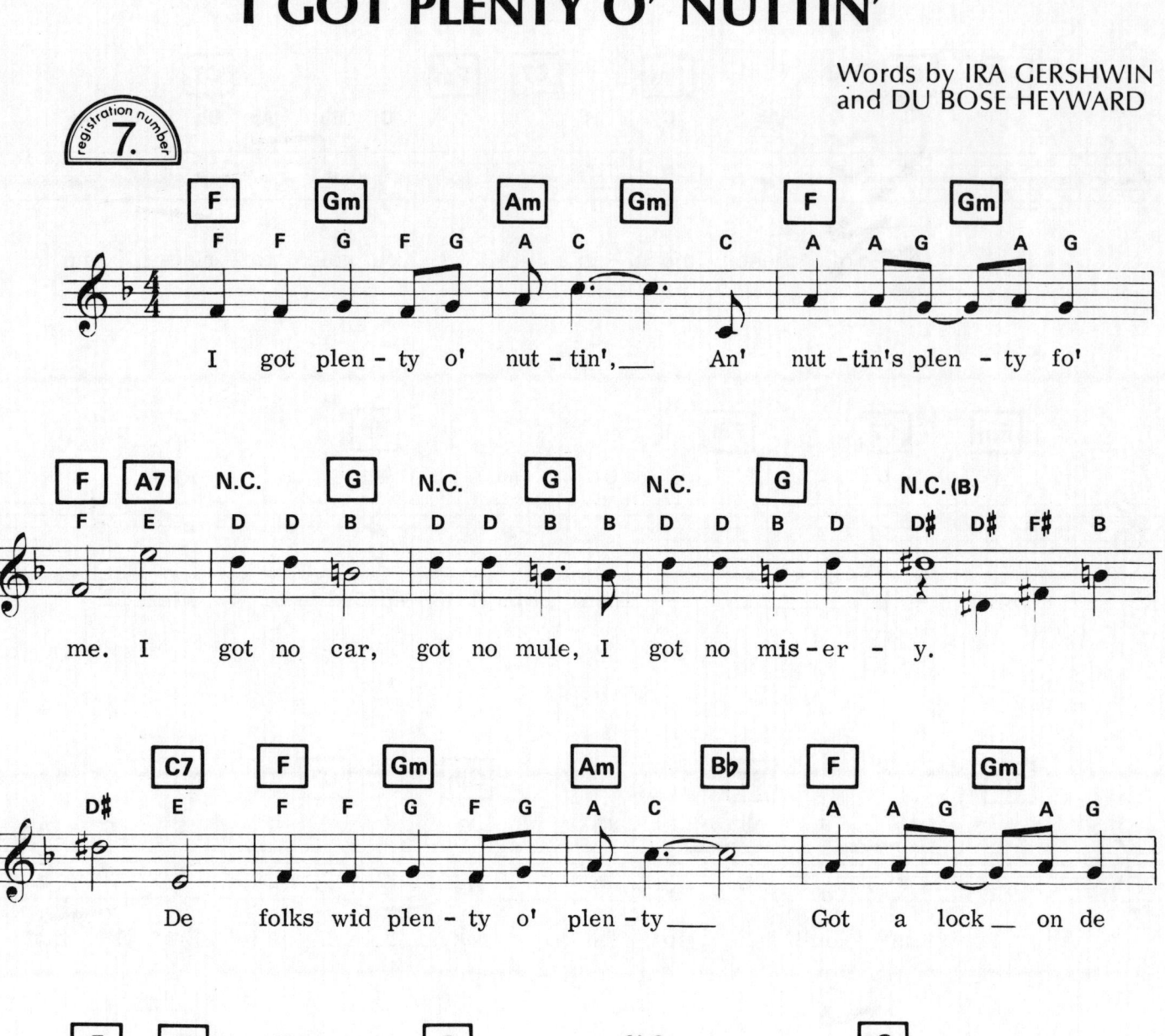

Words by IRA GERSHWIN and DU BOSE HEYWARD

registration number 7.

I got plen-ty o' nut-tin', An' nut-tin's plen-ty fo' me. I got no car, got no mule, I got no mis-er-y. De folks wid plen-ty o' plen-ty Got a lock on de door, Dey's 'fraid some-bod-y's a-go-in' to rob 'em while dey's out a-mak-in' more. What for?

Copyright©1935 by Gershwin Publishing Corporation
Copyright Renewed
Published in the United States by joint agreement with Gershwin Publishing Corporation and Chappell & Co., Inc.
Used by HAL LEONARD PUBLISHING CORPORATION, Winona, MN 55987 by Permission
Made in U.S.A.   International Copyright Secured   All Rights Reserved

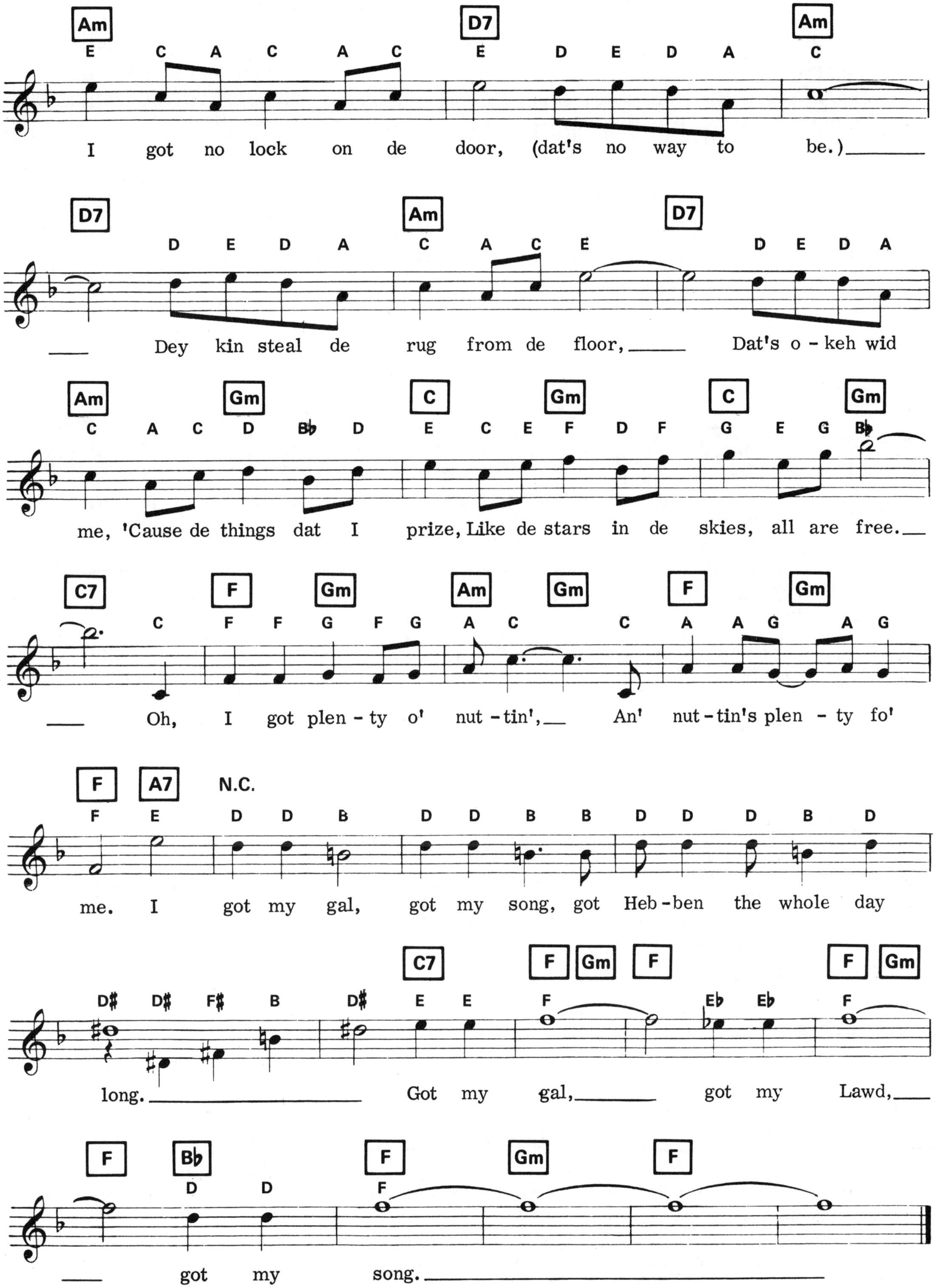
Am D7 Am
E C A C A C E D E D A C
I got no lock on de door, (dat's no way to be.)
D7 Am D7
D E D A C A C E D E D A
Dey kin steal de rug from de floor, Dat's o - keh wid
Am Gm C Gm C Gm
C A C D B♭ D E C E F D F G E G B♭
me, 'Cause de things dat I prize, Like de stars in de skies, all are free.
C7 F Gm Am Gm F Gm
C F F G F G A C C A A G A G
Oh, I got plen - ty o' nut - tin', An' nut - tin's plen - ty fo'
F A7 N.C.
F E D D B D D B B D D D B D
me. I got my gal, got my song, got Heb - ben the whole day
C7 F Gm F F Gm
D♯ D♯ F♯ B D♯ E E F E♭ E♭ F
long. Got my gal, got my Lawd,
F B♭ F Gm F
D D F
got my song.

I LOVES YOU PORGY

Words by IRA GERSHWIN
and DU BOSE HEYWARD
Music by GEORGE GERSHWIN

registration number 2.

F D7 G7
C D E♭ F G F E♭ C C C C E♭ D
It's goin' to be like dy - in', Por - gy, deep in - side me.
C7 F Fm C7 N.C.
E E E F F D D D D E♭ C F A C
But when he calls, I know I have to go. I loves you,
F B♭ Gm
E G F C A A C D F A C E E C A F
Por-gy, don' let him take me, Don' let him han-dle me with his hot
F Am D7 Gm
A D F A C E C A F♯ F A B♭ D F
han'. If you can keep me, I wants to stay here wid you for -
C7 Gm F B♭ F
A C A F D F
ev - er. I got my man.

I LOVE PARIS

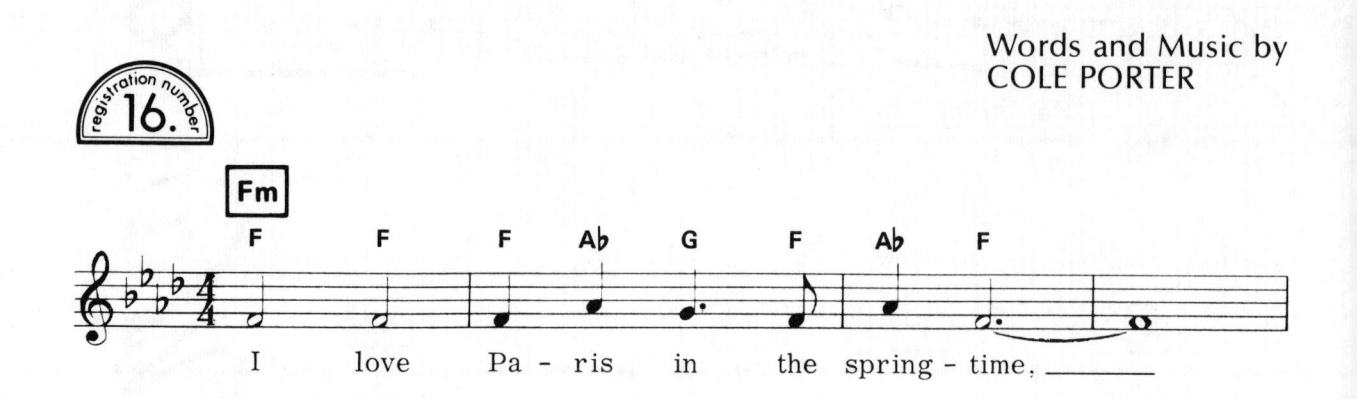

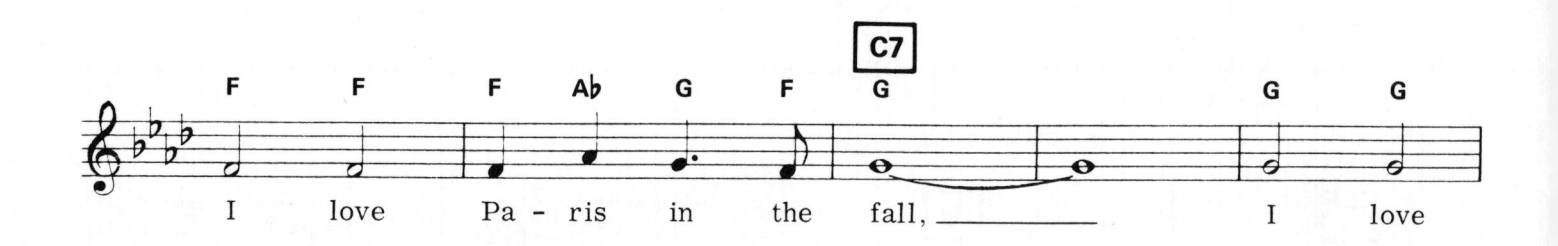

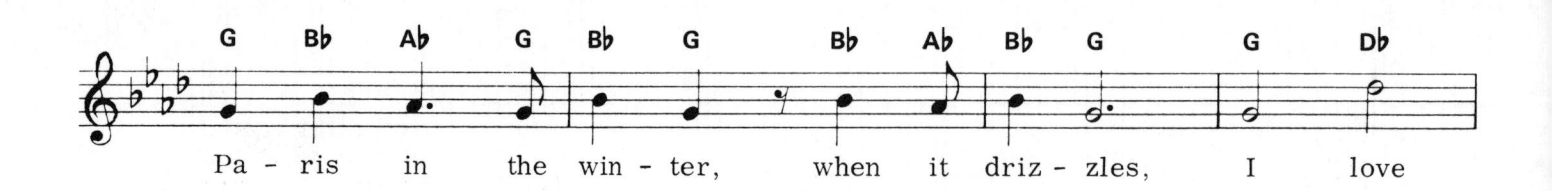

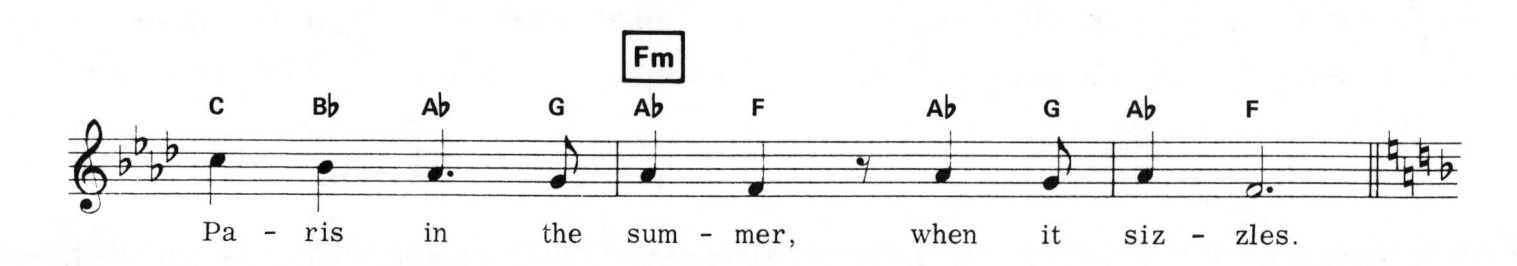

Words and Music by
COLE PORTER

Copyright © 1953 by Cole Porter
Chappell & Co., Inc., publisher and owner of publication and allied rights throughout the world
Used by HAL LEONARD PUBLISHING CORPORATION, Winona, MN 55987 by Permission
Made in U.S.A.   International Copyright Secured   All Rights Reserved

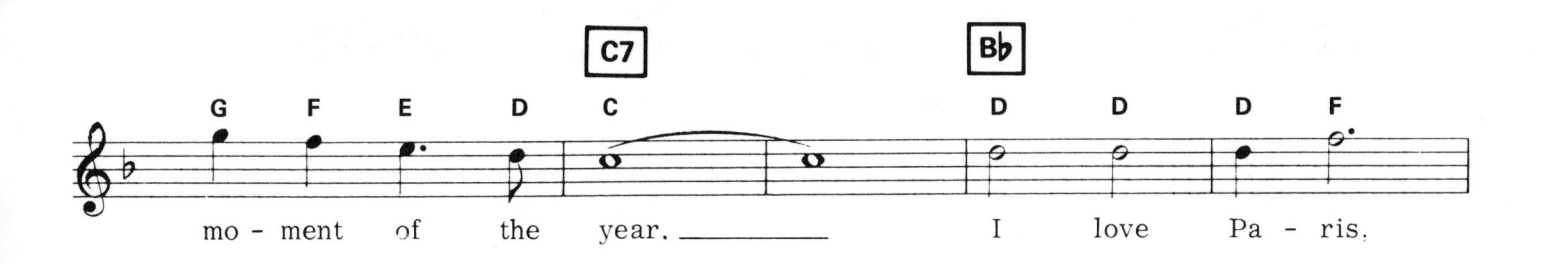

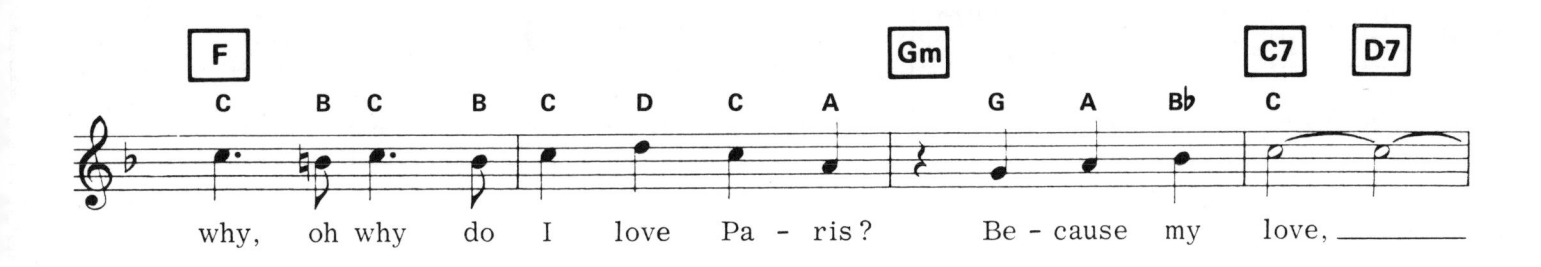

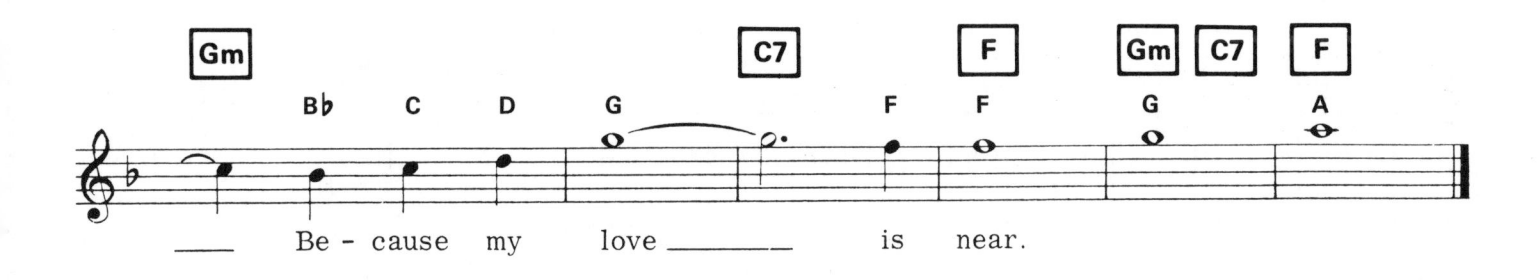

I love Paris ev-'ry mo-ment, ev-'ry moment of the year. I love Paris why, oh why do I love Paris? Because my love, Because my love is near.

C'EST MAGNIFIQUE

Words and Music by
COLE PORTER

registration number 2.

When love comes in and takes you for a spin, oo la, la, la, ___ C'est mag-ni-fi-que. ___ When ev-'ry night your loved one holds you tight, oo la, la, la, ___

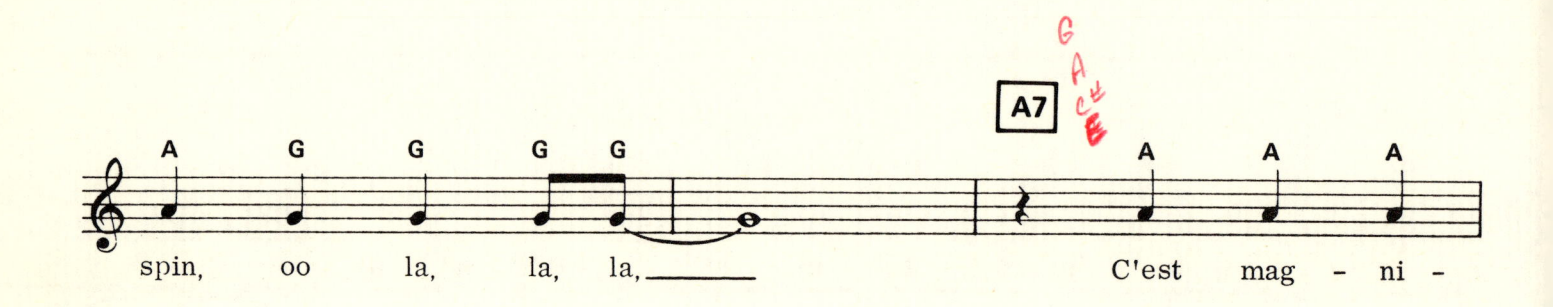

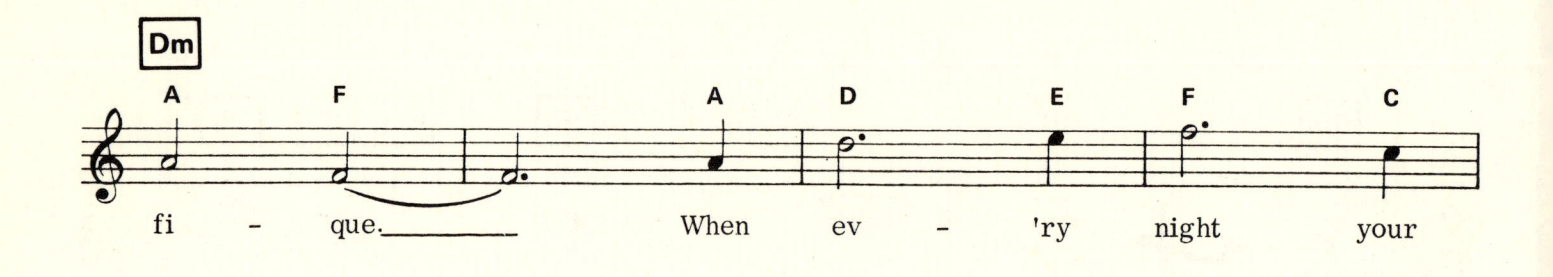

Copyright ©1935 by Cole Porter
Chappell & Co., Inc., publisher and owner of publication and allied rights throughout the world
Used by HAL LEONARD PUBLISHING CORPORATION, Winona, MN 55987 by Permission
Made in U.S.A.   International Copyright Secured   All Rights Reserved

135

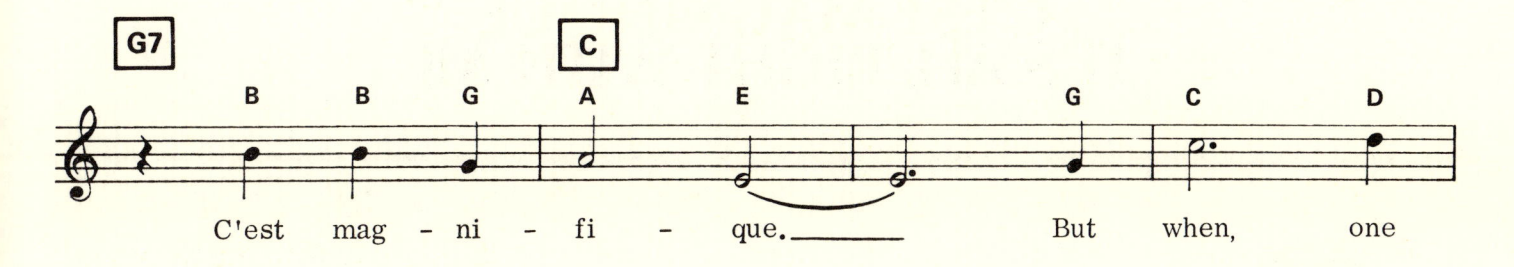

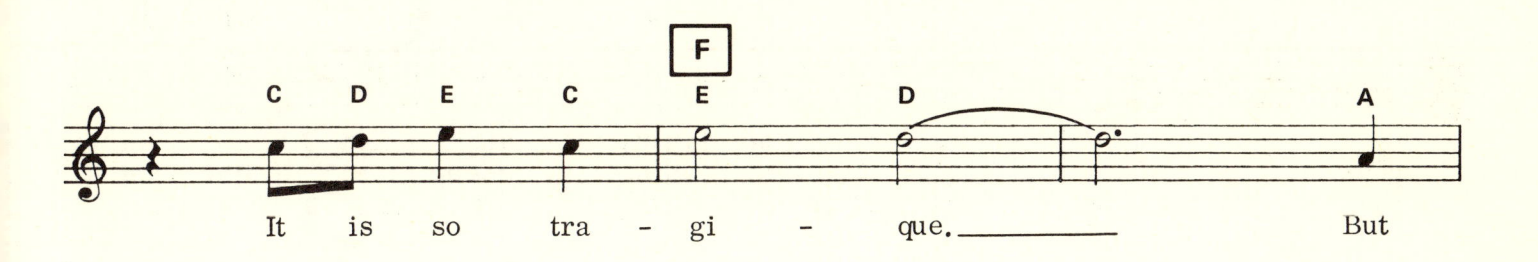

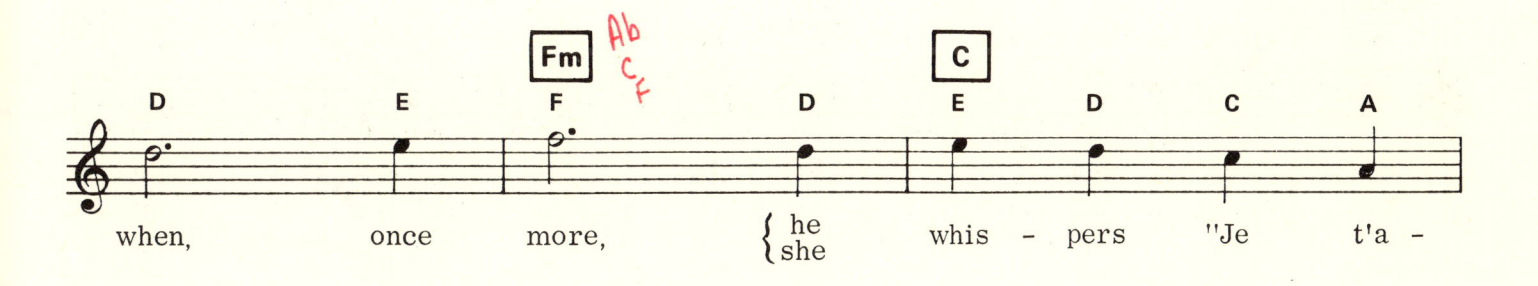

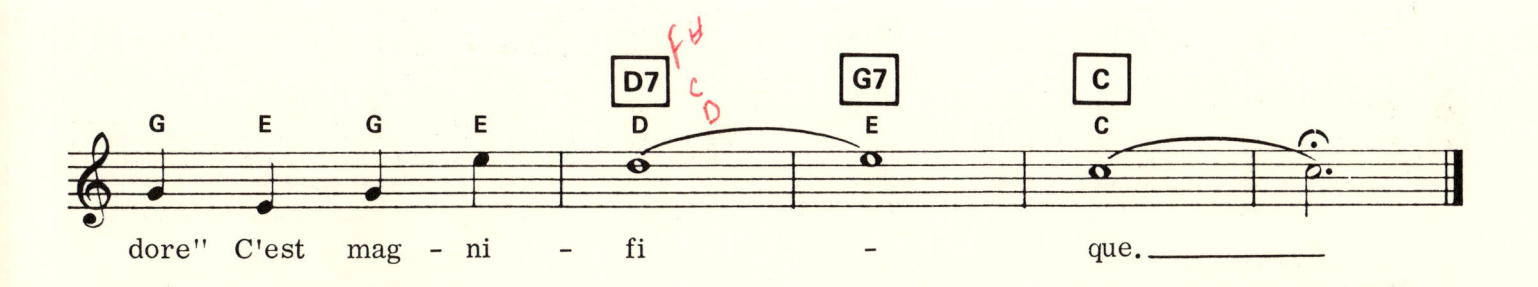

IT'S ALL RIGHT WITH ME

Words and Music by
COLE PORTER

registration number 5.

It's the wrong time and the wrong place, tho' your face is charm-ing, it's the wrong face, it's not her face but such a charm-ing face that it's all right with me. It's the

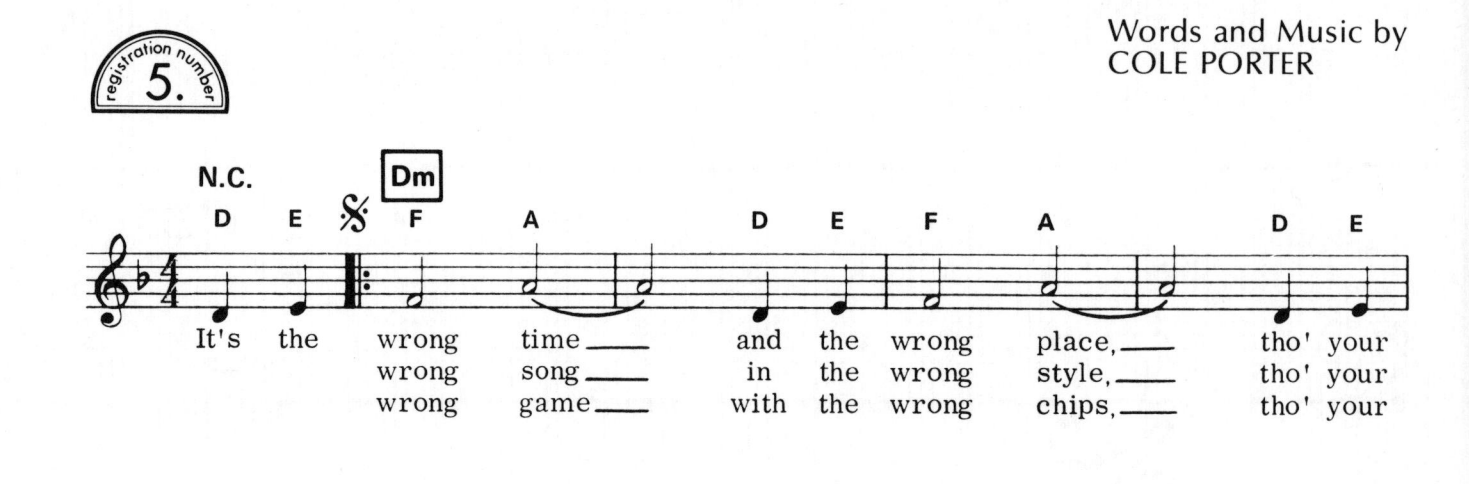

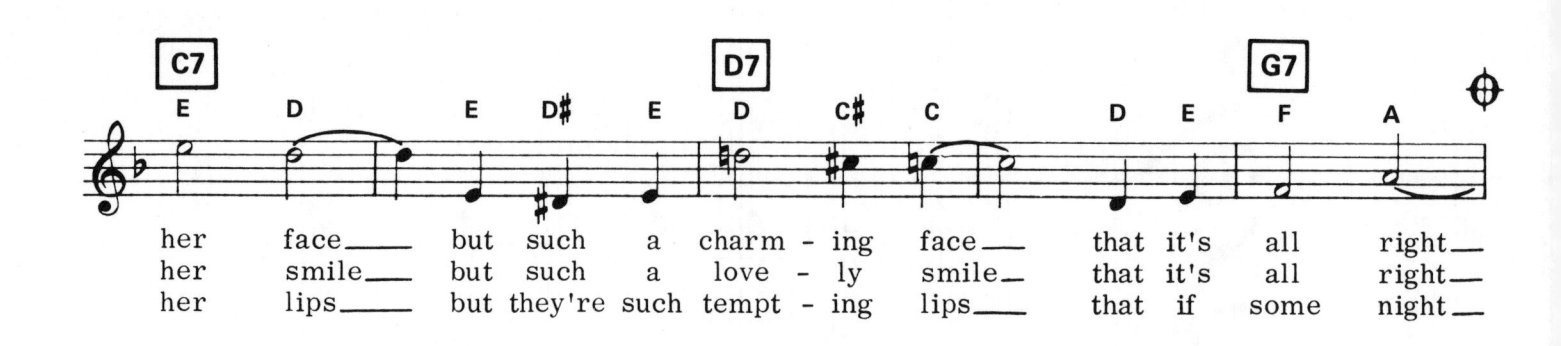

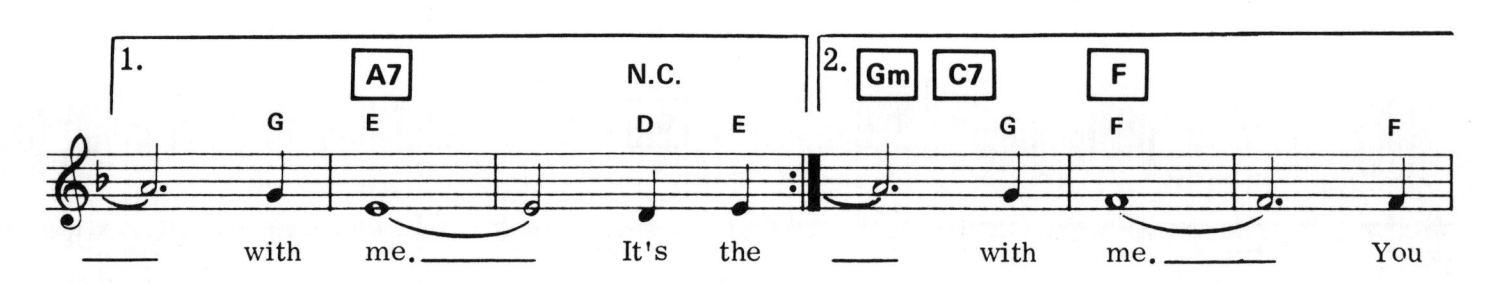

wrong song in the wrong style, tho' your smile is love-ly, it's the wrong smile, it's not her smile but such a love-ly smile that it's all right with me. You

wrong game with the wrong chips, tho' your lips are tempt-ing, they're the wrong lips. They're not her lips but they're such tempt-ing lips that if some night

Copyright ©1953 by Cole Porter
Copyright assigned to, and Copyright ©1970 by John F. Wharton, as trustee (of Literary and Musical Trusts under declaration of trust by Cole Porter dated July 6, 1961, as amended)
Chappell & Co., Inc., owner of worldwide publication and allied rights
Used by HAL LEONARD PUBLISHING CORPORATION, Winona, MN 55987 by Permission
Made in U.S.A.   International Copyright Secured   All Rights Reserved

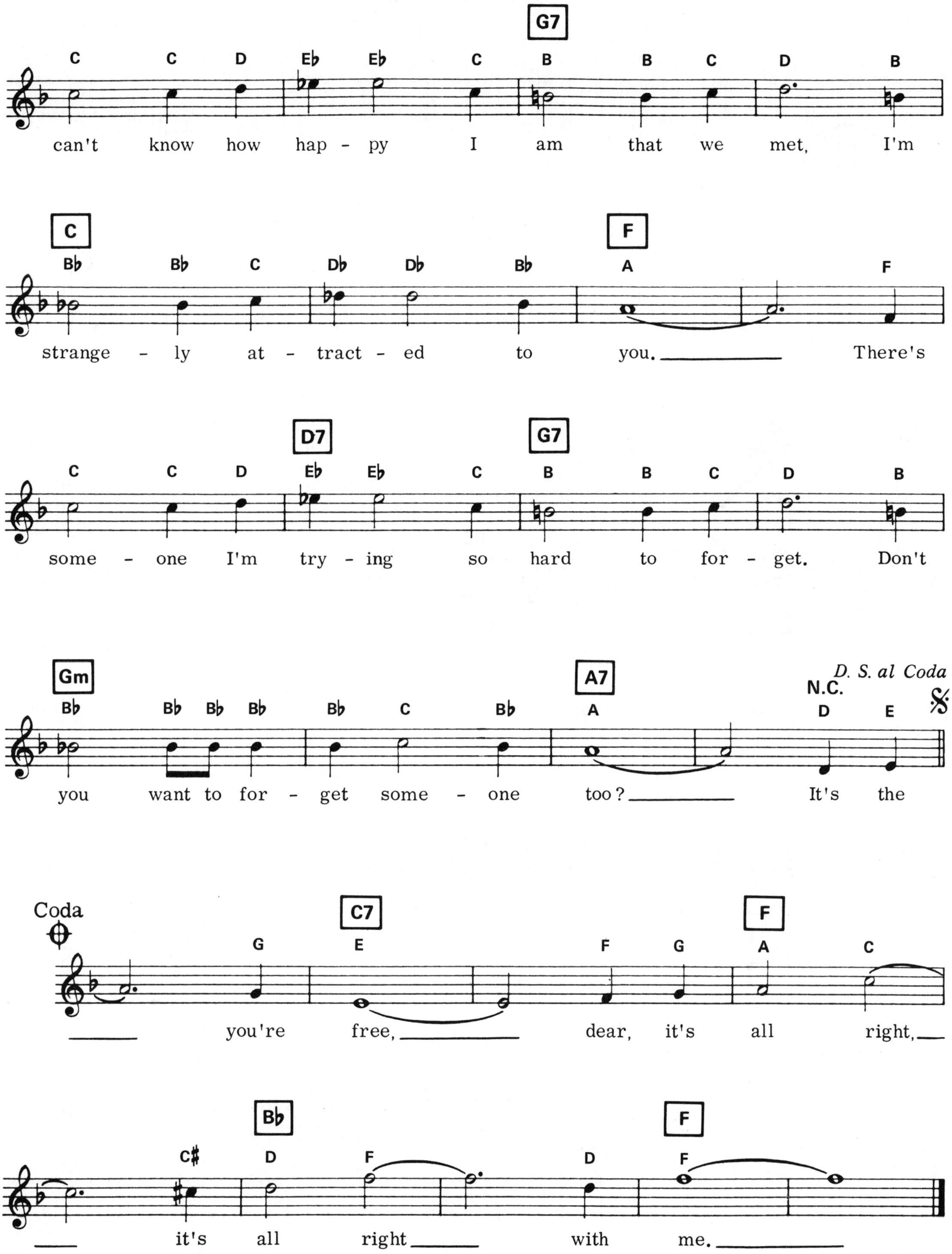
G7
C C D E♭ E♭ C B B C D B
can't know how hap - py I am that we met, I'm
C F
B♭ B♭ C D♭ D♭ B♭ A F
strange - ly at - tract - ed to you. There's
D7 G7
C C D E♭ E♭ C B B C D B
some - one I'm try - ing so hard to for - get. Don't
Gm A7
D. S. al Coda
N.C.
B♭ B♭ B♭ B♭ B♭ C B♭ A D E
you want to for - get some - one too? It's the
Coda
C7 F
G E F G A C
you're free, dear, it's all right,
B♭ F
C♯ D F D F
it's all right with me.

ALLEZ-VOUS-EN, GO AWAY

Words and Music by
COLE PORTER

registration number 14.

Al - lez - vous - en, al - lez - vous - en, Mam' - selle,_____ Al - lez - vous - en, go a - way._____ Al - lez - vous - en, al - lez - vous - en, Mam' - selle,_____ I have no time for

Copyright © 1953 by Cole Porter
Chappell & Co., Inc., publisher and owner of publication and allied rights throughout the world
Used by HAL LEONARD PUBLISHING CORPORATION, Winona, MN 55987 by Permission
Made in U.S.A.   International Copyright Secured   All Rights Reserved

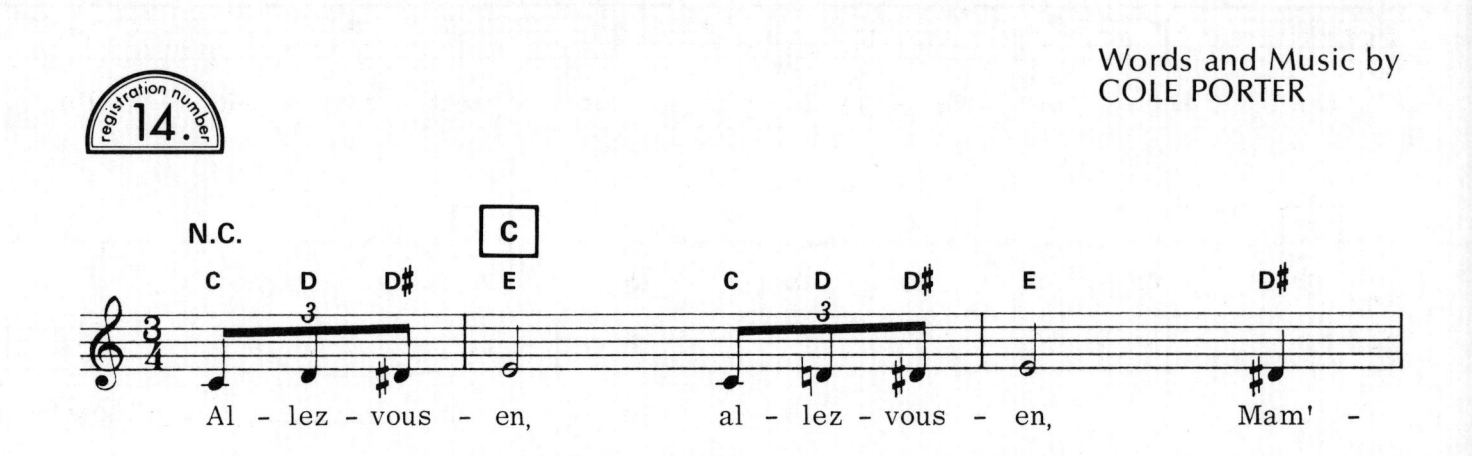

G7 C
B G E C D D♯ E C D D♯
3 3
you to - day. Do be a dear, just dis - ap -
E D♯ E E F F♯
3
pear, Mam' - selle, Bid me good -
C7 F
G D C A A B♭ B
3
bye, do, do, do. Al - lez - vous-
C
C D C B A C G C D
3
en, please go a - way, Mam' - selle, or I
D7 G7 C
E D C B D C
may go a - way with you.

DO I LOVE YOU?

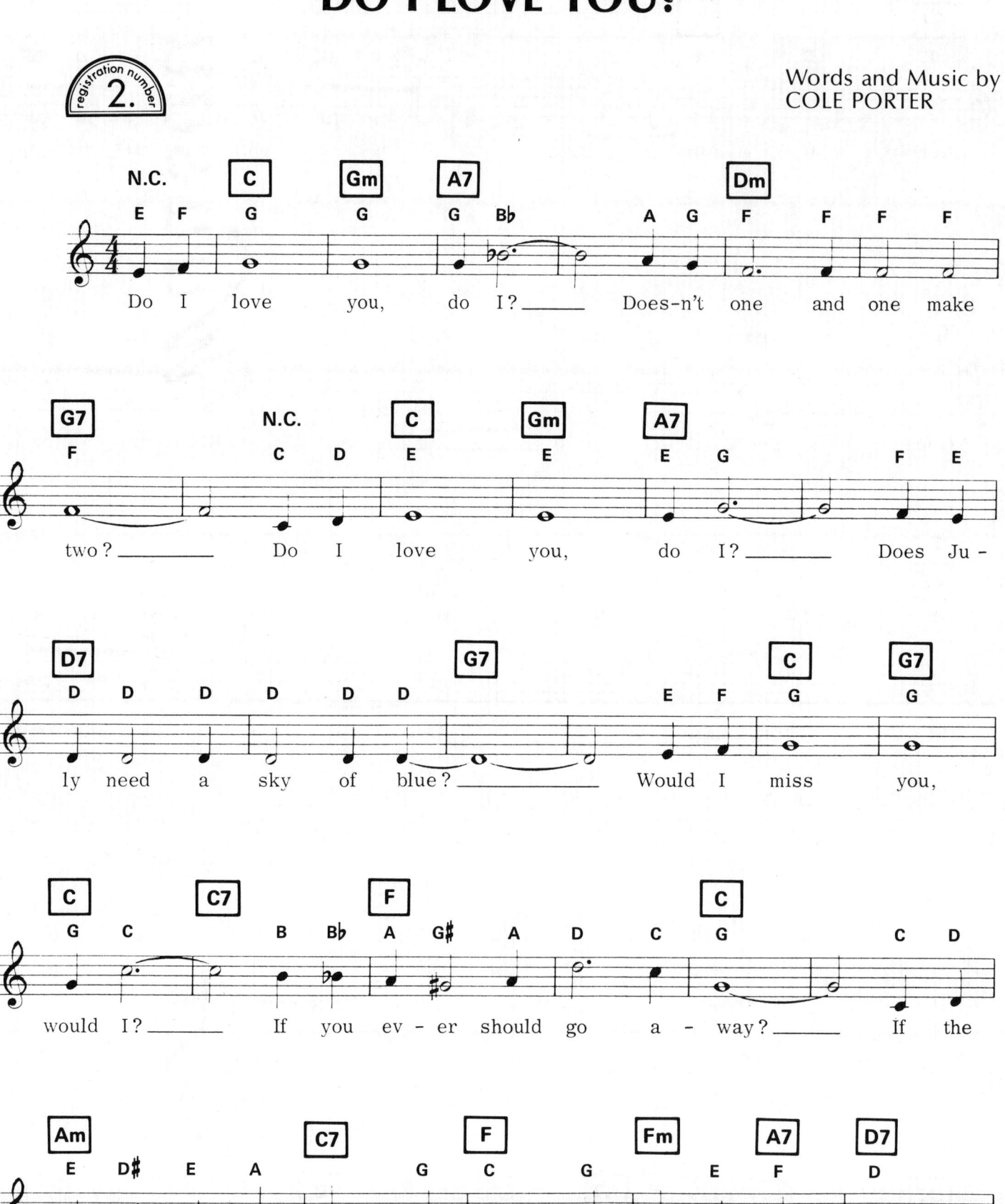

Words and Music by
COLE PORTER

registration number 2.

Do I love you, do I? Doesn't one and one make two? Do I love you, do I? Does Ju-ly need a sky of blue? Would I miss you, would I? If you ev-er should go a-way? If the sun should de-sert the day, What would life be?

Copyright ©1939 by Chappell & Co., Inc.,
Copyright Renewed
Copyright ©1962 by Chappell & Co., Inc.,
Used by HAL LEONARD PUBLISHING CORPORATION, Winona, MN 55987 by Permission
Made in U.S.A.   International Copyright Secured   All Rights Reserved

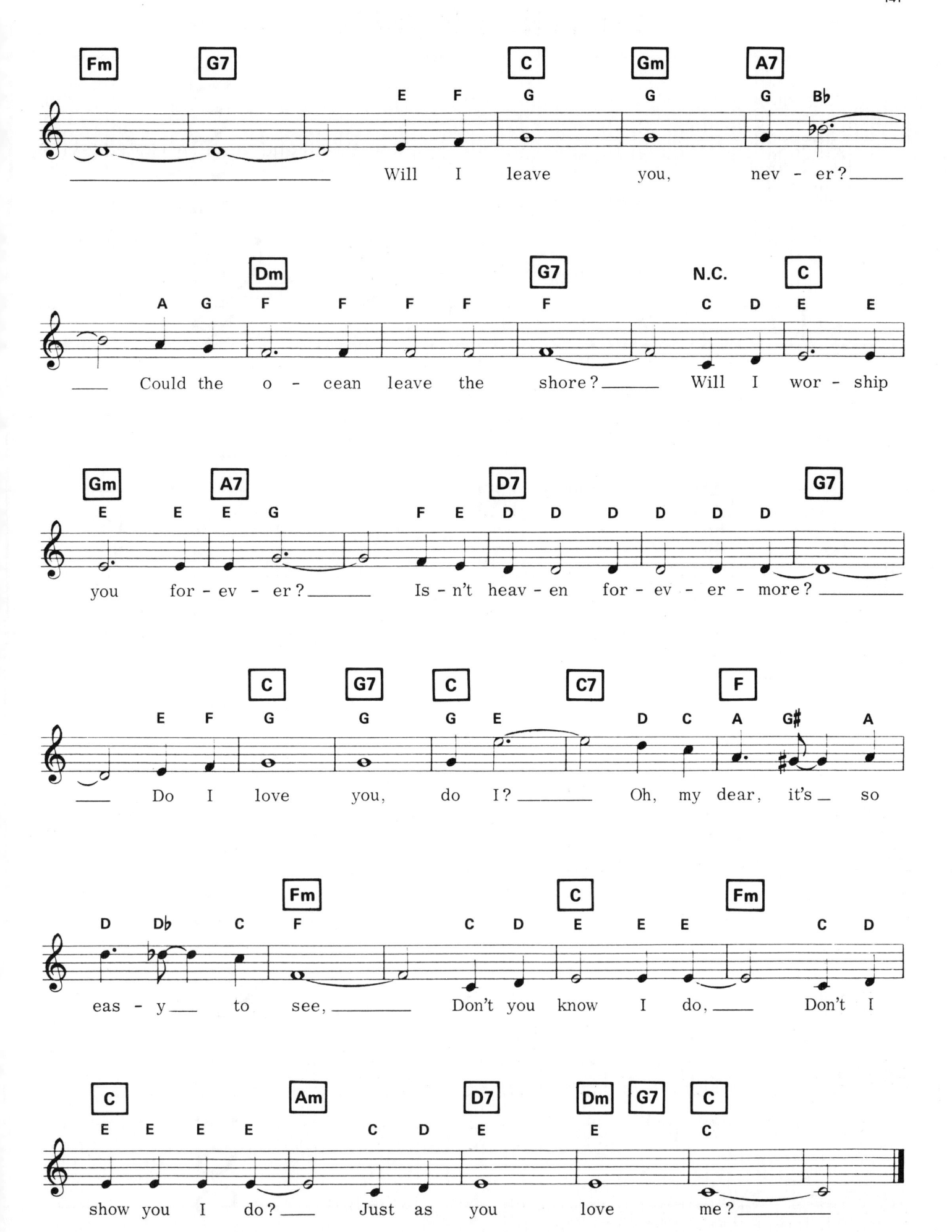

Will I leave you, nev-er? Could the o-cean leave the shore? Will I wor-ship you for-ev-er? Is-n't heav-en for-ev-er-more? Do I love you, do I? Oh, my dear, it's so eas-y to see, Don't you know I do, Don't I show you I do? Just as you love me?

FROM THIS MOMENT ON

Words and Music by COLE PORTER

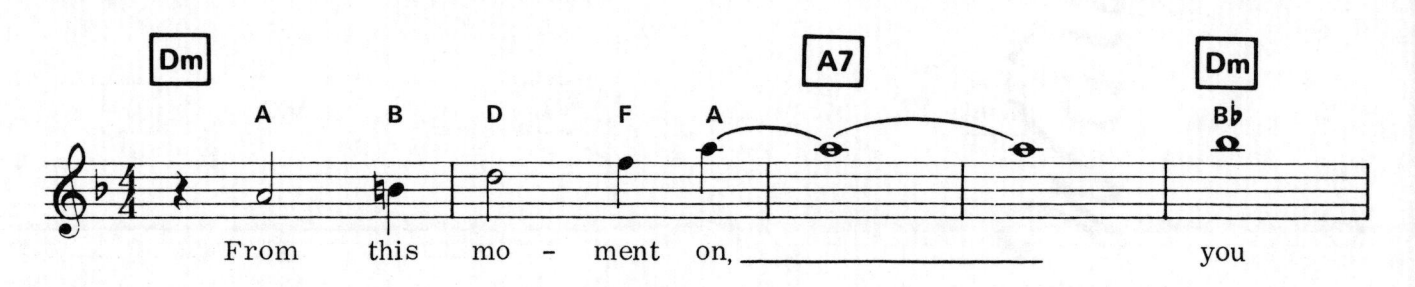

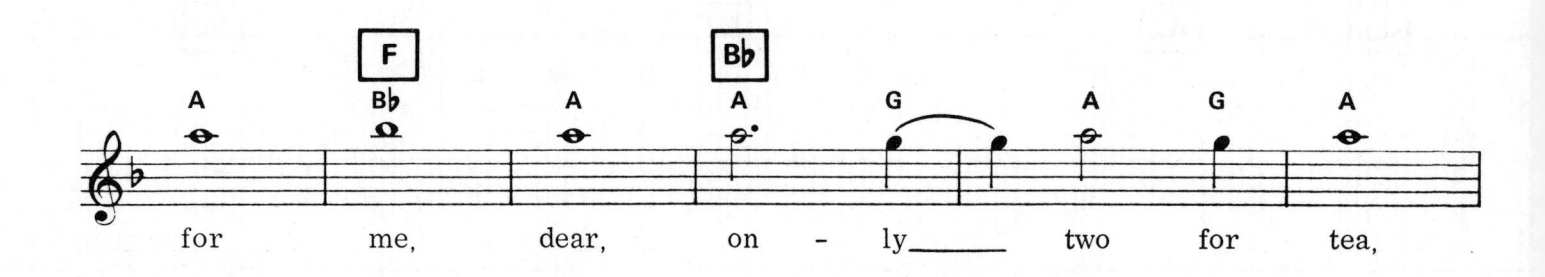

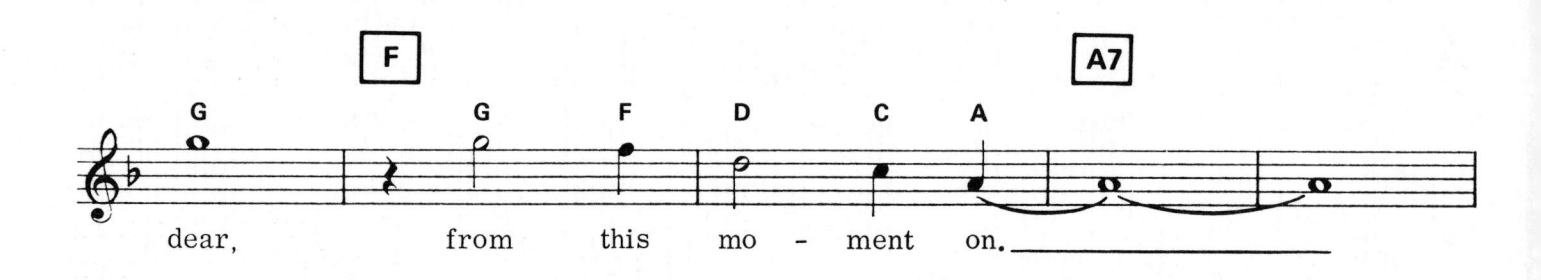

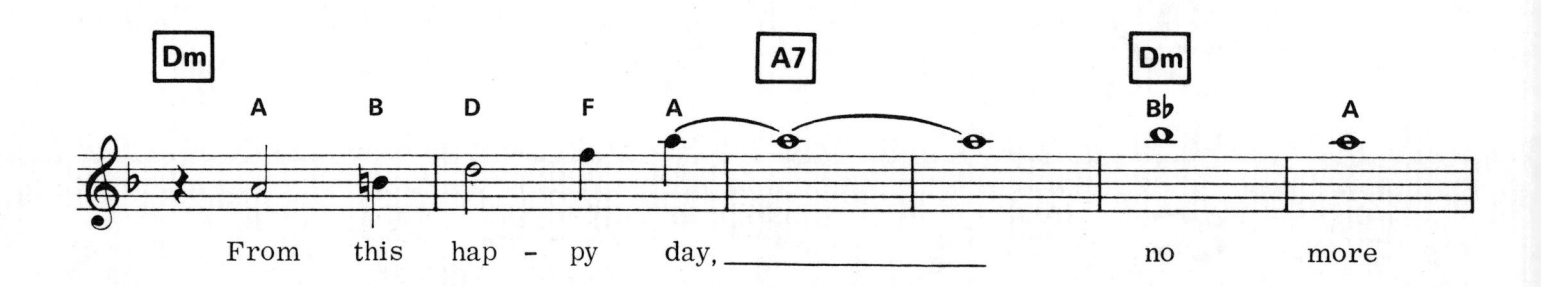

registration number 3.

From this moment on, you for me, dear, only two for tea, dear, from this moment on. From this happy day, no more blue songs, on-ly whoop-dee-doo songs, from this mo-ment on. For you've got the love I need so much, Got the skin I love to touch, Got the arms to hold me tight,

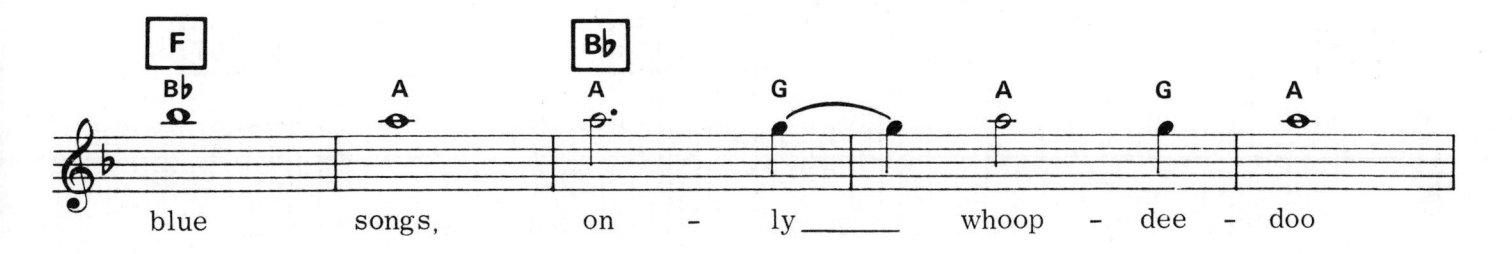

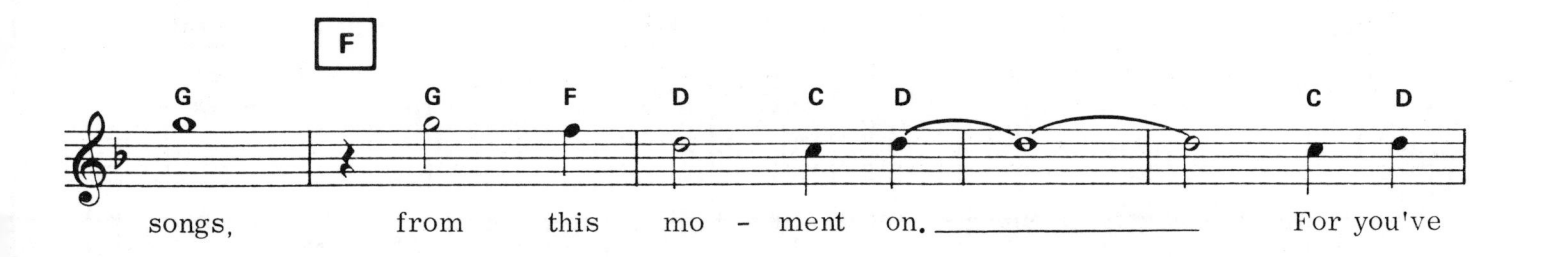

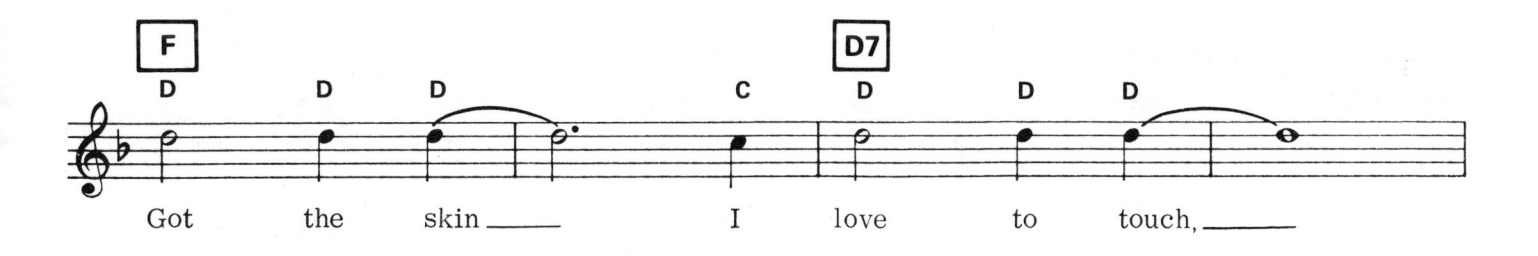

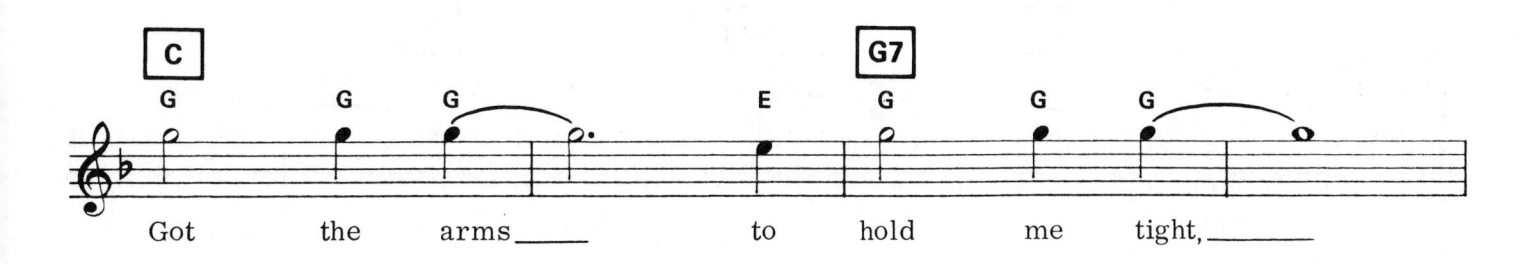

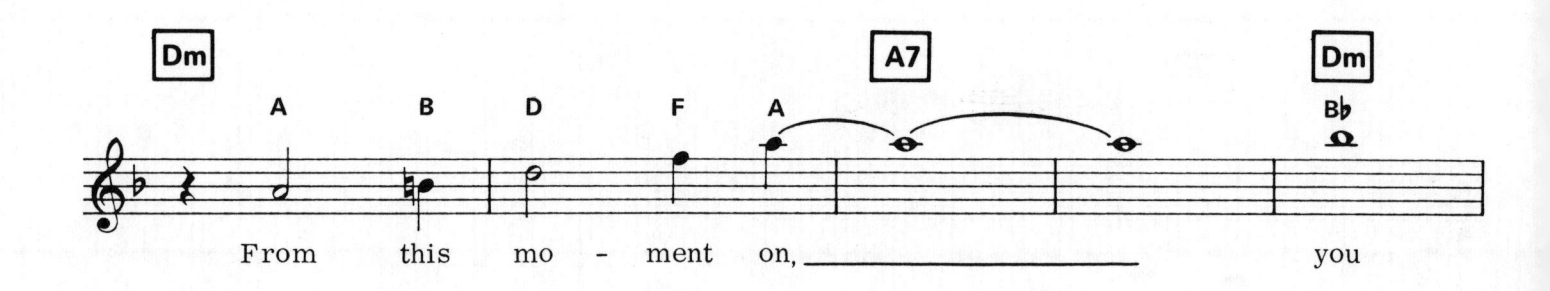

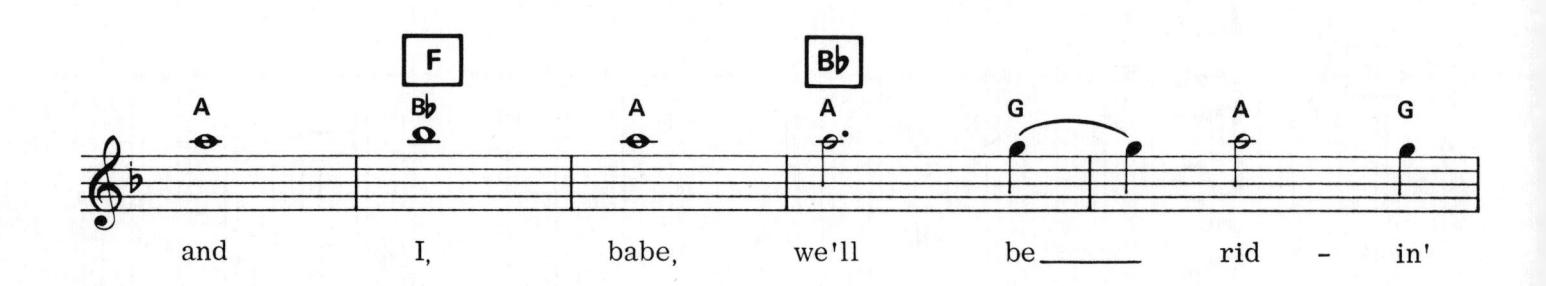

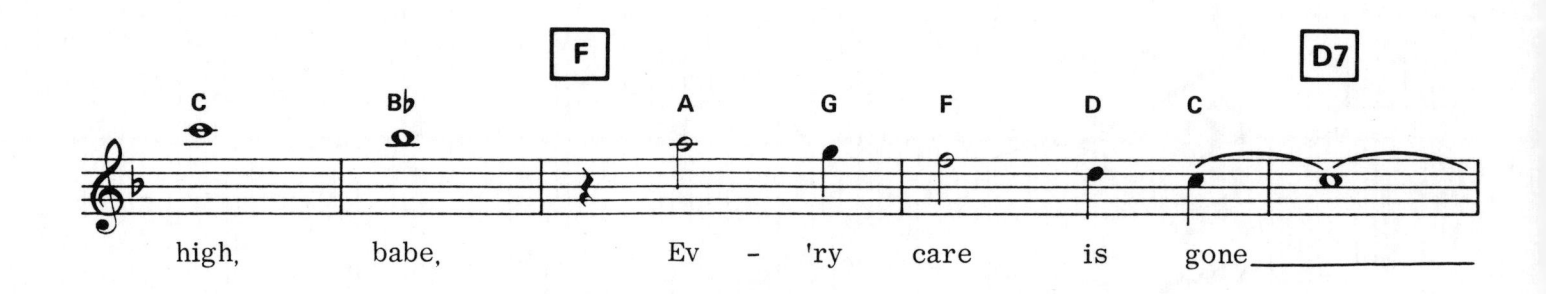

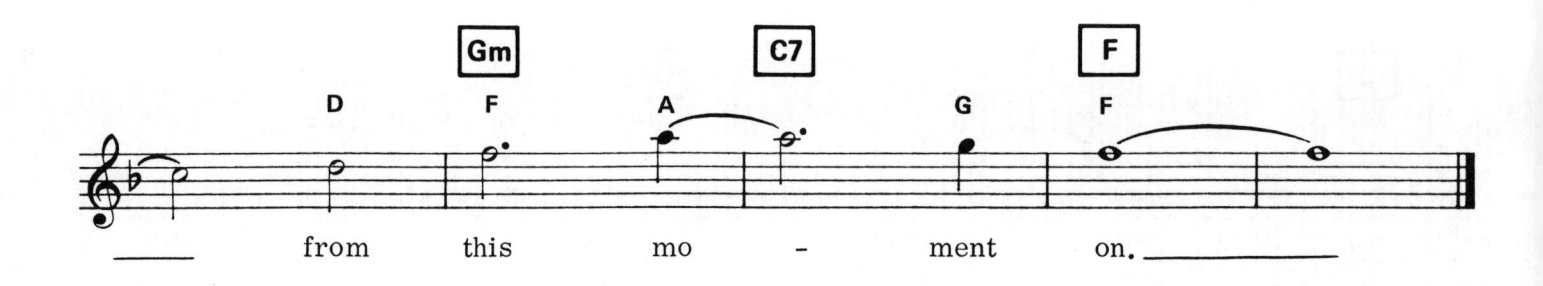

Got the sweet lips to kiss me good-night. From this moment on, you and I, babe, we'll be ridin' high, babe, Ev-'ry care is gone from this moment on.

LOOK TO THE RAINBOW

Words by E. Y. HARBURG
Music by BURTON LANE

Look, look, look to the rain-bow, Fol-low it o-ver the hill___ and stream. Look, look, look to the rain-bow, Fol-low the fel-low who fol-lows a dream, Fol-low the fel-low, Fol-low the fel-low, Fol-low the fel-low who fol-lows a dream.

Copyright © 1946 by Chappell & Co., Inc.,
Copyright Renewed
Copyright © 1968 by Chappell & Co., Inc.,
Used by HAL LEONARD PUBLISHING CORPORATION, Winona, MN 55987 by Permission
Made in U.S.A.   International Copyright Secured   All Rights Reserved

For Inspiration

ONE MORE SONG FOR JESUS

TOM T. HALL

1. We've trav-eled this world o-ver in our day and in our time. We've heard some songs that made no sense and some that did not rhyme. We may nev-er sing an-oth-er song, there ain't no way to know. But let's have one more song for Je-sus be-fore we go.

2. say they're gon-na burn us in a not too dis-tant day. I don't think we should but that 'cause it just ain't Je-sus' way. They say He's mean and vi-cious and there's noth-ing that He won't do. They must know a dif-f'rent Je-sus than we do.

3. a-the-ist may tell us He was just an-oth-er man. Some say that He's a su-per-star and they're His big-gest fans. He means so much to so man-y that I think you will a-gree, We ought-a have one more song for Je-sus, if you please.

Oh, we may not live the

Copyright © 1972 by Hallnote Music
Used by permission of copyright owner
Used by HAL LEONARD PUBLISHING CORPORATION, Winona, MN 55987 by Permission
Made in U.S.A. International Copyright Secured All Rights Reserved

letter of the law and live that true,— Judged and criti-
cized for almost ev-'ry-thing we do.—— But they
cannot stop our singing, though they're ho-li-er than we.— Let's have
one more song for Je-sus, if you please.— 2. They
3. Some please.—

AMAZING GRACE

TRADITIONAL

A-maz-ing grace! How sweet the sound That saved a wretch like me.—
'Twas grace that taught my heart to fear, And grace my fears re-lieved,—
— I once was lost, but now am found, Was blind but now I see.
— How pre-cious did that grace ap-pear The hour I first be-lieved!

Copyright ©1973 by Chappell & Co., Inc.
Used by HAL LEONARD PUBLISHING CORPORATION, Winona, MN 55987 by Permission
Made in U.S.A.   International Copyright Secured   All Rights Reserved

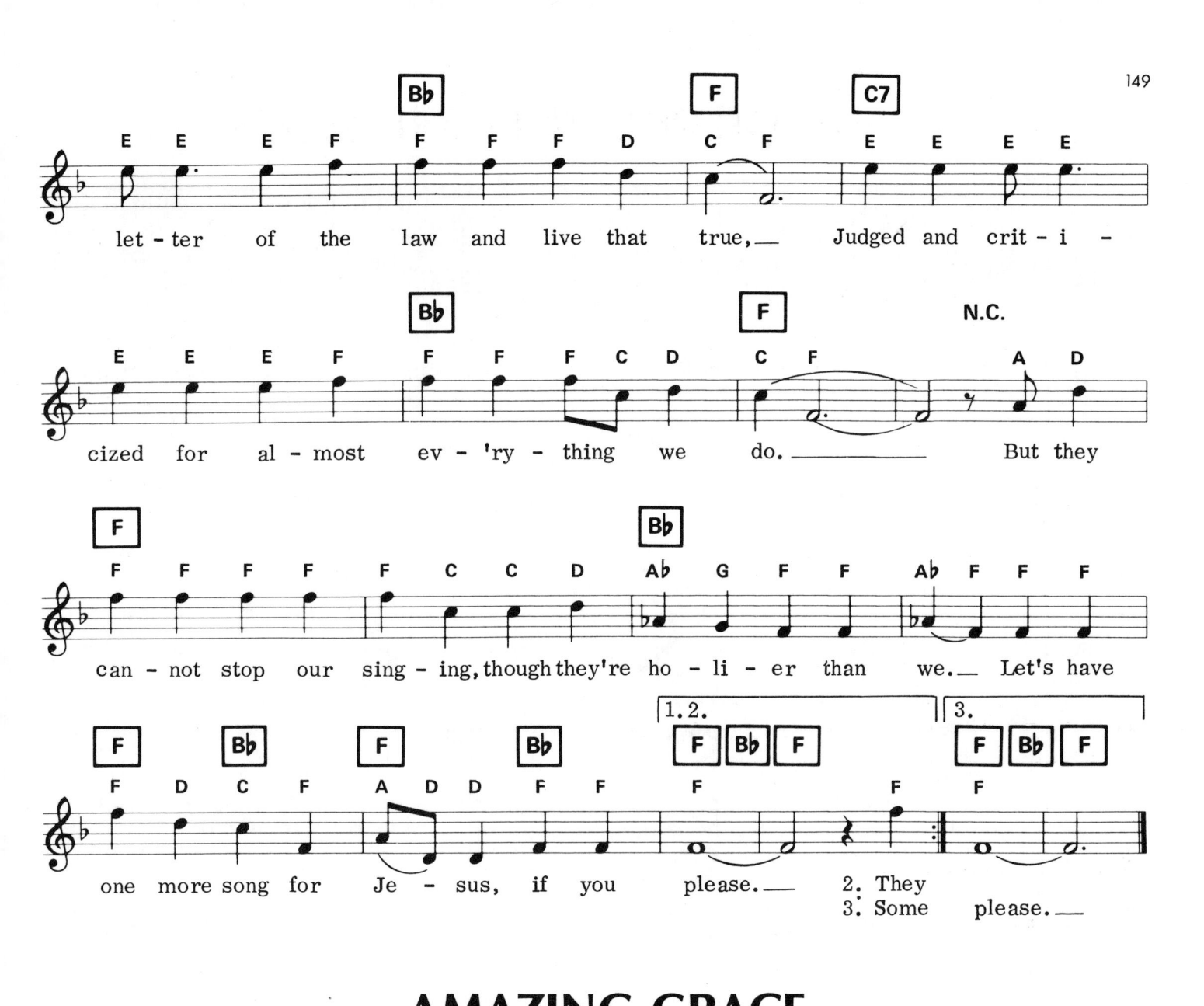

DIDN'T HE SHINE

ALLEN REYNOLDS and BOB McDILL

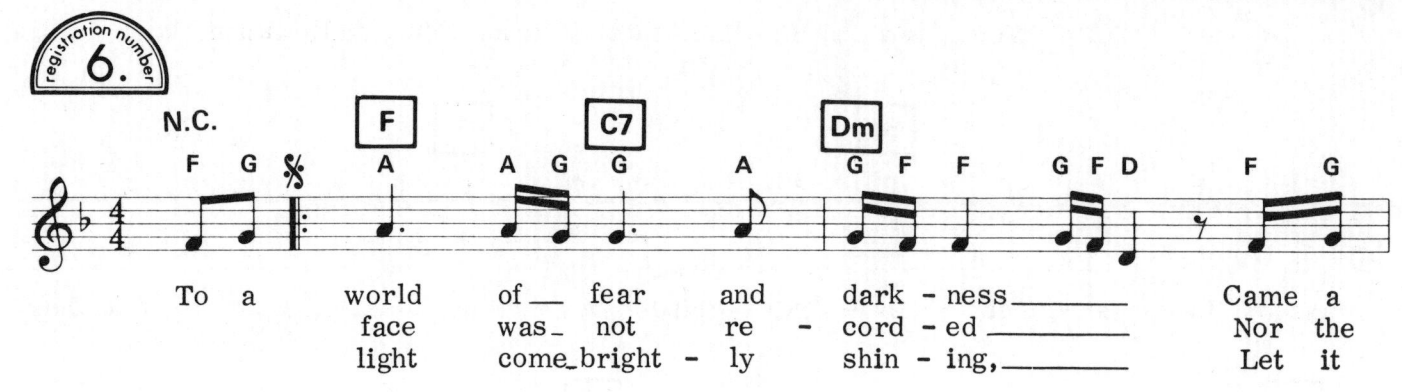

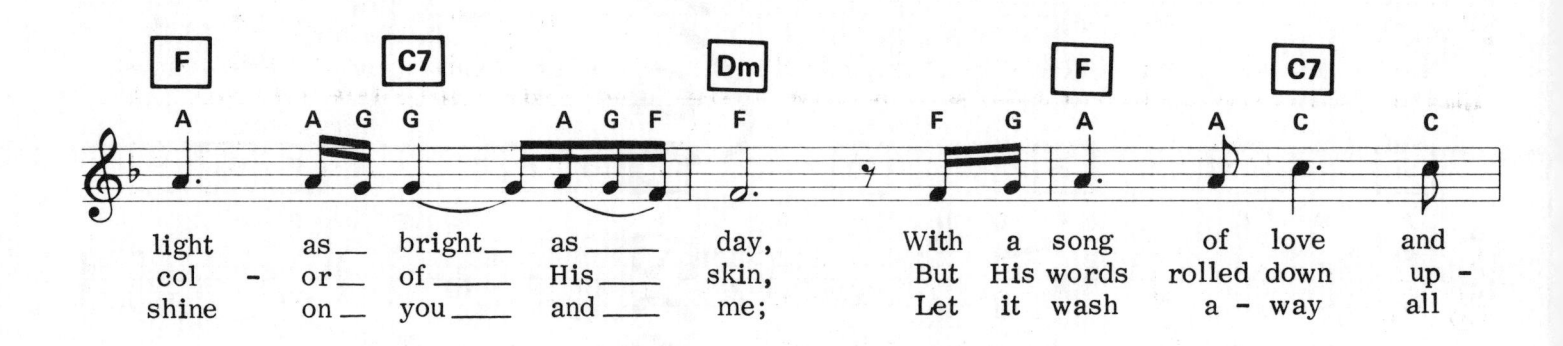

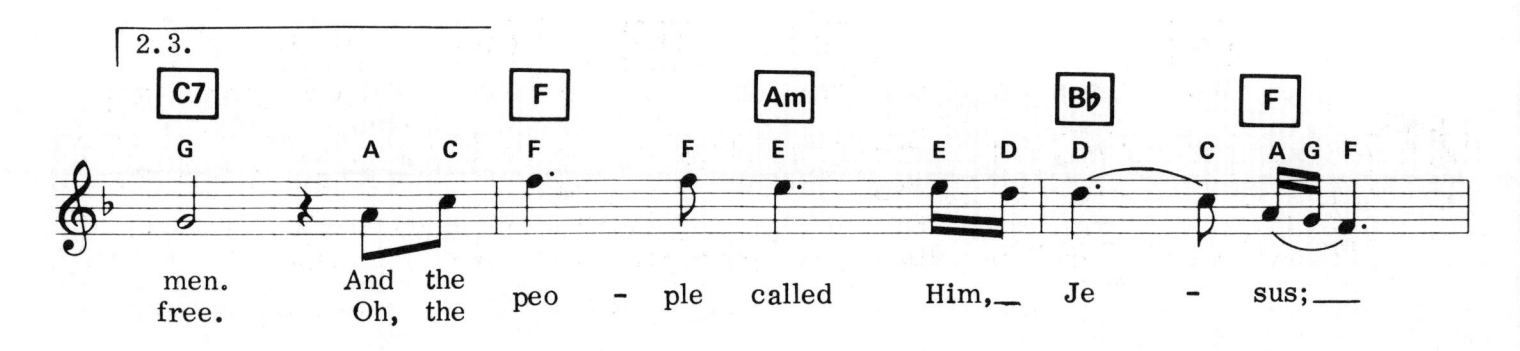

To a world of fear and darkness, Came a
face was not re-cord-ed, Nor the
light come bright-ly shin-ing, Let it

light as bright as day, With a song of love and
col-or of His skin, But His words rolled down up-
shine on you and me; Let it wash a-way all

words of kind-ness He came to show the way. Oh, His
on the dark-ness And touched the hearts of
fear and sor-row, Let it set us

men. And the
free. Oh, the peo-ple called Him, Je-sus;

Copyright © 1970 by Jack Music, Inc.
Used by permission
Used by HAL LEONARD PUBLISHING CORPORATION, Winona, MN 55987 by Permission
Made in U.S.A.   International Copyright Secured   All Rights Reserved

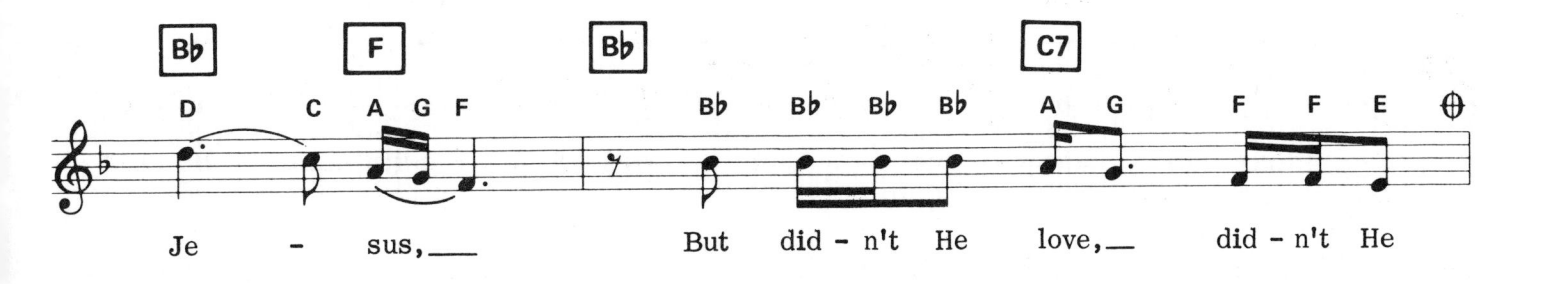

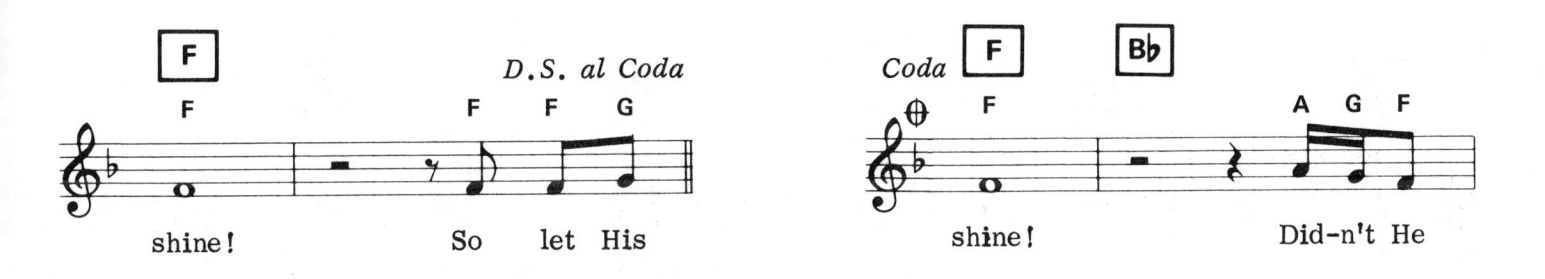

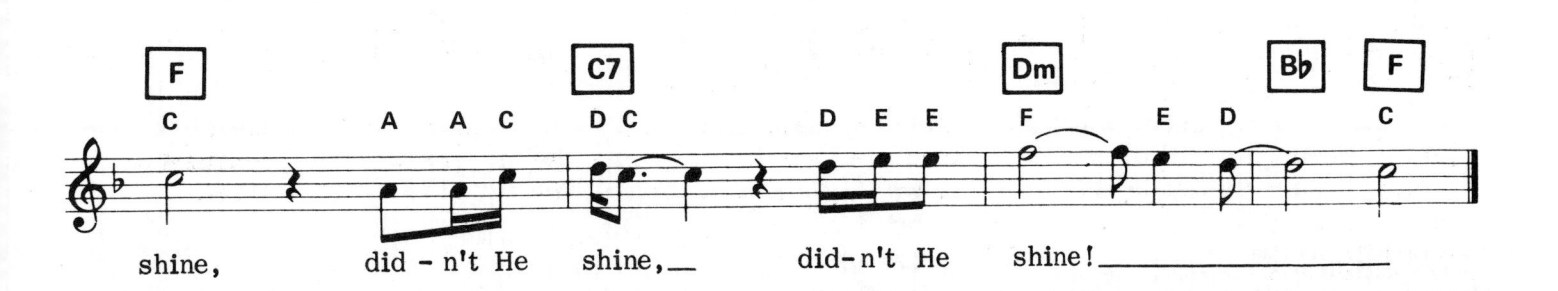

He was a man for all time, Just a simple man called Je-sus, But did-n't He love, did-n't He shine!

D.S. al Coda

So let His shine!

Coda Did-n't He shine, did-n't He shine, did-n't He shine!

ME AND JESUS

TOM T. HALL

Well, me and Jesus got our own thing going, Me and Jesus got it all worked out; Me and Jesus got our own thing going, We don't need anybody to tell us what it's all about.

I know a man, once was a sinner, I know a man
Jesus brought me through all of my troubles, Jesus brought me
We can't afford any fancy preachin', We can't afford

Copyright©1971 by Hallnote Music
Used by permission of copyright owner
Used by HAL LEONARD PUBLISHING CORPORATION, Winona, MN 55987 by Permission
Made in U.S.A.   International Copyright Secured   All Rights Reserved

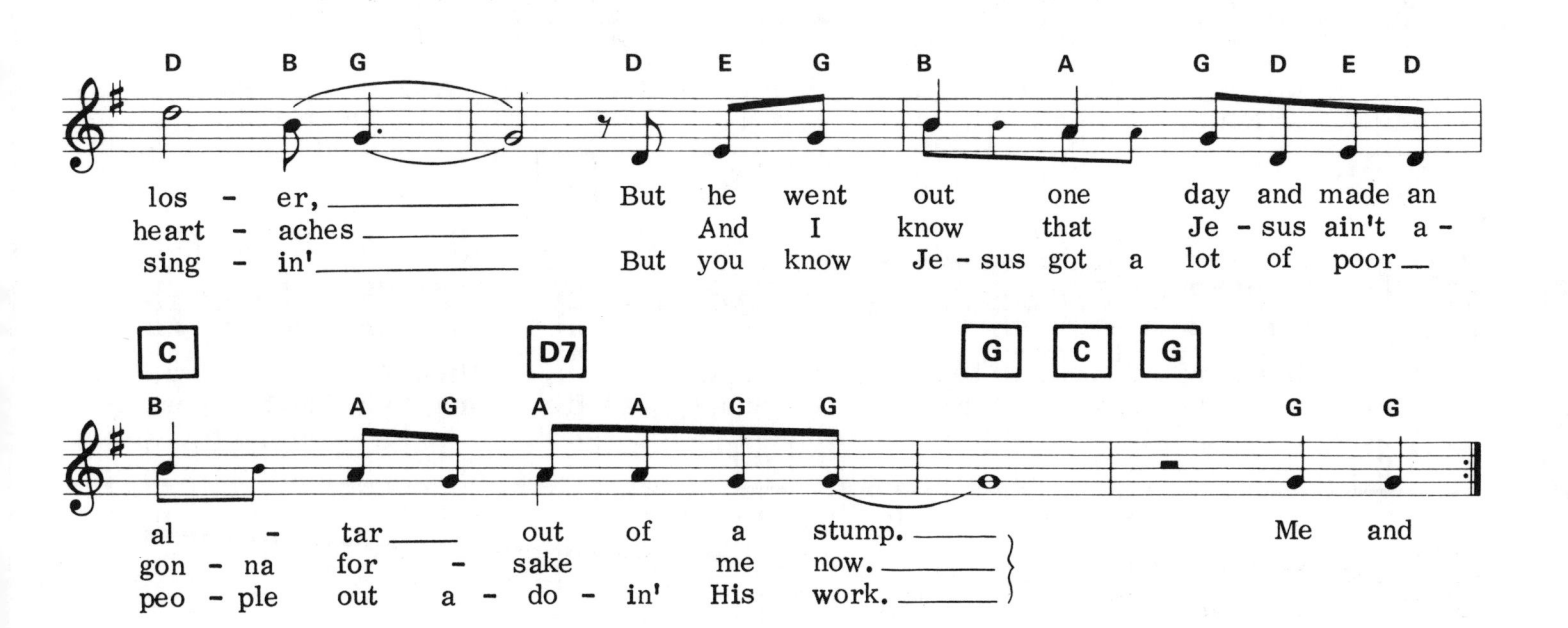

that once was a drunk; I know a man, once was a
through all of my trials; Je-sus brought me_ through all of my
an-y fan-cy_ church; We can't af-ford an-y fan-cy

los - er,_____ But he went out one day and made an
heart - aches_____ And I know that Je-sus ain't a-
sing - in'_____ But you know Je-sus got a lot of poor_

al - tar_ out of a stump._ Me and
gon - na for - sake me now._
peo - ple out a - do - in' His work._

SUN OF MY SOUL

W. H. Monk

Sun of my soul,_Thou Sav-iour dear, It is not night_ if Thou_ be near.

Oh, may no earth-born cloud a-rise To hide Thee from Thy ser-vant's eyes.

Copyright © 1973 by Chappell & Co., Inc.
Used by HAL LEONARD PUBLISHING CORPORATION, Winona, MN 55987 by Permission
Made in U.S.A.   International Copyright Secured   All Rights Reserved

JESUS MADE ME HIGHER

MICHAEL S. OMARTIAN

Day be-gins, my trou-ble gone a-way;
Now I can love and know it's from with-in,

Can't re-mem-ber how it was. Used to wor-ry
No need to hide an-y more. Lis-ten, my broth-ers,

al-most ev-'ry day But some-thing's made me high-er than
we can all be-gin To love one an-oth-er like we

all the words I can say. So take my hand,
nev-er have be-fore.

I will tell you 'bout new life and so much more, 'Cause

Je-sus made me high-er than I've ev-er been be-fore.

Copyright © 1971 by Grob Music Company
Chappell & Co., Inc., publisher
Used by HAL LEONARD PUBLISHING CORPORATION, Winona, MN 55987 by Permission
Made in U.S.A.   International Copyright Secured   All Rights Reserved

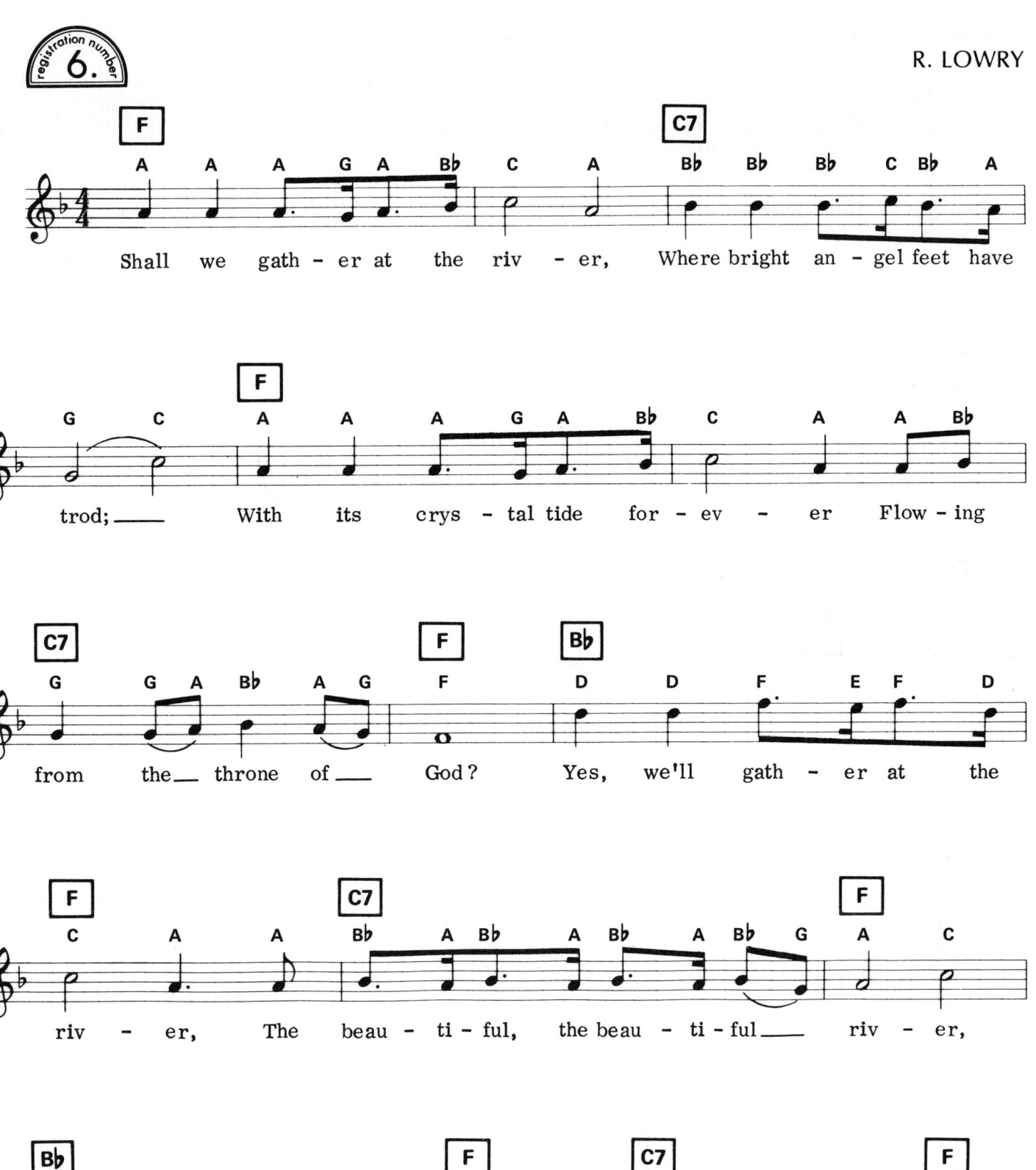

SHALL WE GATHER AT THE RIVER

R. LOWRY

Shall we gath-er at the riv-er, Where bright an-gel feet have trod;___ With its crys-tal tide for-ev-er Flow-ing from the___ throne of___ God? Yes, we'll gath-er at the riv-er, The beau-ti-ful, the beau-ti-ful___ riv-er, Gath-er with the saints___ at the riv-er, That flows from the throne of___ God.

Copyright © 1973 by Chappell & Co., Inc.
Used by HAL LEONARD PUBLISHING CORPORATION, Winona, MN 55987 by Permission
Made in U.S.A.   International Copyright Secured   All Rights Reserved

All-time Favorites

TRY TO REMEMBER

Words by TOM JONES
Music by HARVEY SCHMIDT

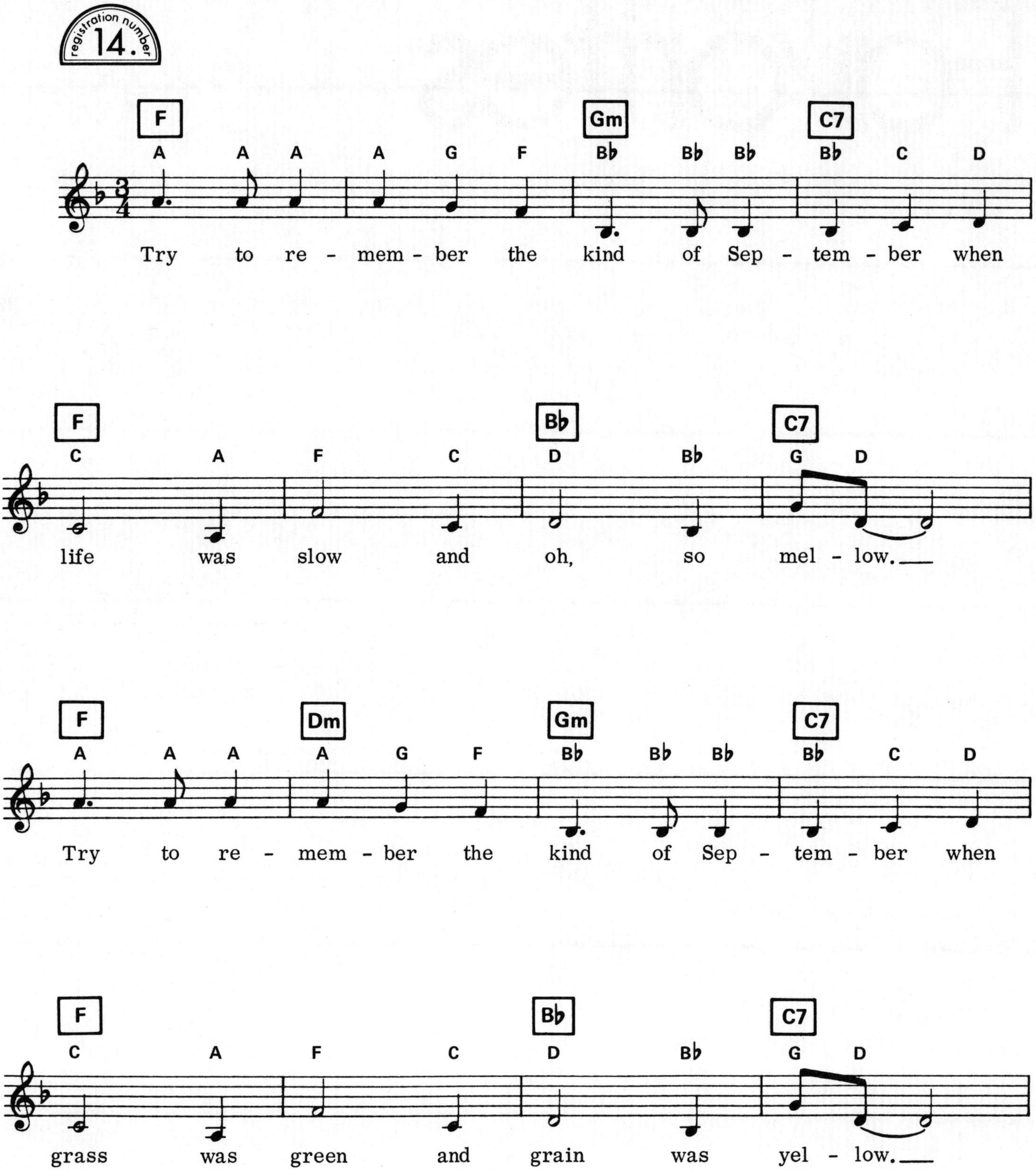

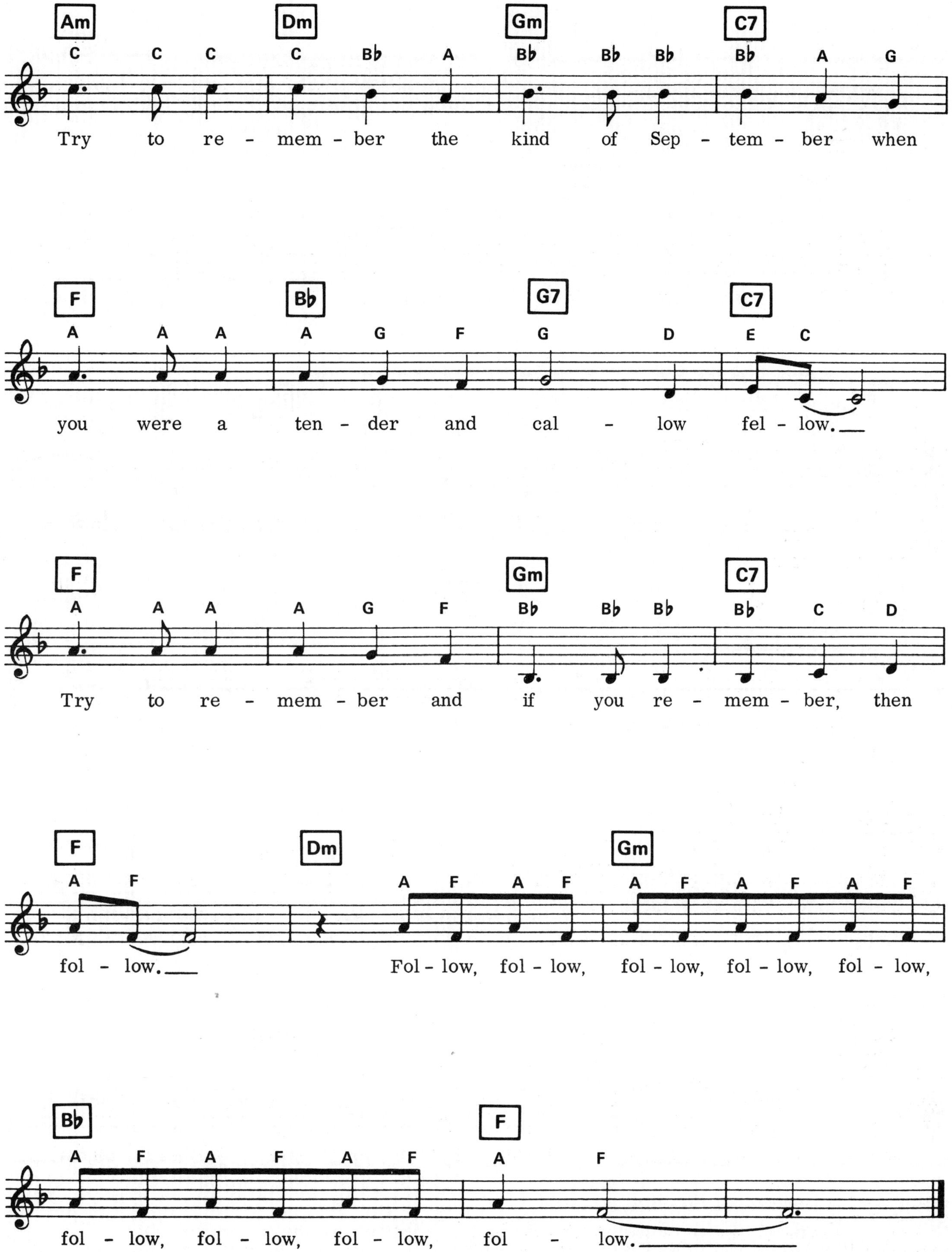

Am Dm Gm C7
C C C C B♭ A B♭ B♭ B♭ B♭ A G
Try to re - mem - ber the kind of Sep - tem - ber when
F B♭ G7 C7
A A A A G F G D E C
you were a ten - der and cal - low fel - low.
F Gm C7
A A A A G F B♭ B♭ B♭ B♭ C D
Try to re - mem - ber and if you re - mem - ber, then
F Dm Gm
A F A F A F A F A F A F
fol - low. Fol - low, fol - low, fol - low, fol - low, fol - low,
B♭ F
A F A F A F A F
fol - low, fol - low, fol - low, fol - low.

HARBOR LIGHTS

Words and Music by
JIMMY KENNEDY and HUGH WILLIAMS

registration number 11.

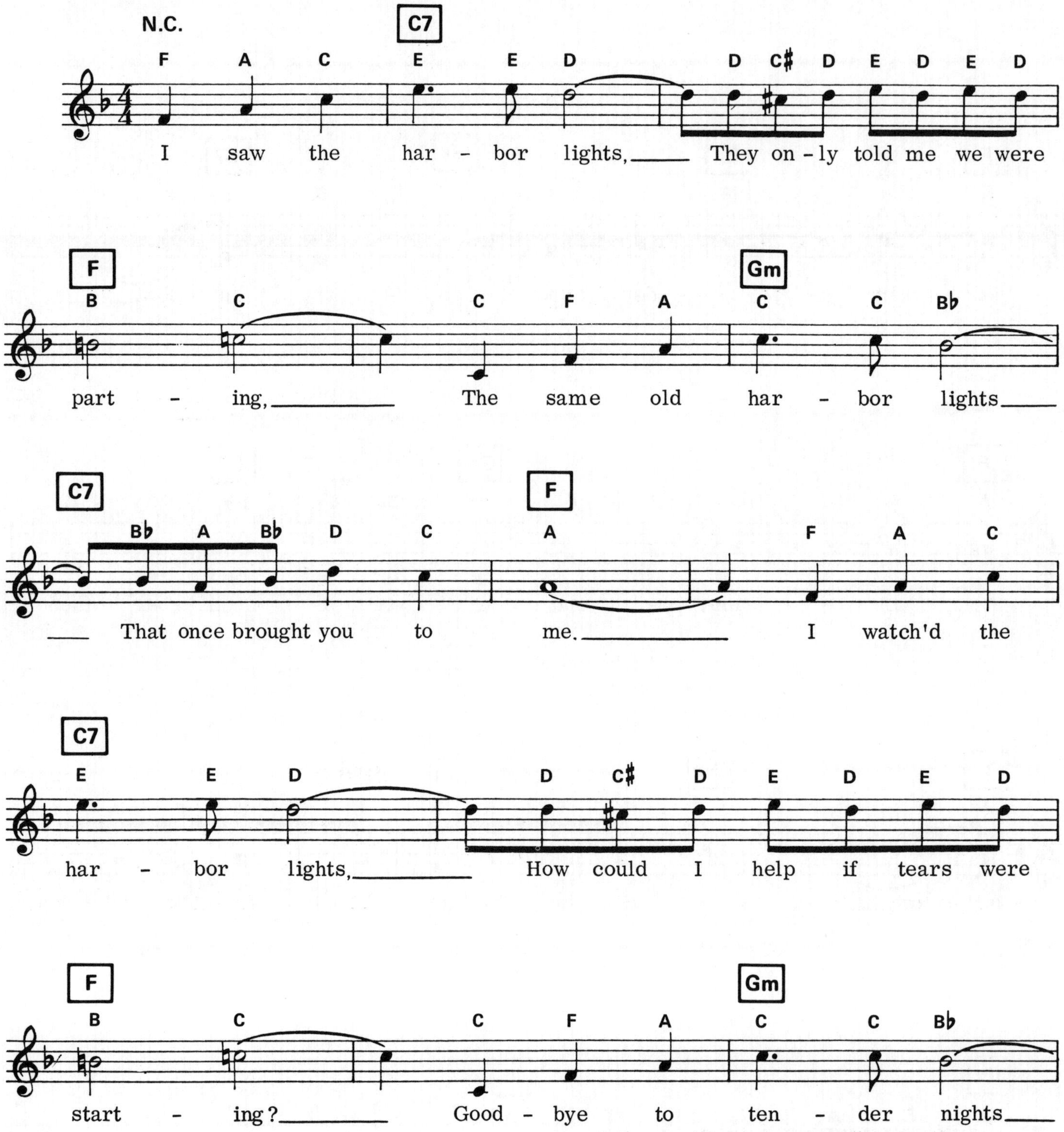

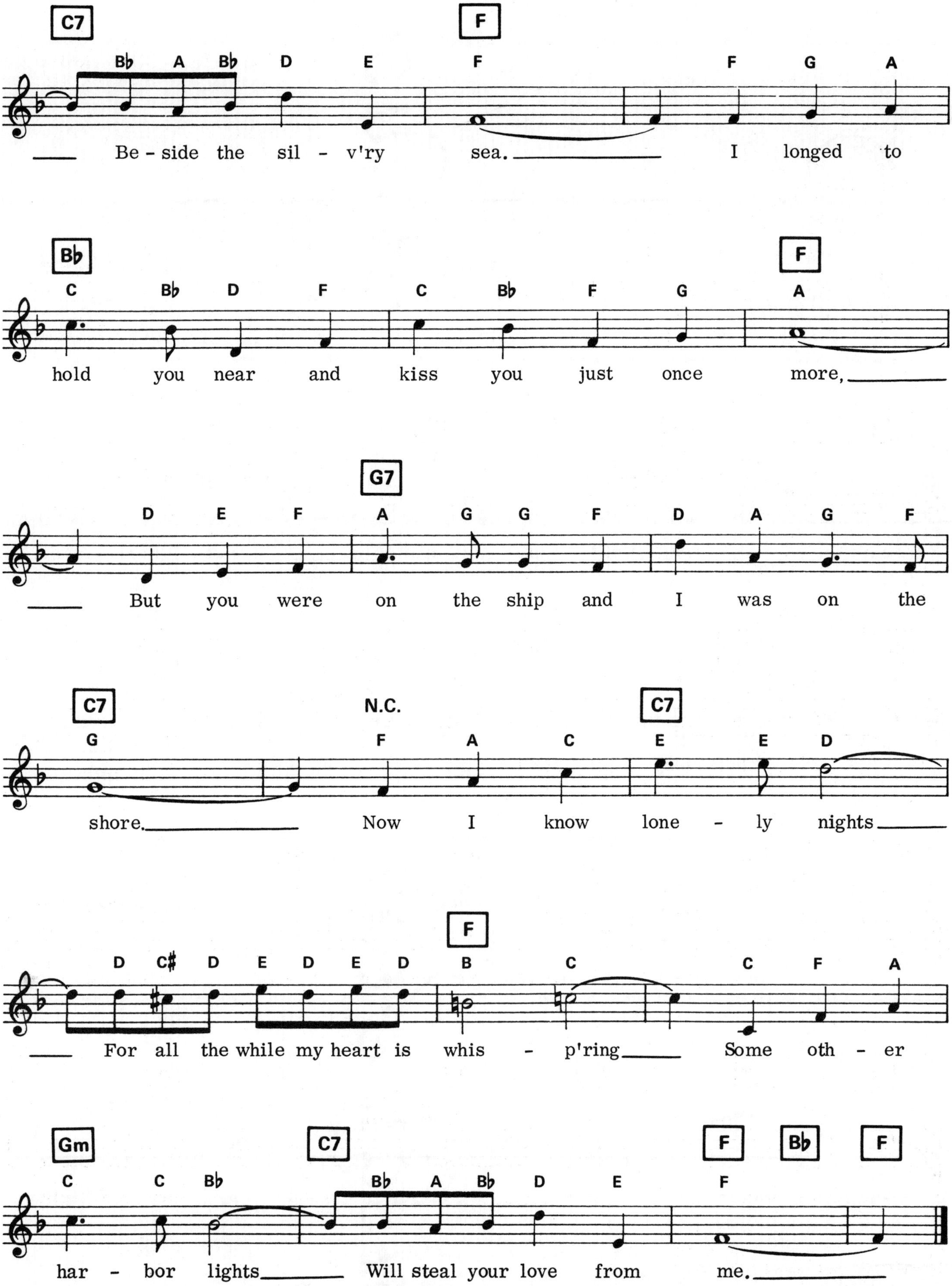
C7 F
B♭ A B♭ D E F F G A
Be - side the sil - v'ry sea. I longed to
B♭ F
C B♭ D F C B♭ F G A
hold you near and kiss you just once more,
G7
D E F A G G F D A G F
But you were on the ship and I was on the
C7 N.C. C7
G F A C E E D
shore. Now I know lone - ly nights
F
D C♯ D E D E D B C C F A
For all the while my heart is whis - p'ring Some oth - er
Gm C7 F B♭ F
C C B♭ B♭ A B♭ D E F
har - bor lights Will steal your love from me.

I CAN'T GET STARTED

Words by IRA GERSHWIN
Music by VERNON DUKE

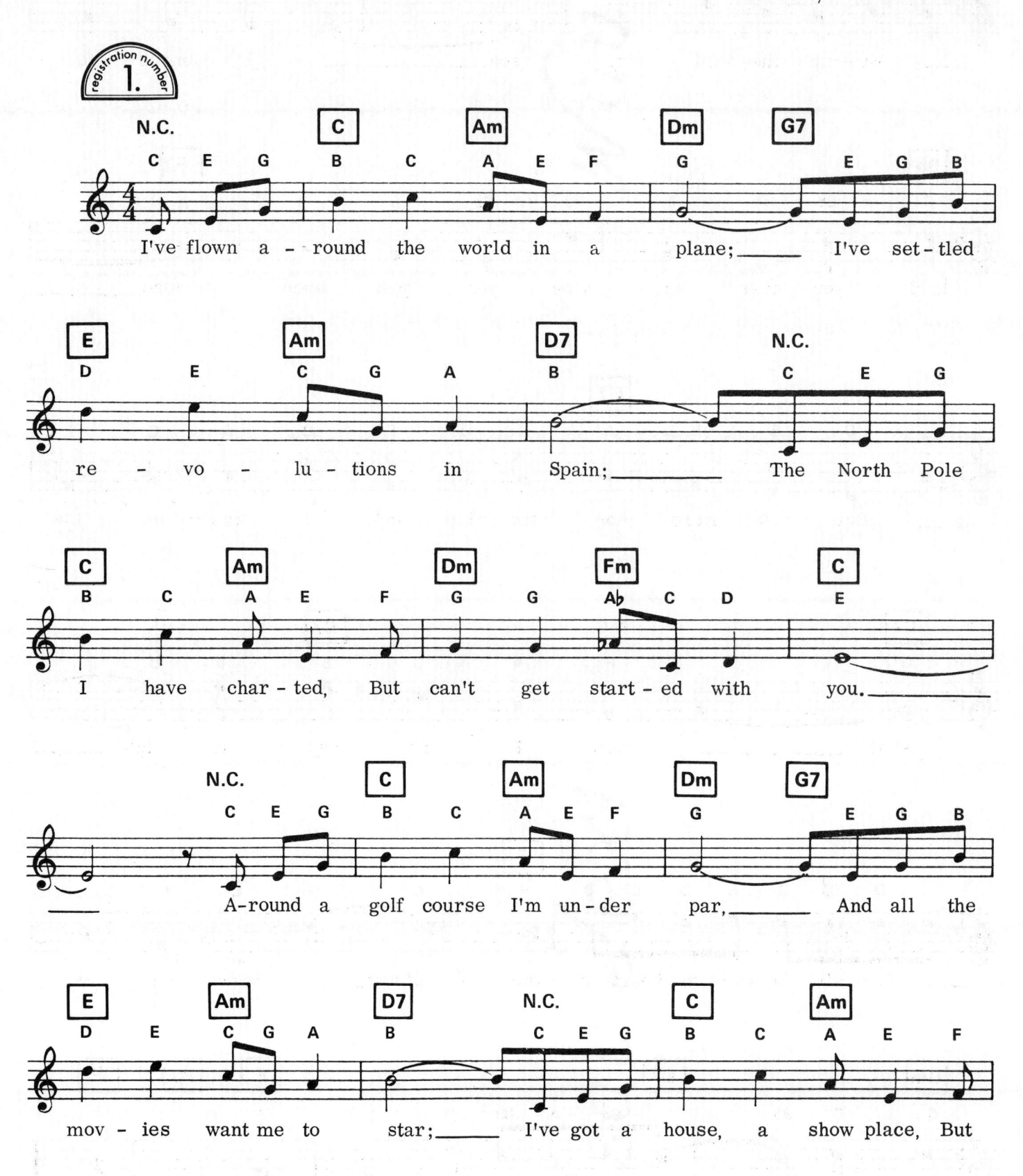

I've flown a-round the world in a plane; I've set-tled re-vo-lu-tions in Spain; The North Pole I have char-ted, But can't get start-ed with you. A-round a golf course I'm un-der par, And all the mov-ies want me to star; I've got a house, a show place, But

Copyright © 1935 by Chappell & Co., Inc.
Copyright Renewed
Used by HAL LEONARD PUBLISHING CORPORATION, Winona, MN 55987 by Permission
Made in U.S.A.   International Copyright Secured   All Rights Reserved

163

I get no place with you. You're so supreme, lyrics I write of you, Scheme just for a sight of you, Dream both day and night of you And what good does it do? In nineteen twenty-nine I sold short; In England I'm presented at court, But you've got me downhearted 'Cause I can't get started with you.

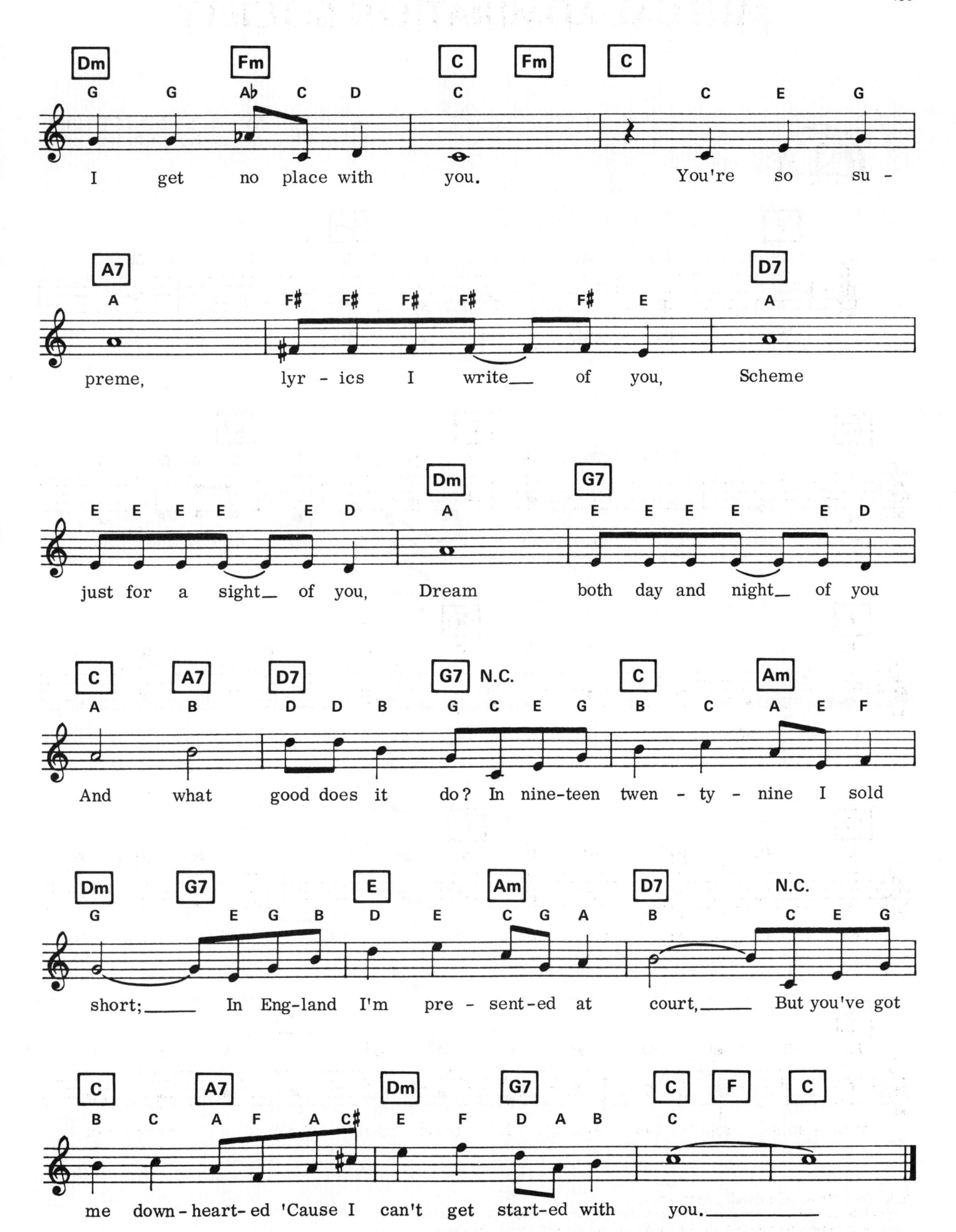

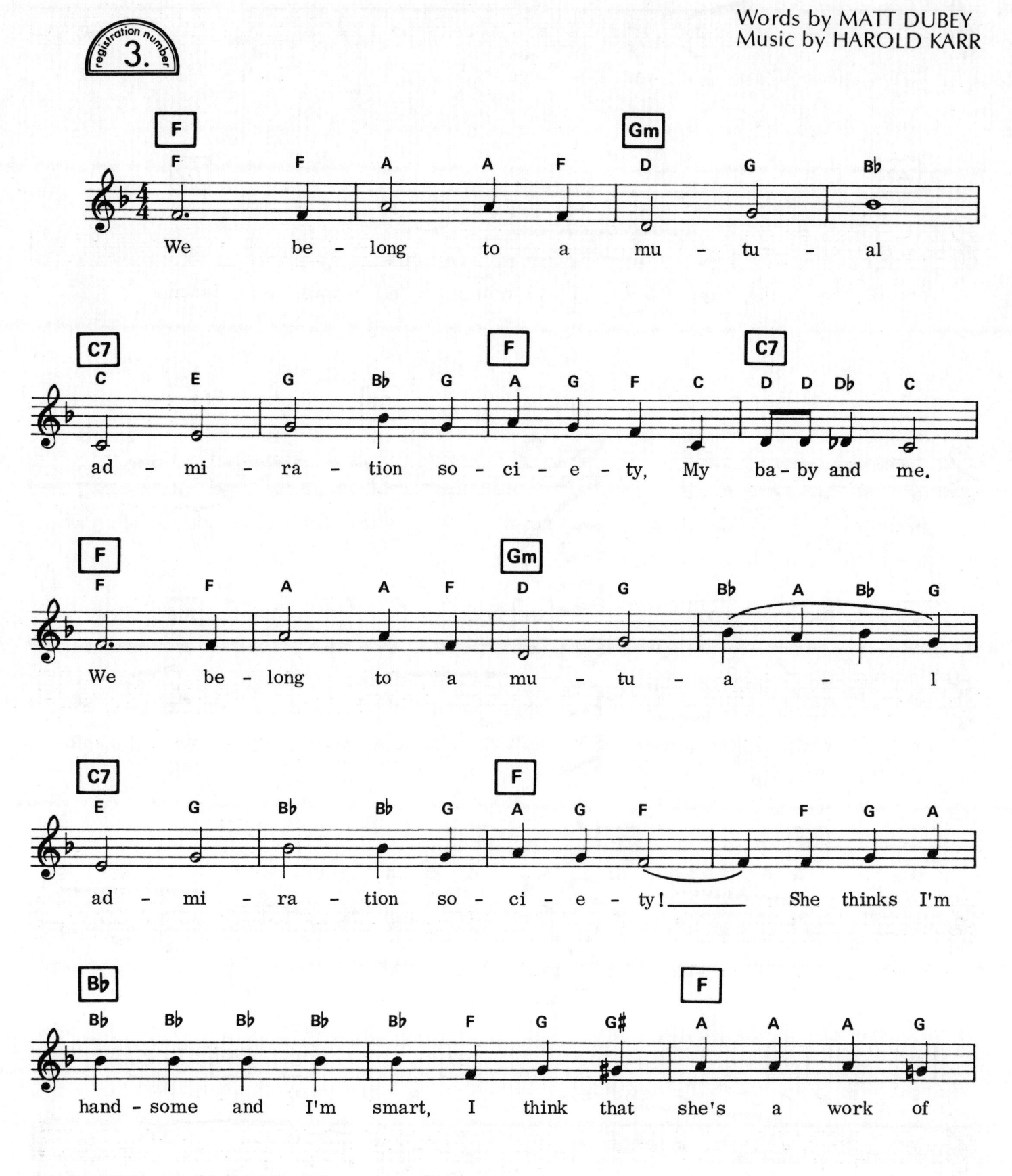

MUTUAL ADMIRATION SOCIETY

Words by MATT DUBEY
Music by HAROLD KARR

registration number 3.

We be-long to a mu-tu-al ad-mi-ra-tion so-ci-e-ty, My ba-by and me. We be-long to a mu-tu-a-l ad-mi-ra-tion so-ci-e-ty! She thinks I'm hand-some and I'm smart, I think that she's a work of

Copyright © 1956 by Matt Dubey and Harold Karr
Chappell & Co., Inc., owner of publication and allied rights throughout the world
Used by HAL LEONARD PUBLISHING CORPORATION, Winona, MN 55987 by Permission
Made in U.S.A.   International Copyright Secured   All Rights Reserved

art. She says that I'm the great-est man, and like-wise, I'm her big-gest fan. I say her kiss-es are like wine, she says they're not as good as mine, And that's the way we pass the time of day! My ba-by and me, Oh we be-long to a mu-tu-al ad-mi-ra-tion so-ci-e-ty! My ba-by and me!

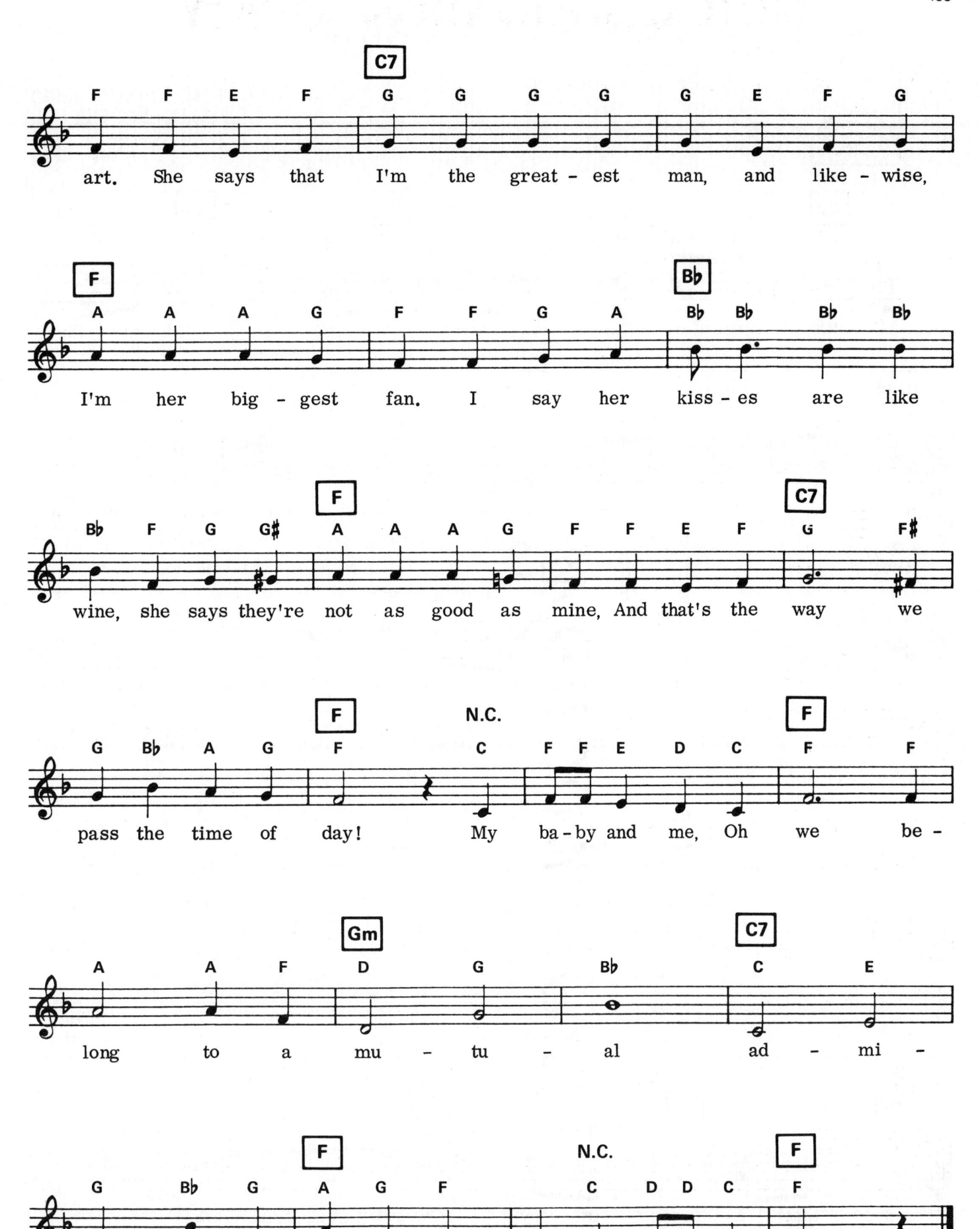

ROSES OF PICARDY

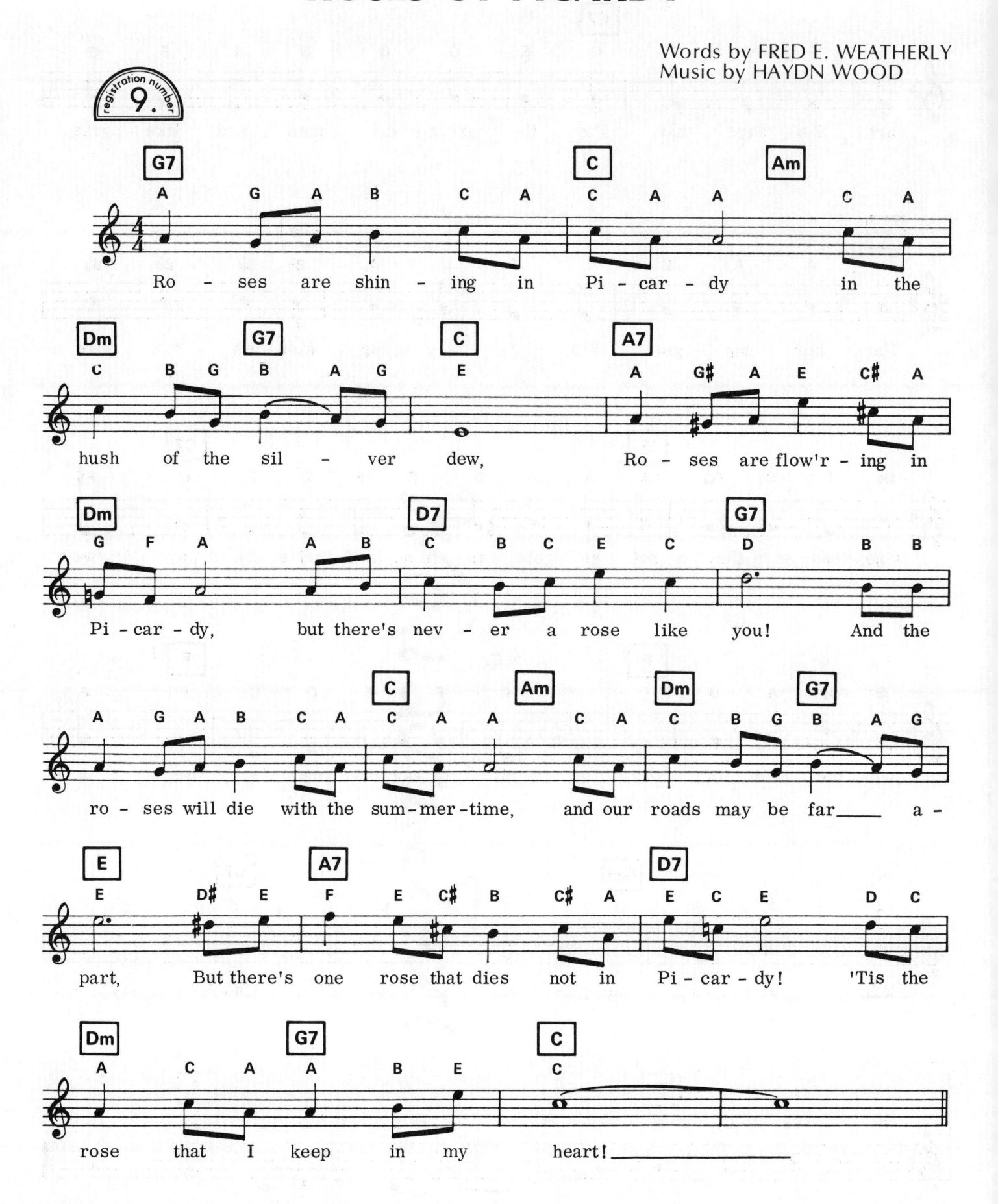

Words by FRED E. WEATHERLY
Music by HAYDN WOOD

Ro-ses are shin-ing in Pi-car-dy in the hush of the sil-ver dew, Ro-ses are flow'r-ing in Pi-car-dy, but there's nev-er a rose like you! And the ro-ses will die with the sum-mer-time, and our roads may be far a-part, But there's one rose that dies not in Pi-car-dy! 'Tis the rose that I keep in my heart!

Copyright © 1916 by Chappell & Co., Ltd., London
Copyright Renewed

Used by HAL LEONARD PUBLISHING CORPORATION, Winona, MN 55987 by Permission
Made in U.S.A.   International Copyright Secured   All Rights Reserved

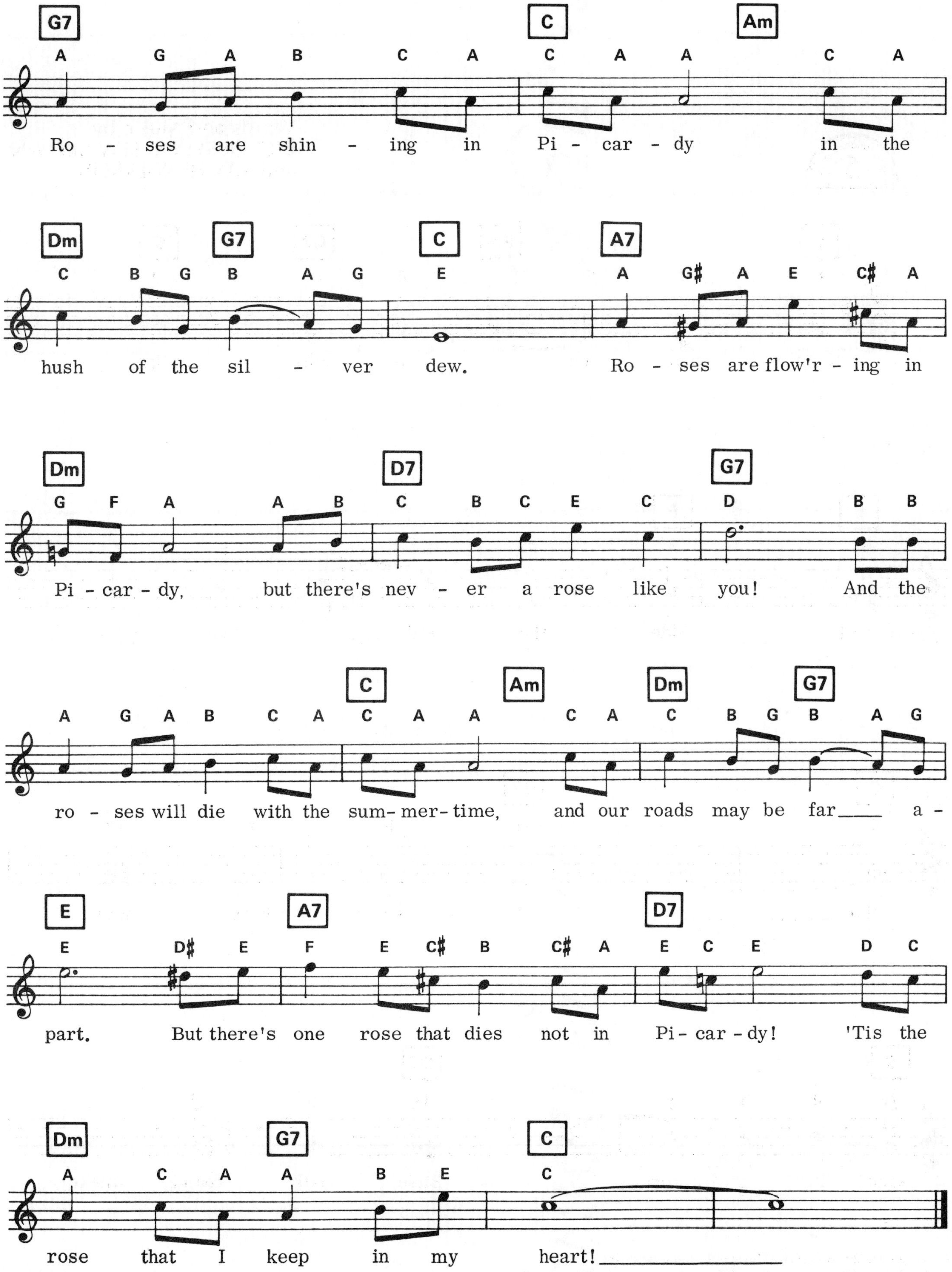
G7 C Am
A G A B C A C A A C A
Ro - ses are shin - ing in Pi - car - dy in the
Dm G7 C A7
C B G B A G E A G# A E C# A
hush of the sil - ver dew. Ro - ses are flow'r - ing in
Dm D7 G7
G F A A B C B C E C D B B
Pi - car - dy, but there's nev - er a rose like you! And the
C Am Dm G7
A G A B C A C A A C A C B G B A G
ro - ses will die with the sum - mer - time, and our roads may be far a -
E A7 D7
E D# E F E C# B C# A E C E D C
part. But there's one rose that dies not in Pi - car - dy! 'Tis the
Dm G7 C
A C A A B E C
rose that I keep in my heart!

SUNNY SIDE UP

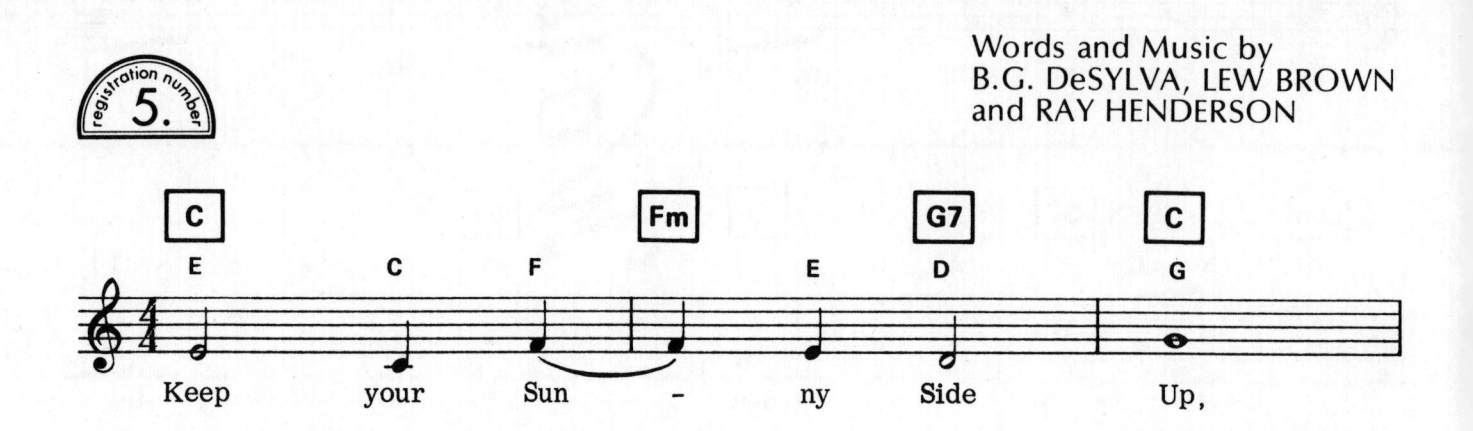

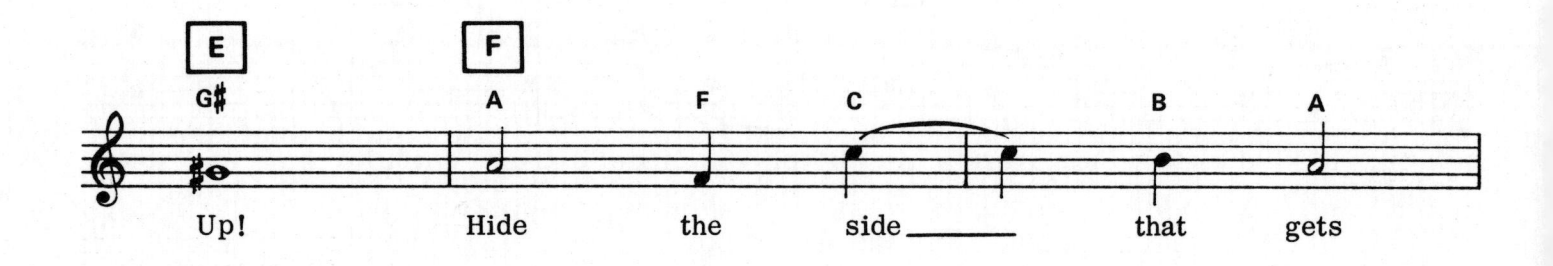

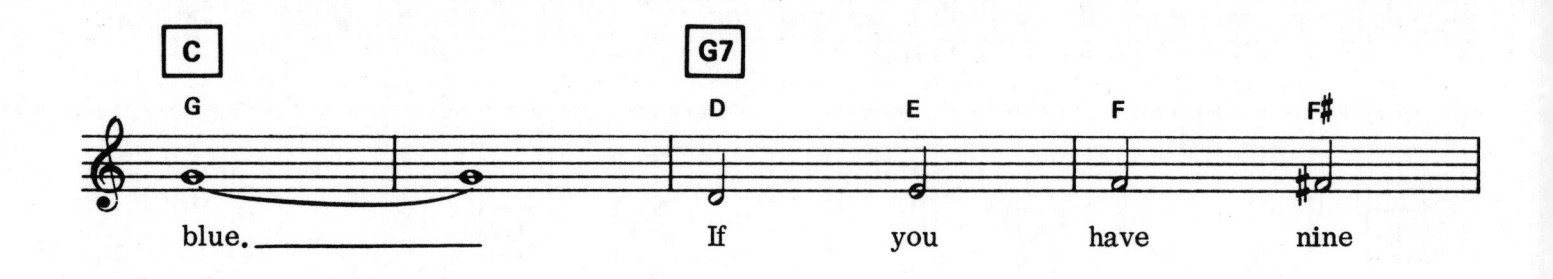

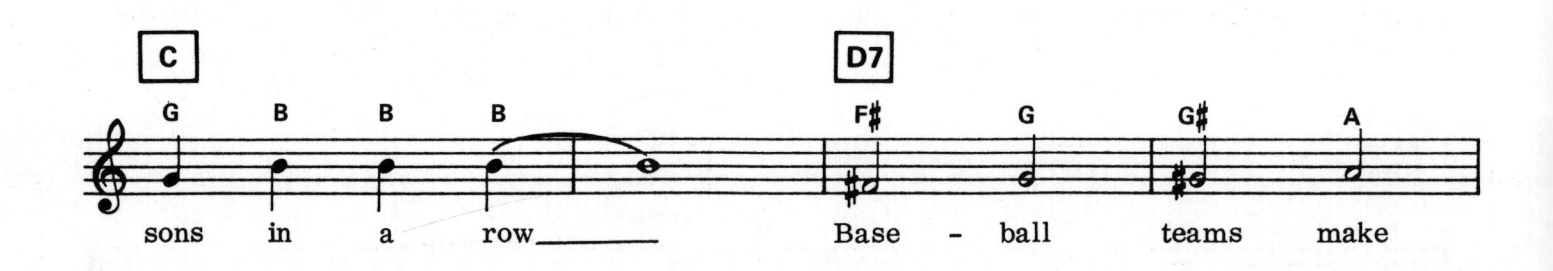

Words and Music by
B.G. DeSYLVA, LEW BROWN
and RAY HENDERSON

registration number 5.

Keep your Sun - ny Side Up, Up! Hide the side that gets blue. If you have nine sons in a row Base - ball teams make

Copyright © 1929 by DeSylva, Brown & Henderson, Inc.
Copyright Renewed, assigned to Chappell & Co., Inc.
Published in the United States by joint agreement with Anne-Rachel Music Corporation and Chappell & Co., Inc.
Used by HAL LEONARD PUBLISHING CORPORATION, Winona, MN 55987 by Permission
Made in U.S.A.   International Copyright Secured   All Rights Reserved

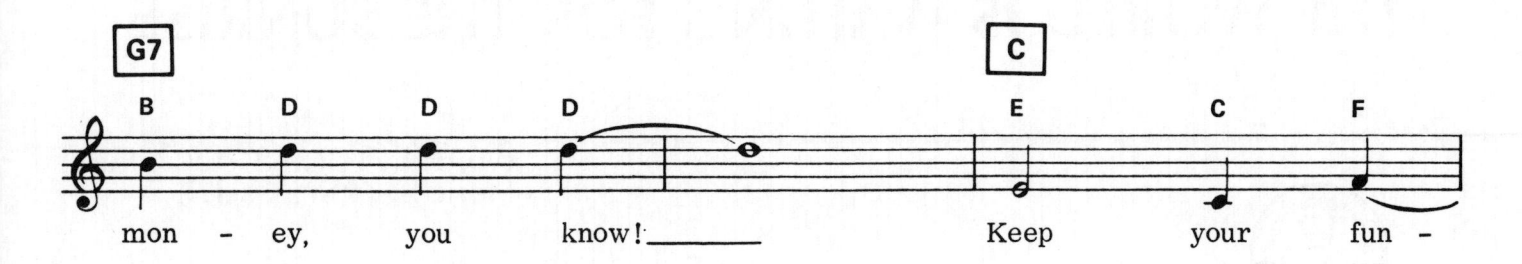

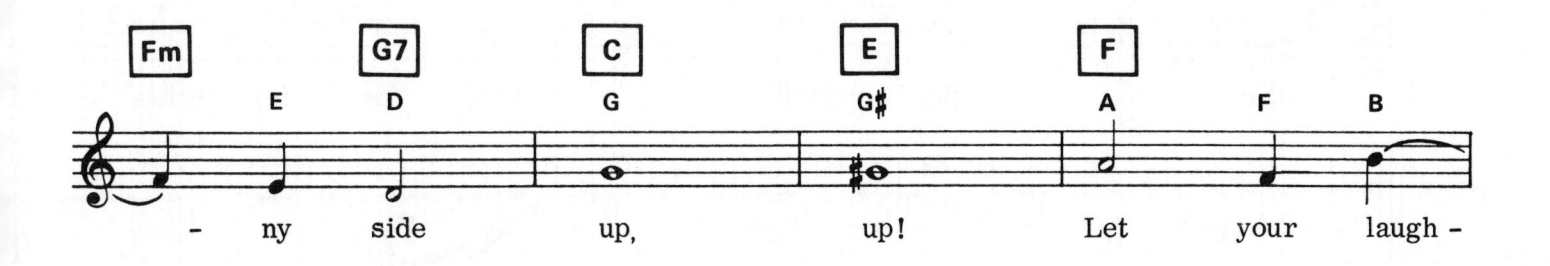

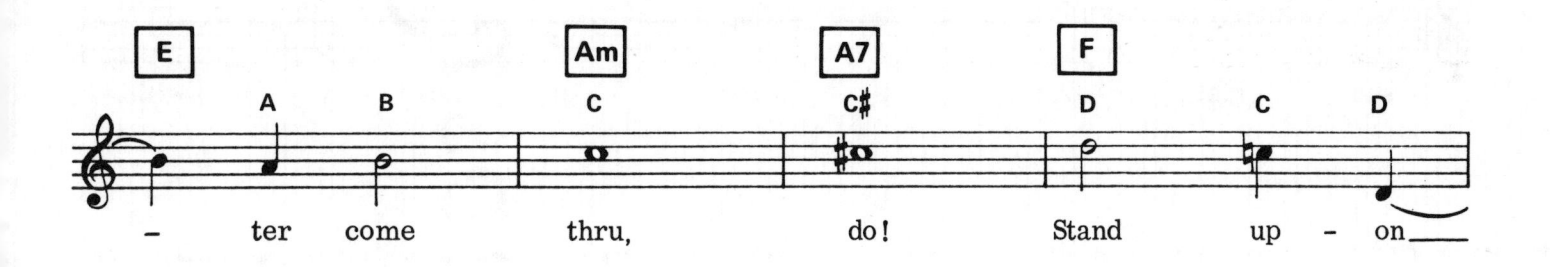

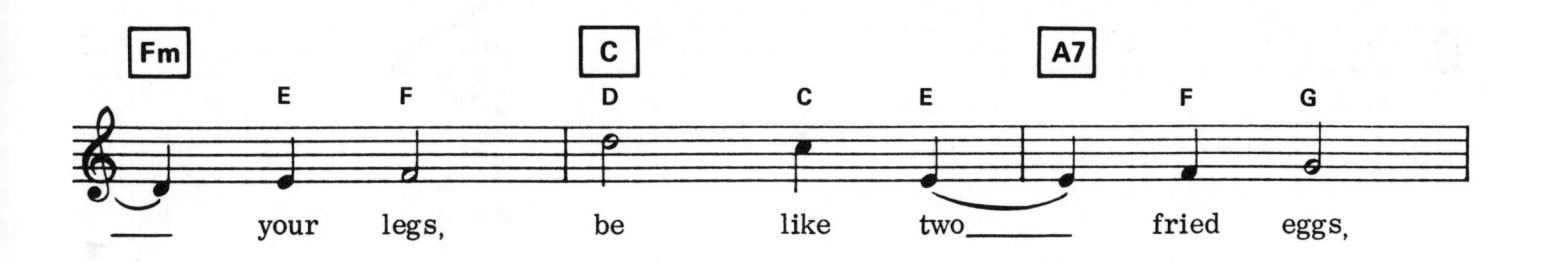

mon - ey, you know! Keep your fun - ny side up, up! Let your laugh - ter come thru, do! Stand up - on your legs, be like two fried eggs, Keep your Sun - ny Side Up!

THE WORLD IS WAITING FOR THE SUNRISE

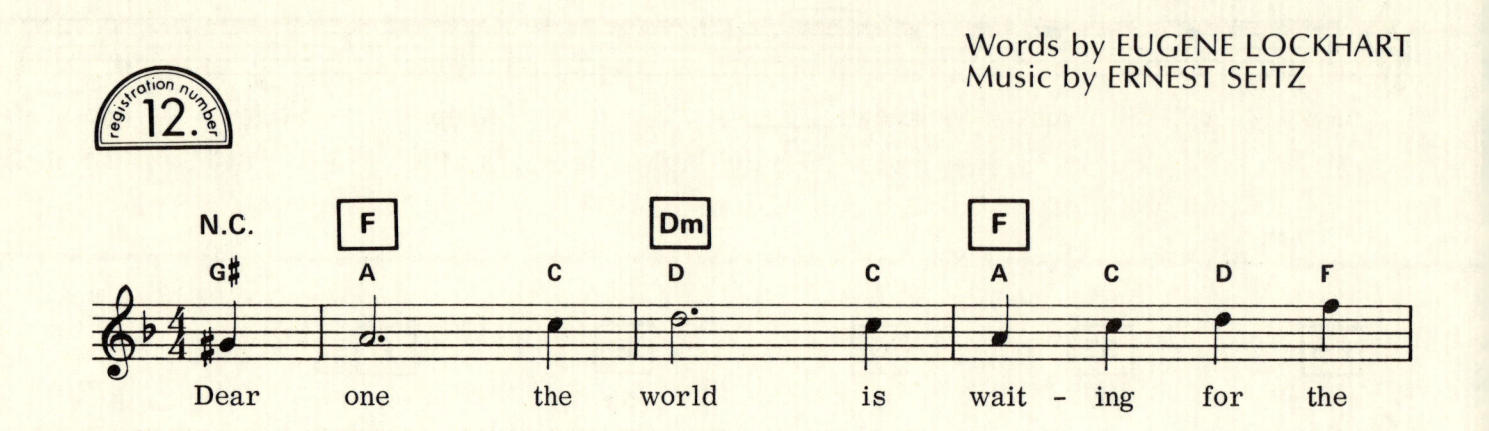

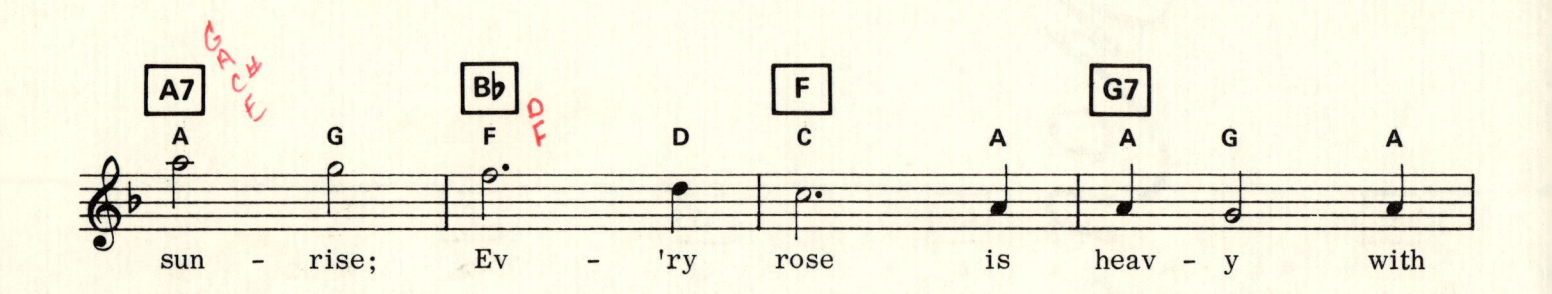

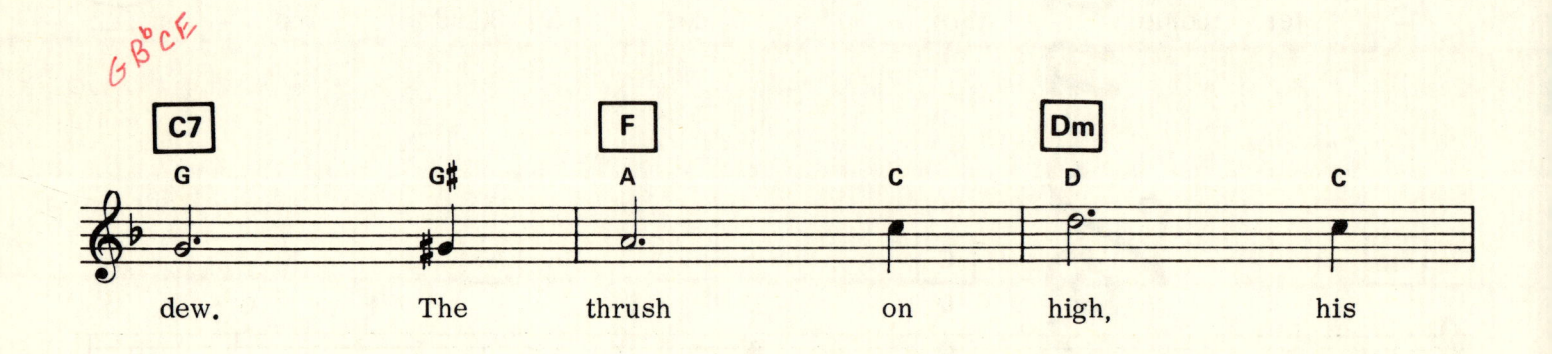

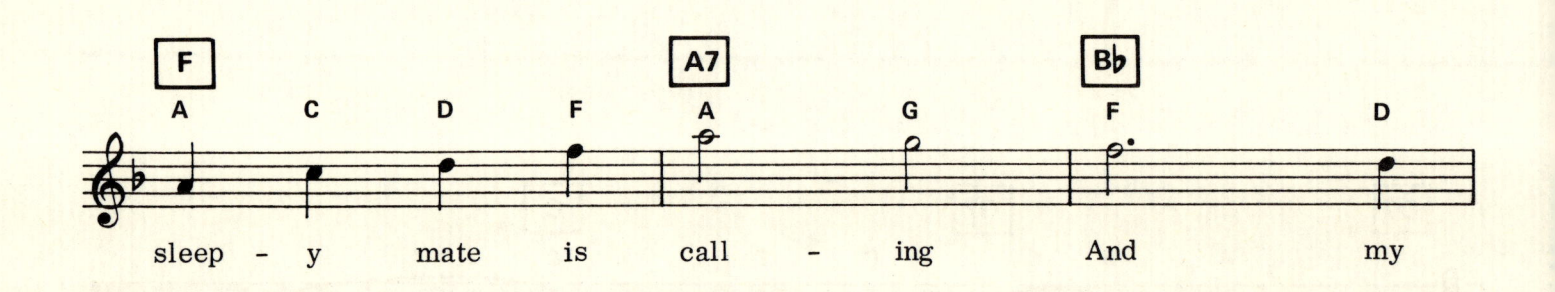

Words by EUGENE LOCKHART
Music by ERNEST SEITZ

registration number 12.

171

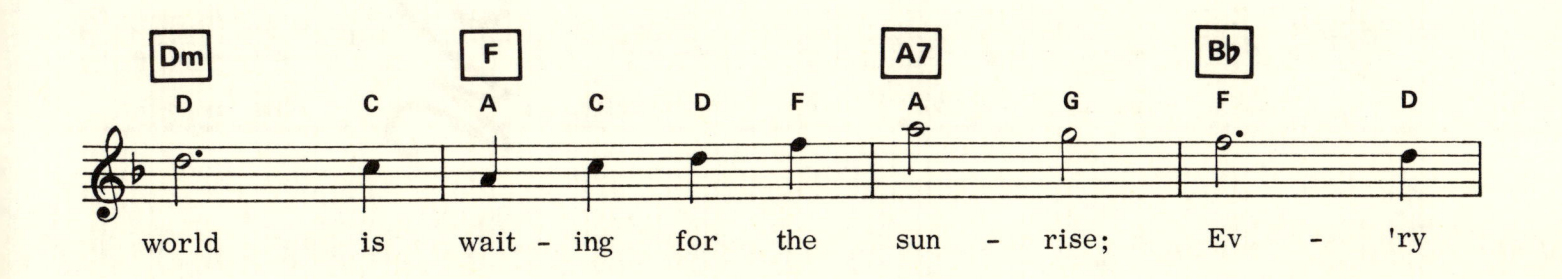

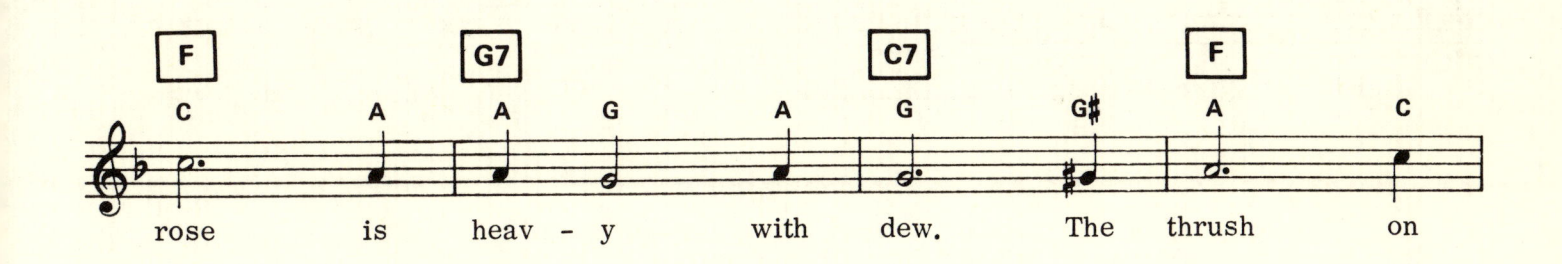

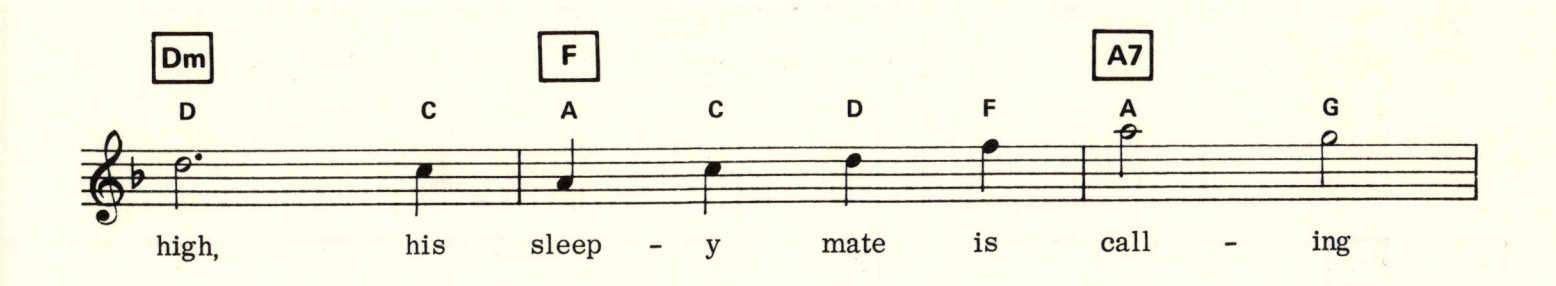

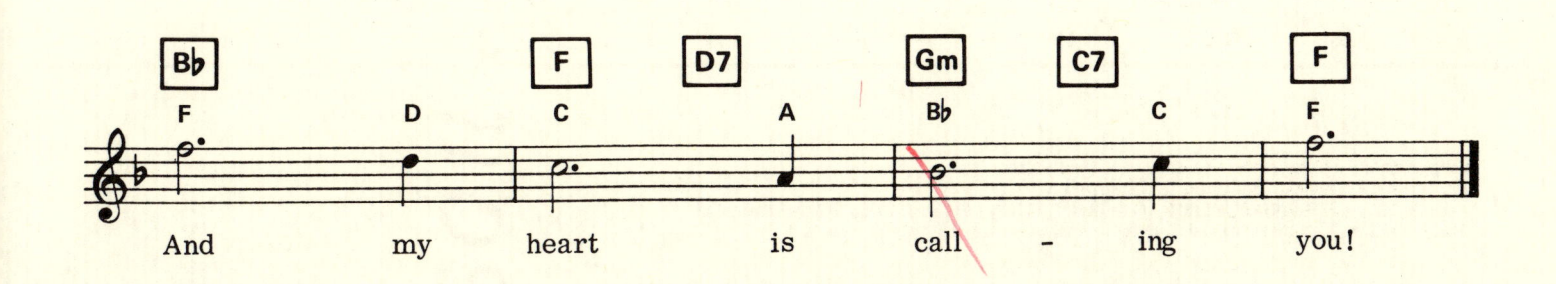

BY MYSELF

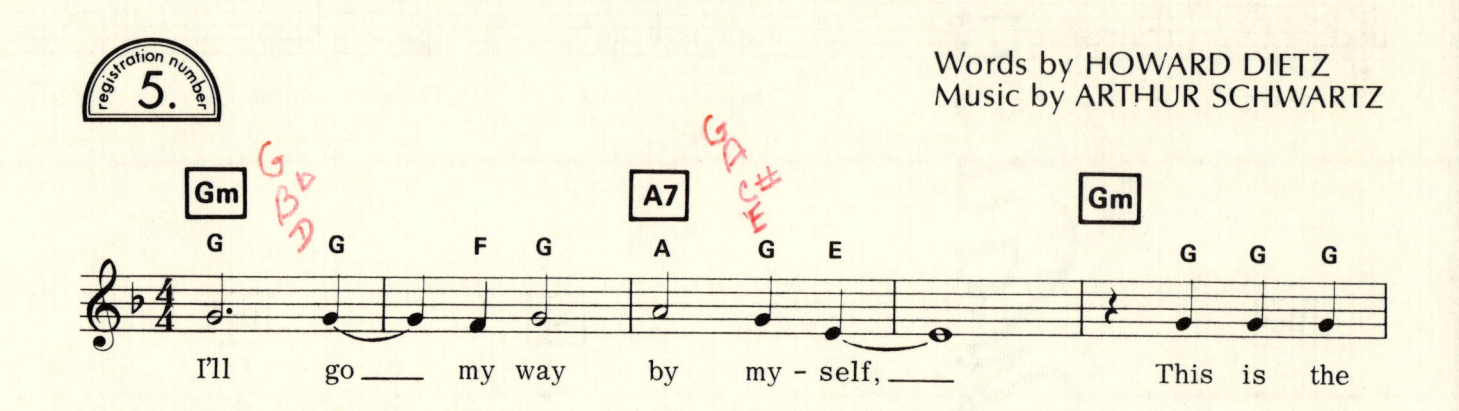

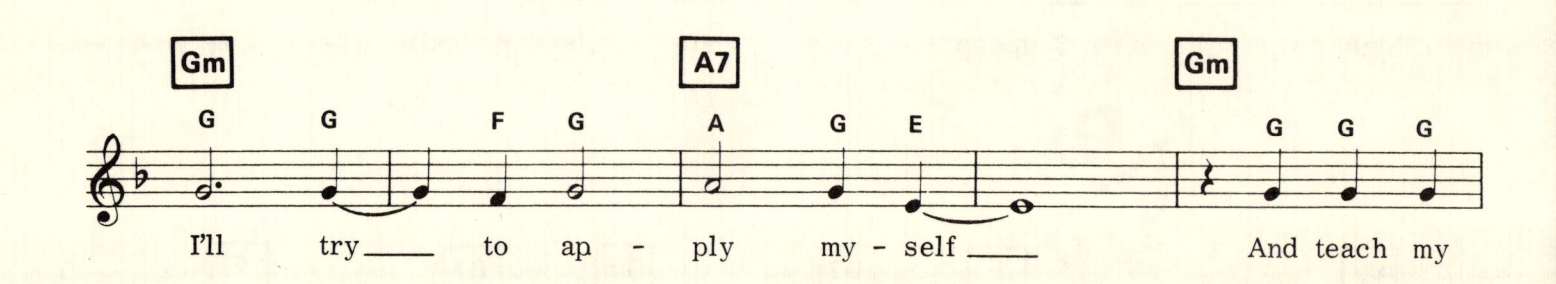

Words by HOWARD DIETZ
Music by ARTHUR SCHWARTZ

registration number 5.

Gm	A7	Gm
G G F G	A G E	G G G

I'll go my way by my-self, This is the

	A7	F
G F G A	A A G A	

end of ro-mance. I'll go my way

Dm	B♭	Gm	C7	F
C A G		B♭ G F G A		C

by my-self, Love is on-ly a dance.

Gm	A7	Gm
G G F G	A G E	G G G

I'll try to ap-ply my-self And teach my

Copyright©1937 by DeSylva, Brown & Henderson, Inc.
Copyright Renewed, assigned to Chappell & Co., Inc.
Used by HAL LEONARD PUBLISHING CORPORATION, Winona, MN 55987 by Permission
Made in U.S.A.   International Copyright Secured   All Rights Reserved

heart how to sing. _____ I'll go ____ my way

by my-self, ____ Like a bird ___ on the wing. ____

I'll face ____ the un - known, _____ I'll build a

world of my own; _____ No one knows bet-ter than

I my-self, ____ I'm by my-self ___ a - lone. ____

LOVE THY NEIGHBOR

Words by MACK GORDON
Music by HARRY REVEL

Love thy neigh-bor, Walk up and say, "How be ya! Gee! but I'm glad to see ya; Pal, how's tricks? What's new?" Love thy neigh-bor, of-fer to share his bur-den, Tell him to say the word 'n' you will see him through,___ Es-

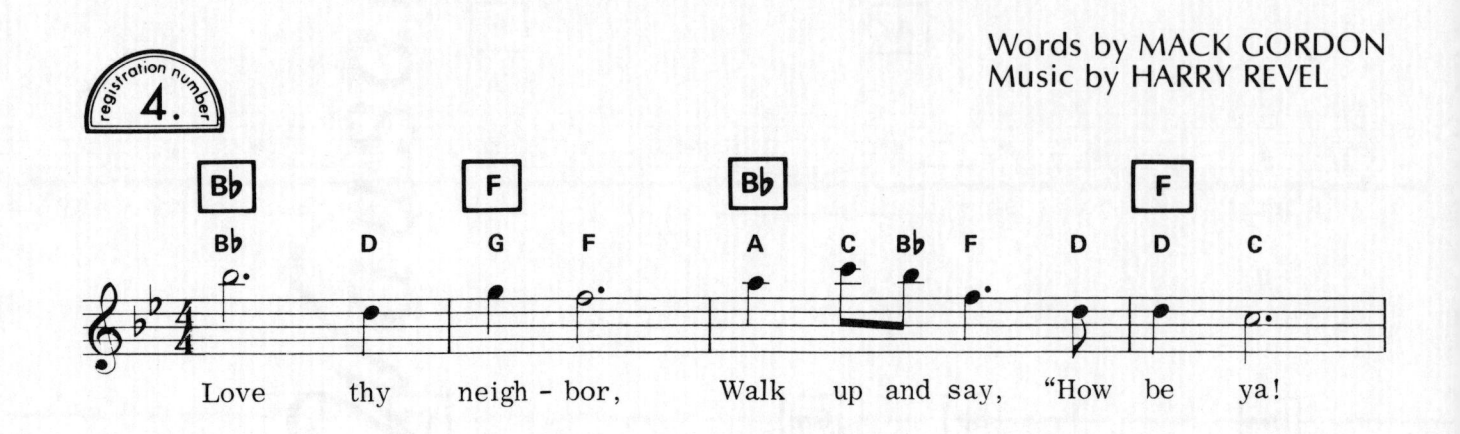

Copyright ©1934 by DeSylva, Brown & Henderson, Inc.
Copyright Renewed, assigned to Chappell & Co., Inc.
Copyright ©1968 by Chappell & Co., Inc.
Used by HAL LEONARD PUBLISHING CORPORATION, Winona, MN 55987 by Permission
Made in U.S.A.   International Copyright Secured   All Rights Reserved

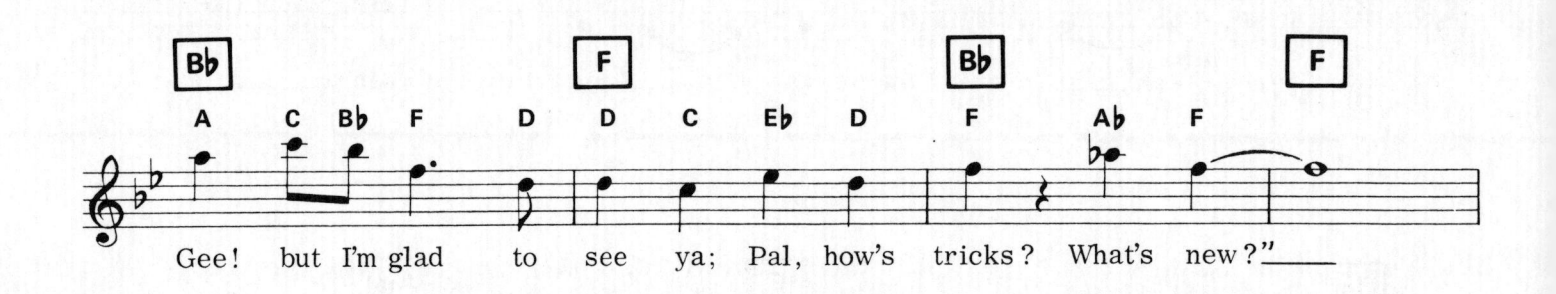

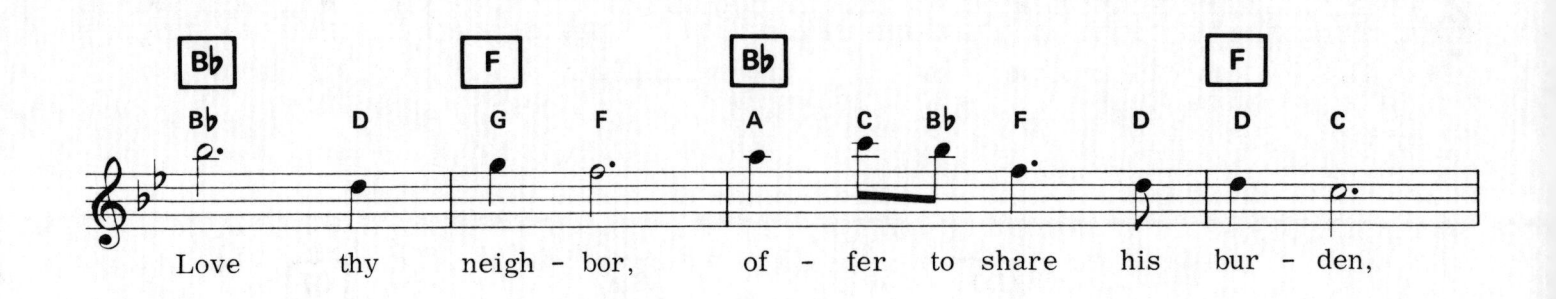

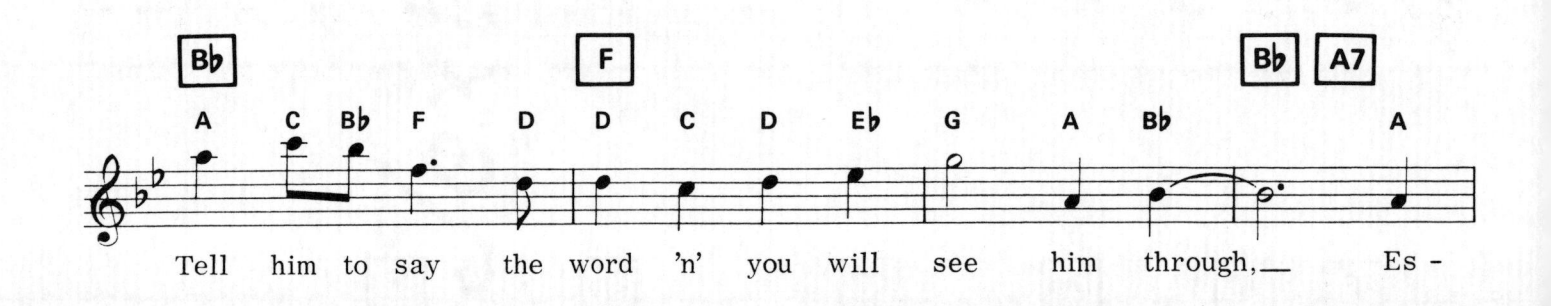

175

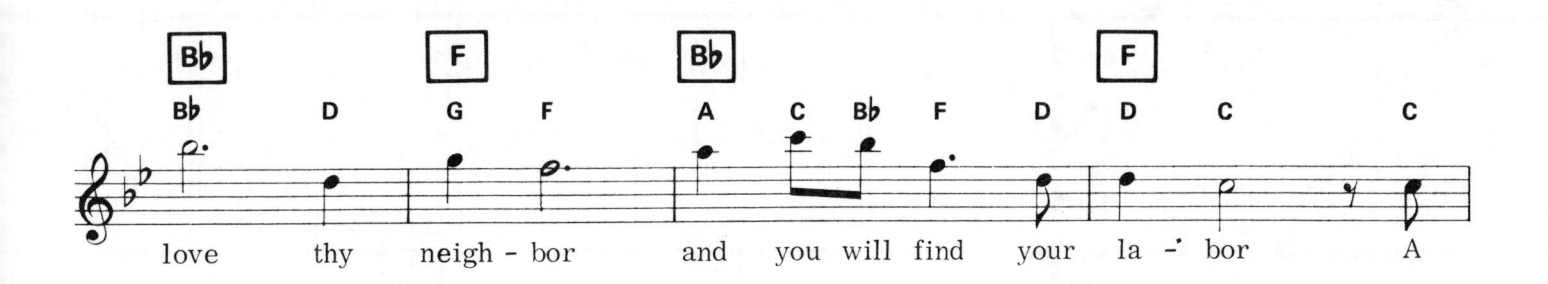

DID YOU EVER SEE A DREAM WALKING?

Words by MACK GORDON
Music by HARRY REVEL

Did you ev-er see a dream walk-ing? Well, I did!

Did you ev-er hear a dream talk-ing? Well, I did!

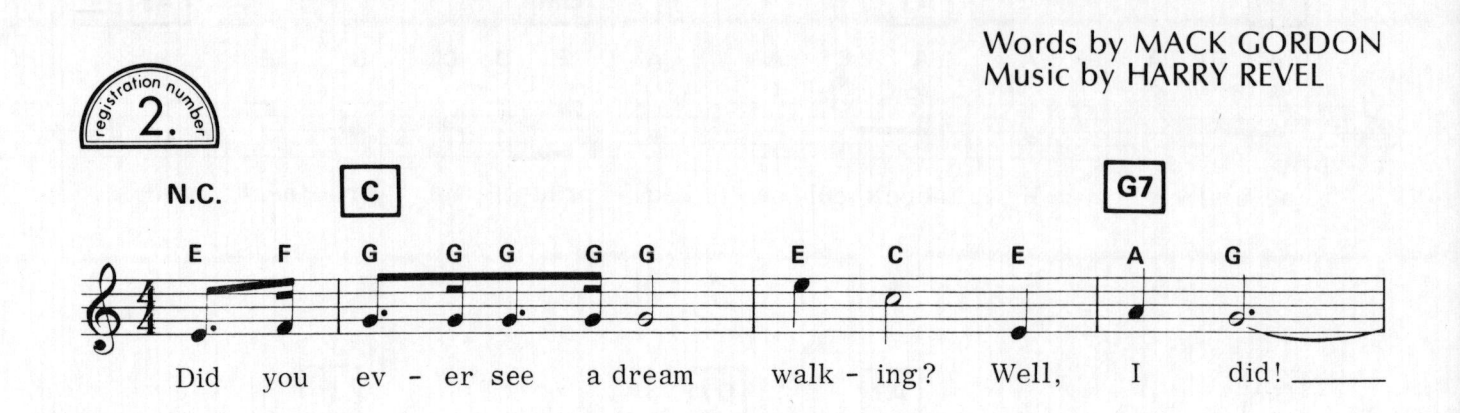

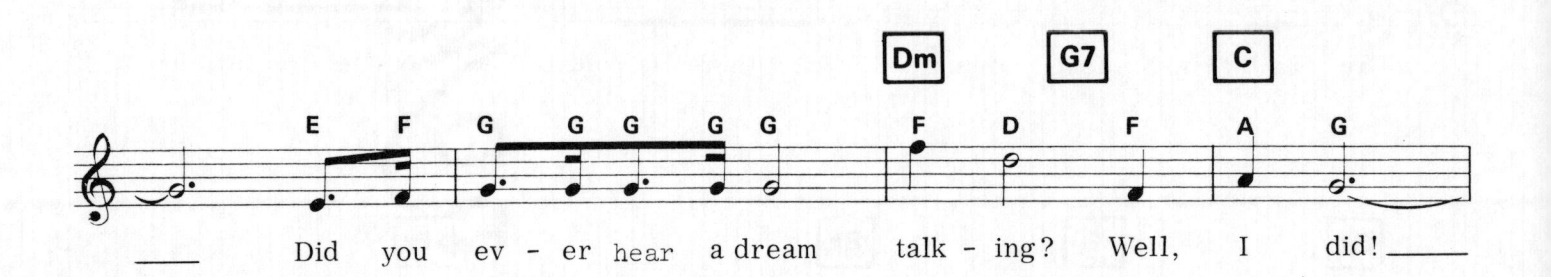

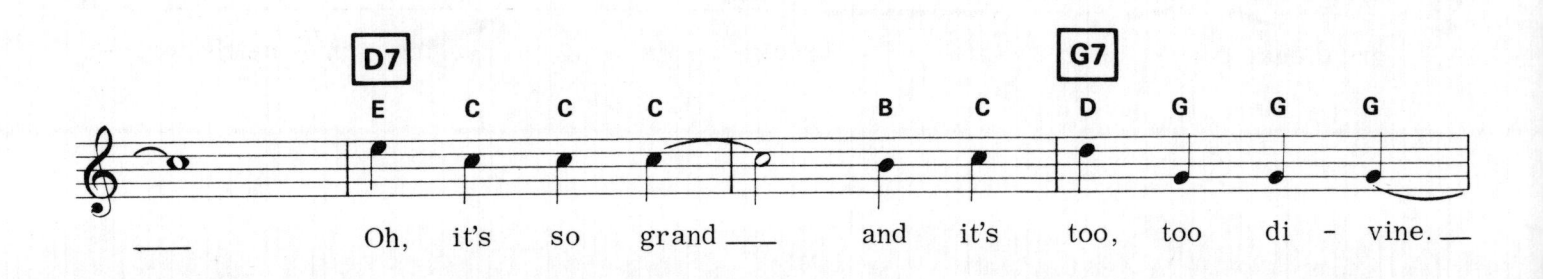

Did you ev-er have a dream thrill you with "Will you be mine?"

Oh, it's so grand and it's too, too di-vine.

Copyright©1933 by DeSylva, Brown & Henderson, Inc.
Copyright Renewed, assigned to Chappell & Co., Inc.
Copyright©1960 by Chappell & Co., Inc.
Used by HAL LEONARD PUBLISHING CORPORATION, Winona, MN 55987 by Permission
Made in U.S.A.   International Copyright Secured   All Rights Reserved

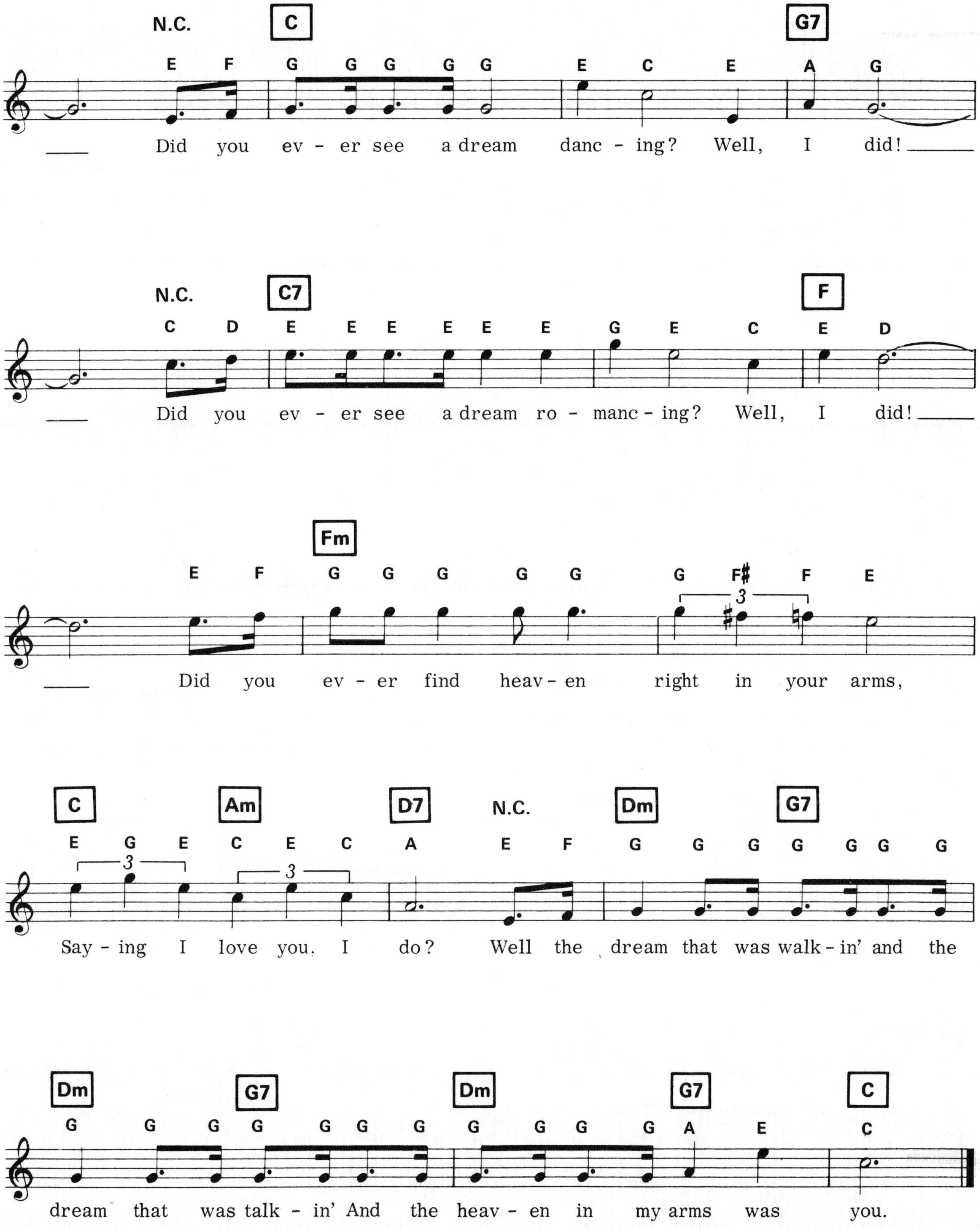
N.C. C G7
E F G G G G G E C E A G
Did you ev - er see a dream danc - ing? Well, I did!
N.C. C7 F
C D E E E E E E G E C E D
Did you ev - er see a dream ro - manc - ing? Well, I did!
Fm
E F G G G G G G F♯ F E
3
Did you ev - er find heav - en right in your arms,
C Am D7 N.C. Dm G7
E G E C E C A E F G G G G G G G
3 3
Say - ing I love you, I do? Well the dream that was walk - in' and the
Dm G7 Dm G7 C
G G G G G G G G G G G A E C
dream that was talk - in' And the heav - en in my arms was you.

PARIS IN THE SPRING

Words by MACK GORDON
Music by HARRY REVEL

Par-is in the spring, Mm, ___ mm, ___ Love is in the air, Mm, ___ mm, ___ Life's a love af-fair And ev-'ry pair of arms a ren-dez-vous For two. Par-is in the spring, Mm, ___ mm, ___ Hearts be-gin to dance, Mm, ___ mm, ___ And in ev-'ry glance you'll find an in-vi-ta-tion to ro-

Copyright © 1935 by DeSylva, Brown & Henderson, Inc.
Copyright Renewed, assigned to Chappell & Co., Inc.
Copyright © 1968 by Chappell & Co., Inc.
Used by HAL LEONARD PUBLISHING CORPORATION, Winona, MN 55987 by Permission
Made in U.S.A.   International Copyright Secured   All Rights Reserved

mance. You must fall. You simply can't evade love. The moon is there to aid love, Find someone you can call your own. You're to blame if you're alone. Mm, It's grand, it's new, Mm, It's me, it's you; Ev-'ry beating heart becomes a part of Paris in the spring.

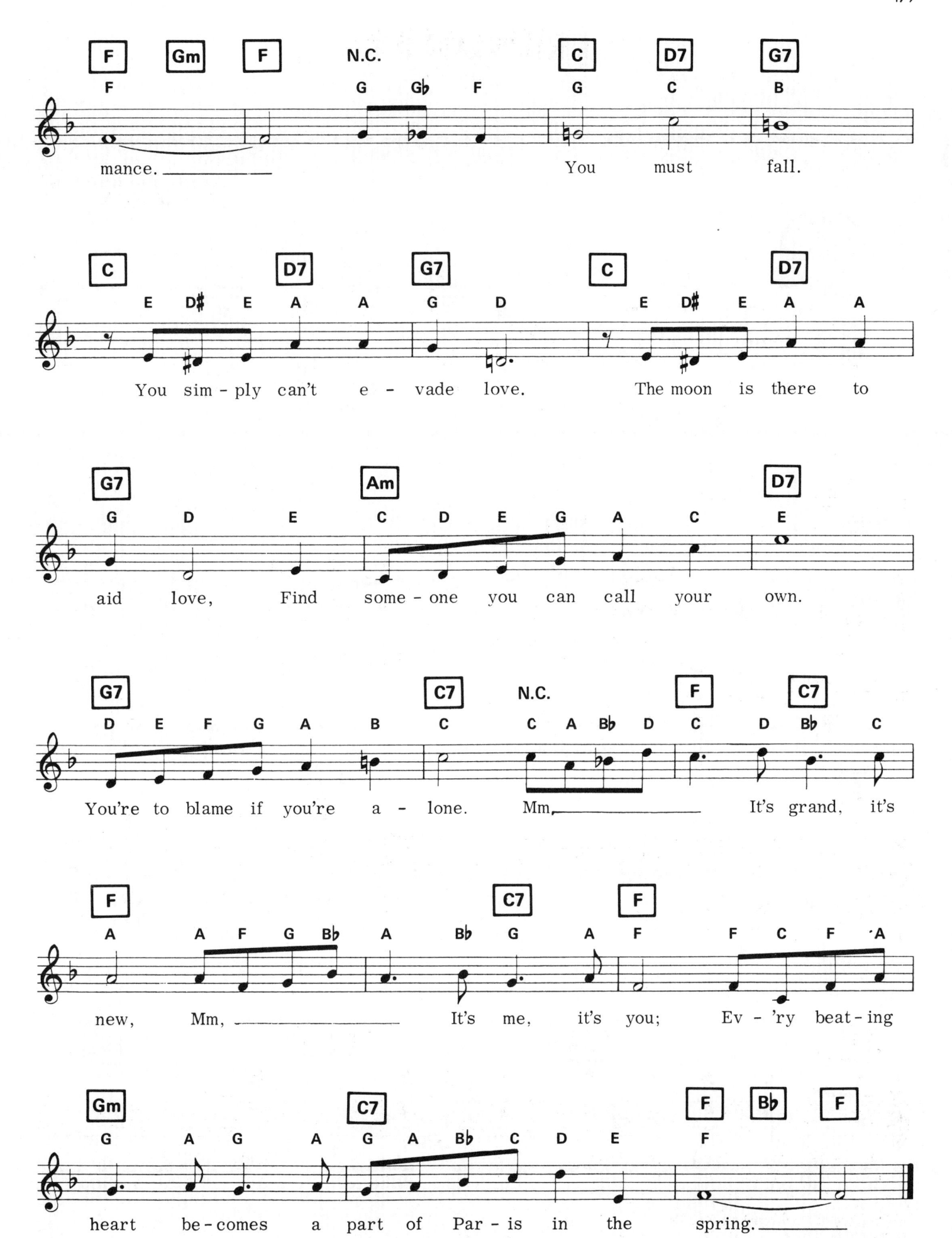

FRIENDSHIP

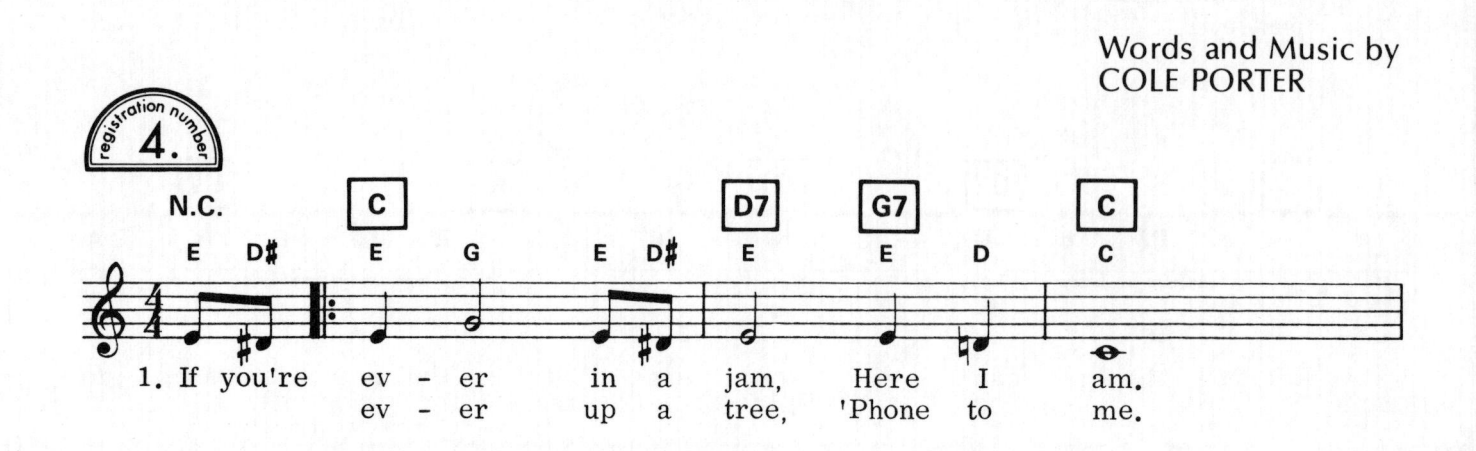

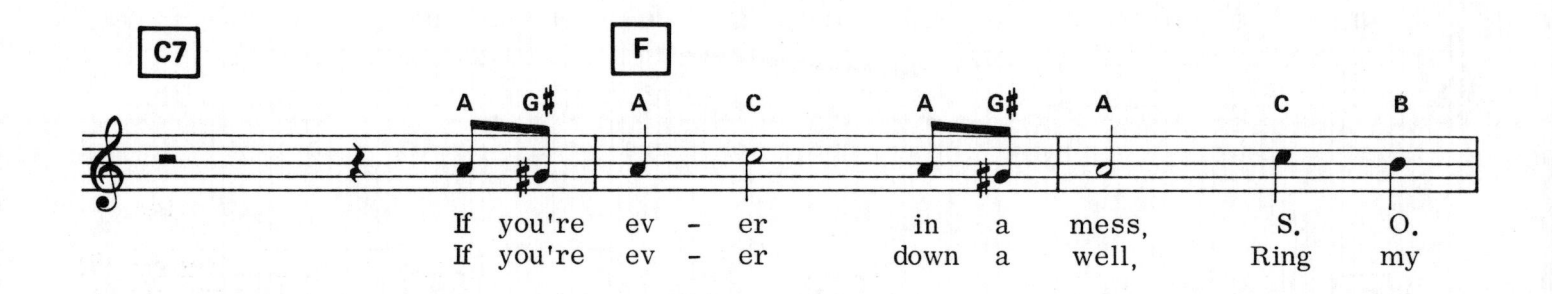

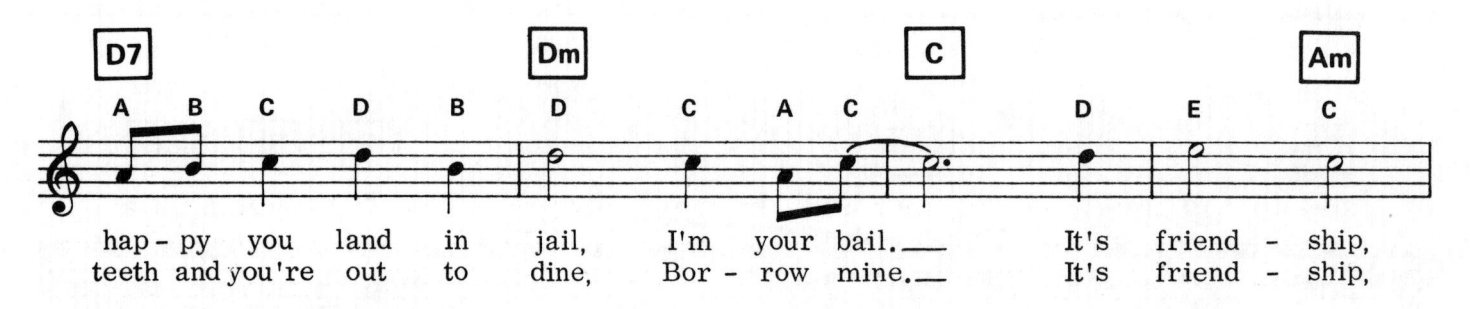

Words and Music by
COLE PORTER

1. If you're ev-er in a jam, Here I am.
   ev-er up a tree, 'Phone to me.

If you're ev-er in a mess, S. O.
If you're ev-er down a well, Ring my

S.
bell. If you ev-er feel so
If you ev-er lose your

hap-py you land in jail, I'm your bail.__ It's friend-ship,
teeth and you're out to dine, Bor-row mine.__ It's friend-ship,

Copyright ©1939 by Chappell & Co., Inc.
Copyright Renewed
Used by HAL LEONARD PUBLISHING CORPORATION, Winona, MN 55987 by Permission
Made in U.S.A.   International Copyright Secured   All Rights Reserved

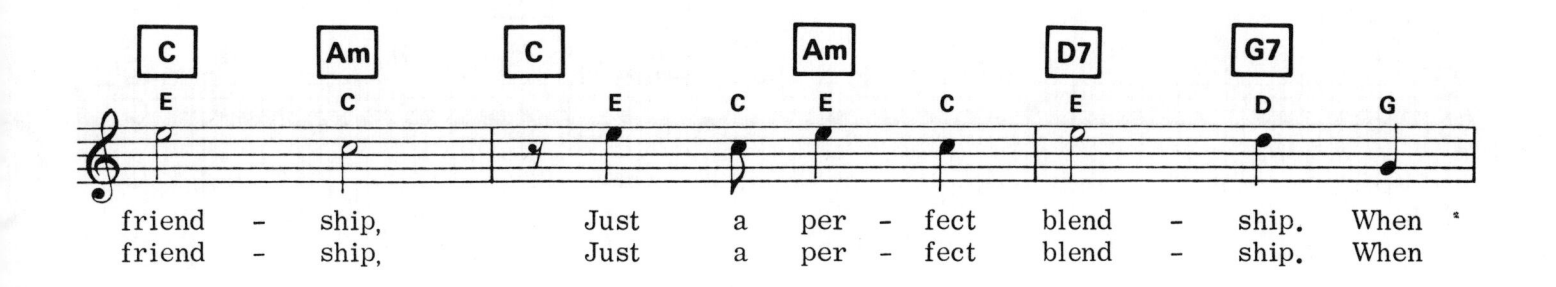

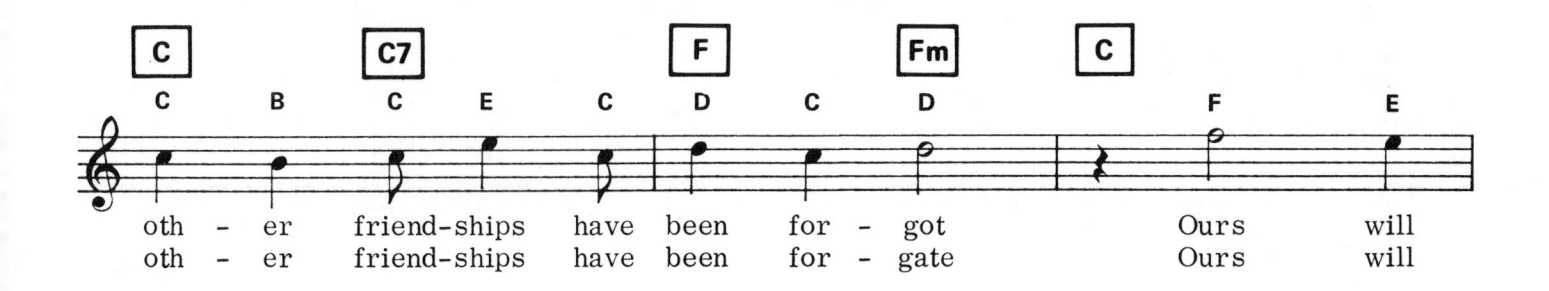

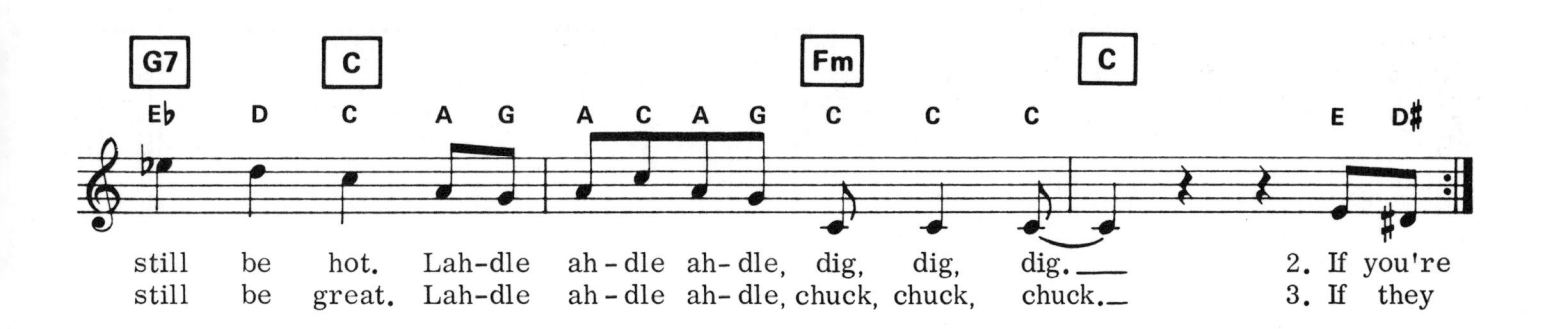

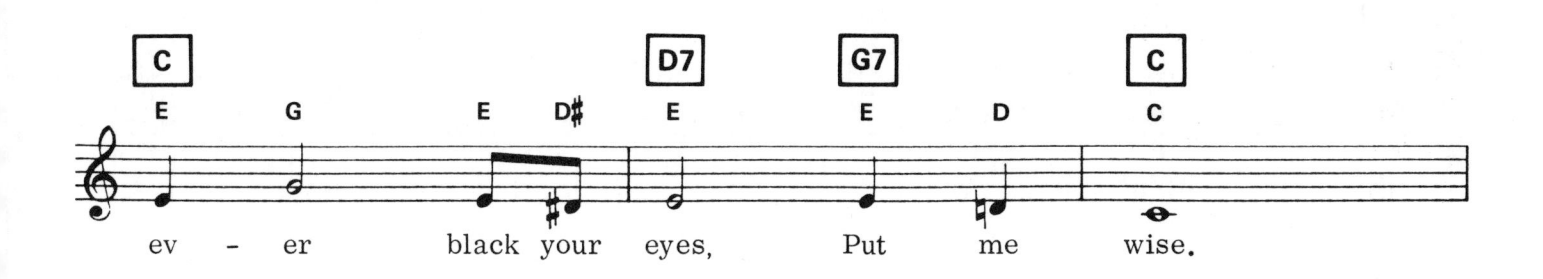

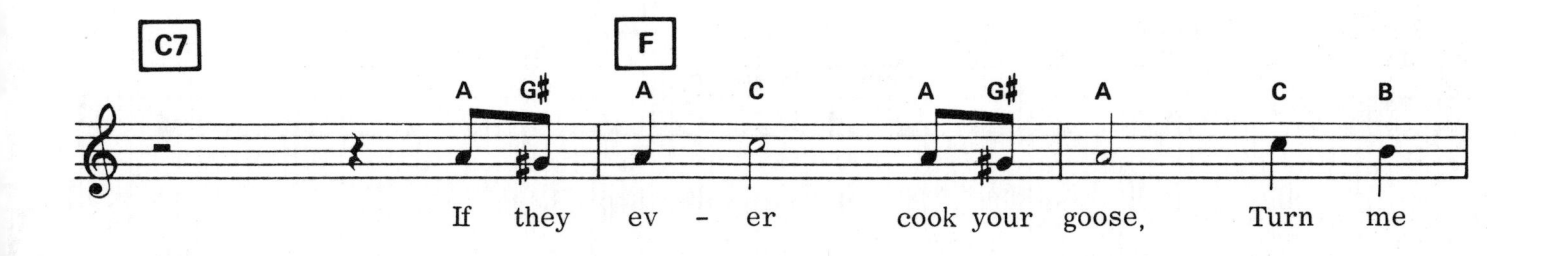

friend - ship, Just a per - fect blend - ship. When
friend - ship, Just a per - fect blend - ship. When

oth - er friend-ships have been for - got Ours will
oth - er friend-ships have been for - gate Ours will

still be hot. Lah-dle ah-dle ah-dle, dig, dig, dig. 2. If you're
still be great. Lah-dle ah-dle ah-dle, chuck, chuck, chuck. 3. If they

ev - er black your eyes, Put me wise.

If they ev - er cook your goose, Turn me

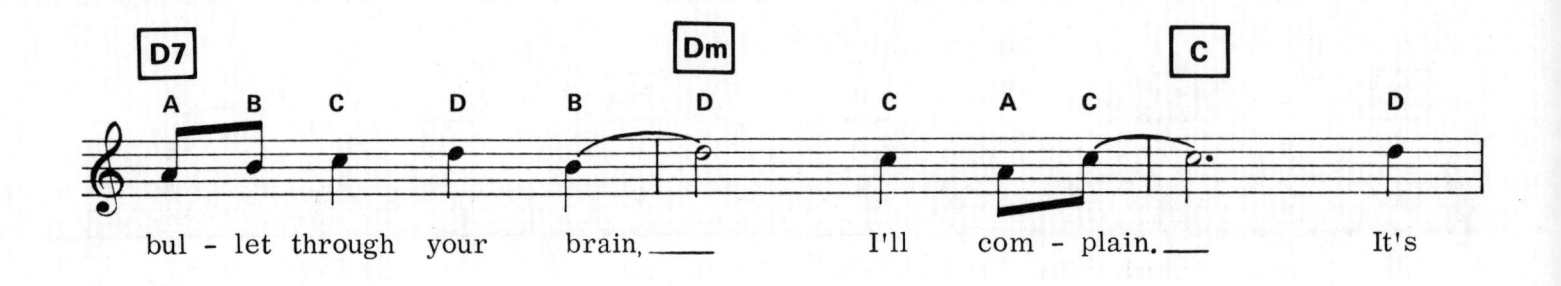

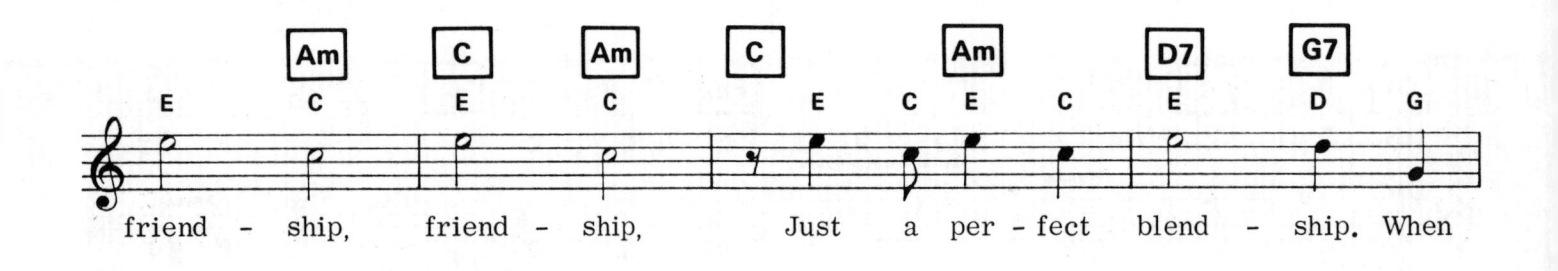

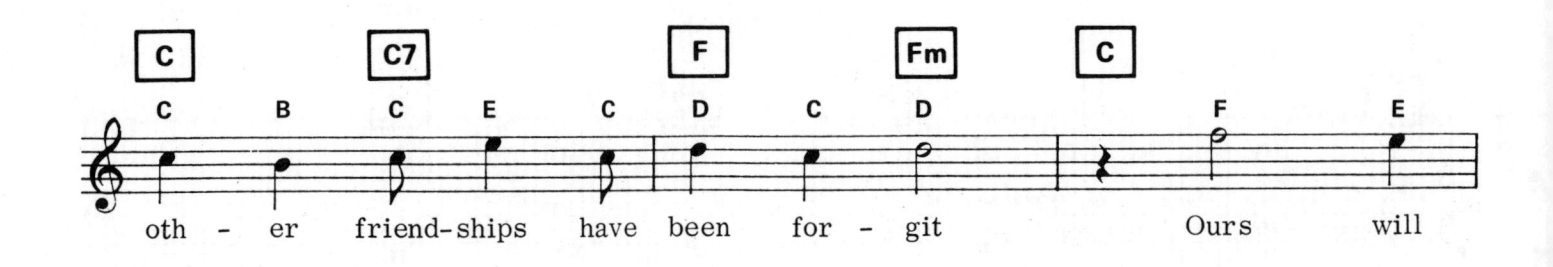

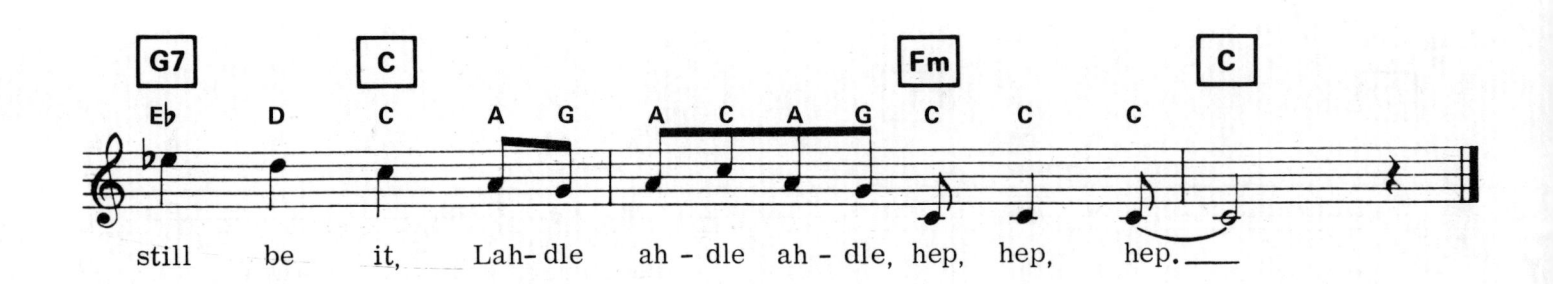

loose. If they ev-er put a bul-let through your brain, I'll com-plain. It's friend-ship, friend-ship, Just a per-fect blend-ship. When oth-er friend-ships have been for-git Ours will still be it, Lah-dle ah-dle ah-dle, hep, hep, hep.

THE BEST THINGS IN LIFE ARE FREE

registration number 4.

Words and Music by
B.G. DeSYLVA, LEW BROWN
and RAY HENDERSON

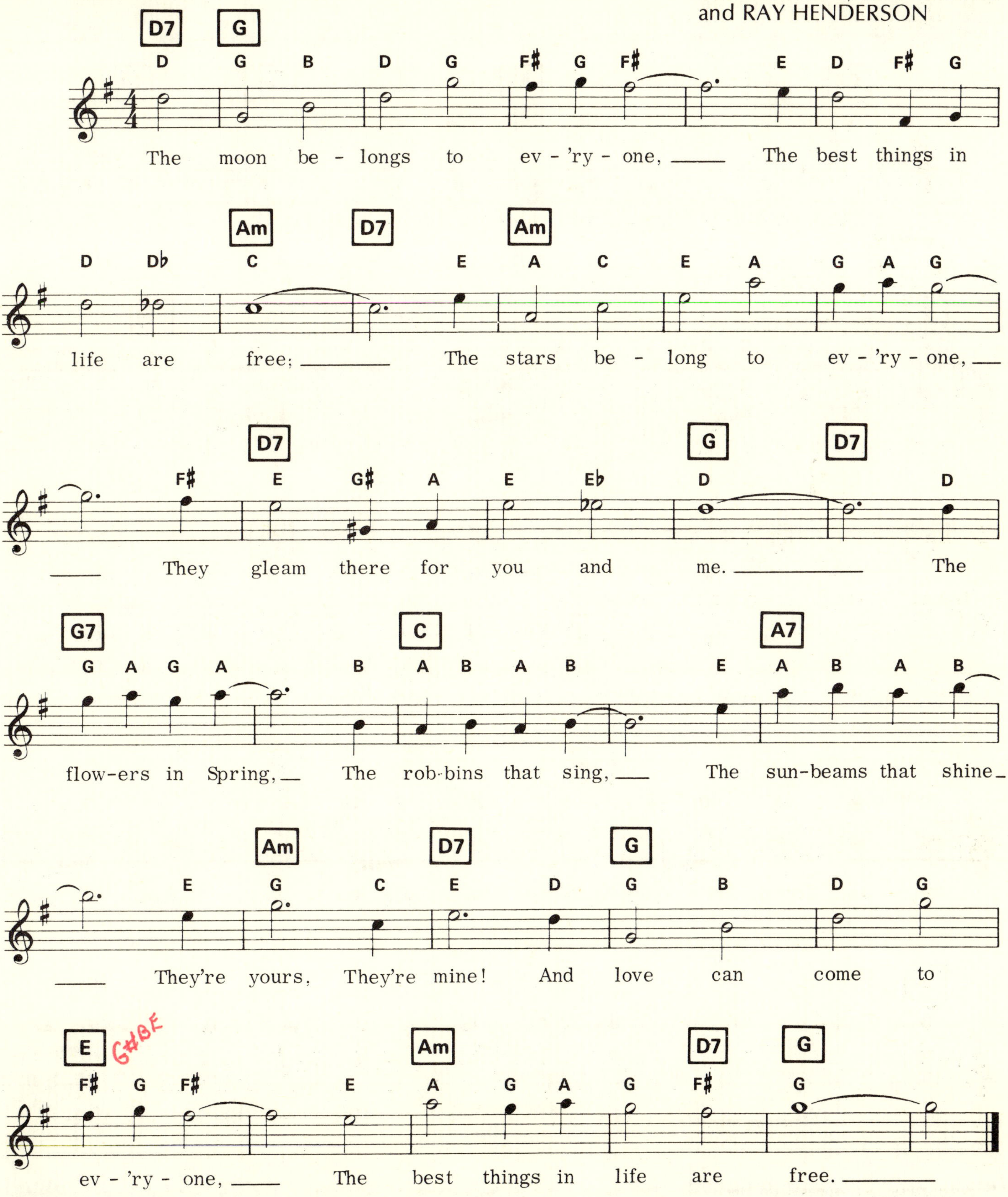

IT'S DE-LOVELY

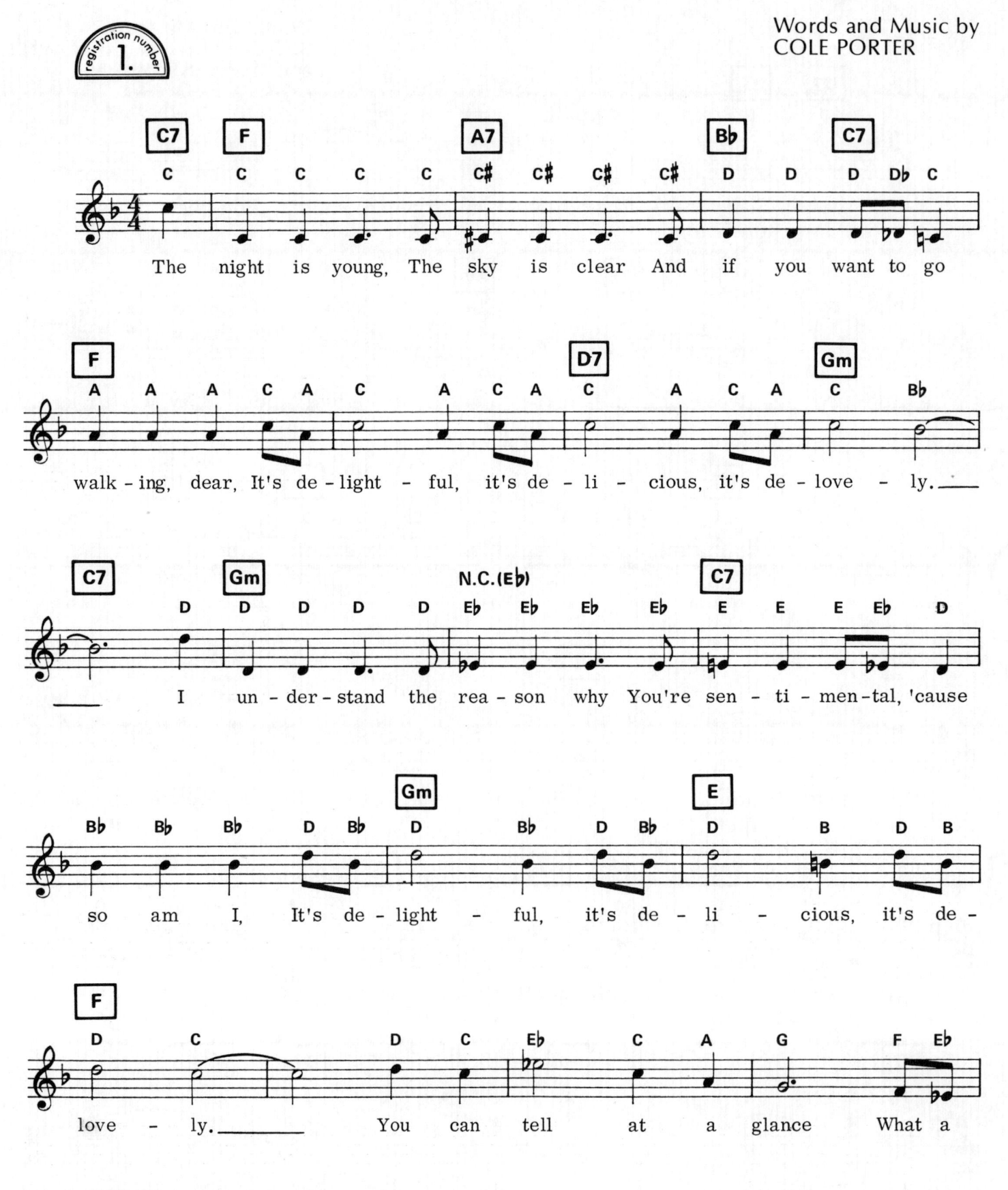

Words and Music by
COLE PORTER

The night is young, The sky is clear And if you want to go walking, dear, It's de-light-ful, it's de-li-cious, it's de-love-ly. I un-der-stand the rea-son why You're sen-ti-men-tal, 'cause so am I, It's de-light-ful, it's de-li-cious, it's de-love-ly. You can tell at a glance What a

Copyright © 1936 by Chappell & Co., Inc.
Copyright Renewed
Used by HAL LEONARD PUBLISHING CORPORATION, Winona, MN 55987 by Permission
Made in U.S.A.   International Copyright Secured   All Rights Reserved

Bb
N.C. (Eb)
D Eb E F G Bb D C Bb Db Bb G F
swell night this is for ro - mance,_ You can hear dear Moth - er
C7
Db Bb G F Db C C C C C C
Na - ture mur - mur - ing low, "Let your - self go." So
F A7 Bb C7
C C C C C# C# C# C# D D D Db C
please be sweet, my chick - a - dee, And when I kiss you, just
F Am
A A A C A C A C A C A C A
say to me "It's de - light - ful, it's de - li - cious, It's de -
D7 Gm
C C A C A C C A C A C A C A C A
lec - ta - ble, it's de - lir - i - ous, It's di - lem - ma, it's_ de - li - mit,
C7 F
C A C D C D F F
It's de - luxe, it's de - love - ly."

MY HEART BELONGS TO DADDY

Words and Music by
COLE PORTER

While tear-ing off___ A game of golf___ I may make a play for the cad-dy;___ But when I do___ I don't fol-low through 'Cause my heart be-longs___ to Dad-dy.___ If I in-vite___ A boy some night___ To dine on my fine fin-nan had-die,___ I just a-dore___ His ask-ing for more,___ But my

Copyright © 1938 by Chappell & Co., Inc.
Copyright Renewed
Used by HAL LEONARD PUBLISHING CORPORATION, Winona, MN 55987 by Permission
Made in U.S.A. International Copyright Secured All Rights Reserved

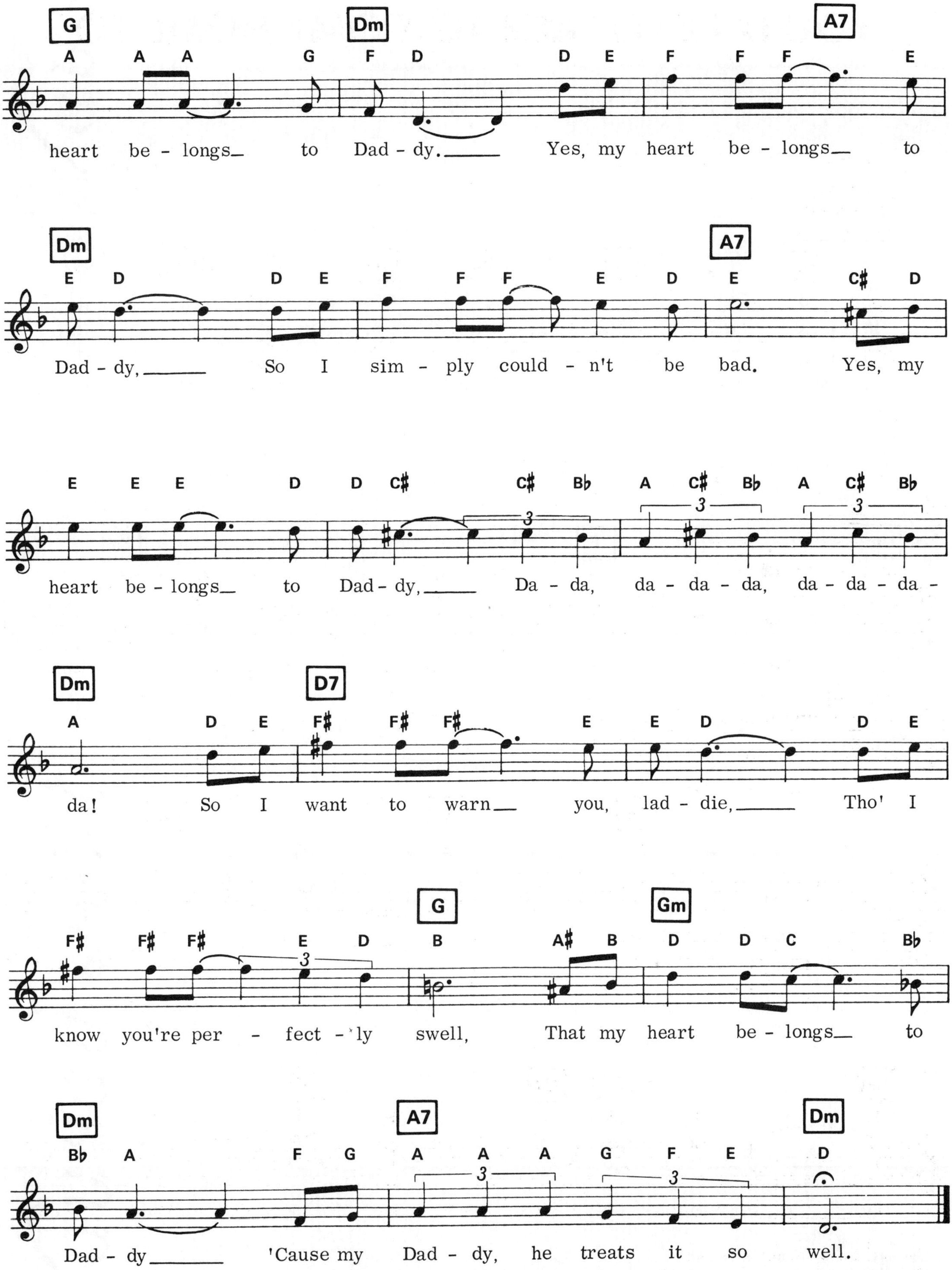
G Dm A7
A A A G F D D E F F F E
heart be - longs to Dad - dy. Yes, my heart be - longs to
Dm A7
E D D E F F F E D E C♯ D
Dad - dy, So I sim - ply could - n't be bad. Yes, my
E E E D D C♯ C♯ B♭ A C♯ B♭ A C♯ B♭
heart be - longs to Dad - dy, Da - da, da - da - da, da - da - da -
Dm D7
A D E F♯ F♯ F♯ E E D D E
da! So I want to warn you, lad - die, Tho' I
G Gm
F♯ F♯ F♯ E D B A♯ B D D C B♭
know you're per - fect - ly swell, That my heart be - longs to
Dm A7 Dm
B♭ A F G A A A G F E D
Dad - dy 'Cause my Dad - dy, he treats it so well.

YOU'D BE SO NICE TO COME HOME TO

Words and Music by
COLE PORTER

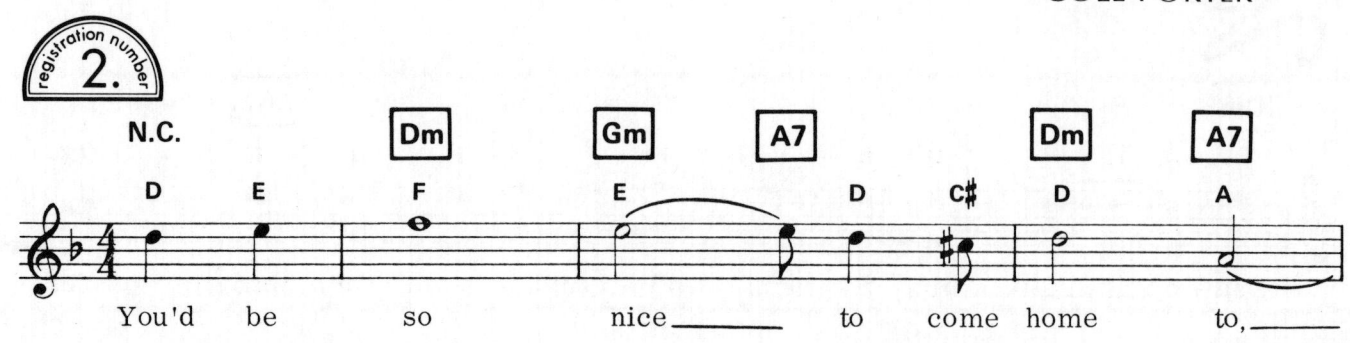

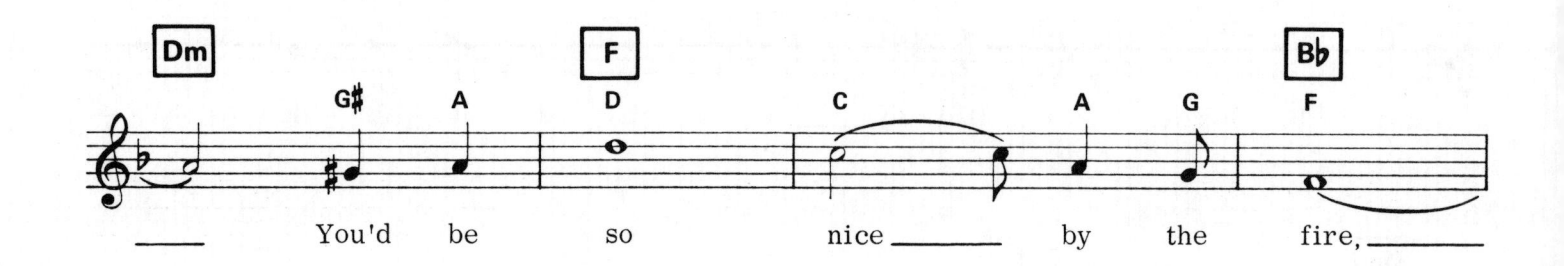

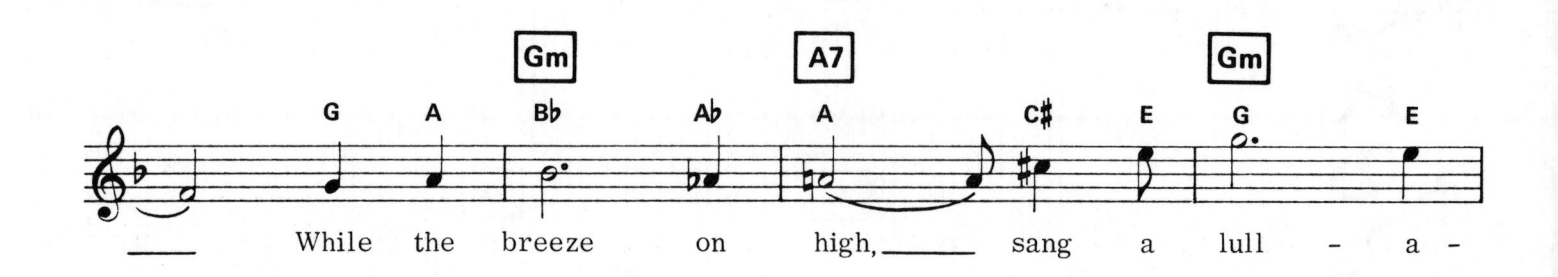

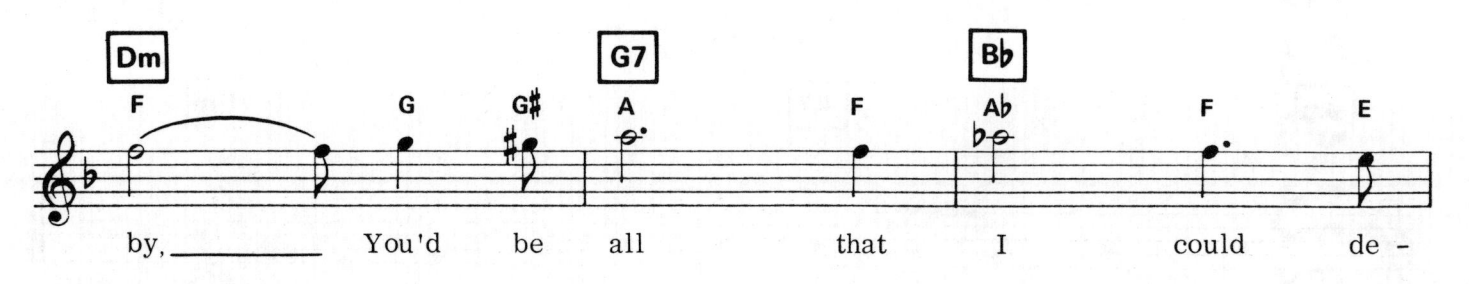

You'd be so nice to come home to,
You'd be so nice by the fire,
While the breeze on high, sang a lull-a-by, You'd be all that I could de-

Copyright © 1942 by Chappell & Co., Inc.
Copyright Renewed
Used by HAL LEONARD PUBLISHING CORPORATION, Winona, MN 55987 by Permission
Made in U.S.A.   International Copyright Secured   All Rights Reserved

sire._____ Un-der stars chilled_____ by the win-ter,_____ Un-der an Aug-ust moon Burn-ing a-bove,_____ You'd be so nice,_____ You'd be par-a-dise to come home to_____ and love._____

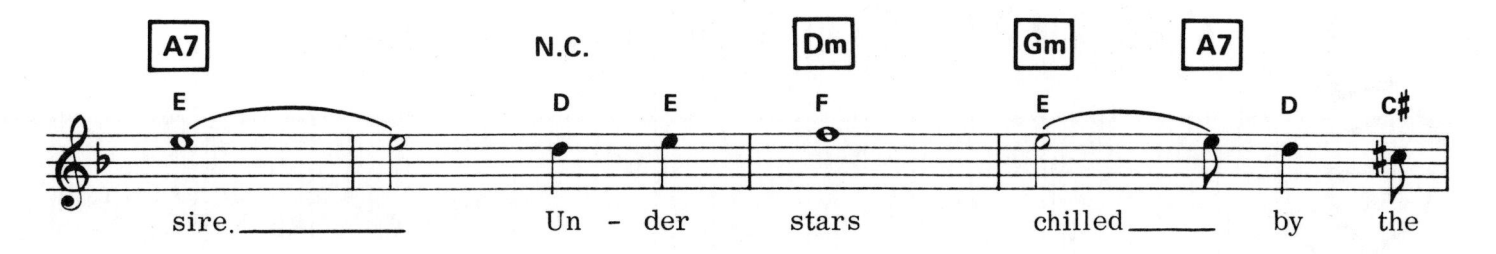

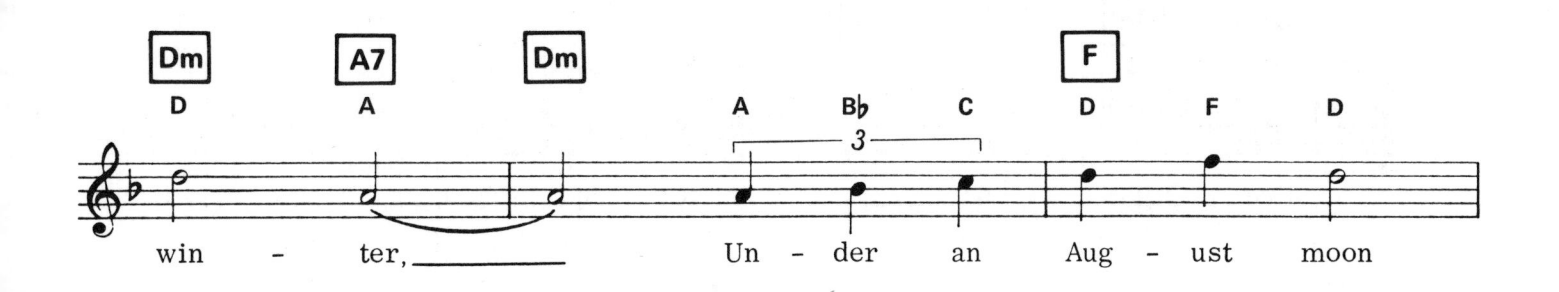

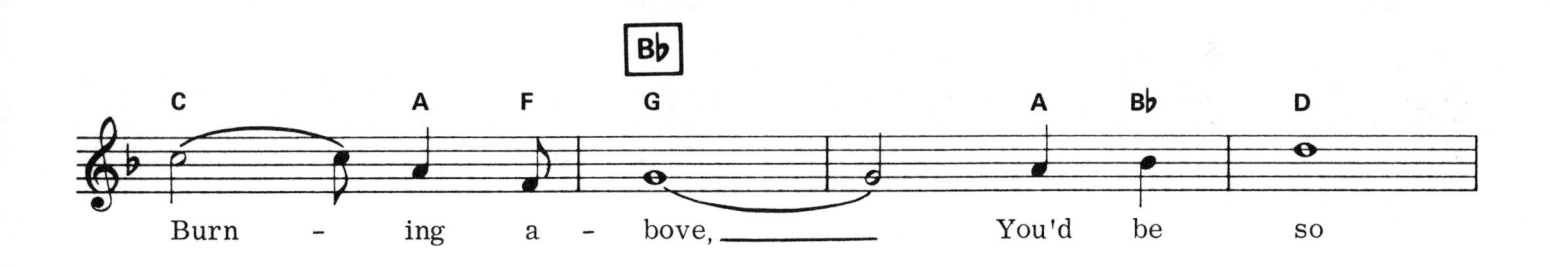

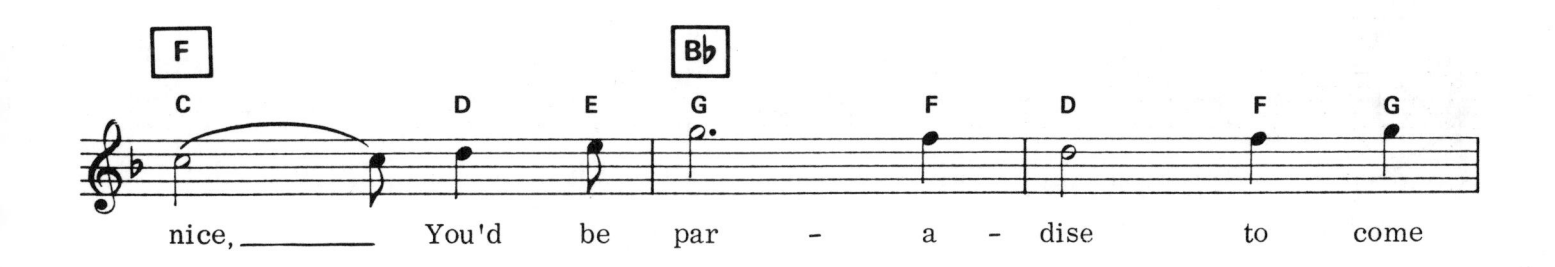

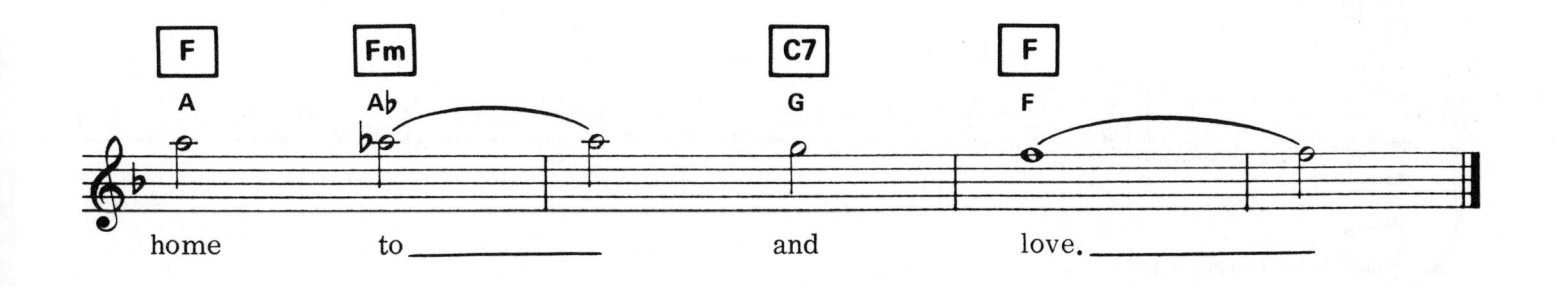

I'VE GOT YOU UNDER MY SKIN

Words and Music by
COLE PORTER

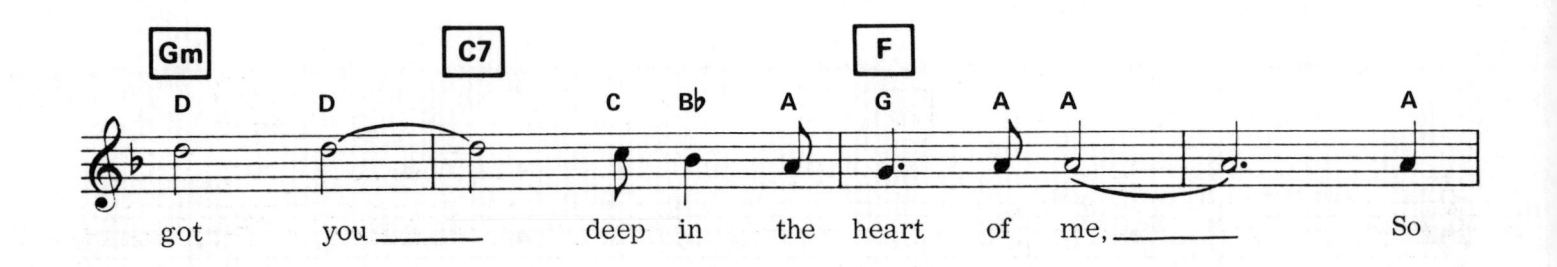

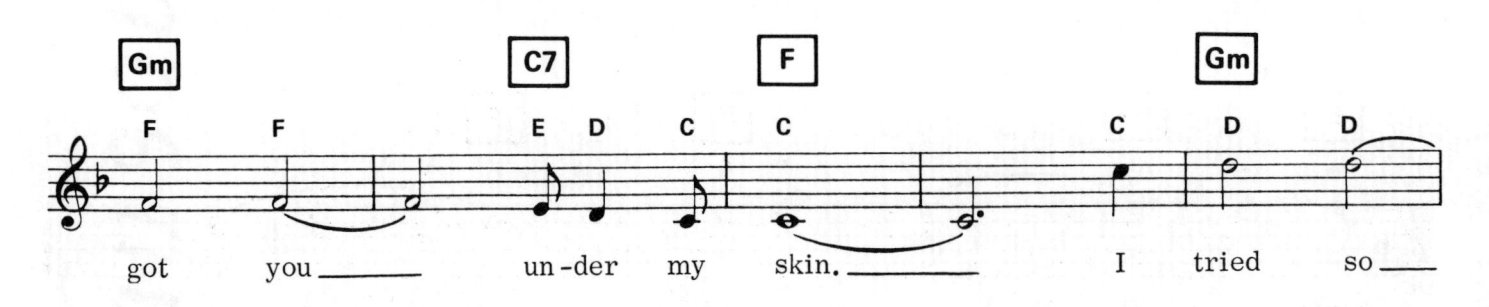

registration number 2.

N.C. | **Gm** | **C7** | **F**
C D | D C Bb A | A | C
I've got you under my skin, I've

Gm | **C7** | **F**
D D | C Bb A G | A A | A
got you deep in the heart of me, So

Gm | **C7** | **F**
Bb Bb Bb Bb | A A G F | E D D | E
deep in my heart, You're really a part of me. I've

Gm | **C7** | **F** | **Gm**
F F | E D C C | C | C D D
got you under my skin. I tried so

Copyright © 1936 by Chappell & Co., Inc.
Copyright Renewed
Used by HAL LEONARD PUBLISHING CORPORATION, Winona, MN 55987 by Permission
Made in U.S.A.   International Copyright Secured   All Rights Reserved

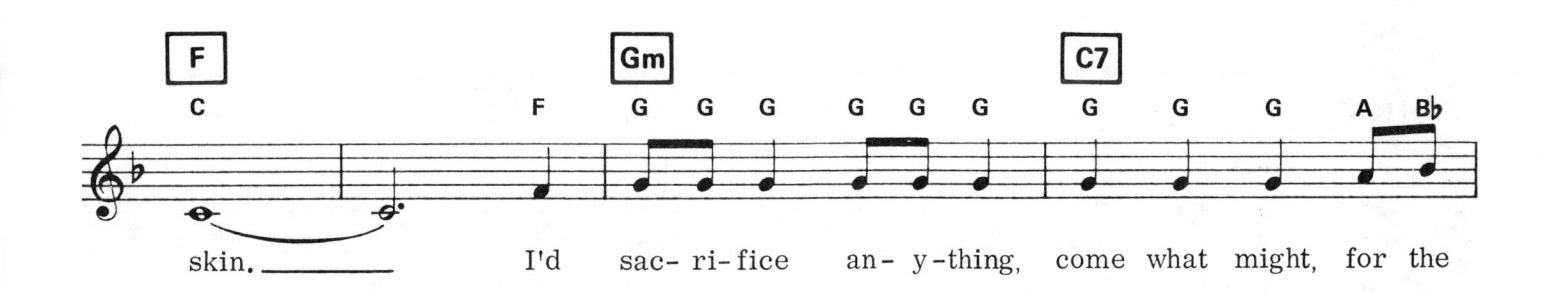

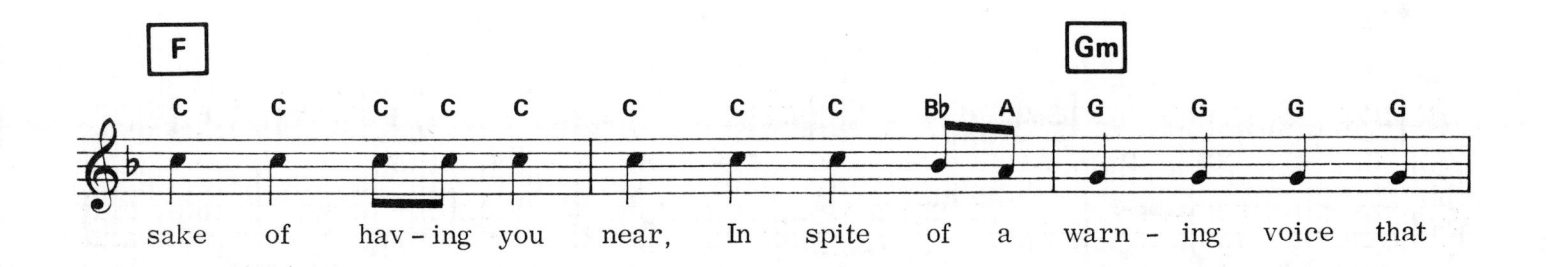

not to give in, I said to my-self, 'This af-fair nev-er will go so well." But why should I try to re-sist when, dar-ling, I know so well I've got you un-der my skin. I'd sac-ri-fice an-y-thing, come what might, for the sake of hav-ing you near, In spite of a warn-ing voice that comes in the night And re-peats and re-peats in my ear: "Don't you know, lit-tle fool, you nev-er can win, Use your men-tal-i-ty, Wake up to re-al-i-ty." But each time I do, just the thought of you makes me stop, Be-fore I be-gin, 'Cause I've got you un-der my skin.

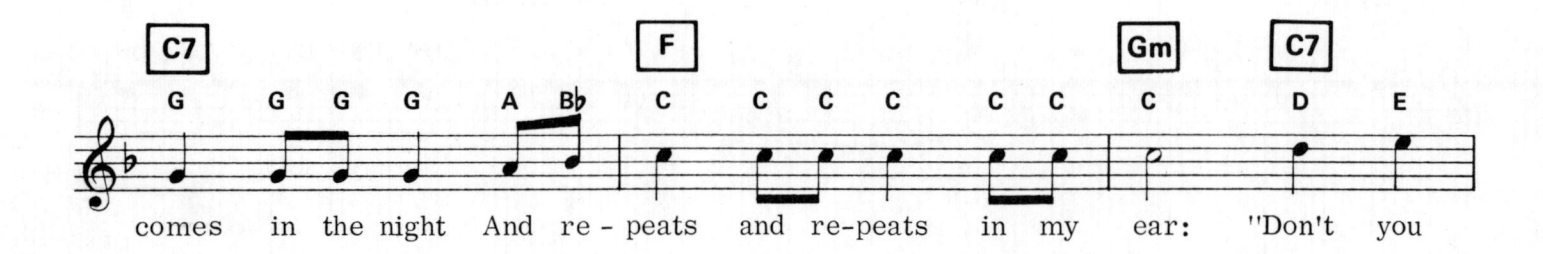

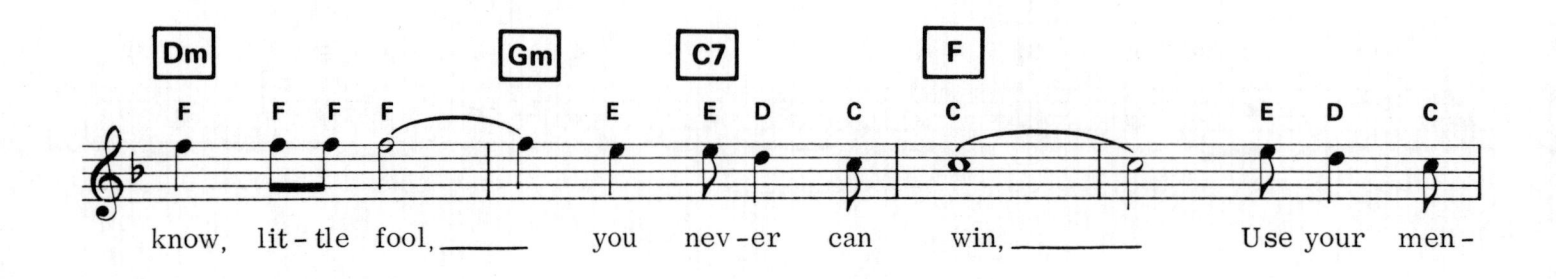

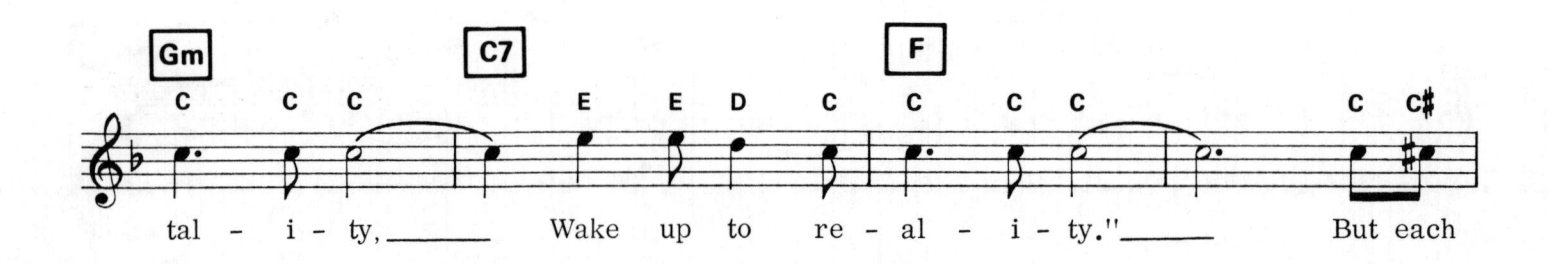

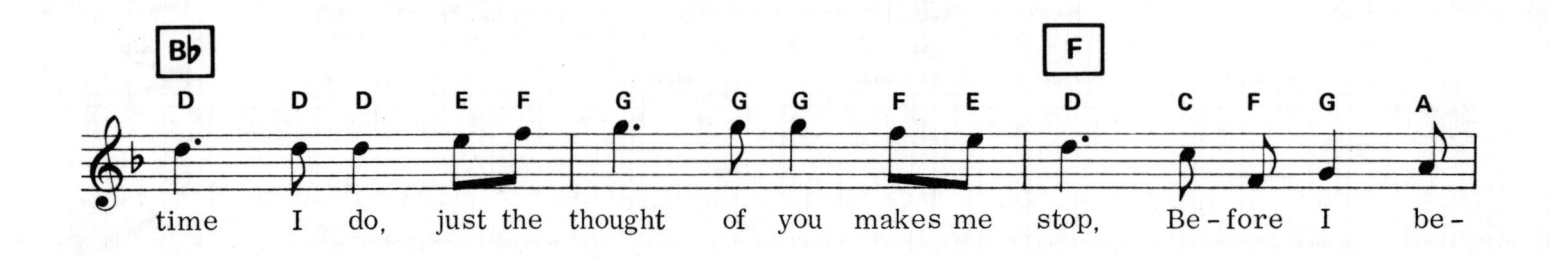

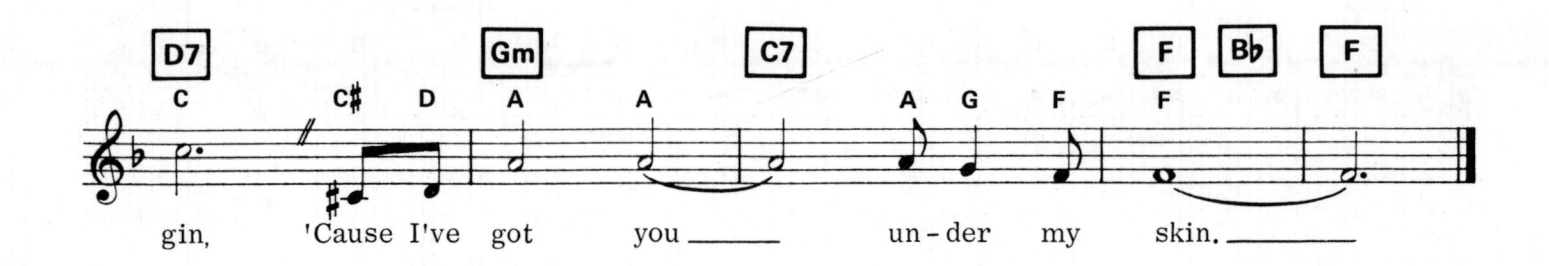

THE WAY OF LOVE

English words by AL STILLMAN
Music by JACK DIEVAL

registration number 2.

When you meet a boy that you like a lot, And you fall in love but he loves you not, If a flame should start as you hold him near, Better keep your heart out of danger, dear. For the way of love is a way of woe, And the day may come when you'll see him go. Then what will you do when he sets you free Just the way that you said goodbye to me. That's the way of love, the way of love.

Copyright © 1965 by Chappell S.A.
Chappell & Co., Inc., owner of publication and allied rights for the United States and Canada
Used by HAL LEONARD PUBLISHING CORPORATION, Winona, MN 55987 by Permission
Made in U.S.A.   International Copyright Secured   All Rights Reserved

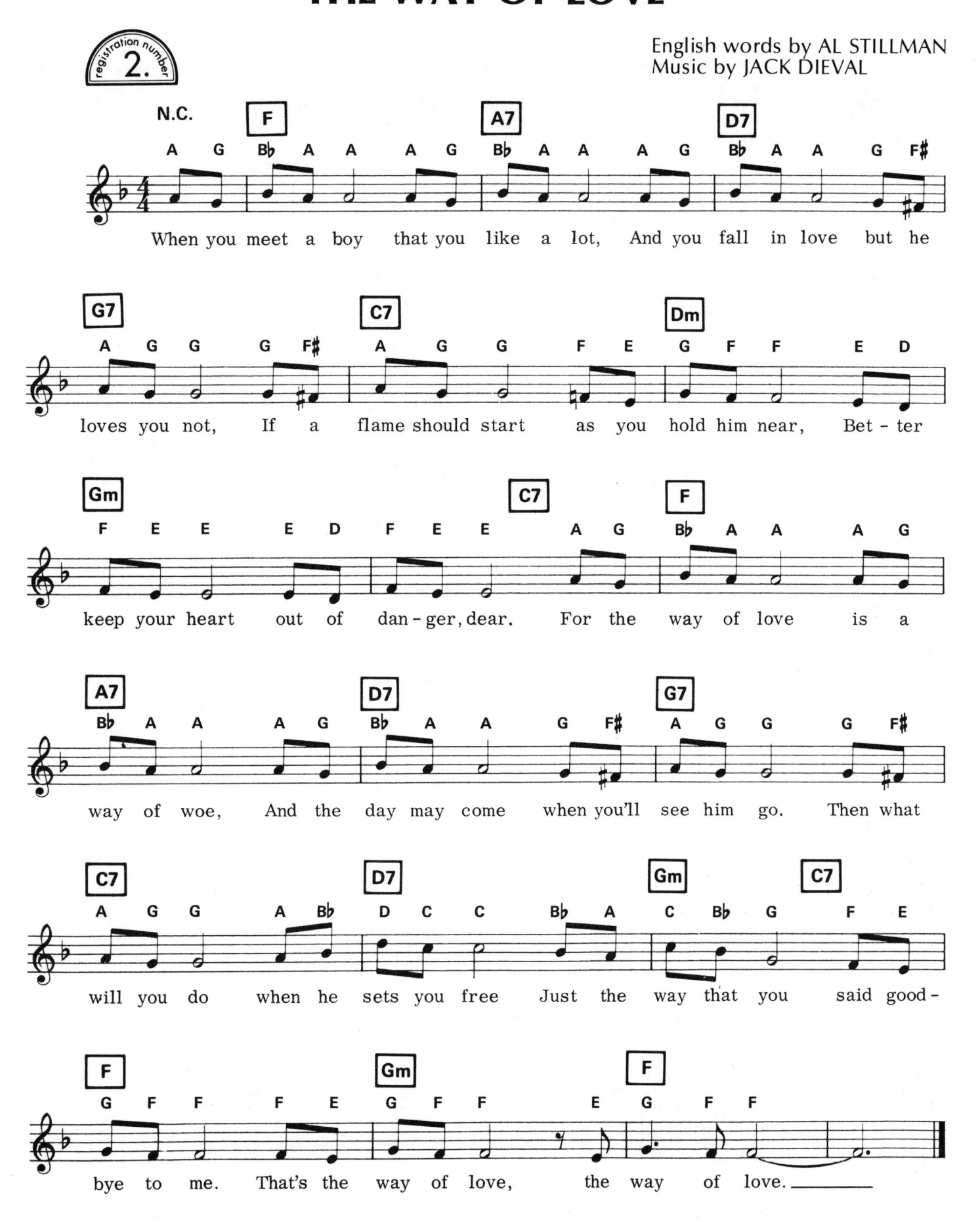

LITTLE OLD LADY

Words and Music by
HOAGY CARMICHAEL & STANLEY ADAMS

Lit-tle old la-dy pass-ing by, Catch-ing ev-'ry one's eye, You have such a charm-ing man-ner, sweet and shy. Lit-tle old bon-net set in place, And a smile on your face; You're a per-fect pic-ture in your

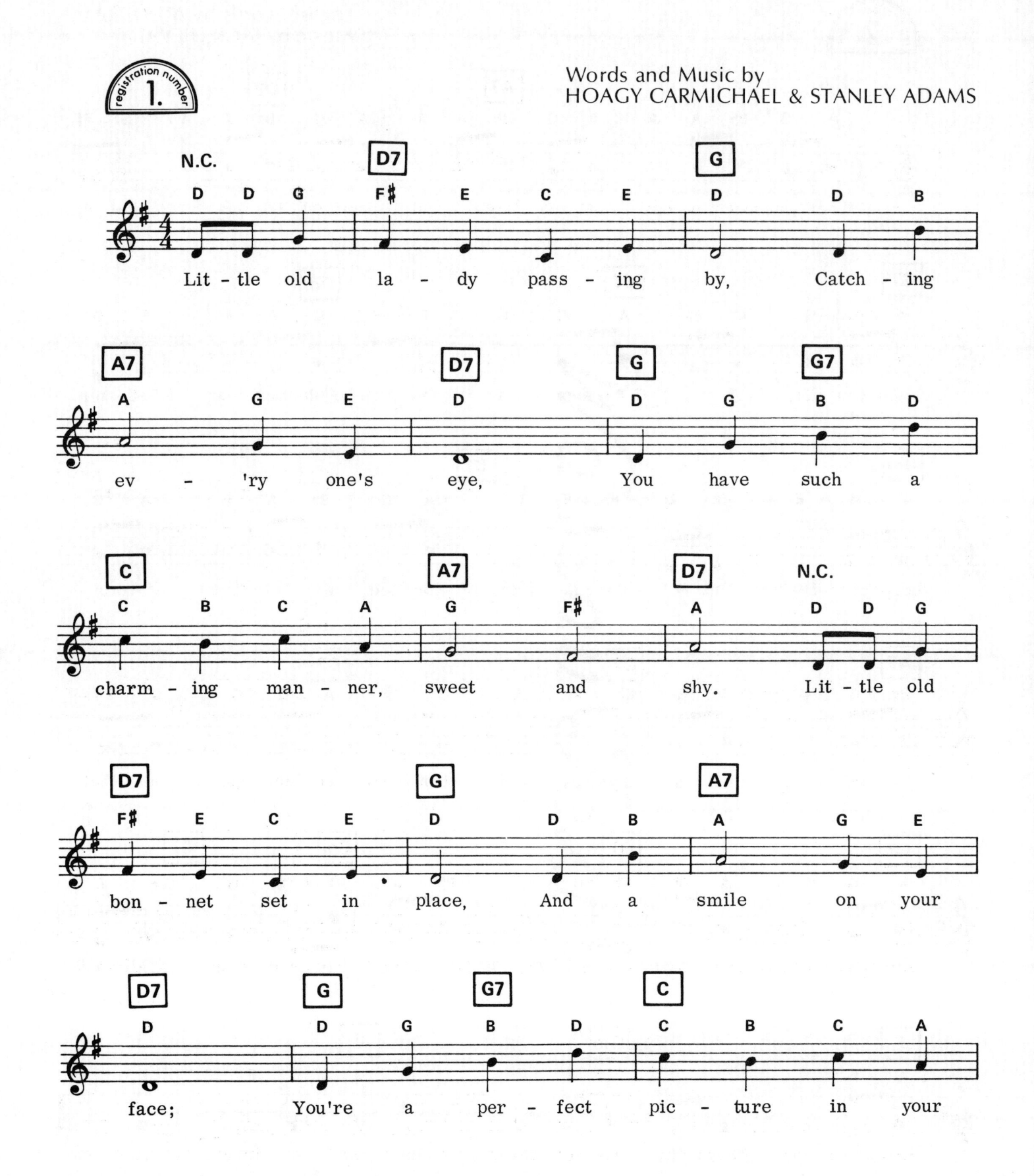

Copyright © 1936 by Chappell & Co., Inc.
Copyright Renewed
Used by HAL LEONARD PUBLISHING CORPORATION, Winona, MN 55987 by Permission
Made in U.S.A.   International Copyright Secured   All Rights Reserved

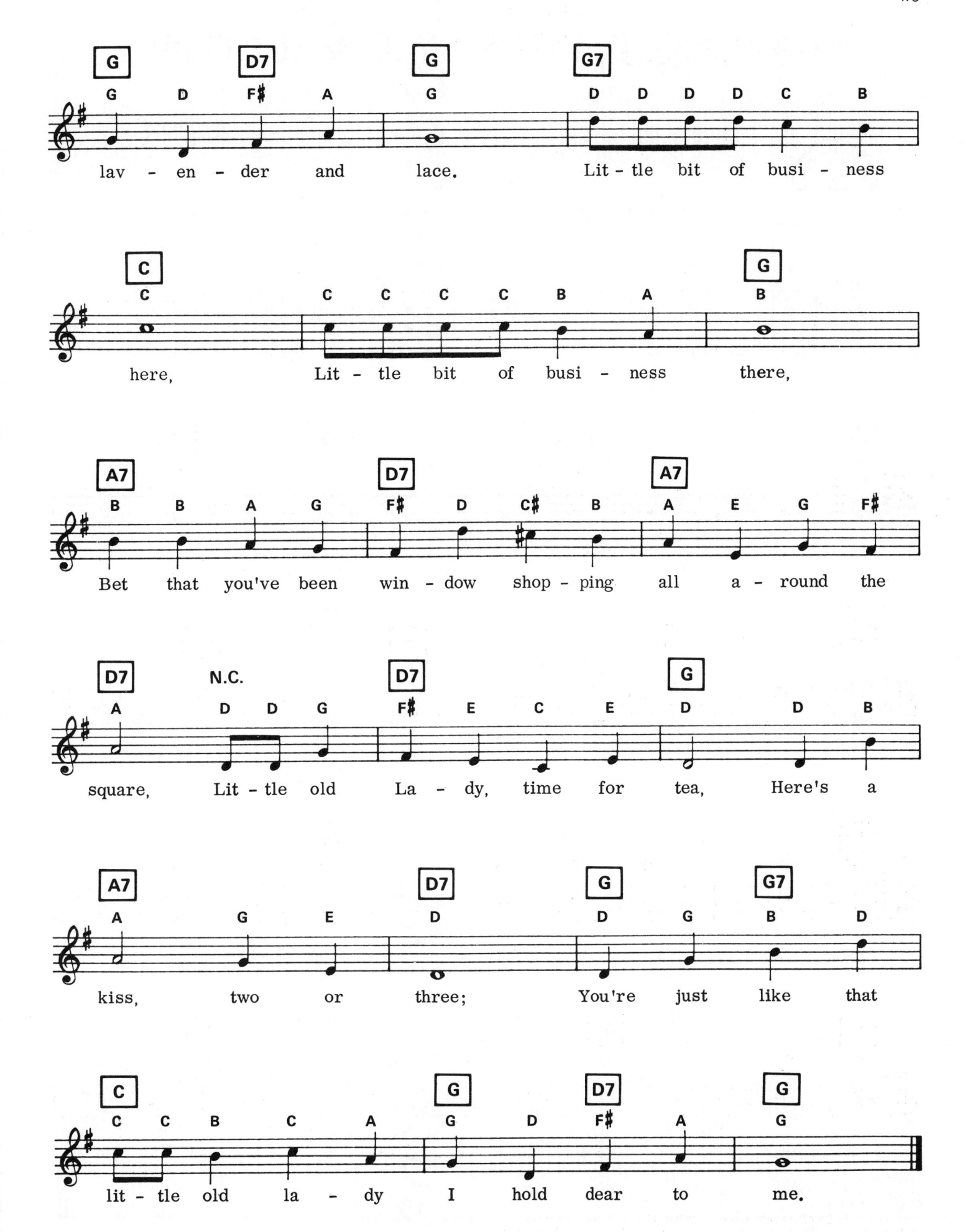

lav - en - der and lace. Lit - tle bit of busi - ness here, Lit - tle bit of busi - ness there, Bet that you've been win - dow shop - ping all a - round the square, Lit - tle old La - dy, time for tea, Here's a kiss, two or three; You're just like that lit - tle old la - dy I hold dear to me.

DARLING, JE VOUS AIME BEAUCOUP

Words and Music by
ANNA SOSENKO

Dar - ling, je vous aime beau - coup, Je ne sais pas What to do. You know you've com - plete - ly stol - en my heart.

Morn - ing, noon and night - time too, Tou - jours won - d'ring What you do. That's the way I've felt right from the

Copyright © 1935 by Publications Francis-Day S.A.
Copyright © 1936 by Chappell & Co., Inc.
Copyrights Renewed
Used by HAL LEONARD PUBLISHING CORPORATION, Winona, MN 55987 by Permission
Made in U.S.A.   International Copyright Secured   All Rights Reserved

start._____ Ah, Cher-ie! my love for you is très, très fort;_____ Wish my French were good e-nough, I'd tell you so much more. But I hope that you com-pree All the things you mean to me. Dar-ling, je vous aime beau-coup, I love you, yes, I do.

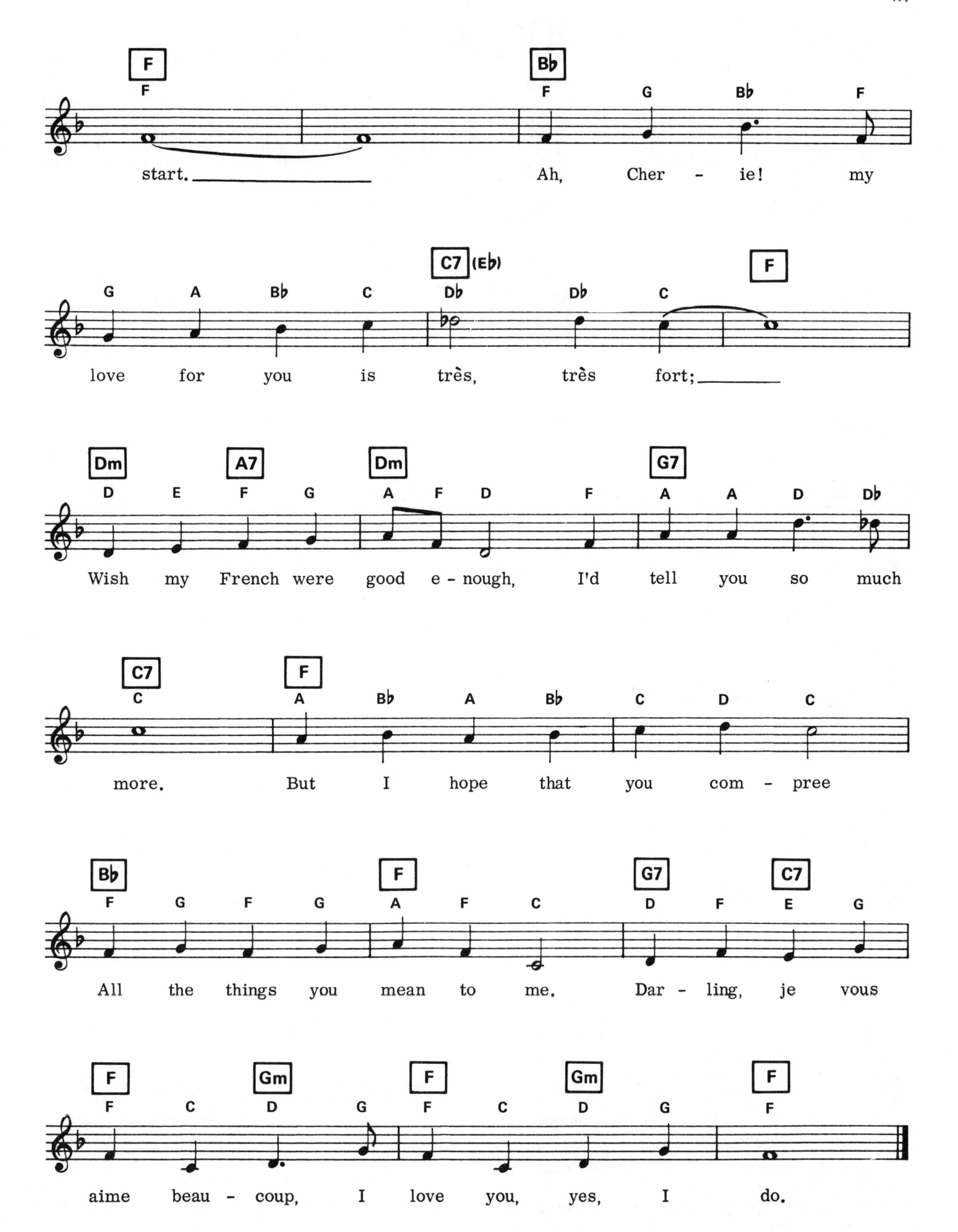

BLUEBERRY HILL

Words and Music by
AL LEWIS, LARRY STOCK & VINCENT ROSE

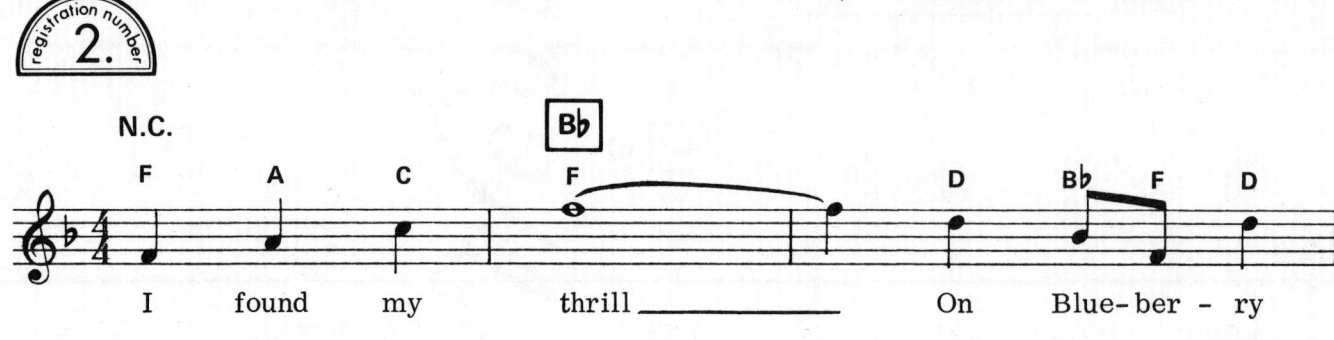

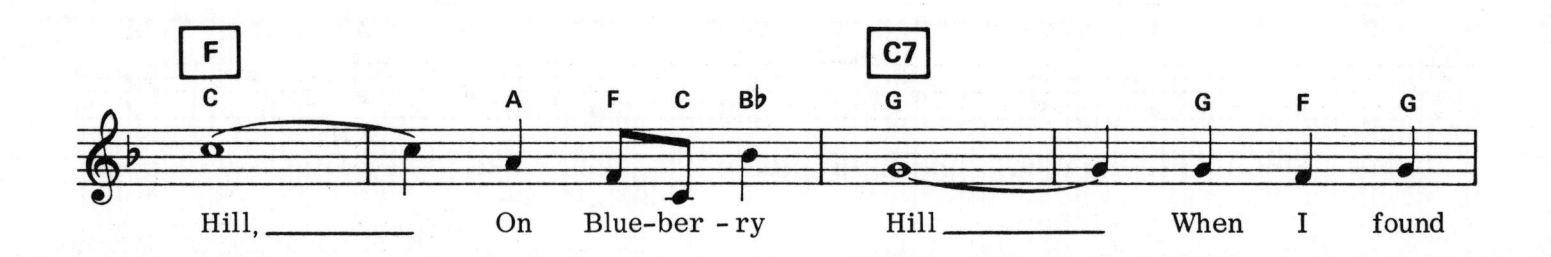

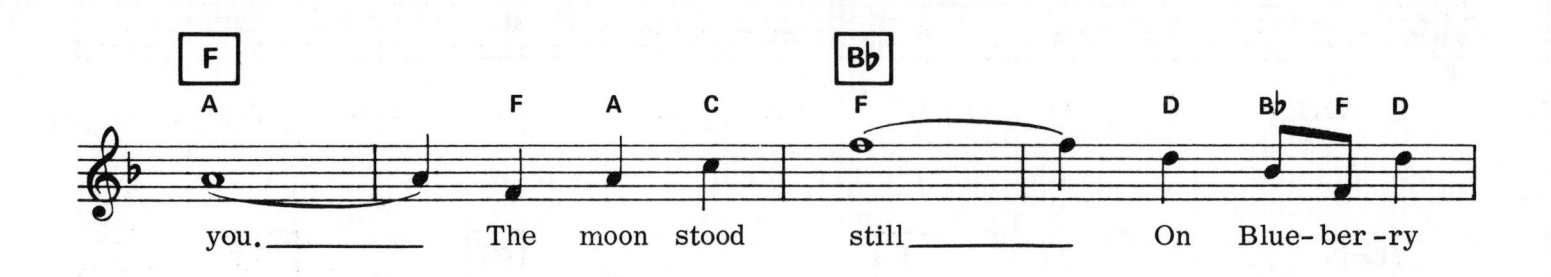

Registration number 2.

I found my thrill On Blueberry Hill, On Blueberry Hill When I found you. The moon stood still On Blueberry Hill, And lingered until my dreams came

Copyright © 1940 by Chappell & Co., Inc.
Copyright Renewed
Copyright © 1970 by Chappell & Co., Inc.
Used by HAL LEONARD PUBLISHING CORPORATION, Winona, MN 55987 by Permission
Made in U.S.A.   International Copyright Secured   All Rights Reserved

199

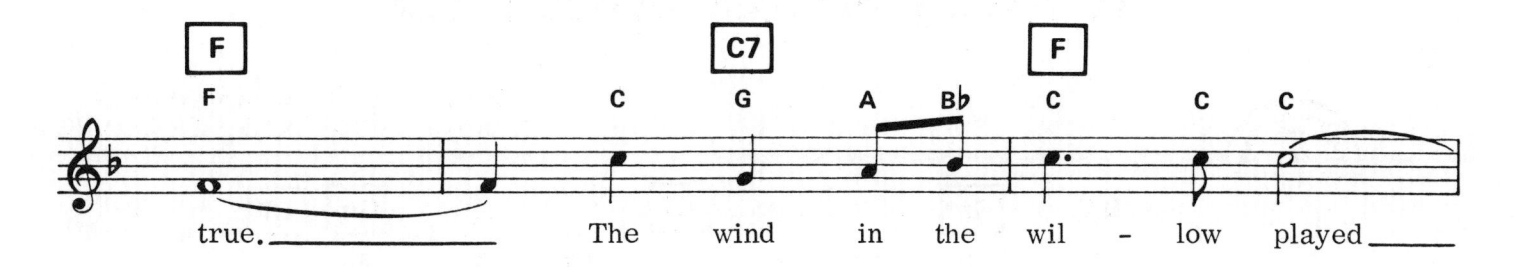

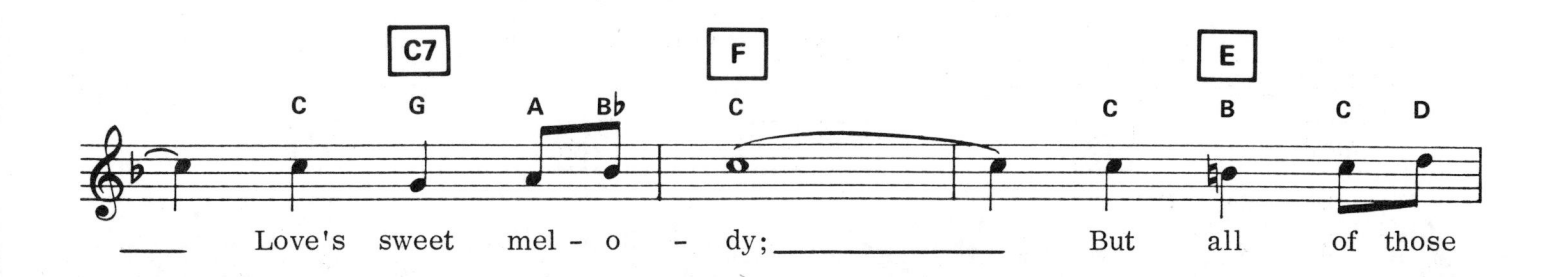

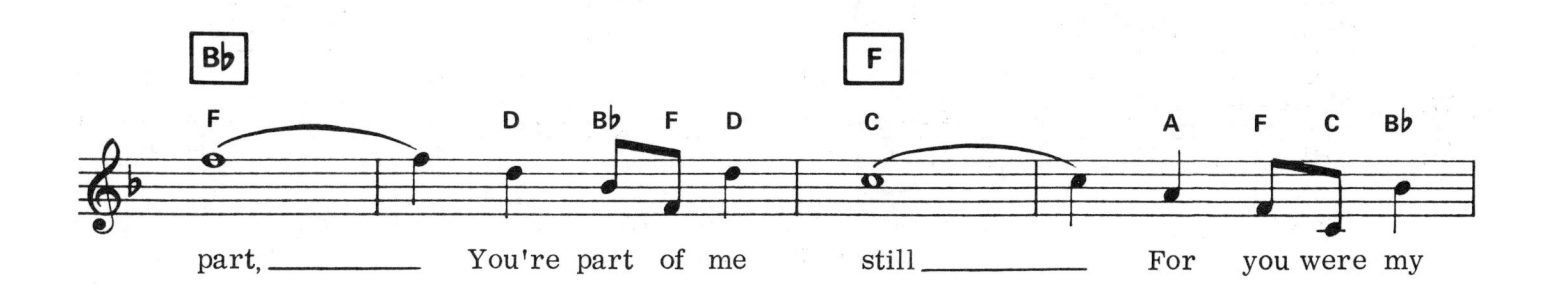

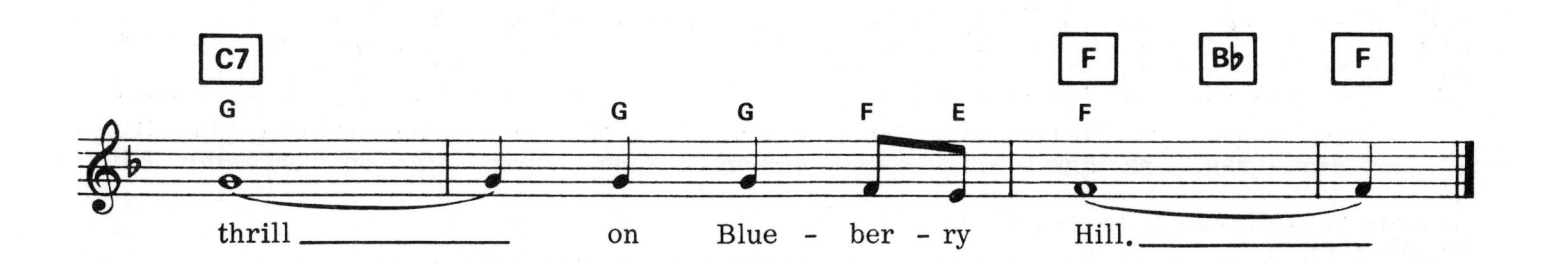

IT AIN'T NECESSARILY SO

Words by IRA GERSHWIN
Music by GEORGE GERSHWIN

It ain't ne-ces-sa-ri-ly so, It ain't ne-ces-sa-ri-ly so, De t'ings dat yo' li'-ble To read in de Bi-ble, it ain't ne-ces-sa-ri-ly so. Li'l

Da-vid was small, but oh my! Li'l Da-vid was small, but oh my! He fought big Go-li-ath Who lay down an' di-eth! Li'l Da-vid was small, but oh my!

Oh, Jo-nah, he lived in de whale, Oh, Jo-nah, he lived in de whale, Fo' he made his home in Dat

Mo-ses was found in a stream. Li'l Mo-ses was found in a stream, He float-ed on wa-ter Till

Copyright © 1965 by Gershwin Publishing Corporation
Copyright Renewed
Published in the United States by joint agreement with Gershwin Publishing Corporation and Chappell & Co., Inc.,
Used by HAL LEONARD PUBLISHING CORPORATION, Winona, MN 55987 by Permission
Made in U.S.A.   International Copyright Secured   All Rights Reserved

1.
Gm C7 A7 D7 Gm C7 Gm C7
G Bb G Bb G Bb G Bb G F D F G G
fish - 's ab - do - men. Oh, Jo - nah he lived in de whale. Li'l
Ole Phar - aoh's daugh - ter She fished him, she says from that
2.
Gm C7 Gm C7 Gm C7 Gm C7
G D D Db G C Cb G Bb G
stream. It ain't ne - ces - sa - ri - ly so, It
Gm C7 Gm C7 Gm C7
D Db G C Cb G Bb G D Db G Bb G Bb
ain't ne - ces - sa - ri - ly so. Dey tell all you chil - lun De
Gm C7 A7 D7 Gm
G Bb G Bb G Bb G Bb G F D F G G
deb - ble's a vil - lun, But 'tain't ne - ces - sa - ri - ly so. To
Fm Bb Am D7 Gm
F Eb Db C Bb Ab G F G Ab Bb C D D D D D D
get in - to Heb - ben don' snap for a seb - ben! Live clean! Don' have no fault. Oh,

C7 Fm A7
C B♭ A G F E D C D E F G A A A A
I takes dat gos - pel When - ev - er it's pos'-ble, But wid a grain of
D7 Gm C7 Gm C7
B♭ D D D♭ G C C♭ G B♭ G
salt. Me - thus' - lah lived nine hun - dred years, Me -
Gm C7 Gm C7 Gm C7
D D♭ G C C♭ G B♭ G D D♭ G B♭ G B♭
thus' - lah lived nine hun - dred years, But who calls dat liv - in' When
Gm C7 A7 D7 Gm C7 Gm
G B♭ G B♭ G B♭ G B♭ G F D F G G
no gal will give in to no man what's nine hun - dred years? I'm
D7 Gm C D7
A B♭ C A B♭ C D D E F♯ G G♯ B A
preach - in' dis ser - mon to show, It ain't nes - sa, ain't nes - sa,
G C G C7 G
G A A♯ B D C B C D E E E E
ain't nes - sa, ain't nes - sa, ain't ne - ces - sa - ri - ly so.

LIFE IS JUST A BOWL OF CHERRIES

Words and Music by
LEW BROWN and RAY HENDERSON

registration number 3.

Life is just a bowl of cher-ries,— Don't make it se-ri-ous,— Life's too mys-te-ri-ous.— You work, you save, you wor-ry so, But you can't take your dough when you go, go, go, So keep re-peat-ing it's the ber-ries, The strong-est oak must fall.— The sweet things in life,— To you were just loaned,— So how can you lose— what you nev-er owned?— Life is just a bowl of cher-ries, So live and laugh at it all.

Copyright © 1931 by DeSylva, Brown & Henderson, Inc.
Copyright Renewed, assigned to Chappell & Co., Inc.
Used by HAL LEONARD PUBLISHING CORPORATION, Winona, MN 55987 by Permission
Made in U.S.A.   International Copyright Secured   All Rights Reserved

RIDIN' HIGH

registration number 1.

Words and Music by
COLE PORTER

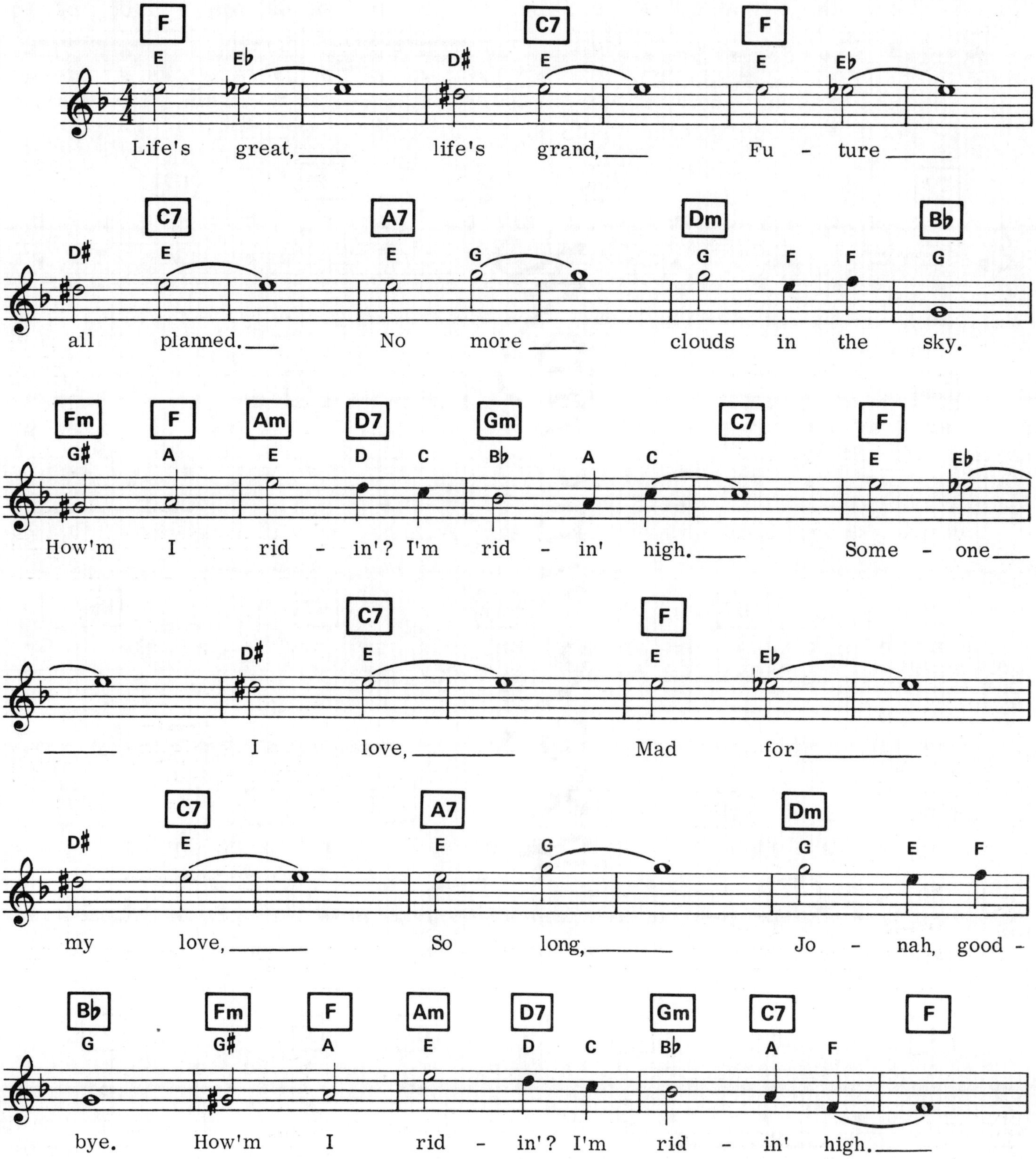

Floating on a starlit ceiling,

Doting on the cards I'm dealing,

Gloating, because I'm feeling

so hap-hap-happy, I'm slap happy. So

ring bells, sing songs, Blow horns,

beat gongs, Our love never will

die, How'm I ridin'? I'm ridin' high.

EVERYTHING I LOVE

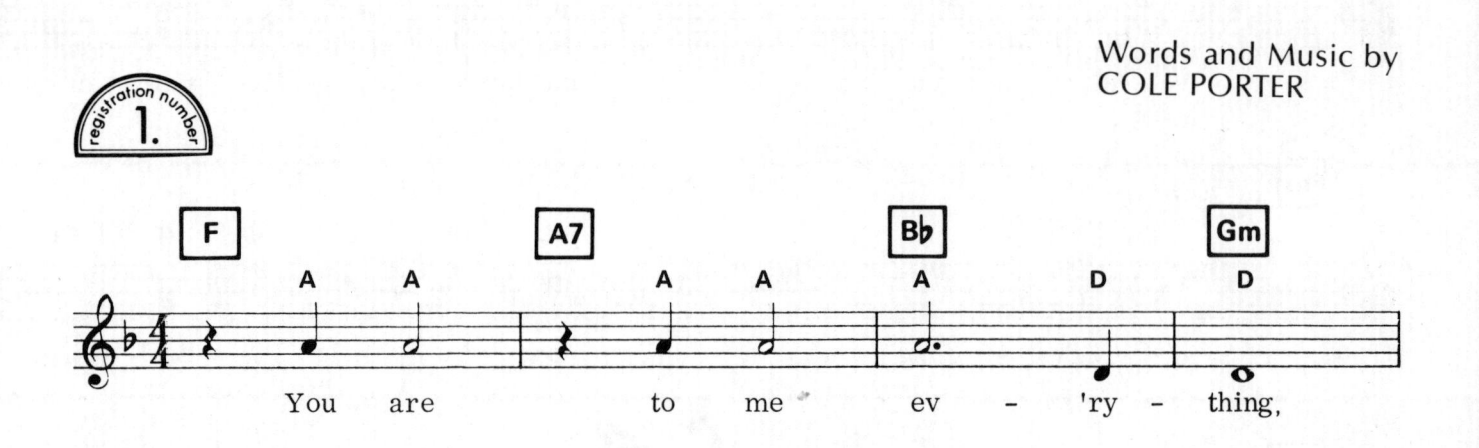

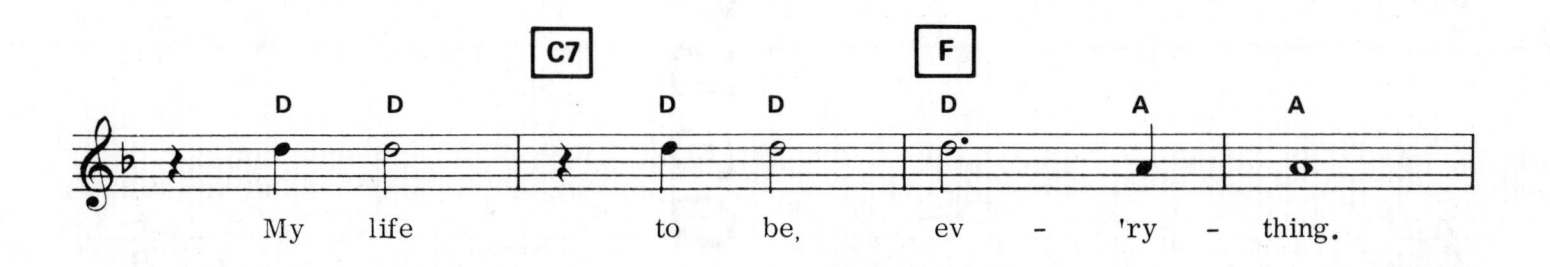

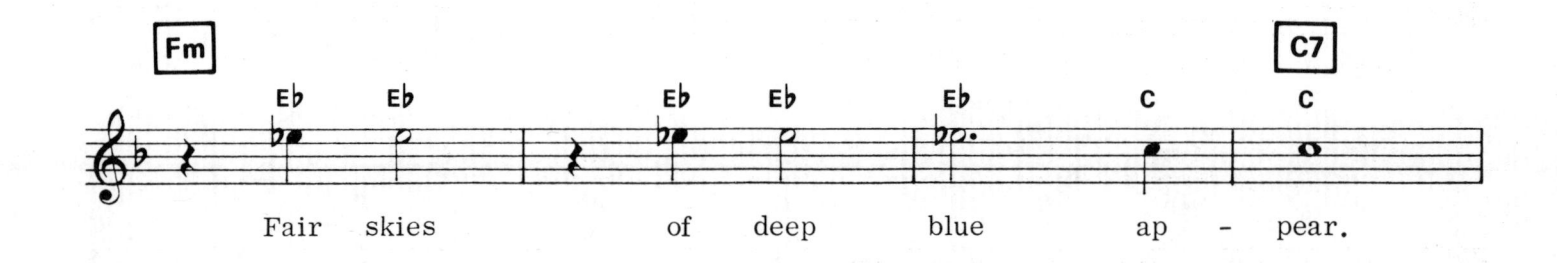

Words and Music by
COLE PORTER

You are to me ev-'ry-thing,
My life to be, ev-'ry-thing.
When in my sleep you ap-pear,
Fair skies of deep blue ap-pear.

Copyright © 1941 by Chappell & Co., Inc.
Copyright Renewed
Used by HAL LEONARD PUBLISHING CORPORATION, Winona, MN 55987 by Permission
Made in U.S.A. International Copyright Secured All Rights Reserved

Each time our lips touch a - gain, I yearn for you oh so____ much a - gain. You are my fav'-rite star,___ My ha - ven in heav - en a - bove, You are ev - 'ry - thing I love.___

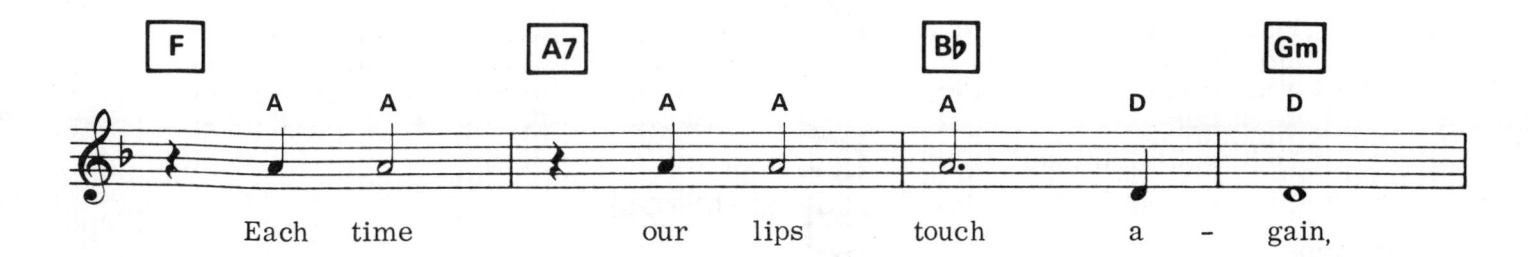

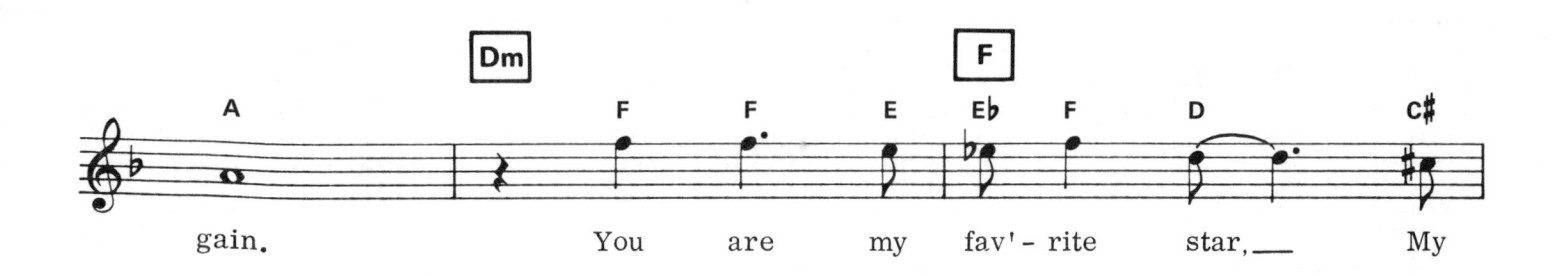

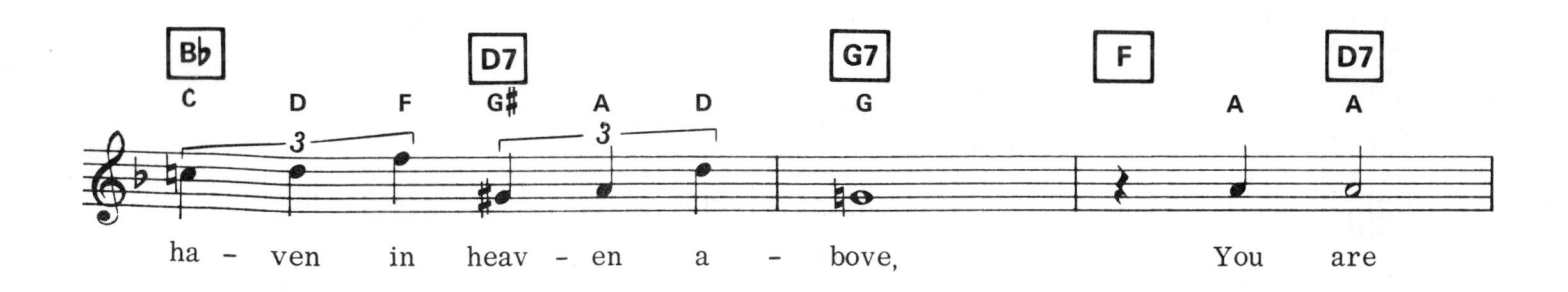

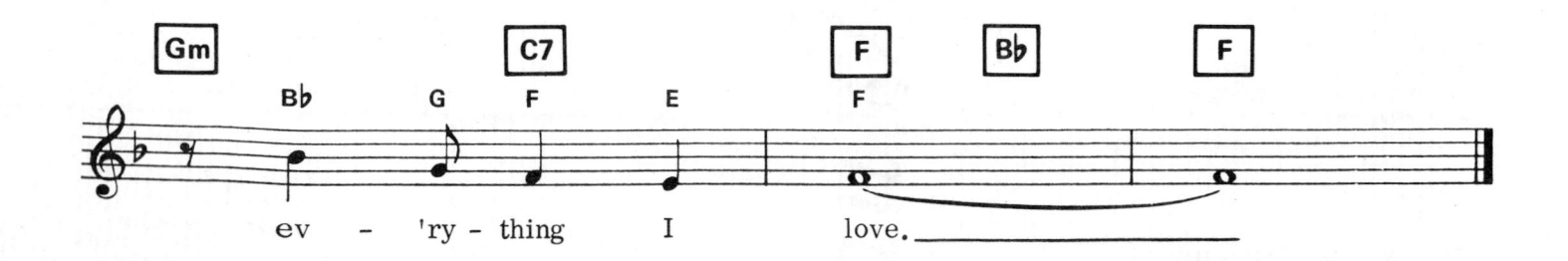

HAVE MORE FUN ON YOUR KIMBALL...
THE KIMBALL *Entertainer* SONGBOOK SERIES

Each songbook contains 20 great tunes in standard music notation — specially arranged and simplified for easy play and adapted for use with the MAGIC CHORD feature on the Entertainer. Kimball organ artists offer their own professional playing hints on registration and automatic rhythms for each ENTERTAINER song selection.

The books are available individually or as bound collections...

COLLECTION ONE

STANDARDS
Airport Love Theme
Call Me
Hawaiian Wedding Song
Heartaches
I Want To Hold Your Hand
Strangers In The Night
Tammy
and more...

POP HITS
Cherish
Didn't We
Joy To The World
Leavin' On A Jet Plane
Put Your Hand In The Hand
Rose Garden
Traces
and more...

SING-ALONGS
Blue-Tail Fly
Give My Regards To Broadway
Sweet Adeline
There Is A Tavern In The Town
Tom Dooley
When You Were Sweet Sixteen
Yellow Rose Of Texas
and more...

COUNTRY SONGS
A Fool Never Learns
I Don't Wanna Play House
It's All Over
The Last Word In Lonesome Is Me
Make The World Go Away
Mountain Of Love
Take Me To Your World
and more...

BALLADS
April Showers
As Time Goes By
Days Of Wine And Roses
Embraceable You
The Man I Love
Night And Day
The Very Thought Of You
and more...

CONTINENTAL HITS
A Man And A Woman
C'est Si Bon
Comme Ci, Comme Ca
Downtown
The Girl From Ipanema
Love Me Tonight
Pigalle
and more...

COLLECTION TWO

MUSICALS
Goodnight, My Someone
Heart
I Ain't Down Yet
Once In Love With Amy
Seventy-Six Trombones
Till There Was You
Wonderful Copenhagen
and more...

POP GALAXY
Ashes To Ashes
Did You Ever Have To Make Up Your Mind
Free As The Wind
I'll Make You Music
Last Night I Didn't Get To Sleep At All
Until It's Time For You To Go
and more...

INTERNATIONAL FAVORITES
Annie Laurie
Dark Eyes
Funiculi, Funicula
Havah Nagilah
I'll Take You Home Again, Kathleen
Juanita
Tales From The Vienna Woods
and more...

BALLROOM MEDLEY
Blue Skies
Cheek To Cheek
How Deep Is The Ocean
I've Got My Love To Keep Me Warm
Remember
There's No Business Like Show Business
They Say It's Wonderful
and more...

HARMONY TIME
Ain't We Got Fun
Bye Bye Blackbird
California Here I Come
Don't Fence Me In
If You Were The Only Girl In The World
In A Shanty In Old Shanty Town
Let The Rest Of The World Go By
and more...

NOSTALGIA
Beer Barrel Polka
Exactly Like You
Let Me Call You Sweetheart
A Marshmallow World
On The Sunny Side Of The Street
Picnic
Side By Side
and more...

SPECIAL EDITIONS
These books are available individually.

HOLIDAY CHEER
Away In A Manger
Hark! The Herald Angels Sing
I'll Be Home For Christmas
Jingle Bells
Let It Snow! Let It Snow! Let It Snow!
Rudolph, The Red-Nosed Reindeer
We Three Kings
and more...

BICENTENNIAL SONGBOOK
America
Battle Hymn Of The Republic
Dixie
Star Spangled Banner
Stars And Stripes Forever
Yankee Doodle Dandy
You're A Grand Old Flag
and more...

TROPICAL BREEZE
Harbor Lights
The Breeze And I
The Moon Of Manakoora
Pearly Shells
Quiet Village
Sleepy Lagoon
Tiny Bubbles
and more...

HOLY, HOLY, HOLY
Ave Maria
Give Me That Old-Time Religion
God Be With You Till We Meet Again
Holy, Holy, Holy
Nobody Knows The Trouble I've Seen
Onward Christian Soldiers
Rock Of Ages
and more...

CLASSICAL FAVORITES
Blue Danube Waltz
Chopin's Nocturne
Liebestraum
Melody In F
My Heart At Thy Sweet Voice
Tales From The Vienna Woods
Toreador Song
and more...

LIVING HITS
Another Somebody Done Somebody Wrong Song
At Seventeen
Feelings
Me And Mrs. Jones
Take Me Home Country Roads
Thank God I'm A Country Boy
You Make Me Feel Brand New
and more...

THAT'S ENTERTAINMENT
That's Entertainment plus 99 other songs from the movies and the best of Broadway, inspirational songs and all-time favorites.